Gender AND AMERICAN POLITICS

Gender AND AMERICAN POLITICS

WOMEN, MEN,
and the
POLITICAL PROCESS

REVISED AND EXPANDED
SECOND EDITION

EDITORS
SUE TOLLESON-RINEHART AND JYL J. JOSEPHSON

M.E.Sharpe
Armonk, New York
London, England

Library of Congress Cataloging-in-Publication Data

Gender and American politics : women, men, and the political process / edited by Sue
Tolleson-Rinehart and Jyl J. Josephson.—Revised and Expanded 2nd ed.
     p. cm.
  Includes bibliographical references and index.
  ISBN 0-7656-1569-X (hardcover : alk. paper) ISBN 0-7656-1570-3 (pbk. : alk. paper)
  1. Sex role—Political aspects—United States. 2. United States—Politics and government.
I. Tolleson-Rinehart, Sue, 1952– II. Josephson, Jyl J., 1960–

HQ1075.5.U6G454 2005
305.3´0973—dc22

                                                                                2004021675

Printed in the United States of America

The paper used in this publication meets the minimum requirements of
American National Standard for Information Sciences
Permanence of Paper for Printed Library Materials,
ANSI Z 39.48-1984.

| BM (c) | 10 | 9 | 8 | 7 | 6 | 5 | 4 | 3 | 2 | 1 |
| BM (p) | 10 | 9 | 8 | 7 | 6 | 5 | 4 | 3 | 2 | 1 |

This book is dedicated to all the scholars,
from Sophonisba Breckenridge onward,
who overcame the skepticism and intellectual neglect
of the discipline of political science,
and slowly convinced those who study politics
of the importance of gender as
an analytical, theoretical, and philosophical construct.

Contents

Part Three. Institutions

List of Tables and Figures

Tables

Figures

Acknowledgments

We would like to thank Patricia Kolb at M.E. Sharpe for her continuing confidence in this volume and its authors and editors, and in the enduring need for scholarly work on gender and political life. We also thank Amy Albert at M.E. Sharpe for her patience and skill in shepherding this volume through the preparation and production process. In addition, we would like to acknowledge the editorial assistance of Natalie Mullen, who read the chapters from a student's perspective and helped prepare the formatted versions of each chapter for publication. We would also like to thank S. Katherine Farnsworth, who provided invaluable assistance with the preparation of the first edition of this book, and Ryan Canney, who helped in the initial stages of the second edition.

We thank also our colleagues who used the first edition of this book in their courses and provided us with valuable feedback regarding ways to make it more useful, including Kathleen Dolan, Georgia Duerst-Lahti, Lynne Ford, R. Claire Snyder, and Diana Zoelle. Thanks to Susan Hansen who, in a generous review of the first edition of this book published in the *Journal of Politics*, suggested that chapters on the media and on legislators would be valuable additions. She stimulated us to approach good colleagues to contribute such chapters. Those chapters, along with a new chapter on gender and national security, prove Susan right. We believe this edition is even stronger and more comprehensive than was the first.

Our pride in this volume is pride in the quality of the scholars who have contributed to it. We could not have been associated with a finer group of researchers, teachers, and colleagues. They were prompt in responding to our requests, patient when production took longer than expected, and good-humored throughout. For that, as well as for their marvelous work, we thank them. Thanks also to Jim Nelson for a careful and timely reading of the concluding chapter.

Laboring in the vineyards of academia requires the support of many senior colleagues and administrators who see value in the study of gender and in encouraging scholars who pursue such work despite the entrenched inertia and resistance of institutions of higher education. We acknowledge the support of scholars and administrators such as Roberta Sigel, M. Kent Jennings, Virginia Sapiro, Jane Winer,

Susan Hendrick, John Tuman, Roberta Trites, Barbara Heyl, Janie Leatherman, Valentine Moghadam, Sandra Harmon, Paula Ressler, Lucinda Beier, Alison Bailey, Cynthia Burack, Lisa Hull, Mary Segers, and Annette Juliano, who have collectively eased our path through multiple institutions. This acknowledgment is much less than each of you deserves.

About the Editors and Contributors

MaryAnne Borrelli is associate professor of government and director of the Holleran Center for Community Action and Public Policy at Connecticut College. Her research interests center on the links among gender, leadership, and organizational culture, which she has investigated through study of the cabinet nomination and confirmation processes, and of the First Lady's Office. In addition to a number of book chapters and journal articles, she is the author of *The President's Cabinet: Gender, Power, and Representation* (2002) and the co-editor of *The Other Elites: Women, Politics, and Power in the Executive Branch* (1997).

M. Margaret Conway is a distinguished professor emeritus at the University of Florida. She is the author of *Political Participation in the United States* (2000) and co-author of *The Politics of Asian American*s (2004) and *Women and Political Participation* (2005), as well as numerous articles on political parties, voting behavior, political participation, and women and politics.

Michael X. Delli Carpini, dean of the Annenberg School for Communication of the University of Pennsylvania, received his B.A. and M.A. from the University of Pennsylvania (1975) and his Ph.D. from the University of Minnesota (1980). Prior to joining the University of Pennsylvania faculty in July of 2003, Professor Delli Carpini was director of the public policy program of the Pew Charitable Trusts (1999–2003) and a member of the political science department at Barnard College and the graduate faculty of Columbia University (1987–2002). He is author of *Stability and Change in American Politics: The Coming of Age of the Generation of the 1960s* (1986) and *What Americans Know About PPolitics and Why It Matters* (1996), as well as numerous articles, essays, and chapters in edited volumes on political communications, public opinion, and political socialization.

Pamela Fiber is assistant professor of political science at California State University, Long Beach. She has published articles on gender and reproductive rights in *Duke Journal of Gender, Law and Policy,* and *Yale Journal of Health Policy, Law, and Ethics,* and has contributed chapters to the *Historical and Multicultural Encyclopedia of Women's Reproductive Rights in the United States* and *The Politics of*

Gay Rights. She is currently working on a study of campaign finance reform and the legislative process.

Richard L. Fox is associate professor of political science at Union College. He is the author of *Gender Dynamics in Congressional Elections* (1997) and *Tabloid Justice* (with Robert Van Sickel, 2001). He has published articles on gender and politics in *Political Research Quarterly, The Journal of Politics, American Journal of Political Science, Political Psychology, Public Administration Review, Women and Politics*, and *Legislative Studies Quarterly*. He is currently working on a study of gender and political ambition.

Jyl J. Josephson is associate professor of political science and director of women's studies at Rutgers, The State University of New Jersey, Newark campus. She is the author of numerous articles on gender and public policy published in journals such as the *Journal of Poverty, New Political Science, Journal of Political Ideologies*, and *Women & Politics.* She is the author of *Gender, Families, and State: Child Support Policy in the United States* (1997) and co-editor of *Fundamental Differences: Feminists Talk Back to Social Conservatives* (2003) with Cynthia Burack. She is currently working with Paula Ressler on a manuscript regarding projects that seek to make schools safer for lesbian, gay, bisexual, and transgender students and their allies. Her two other major projects include a book that examines privacy and intimate life from the perspective of groups whose privacy claims most frequently have been disparaged and foreclosed, and an ongoing research project on the development of a faith-based community organization in west Texas.

Scott Keeter is associate director of the Pew Research Center for the People and the Press in Washington, DC. From 1998 to 2002, he served as chair of the department of public and international affairs at George Mason University. Since 1980 Keeter has been an election night analyst of exit polls for NBC News. He is co-author of three books, and has written articles and book chapters on survey methodology, political communications and behavior, and health care topics. Keeter's current research focuses on civic engagement among youth.

Janie Leatherman is a professor in the department of politics and government at Illinois State University. She is co-director of Peace and Conflict Resolution Studies and coordinator of the Global Studies concentration. Professor Leatherman consults with many national and international organizations on the early warning and prevention of conflict, including the Council on Foreign Relations South Balkans Working Group (New York), The Brookings Institution, Catholic Relief Services, and the United Nations University. She is author of *From Cold War to Democratic Peace* (2003) and co-editor with Julie Webber of *Beyond Global Arrogance: Charting Transnational Democracy* (forthcoming). She is also the lead author of *Breaking Cycles of Violence: Conflict Prevention in Intrastate Crises* (1999).

Dorothy E. McBride is a professor in the department of political science at Florida Atlantic University, Boca Raton, Florida, where she is a founding member of the women's studies faculty and the faculty for the Ph.D. in comparative studies. A specialist in comparative analysis and women and public policy in the United States and Europe, she is the author of *Women's Rights in the USA* (forthcoming) and *Women's Rights in France* (1987) as well as numerous chapters and journal articles. She is co-editor of *Comparative State Feminism* (1995, with Amy G. Mazur) and *Abortion Policy in Comparative Perspective* (1996, with Marianne Githens). A co-convenor of the Research Network on Gender Politics and the State, she edited *Abortion Politics, Women's Movements and the Democratic State: A Comparative Study of State Feminism* (2001) and has written chapters on job training and prostitution policy debates in the United States for the Research Network on Gender Politics and the State (RNGS) state feminism project.

Susan Gluck Mezey is a professor in the political science department and assistant vice president for research at Loyola University Chicago. She is the author of *No Longer Disabled: The Federal Courts and the Politics of Social Security Disability* (1988); *In Pursuit of Equality: Women, Public Policy, and the Federal Courts* (1992); *Children in Court: Public Policymaking and Federal Court Decisions* (1996); *Pitiful Plaintiffs: Child Welfare Litigation and the Federal Courts* (2000); and *Elusive Equality: Women's Rights, Public Policy, and the Law* (2003). She has written numerous articles and book chapters on women and politics and law and the courts. She teaches courses in constitutional law, judicial process, the federal courts, women and law, and children and law.

David Niven is an associate professor of political science at Florida Atlantic University and holds a Ph.D. from Ohio State University. Professor Niven's research on women in politics has been published in several journals, including *Women and Politics*, *Polity*, and *Political Communication*, and in his book *The Missing Majority: The Recruitment of Women as State Legislative Candidates* (1998).

Eric Plutzer is associate professor of political science and sociology at Penn State University, where he teaches courses on public opinion, political behavior, and research methods. He has written extensively on reproductive rights (with Barbara Ryan); on the success of women seeking statewide office (with John Zipp); and the ways that work, gender, and family life interact to influence citizens' opinion, political participation, and voting behavior on reproductive rights. He is currently completing a book-length study (with Michael Berkman) of policy responsiveness in 10,000 U.S. school districts and beginning a major project on how adolescent experiences can hinder or enhance political participation many years later.

Sue Thomas is senior policy researcher at the Pacific Institute for Research and Evaluation. She has previously served as associate professor in the department of government and director of women's studies at Georgetown University. Her research interests center on women and politics, most especially women officeholders. Dr. Thomas's publications include *How Women Legislate* (1994) and *Women and Elective Office: Past, Present and Future* (1998). The second edition of *Women and Elective Office* will be published in 2005.

Sue Tolleson-Rinehart is the program administrator of the Program on Health Outcomes and the Center for Education and Research in Therapeutics at the University of North Carolina at Chapel Hill, where she also holds faculty appointments in political science and public health. She is a former professor of political science at Texas Tech University. She is the author of numerous articles on the political psychology of gender, and of the books *Gender Consciousness and Politics* (1992) and *Claytie and the Lady: Ann Richards, Gender and Politics in Texas* (1994, with Jeanie R. Stanley). She co-edited, with Jyl J. Josephson, the first edition of *Gender and American Politics: Women, Men and the Political Process*. She is a co-author of reports and monographs on aspects of health outcomes and quality of health care. Her current interests include the politics of American health care and the paradoxes of private sector delivery of the public good of health care.

Gender AND AMERICAN POLITICS

1

Introduction
Gender, Sex, and American Political Life

Jyl J. Josephson and Sue Tolleson-Rinehart

"Gender" is a term that describes both men and women, yet books on gender and American political life often read as though gender were a synonym for women. In this volume we address the roles and behaviors of both men and women in political decision making, political institutions, and public policy. We provide an overview of current empirical research on the contours of what is popularly known as the "gender gap": the difference between men and women in voting behavior, political leadership, and political beliefs and commitments. We also look at the role that gender plays in American political institutions by examining gender, men, and women in the executive, legislative, and judicial branches. And we examine the importance of gendered institutions and assumptions in the making of public policy. Overall, then, the essays in this volume look at gender comparatively—that is, comparing men and women—and focus on the differences in men's and women's roles in various aspects of political life and on the way that gender affects them.

This volume has a normative perspective, that of feminism. Virtually all works of gender politics are feminist, tracing their roots to the work of the 1970s (and, rarely, before that time), conducted by scholars who were engaged not only in measuring and reporting women's political roles, but in calling attention to the absence of such recognition in political science and in the wider world. Those who were satisfied with the status quo of the time did not produce what came to be known as "gender politics" research, and those who created such research were doing so, in part, because they were *not* satisfied with women's status.

In the present volume, a feminist perspective, taken at its simplest, means that the authors accept women's inherent right to be full political actors, and their full political equality with men. That assertion might seem less than bold a generation after the most recent renascence of the Women's Movement, and more than a decade after the "Year of the Woman" produced a leap forward in the number of women elected to Congress. It is nonetheless worth noting, particularly because one of the Women's Movement's successes has been the political action of *anti-* or *nonfeminist* women. Feminism has made the careers of Phyllis Schlafly, Margaret Thatcher, and Condoleezza Rice possible, even though these three women might

3

be loathe to acknowledge it. From the days of the suffrage movement, feminists have been opposed by other women, as well as by men, but their success meant that all women were enfranchised, and with this enfranchisement came substantial intrasex debate over "women's issues" and "women's interests," not just the inter-sex debate with which the popular culture has appeared to be more fascinated.

This book takes a mainstream feminist view of "women's interests": women are not "deviant" from some norm of political behavior; rather, empirically observed differences and similarities between men and women provide fruitful ground for analyzing the nature of American political life and the functioning of American political institutions. Our focus is on empirical evidence. In addition to showing differences among women, much of this evidence continues to show differences between the sexes as well: men and women come to political life with different kinds of information, experiences, and priorities. Thus, the differences between men's and women's political behavior are not surprising, just as differences among women are not. The essays in this book will provide the reader with information regarding the contours of those differences. Before we can discuss the effects of gender on politics, however, we must clarify what is meant by the term "gender"—"gender" does not mean "women," contrary to much popular usage.

What Is Gender?

It is important at the outset to note what we mean by gender, to distinguish between "sex" and "gender," and to distinguish those aspects of gender that this volume covers. The most common contemporary use of the term "gender" in academic study and usage, and later in common public discourse, was driven by the theory emanating from the women's movement. As more scholars began to pay attention to the differences that the study of women might bring to the subject matter and to methodological approaches in their own disciplines, the study of women's attitudes and behaviors, and the contexts of their lives, began to emerge as a distinct but important arena of academic inquiry. In turn, scholars began to note that the exclusion of women from consideration had both distorted and denied many significant arenas of knowledge in disciplines as disparate as literature and science and, of course, in political science.

Was the problem simply that women and men are inherently different creatures, destined to live entirely differently lives, in relation to politics as well as all else? Social scientists observed many of the social factors influencing differences between men and women, from the ways that adults treat infants—including dressing boys and girls differently, providing them with different toys, and even holding them differently—to the quite different social roles played by adult men and women. As a result, social scientists began to distinguish between "sex" and "gender." According to this distinction, sex is the characteristic of the biological being; gender is the socially constructed aspect of the self.

Sex is also "sexual." Others have recognized this distinction and have used the term "gender" deliberately to distract their audiences from thinking about the act of sex. Those who dictated Victorian popular culture used "gender" in this way. Ironically, a century after the height of Victorian limitations on women's gender roles, Ruth Bader Ginsburg used "gender" in her foundational sex discrimination arguments before the U.S. Supreme Court (on which she now sits) for similar reasons—but different ends. She too, she said, wanted to keep her audiences' minds off "sex" while she was trying to win support for the equality of the sexes.

As these examples suggest, we might describe sex as "nature" and gender as "nurture," but the matter is a bit more complicated than this. For instance, most people think of "sex" as coming in only two forms: male or female. Yet at least one percent of humans are born as intersexuals: neither male nor female, but with characteristics of both. Sex is thus not quite as dichotomous as it is commonly perceived to be. Similarly, seeing gender as simply "nurture" might fail to recognize potentially important interactions between the biological, the social, and the political, and the complexity of the many institutions that construct gender.

Although we intend this discussion to indicate the complicated nature of "sex" and "gender," for the purposes of the empirical studies in this book, we use the standard distinction between the two, unless explicitly noted otherwise: sex is biological; gender is socially and politically constructed. Thus, for example, as Richard Fox and Pamela Fiber show in their chapter in this volume, it is one thing to note sex differences—or, in the instant case, growing similarities—between men and women who are running in congressional election campaigns. We can determine that female candidates who are running for Congress in open-seat elections now tend to have, on average, the same chance of winning as do male candidates. A candidate's sex, therefore, no longer seems to make a difference in electoral outcomes, at least in open-seat elections for the House of Representatives. It would be quite another matter, however, to assert that women across the country have similar opportunities to those of men to run for Congress; they do not. Significant regional variations in parties' recruitment of women candidates for open-seat elections persist. Further, Fox and Fiber find meaningful differences in fundraising between male and female candidates in open-seat elections, and these differences seem to be about gender.

To cite another example, political scientists have long observed sex differences in political knowledge between men and women. Men, on average, tend to know more about politics than do women, on average. These sex differences have narrowed somewhat as women's roles have changed, but they are remarkably resistant to eradication. What Michael Delli Carpini and Scott Keeter accomplish in their chapter is to locate many of the sources of these sex differences in political knowledge. Their sources are the differently gendered experiences and roles of men and women. In other words, the more interesting question is not the *fact* that men and women have different levels, and different kinds, of political knowledge, but rather the *reason* that they do. The reasons, Delli Carpini and Keeter argue, have to do with continuing structural inequalities in gender roles. When they examine how political knowledge might translate into political opinions, they find that the "gender gap" in opinions actually increases with increased political knowledge. This suggests that many women's lower levels of political knowledge may be preventing them from representing their own policy interests as well as they might wish to do.

Gender affects political life in multiple ways and at multiple levels. Historically, it has shaped the structure and functioning of political institutions. Certainly, as women come to be more included in political life and in positions of political power, the gendered aspects of the institutions will be reshaped. Much of this depends upon the nature of the decision-making structures of the institutions, as demonstrated in the chapters by Sue Thomas and Susan Gluck Mezey on women in legislative office and in the federal judiciary, respectively. Thomas shows that women legislators have indeed made a difference by advancing somewhat different issues and policy priorities. But she also shows that the institutions have not been entirely remade by the presence of women; many aspects of what she terms "gendered institutions" persist. Mezey shows that, though women have significantly increased their numbers on the federal bench, the evidence as to whether women bring a "different voice" to judicial decision making is mixed. Thomas's chapter shows that a relatively small number of women legislators, who after all are still a minority of all legislators, cannot remake an institution; we must wait to see whether a majority of women legislators could do so, and our wait is likely to be a long one. Women's share of legislative seats nationwide has stopped growing in the opening years of the twenty-first century, and remains at the level it had reached by the end of the 1990s. Mezey's chapter suggests that the structure of legal decision making and the career paths of federal judges may limit the ways in which a judge's gender might influence decision making; in this case, even a continually climbing proportion of lawyers who are women may not have an obvious early effect on judicial institutions.

Gender's multiple effects require multiple levels of analysis. As our brief illustration of three of the chapters demonstrates, these essays examine gender at the level of the symbolic, the institutional, and the individual. Some chapters address the way in which gender has structured the institutions of government and the means of delivering services to citizens. Others address the way that men and women as individuals become aware of and active in political life. Still others seek to explain the way in which gender shapes the decision-making processes of public leaders. This volume provides evidence of the profound and subtle effects of gender (and the intersection of gender with other critical sources of identification, such as race) on the way politics is done in the United States.

This volume is divided into three sections: Political Behavior, Public Policy, and Institutions. These three sections reflect three major areas of empirical study of American politics. While each arena is very broad, we believe the essays in this volume provide something of an overview of the state of research and empirical evidence regarding gender in each of these areas. After outlining the changes that have been made for the second edition, we will discuss the arguments of each chapter.

New in the Second Edition

Three new chapters increase the area covered by this edition. First, a significant arena of research on gender and American politics has been examination of the behavior of women and men as representatives in state legislatures and Congress, particularly as these institutions have been transformed by the addition of significant numbers of women. Sue Thomas discusses this important area of research and examines the ways in which legislatures have, and have not, been transformed by the increasing presence of women legislators. Her chapter on women in office is a fine counterpart to the Fox and Fiber chapter on women seeking office. Second, we have added a chapter on gender and the media, authored by David Niven. The interaction between the media and political life is an important area of research, and Niven's chapter, examining the major media's gendering of their coverage of women and men in Congress, is an important addition to this volume. Finally, the first edition did not address gender and U.S. foreign policy. Given events of the past several years, doing so in the second edition seemed imperative. Thus we have added a chapter by Janie Leatherman on hegemonic masculinity as a policy justification for the U.S. invasion of Iraq.

In addition to these three new chapters, all of the chapters in the original volume have been either updated with new data or completely revised. These changes are outlined in the discussion of each chapter, below.

Political Behavior

The chapters in this section of the book explore numerous facets of men's and women's political engagement, including political knowledge and its determinants, as well as the participation (largely through elections) of men and women in political life.

Michael Delli Carpini and Scott Keeter present empirical evidence of differences in men's and women's levels of political knowledge. Political psychologists have long debated whether knowledge—an understanding of the institutions, processes, and actors of politics—engenders political action, or action leads to knowledge (although the two are clearly also reciprocal). Delli Carpini and Keeter take the perspective that political action is driven in significant ways by political knowledge—and, if this is the case, women's comparatively lower levels of political knowledge may leave them at a disadvantage in political behavior as well. Americans generally are not especially knowledgeable about the structure and processes of the American political system. Even given this low bar, however, women are not as knowledgeable, on average, as are men. Delli Carpini and Keeter review the many studies that have found a difference between women's and men's knowledge of national politics, a difference that has persisted over the last half century despite changes in men's and women's roles. Their chapter's special contribution is to limn the dimensions of this gender gap in political knowledge and make its consequences clear. In particular, they seek to explain how differences in political knowledge arise from structural inequities between men and women, by which they mean women's historic exclusion from national politics, and situational inequities, by which they mean the continuing differences between men's and women's lives, such as working for wages, education, and other activities that favor the acquisition of political information. They use data from the National Election Study, from their own national survey, and from Gallup polls to examine changes in men's and women's comparative political knowledge from the 1940s through the 2000 election.

The authors find what seems to be a clear manifestation of gender role socialization differences: the "knowledge gap" is largest at the level of national politics and foreign policy, but the gap diminishes or disappears for issues that might be considered of direct relevance to women, such as health care policy or candidate positions on abortion, or local politics (historically the domain most receptive to women's political action, as the political arena literally "closest to home"), and the gap reverses, favoring women, on questions of local school politics—once again, appearing to reflect gender role expectations about the sexes' interests.

Finally, the authors examine the effect of political knowledge on political attitudes. They find a modest gap in the opinions of men and women with low levels of political knowledge. As political knowledge increases, however, the gender gap in opinion increases as well. More informed men hold more conservative views, and more informed women are more liberal. Extrapolating from these data, they argue that a fully informed citizenry would vote differently and hold different opinions than does the present electorate. They conclude that a better informed citizenry, with no knowledge gaps between the sexes, is necessary to a truly democratic democracy—one that represents its citizens' interests.

M. Margaret Conway's chapter addresses gender differences and similarities in political participation. Conway provides a concise summary of women's historic exclusion from participation in political life before turning to an examination of three classic indicators of electoral engagement: voting, making campaign contributions, and participating in campaign activities. She finds that although women were less likely to vote than men were during the first six decades after they gained the franchise, since 1980 women have been about as likely to vote as have men—but women remain less likely than men to give money and to participate in campaign events.

Conway then examines possible explanations for women's lower levels of political participation. Among explanations that have been offered by scholars are differences in gender role socialization, in available resources, and in social contexts. Conway explores another approach: generational differences in patterns of participation. When she divides voters into four birth cohorts, she finds that men are advantaged in voting by slight but insignificant amounts, but the differences are larger for campaign contributions and activities. Conway speculates that women's varying gender role orientations may explain intrasex differences in participation, as other works have found to be the case, but the two measures available to her—views on equal roles for women, and support of the women's movement—are not sensitive enough to explain those differences. Far from concluding that gender role orientations make no difference to women's politicization, Conway argues that we need better measures. Conway joins others who have found that our major electoral behavior and opinion databases lack sufficient indicators of women's and men's beliefs about their gender roles to enable us to map the relationships among them with any refinement. Those measures we do have, such as the thirty-year-old question in the National Election Studies on the belief that men and women should have equal roles, may no longer be as effective as discriminators as they once were. They may particularly fail to reveal the dynamics behind the political mobilization of "antifeminist" women, such as politically engaged, conservative, religiously active women, whom Conway and others find to be more politically active than some hypotheses about women's behavior would predict.

The chapter by Pam Fiber and Richard Fox is new to this volume, replacing the chapter by Richard Fox in the first edition. Its location has also changed. Because of the chapter's central concern with electoral processes and behaviors, we have taken the opportunity to include it in the section on political behavior. Fiber and Fox note that at 86 percent male, the U.S. Congress trails well behind the national legislative bodies of many other democracies in the progress of women into its ranks. Incumbency is a significant obstacle to women's entry into Congress; when women run in open-seat elections, they are as likely to win as are male candidates. Gender matters, then, in its residual effects: because, until recently, only men were seen as credible candidates, the majority of incumbents are male. Today's female members of Congress also benefit from the incumbency advantage, meaning that, as women run for and win open seats, this particular residual association of gender and incumbency will fade. Fiber and Fox contribute to our understanding of gender in elections by showing how although gender no longer matters at the ballot box in the sense of simple voter discrimination against women candidates, it continues to matter in quite subtle ways to other parts of the electoral process. As they note, both male and female candidates still face "an electorate, a press corps, and a political establishment that often rely on masculine and feminine stereotypes to assess candidates." This means that men's and women's experiences as candidates continue to differ, even if the old voter discrimination against women candidates has evaporated.

In U.S. House elections from 1980 through 2002, they find, male and female candidates amass similar vote totals; the authors thus join other recent researchers in concluding that voter bias for or against female candidates is not a significant factor in congressional election outcomes. Fiber and Fox also find that men and women are roughly equivalently successful as fundraisers. Underneath the national totals, however, we find significant regional variations: some states have substantial representation by women, and others do not. Since the "Year of the Woman" in 1992, the rate of increase in women's electoral success has continued only in the West, while stagnating or remaining constant in other regions. National vote totals and the size of campaign war chests, then, suggest parity between women and men, but regional variation suggests that some differences continue to influence electoral outcomes.

The second section of the chapter turns to these more subtle ways in which gender does still matter. In particular, Fiber and Fox examine men's and women's different experiences of campaigning. They divide their analysis of open-seat elections, where incumbency cannot obscure the picture, into the two distinctly different periods of 1980 to 1990 and 1992 to 2000. Both parties run more women candidates in the latter period, although the Democratic party runs significantly more women candidates than does the Republican party. One of the subtle differences makes itself evident in funding. Although women actually raised more money on average than did men, in races featuring male–female competition (as opposed to male–male or female–female races), the authors find that men raise about $100,000 more than do their female opponents, and they raise the money from different sources. Women tend to raise more of their campaign funds from individuals, from labor, and from out-of-state individuals. The final group is explained by the influence of national women's candidacy advocacy groups like EMILY's List and WISH List, who recruit women donors nationwide and ask them to donate to targeted races. Some other differences in the sources of campaign funds may be attributable to candidates' party affiliations, but Fiber and Fox find a residual advantage for men in all fundraising categories except that of out-of-state funds. Further, both female and male candidates raise more money when their opponent is a woman than when either runs against a man. Fiber and Fox suggest that women candidates may be competing in "particularly intense electoral environments," and they invite us to pay more attention to these subtle gender differences in congressional campaigns.

In the final chapter of the political behavior section, Eric Plutzer investigates the implications of the discussion of gender and moral decision making stimulated by Carol Gilligan's book, *In a Different Voice.* Plutzer links this theorizing about decision making to the pessimism about citizen competence in democratic decision making articulated by James Madison and other framers of the U.S. Constitution. He argues that debate about public policy in the United States is often motivated by an underlying evaluation of the capacity of citizens to make their own choices on matters that may be of public import or concern. Concern about women's capacity to make informed moral judgments (or the lack thereof, as some earlier theories and popular understandings have had it) has been a backdrop to many public policy debates, including debates over abortion policy.

Plutzer studies the question by using data from a survey he and Barbara Ryan conducted in the 1980s on the decision-making process of women who had chosen to have an abortion. In their study, they examined the decision about whether to tell the co-conceiver of the child of the pregnancy and of their decision to abort. Plutzer and Ryan asked a series of questions in the context of the counseling sessions that all patients underwent prior to receiving services. Their data come from about equal numbers of women who chose to tell, and who chose not to tell, the co-conceiver.

Plutzer is interested in the reasons women give for telling, and for not telling, and especially in the decision-making process that women go through. As Plutzer notes, Carol Gilligan's book laid out a framework of moral reasoning based on an ethic of care versus moral reasoning based on an ethic of rights. Scholars and the public alike seemed frequently, and incorrectly, to have reached the superficial conclusion that Gilligan was associating the former kind of reasoning with women, and the latter kind with men. Plutzer uses a more refined understanding of Gilligan's "multiple moral voices" to assess which type of reasoning predominates, and under what circumstances, in women's decision making about whether to tell of pregnancy and the decision to abort. He finds that both those who chose to tell and those who chose not to tell use both modes of reasoning in their decision making. In addition, the context of the relationship between the woman and her co-conceiver was a critical variable in the decision-making process. Plutzer's findings support the conclusion that both men and women use both modes of reasoning, and he warns us to be skeptical of efforts to essentialize decision making according to gender. Plutzer notes that women who chose not to tell were often more concerned with rights and principles, and with their own autonomy, given the context of the relationship. However, he argues, this study shows the tremendously contextual nature of ethical reasoning: it is affected by power and by the nature of the relationships involved—especially the relative power of the persons involved in the decision. Thus, what is perhaps most important in examining moral or ethical decisions as they relate to public life is the context in which decisions are made. Gender is an important part of this context.

Plutzer's chapter in the first edition was limited to women subjects. For this edition he adds a brief section regarding men and decisions regarding abortion. Plutzer concludes from available evidence on studies of "waiting room men"—men who accompany their partners to the abortion clinic—that men, as well as women, hear moral voices related to both justice and care. Moral decision making and gender have more complex interactions than is often recognized by many who have invoked Gilligan's work.

Public Policy

Given some of the observed differences as well as similarities in political behavior of men and women, what difference does gender make to public policy? How is gender reflected in the institutions created by public policy and in the policymaking process? The chapters in this section provide some answers to those questions.

The first chapter tackles gender in U.S. foreign policy. Janie Leatherman uses the construct of "hegemonic masculinity," or the articulation of aggressive nation-alism and the doctrine of superiority, and the rhetorical and policy initiatives used to "feminize" foreign policy strategies that emphasize consensus building and multilateralism, to explore the Bush strategic doctrine behind the U.S. invasion of Iraq. Leatherman finds that hegemonic masculinity, a doctrine used by most of the world's powers when they have engaged in war-making, may have short-term mili-tary advantages, but it comes with long-term costs to the U.S. position in the inter-national community and to our credibility as the superpower, to the troops who are sent to fight, and, not least, to the lives of the noncombatants who find themselves in the path of the conflict.

The international community, Leatherman says, is finally beginning to express a willingness to reexamine the appropriateness of hegemonic masculinity. In 2000, for example, the United Nations engaged in the first systematic examination of the unique effects of war on women and girls, resulting in the adoption of Resolution 1325, which affirms women not only as victims of war's cruelties, especially rape, which women have historically endured, but as agents who must be seen as genu-ine actors both in war and in the making of peace.

In the chapter that follows, Dorothy E. McBride uncovers the role of gender in the debates in three policy areas: welfare reform, abortion, and trafficking in women and girls. McBride seeks to address the substantive representation of feminist ideas in the policymaking process by evaluating the impact of feminist policy advocates on the shape of these policies. She treats policymaking as a process in which there are regular patterns in the conflict of ideas surrounding policy formulation and implementation. McBride is especially interested in the framing of policy debates. She argues that feminist advocates seek both to place their policy concerns higher on the government's agenda and to influence the way that policy debates are framed on issues related to gender.

To begin her examination of the role that feminist advocates play in policy debates where gender is a significant issue, McBride analyzes debates over wel-fare reform, particularly in the process that led to the 1996 Personal Responsibility and Work Opportunity Reconciliation Act (PRWORA). This legislation ended the Aid to Families with Dependent Children (AFDC) program and replaced it with a new program focused on time-limited benefits and work requirements. Despite feminists' efforts to intervene in both the framing of the debate and the policy outcome, McBride concludes, the passage of PRWORA represented an almost complete defeat for the feminist policy stance. With respect to abortion, McBride analyzes the debate over the Partial-Birth Abortion Ban Act of 1995. The debate, McBride argues, placed feminist advocates outside of the policy process and marks a shift in abortion politics from a focus on women's privacy rights to a focus on abortion procedures themselves. Despite feminist efforts to introduce ideas of women's health and self-determination, these were not the dominant frames of the debate. Of course, the act was vetoed by then President Clinton, but passed again, in similar form, in 2003, when it was signed into law by President Bush.

Finally, McBride examines the issue of trafficking in women and girls—like rape in war, one of the more horrific consequences of state sanctioning of, or indifference to, the treatment of women and girls as less than human beings vested with full rights. While trafficking—the practice of bringing women and girls into forced work in the sex industry—has a long history, it received new attention in international and domestic policy arenas beginning in the 1990s. McBride argues that because this issue was reframed in gendered terms from the beginning of the new policy debate on it, both feminist groups and the President's Interagency Council on Women had a significant influence on the policy outcome in the Traffic in Persons Protection Act of 2000. McBride concludes that all three policy arenas show both the complexity of the interaction of feminist advocates with government officials in the policymaking process, and the significance of language and ideas in the agenda-setting process.

Jyl J. Josephson addresses in her chapter the shaping influence of gender on social policy, especially with respect to policy termination and to the justifications provided for ending policies targeted toward specific groups. Her chapter draws on a model developed by Anne Schneider and Helen Ingram that argues that the political power and positive or negative perceptions of populations targeted by public policies affect policy formation and implementation. Josephson applies their model to social policy. Specifically, she addresses two policy terminations of the 1990s: the termination of the General Assistance program in Michigan in 1991—a program perceived to be targeted primarily toward able-bodied men—and the termination of the federal AFDC program in 1996—a program perceived to be targeted primarily toward poor women.

Josephson notes that gender played an important role in the formation of social policy as a whole in the United States: several of the social programs of the New Deal can be characterized as targeted either toward men in their role as workers or toward women in their role as mothers. She then traces the history of the termination of Michigan's General Assistance program and the federal AFDC program, arguing that, although budget shortfalls and political ideology placed termination on the agenda in the case of both programs, other programs, also targeted for termination, escaped that fate. General Assistance and AFDC could be terminated because policymakers could depict the recipients of each program as deviant. The "deviance" of each target population emanated in part from its failure to comply with gender roles perceived as appropriate for that population. In the case of General Assistance, recipients were depicted as able-bodied minority men who were simply unwilling to work; in the case of AFDC, recipients were depicted both as able-bodied women unwilling to work and as bad mothers who were not providing proper care for their children. Josephson shows that the empirical evidence about the characteristics of each population differs decidedly from their depiction by policymakers.

Although the law that terminated AFDC and created Temporary Assistance for Needy Families is still in effect, Josephson concludes her chapter by examining the proposed reauthorization legislation for this program, which is still pending before Congress at this writing. In particular, she assesses the provisions for promoting marriage and "responsible fatherhood" and the assumptions embedded in these proposals, comparing them again to the empirical evidence regarding low-income families.

Sue Tolleson-Rinehart's chapter addresses the gendering of health policy by evaluating the difficulty of treading the line between similarity and difference in health care for men and for women. Tolleson-Rinehart notes that the adage among health care providers used to be that "women get sicker, men die quicker," and that, except in the case of reproduction, neither health care providers nor policymakers took much more account than that of women's health. For example, the history of medical research has been one of excluding women from most clinical trials (on the grounds of possible harm to fetuses, should women in research trials become pregnant), but then unreflectively applying the results of trials on men to women. Sometimes such "gender-blind" applications are harmless, but at other times, as in the recognition and treatment of heart disease, they have harmful consequences.

Recently, "women's health" has gained high salience in the public and the policymaking arena alike, but even in this case, the attention has been to women's breast and reproductive health, suggesting that health policy is still perhaps inappropriately gendered. That is, we have had new attention to "women's health," but framed in such a way that there appears to be "health," which only applies to men, and "women's health," which is only reproductive health. Even the new attention to women's health is not without controversy, as Tolleson-Rinehart demonstrates with brief case studies of breast cancer screening and the treatment of pre-term labor. At present, the health policy community—including women's health advocates—is beginning to acknowledge that both sex and gender matter to some aspects of women's and men's health, and are not relevant to others.

For example, some of the most powerful threats to women's health are not related to reproductive health; heart disease, for example, kills vastly more women each year than does breast cancer, but women's experience of heart disease may nonetheless be different from the experience of men for sex-related reasons we do not yet fully understand. In other cases, gender still matters: women are poorer than are men because of the inequities arising out of gendered political and social structures, and poverty is associated with poor health, poor access to health care, and, possibly, poorer quality of the care the poor do receive. In order to make the best health policy for both women and men, Tolleson-Rinehart concludes, we must be alert to the contexts in which sex matters, those in which gender does, and those for which neither is a factor.

Institutions

The final section of the book addresses men's and women's roles in each branch of government. These chapters determine the influence of gender on the behavior of men and women in elective and appointive office, with a special focus on representation: does it matter, and if so how, whether both women and men hold public office? Since women have historically been excluded from most top government positions, what difference does it make, if any, that more women hold positions in the federal judiciary, in Congress, and in the Cabinet, than has been true in the past? In what ways do men and women bring gender into the public arena in decision making, and what can an analysis of gender contribute to our understanding of public officials in American political life?

MaryAnne Borrelli here offers a completely revised and updated study of the role of gender in the Cabinet in her chapter for this edition. Borrelli examines the history of the appointment of women to Cabinet positions and the role that gender plays as women increasingly assume these roles. After briefly reviewing the history of presidential appointment of women to Cabinet positions, Borrelli focuses on a comparison of appointments in the Clinton and George W. Bush administrations. Borrelli argues that Cabinet nominations are in part an indication of how responsive presidents are to pluralism in the United States. Thus, cabinet designees provide one way of measuring the representativeness of the executive branch. To provide an analytic focus for the role that gender plays in Cabinet nominations, Borrelli argues that, given the history of the Cabinet as a male-gendered institution, and one that is still dominated by male nominees, women nominees might be seen as either contributing to the regendering, or the transgendering, of the Cabinet. By regendering, Borrelli means that the woman nominee's position reinforces traditional gender patterns in the executive branch; by transgendering, she means that the woman nominee's position challenges the historic gender patterns of the Cabinet.

Borrelli argues that prior to the Clinton administration, given that the overwhelming majority of women Cabinet members were policy generalists and thus dependent on the White House, the Cabinet was not significantly altered by the presence of women. However, during the Clinton administration, Borelli says, a set of fortuitous circumstances and an increase in the number of women produced a transgendering effect. Although it is still early to assess the record of the current administration, Borrelli argues that both transgendering and regendering of the Cabinet are occurring as a result of appointments made by George W. Bush.

Susan Gluck Mezey's chapter on the federal judiciary details both the number of men and women appointed to the bench and the degree to which gender may influence their judicial decision making. The chapter distinguishes between descriptive representation, achieved when public officials have superficial characteristics similar to those characteristics in the population, and substantive representation, which occurs when public officials seek to accomplish the goals of the group that they represent. Mezey is primarily concerned with the extent to which women judges act as substantive representatives for women as a group.

Mezey, like Plutzer, addresses the uses to which Carol Gilligan's work in moral theory has been put. In this case, some legal scholars have assumed that female judges might speak, and make decisions, in a "different voice." The empirical tests of these claims have yielded decidedly mixed results: women judges sometimes speak in Gilligan's different voice of care and connection rather than in the voice of rules and legalism, but men judges also speak in this different voice at times. Similarly, both women and men can, and sometimes must, render decisions in formal legalistic terms. Thus, the literature on whether women have different or distinctly female approaches to decision making is mixed.

Mezey then traces the history of appointments of women judges to the federal bench. She notes that the first presidential administration to appoint substantial numbers of women to federal judgeships was the Carter administration, which made a total of ninety-three appointments of women to the bench. After the Carter administration increases, the question of whether gender makes a difference in how judges make decisions becomes much more subject to valid scientific analysis. One way to translate the question of gender difference into judicial terms is to ask whether women judges are more likely to be judicial activists, or judges willing to make policy from the bench—especially liberal policy, and especially with regard to sex and race discrimination. Mezey reviews the studies that have addressed this question, noting that most have found little difference in the judicial activism of women and men, or between racial minority and racial majority judges' activism on the bench. Mezey provides profiles of the two most prominent women federal judges, United States Supreme Court Associate Justices Sandra Day O'Connor and Ruth Bader Ginsburg, before concluding that the tenets of legal education, and the institutional and professional constraints surrounding the federal judiciary, limit the potential influence of gender on judicial decision making.

New to this edition is the chapter by Sue Thomas on the behavior of women legislators. Thomas begins with an overview of the types of questions that scholars have asked with respect to women in legislative bodies at the state and national level in the United States. The chapter then outlines the findings of several decades of research on women and men in legislative office. Her review reveals, for example, that men and women have tended to come from different backgrounds and to have taken different career paths to legislative office, although these differences have diminished as more women have won office. A persistent dissimilarity, however, is in differences between men and women with respect to their private lives; women legislators remain less likely to be married, and to have children, than is true of their male counterparts.

Thomas turns next to the impact that women have had as legislators, perhaps the question on which the largest amount of scholarly energy has been lavished in all of gender politics research. The findings to date indicate that women have indeed focused on somewhat different issues than have their male counterparts, even accounting for party affiliation. Indeed, as Thomas points out, women legislators have placed many issues formerly considered to be "private," such as sexual harassment and domestic violence, squarely on the public agenda. More recent work also indicates that women legislators have become more active in all aspects of the legislative process, and that women are also beginning to move to committee and institutional leadership positions. Thomas also discusses the question of whether a "critical mass" of women is required to influence policy in particular directions. The evidence on this is mixed, and may require both more study and more legislatures with a critical mass of women before we can draw firm conclusions.

Thomas then turns to what she terms "environmental factors" with respect to legislatures: how does the institutional, political, and societal context of gender shape women's experiences as legislators? Data from her own highly regarded study of women state legislators enables Thomas to concur with other researchers who find that women legislators persistently identify gender as a significant barrier to women's success in the institution. Interestingly, no male legislators saw gender as an issue, evidence that those in the "unmarked" gender category—men— are unaware of the advantages they accrue from gender hierarchies. Thomas also finds that women tend to lead and engage in decision making in ways somewhat different from the ways of male legislators, which puts women at odds with the male-dominated culture of legislative bodies. She also finds that women legislators must still negotiate traditionally gendered social roles. Thomas leaves us with a picture of women officeholders coping with change as well as with enduring, and limiting, patterns in the gendered structure of legislatures.

David Niven's chapter, also new to this volume, addresses gender bias, and gendered expectations, in the media. Niven looks specifically at media treatments of male and female members of Congress. He restricts his study to elected officials rather than candidates because coverage of them is ongoing, not seasonal, and because the treatment of officeholders reveals more about the current and future political context than does the treatment of candidates. The chapter is in three sections: Niven looks first to scholarly findings with respect to gender bias in the media. He then turns to his own content analysis of newspaper coverage of members of Congress. Finally, he compares this coverage to members' own websites as a way to compare media coverage to officeholders' self-presentation.

Much of the academic study of gender and the media has focused on candidates. There, scholars have found persistent differences in the way that male and female candidates are treated. These studies find that women receive less coverage, are portrayed differently than are male candidates, are subject to much more discussion of their sex, personality, and personal characteristics, and have more trouble getting coverage of their key campaign issues. In short, the press reinforces gender stereotypes in its coverage of men and women candidates. These findings reinforce Niven's findings from an earlier study of press secretaries. Press secretaries who work for women members of Congress had persistent concerns regarding media gender bias in coverage of their bosses. Press secretaries for male members of Congress offered no complaints about gender bias.

Next, Niven turns to a content analysis of print coverage of male and female members of Congress. He identifies the sample of all 73 women who served in the Senate and House between May 1 of 2001 and April 30 of 2003, and matches them with a sample of 73 men on party, ideology, and regional characteristics. He then compares media coverage of the women and men over the study period in five major national and five home-state newspapers, measuring amount of coverage, how the priorities of the members were depicted, descriptions of members' qualifications and accomplishments, descriptions of political motivations of members, how the members' personal lives were discussed, and the overall tone of the coverage.

Niven finds that male members of Congress received more coverage than did women in both national and state newspapers. In some cases the differences are extreme, such as in the case of the two senators from Michigan, both liberal Democrats. In the time period studied, Senator Debbie Stabenow was the subject of 19 articles in major newspapers, compared to 154 articles on Senator Carl Levin. Niven finds some interesting trends in the coverage of issues, some of which seem to maintain gender differences and others of which may indicate some changes. For example, children's issues are salient in the coverage of men as well as women. Niven finds that women are depicted less favorably and with less respect than are men. He notes especially the coverage of Nancy Pelosi's ascendancy to the position of minority leader in the House, in which the *Los Angeles Times* depicted her, in its headline, as an "Airhead." He also finds persisting gender differences in coverage of the personal lives and traits of members of Congress. Women's clothing, physical appearance, and hair are frequently mentioned. When men's personal appearance is mentioned, Niven notes that it is done in the context of illustrating "their high stature and suitability for the job," as in mentions of Senator John Cornyn's "senatorial" hair.

Comparing the press coverage to members' own websites, Niven finds that men and women depict their commitment to issues and priorities and their accomplishments in very similar terms, but that women actually devote less space and attention on their websites to family and personal lives than do men. Niven concludes that the differences between coverage of male and female members of Congress is an artifact of media bias, and not instigated by members' own actions and preferences. Further, these differences do contribute to influencing constituents' perceptions of members. Media gender bias remains a significant problem for women members of Congress.

Conclusion

The chapters in this book provide the reader with an overview and analysis of the role of gender in virtually all the domains of American political life. They offer insight into the significant role that gender plays in governmental decision making and the political process, as well as in parties, elections, and in political behavior. They illustrate the importance of the context in which political decisions are made, and the power of both sex and gender to shape American politics.

Part One
Political Behavior

2

Gender and Political Knowledge

Michael X. Delli Carpini and Scott Keeter

According to many indicators, the integration of women into the U.S. political system proceeds apace. Voter turnout among women now exceeds that of men, and the trend is for this gap to increase (Leighley and Nagler 1991). The number of female candidates for political office at all levels of government continues to rise, and women's chance for success at the polls appears greater as well (Delli Carpini and Fuchs 1993). The increasing presence of women in the work force, and in politically relevant professions such as the law, portends greater participation as candidates and activists in the future (Darcy, Welch, and Clark 1987; Taeuber 1991).

At the same time, women are becoming increasingly differentiated from men in their political views and preferences. The "gender gap" in partisanship and vote choice, rarely seen prior to the late 1970s, is larger than ever. Gender differences in attitudes on a variety of issues show no sign of diminishing (Shapiro and Mahajan 1986; Erikson and Tedin 1995, 209–12; Pew Research Center 2003). The combination of greater participation and a distinctive agenda suggests the potential for women to exert a powerful influence in contemporary politics.

However, there remain important differences between women and men in the resources that fuel effective political action. Men still earn more than women, even in jobs requiring comparable training and skills. Child care responsibilities often restrict career progress for women, especially those who are single. Women are still less likely than men to engage in a variety of modes of political participation beyond voting, though the definition of "political" in this context is controversial (Verba 1990; Bourque and Grossholtz 1984). And there is growing evidence that even when women are granted nominal access to power, their effectiveness is undermined by gendered expectations and practices (Kathlene 1994; Mattei 1998).

This chapter focuses on a fundamental resource for political action: knowledge about politics. While several studies of political knowledge have found that men are better informed than women about national politics (Glenn 1972; Sigelman and Yanarella 1986; Bennett 1988; Delli Carpini and Keeter 1996; Kenski and Jamieson 2000; Kenski 2003; but see Anderson, Canache, and Mondak 2002), few have explored the size, significance, and sources of this "gender gap" in any detail. In the present study, we draw on a number of recent surveys—including several specifically designed to tap factual knowledge about politics—to document the nature and extent of the current gender gap in political knowledge. We also examine whether or not this gender gap has increased or decreased over the past thirty to forty years. We then test several explanations for the knowledge gap between men and women. Finally, we assess the political implications of gender differences in political knowledge.[1]

The Importance of Political Knowledge

The value of political knowledge has been attested to by numerous studies. First, knowledge stimulates and facilitates political participation. Both Neuman (1986, 84–89, 99–103) and Palfrey and Poole (1987, 524–29) found knowledge of politics—controlling for socioeconomic status—to be highly predictive of voting turnout. And Junn found a reciprocal relationship between knowledge and participation, with knowledge eclipsing most other predictors of a variety of forms of participation (1991, 203–9).

Second, political knowledge has a powerful impact on the formation of political opinions and the processing of new information. Elaborating on Converse's (1962) classic work on the role of stored information in mediating the effects of political communication, Zaller has developed a general model of the effects of knowledge on attitude change in a variety of settings (1991, 1992). Of specific relevance to our interests, he noted that gender differences in attitudes about the Vietnam war—with women less supportive than men—were manifested chiefly among individuals with high levels of knowledge, and concluded that high information levels were "necessary for the effective translation of political predispositions into appropriate policy preferences" (Zaller 1991, 1229). Several studies have also documented differences in how better and lesser informed individuals reason about political issues and decisions, demonstrating that political knowledge improves the speed and efficiency of information processing, and renders citizens less vulnerable to priming and other media effects (Fiske, Lau, and Smith 1990; Lodge, McGraw, and Stroh 1989; McGraw and Pinney 1990; Sniderman, Brody, and Tetlock 1991, esp. ch. 3, 4, and 7; Lanoue 1992).[2]

Third (and perhaps as a specific application of the previous point), the process of voter decision making among the well informed is very different from that of the less informed. Compared with uninformed voters, informed voters are likely to use a broader range of considerations in reaching a candidate choice and are much more likely to use issues as a criterion (Moon 1990; Sniderman, Brody, and Tetlock 1991; Brady and Ansolabehere 1989).

Thus, political knowledge facilitates more effective citizenship in several ways. It promotes participation and engagement in politics. It enables citizens to comprehend the political world and to develop attitudes about politics that are consistent with one's basic values and orientations. And it is critical to an effective linkage between attitudes and political behavior.

Measuring Political Knowledge

The analyses in this chapter utilize a variety of data, nearly all of which were gathered by telephone or in-person surveys of random samples of the public. Four major national surveys are at the center of much of the analysis: one is a telephone survey of 610 adults, designed by the authors and conducted in 1989 by a university-based survey research center; the other three are the 1992, 1996, and 2000 National Election Studies (NES), conducted through in-person interviews by the Center for Political Studies at the University of Michigan (Miller and the National Election Studies 1992, 1996; Burns, Kinder, Rosenstone, Sapiro, and the National Elections Studies 2001).

Our national survey included fifty-one knowledge questions covering a broad range of political topics, as well as an extensive set of attitudinal, behavioral, and demographic items. Our approach was to include questions of varying format and difficulty, covering several different topic areas. Following James David Barber's notion that citizens "need to know what the government *is* and *does*" (1973, 44, emphasis added), a large part of the questionnaire covered "the rules of the game" and "the substance of politics." A third important area, linked to the citizen's responsibility in a representative democracy, is the set of "people and players" in politics.[3] The specific topics covered by our survey, along with the percentage of men and women correctly answering each question, are provided in Table 2.1 (discussed below).[4] In addition to using the questions individually, we also created a knowledge index by summing the number of correct answers to the questions (and assigning partial credit on some topics where appropriate). This index varied from 3 to 43 in the sample (with a theoretical range of 0 to 51), with a mean of 23.7 and a median of 24.[5]

The NES surveys typically devote relatively few direct questions to the measurement of political knowledge. However, because of the relative unidimensionality of the concept (see note 5), a good knowledge index can be constructed by combining the available direct knowledge items with other questions that also tap awareness and understanding of political phenomena (Delli Carpini and Keeter 1992, 1993, 1996; Zaller 1986). Using the 1996 NES we constructed a sixteen-item knowledge index, to which we added the two interviewer ratings of respondent's information level (pre-election and post-election waves).[6] The resulting index varies from 0 to 24 in the sample, with a mean of 14.3 and a median of 15. The content is narrower than in our national survey, with no questions focusing on "civics knowledge," but this data set has the advantage of a large sample size and an extensive set of attitudinal and behavioral questions.[7] Table 2.2 shows the percentage of men and women correctly answering each of the items.

Past and Present Gender Differences in Knowledge of National Politics

In both of the national surveys, men as a group were more knowledgeable than women on nearly all of the factual political questions.[8] In our 1989 survey (Table 2.1), the

Table 2.1

Gender Differences in Knowledge of National Politics, 1989 National Survey (percent correct)

	Men	Women	Difference	Odds ratio
What is the Superfund?	18	4	14	5.3
Percent unemployed	41	14	27	4.3
Percent vote required for veto override	50	21	29	3.8
Does U.S. have a trade deficit?	91	73	18	3.7
Percent black in U.S.	19	7	12	3.1
Contras are rebels	69	42	27	3.1
Sandinistas control Nicaraguan government	58	32	26	2.9
What is a veto?	94	85	9	2.8
Can veto be overridden?	89	75	14	2.7
Did U.S. support Contras?	80	60	20	2.7
Name governor	81	66	15	2.2
Describe recent arms agreement	57	39	18	2.1
Can Communist run for President?	59	41	18	2.1
Define the New Deal	20	11	9	2.0
Federal budget: percent for education	24	14	10	1.9
Name both U.S. senators	31	19	12	1.9
Rehnquist's ideology	37	24	13	1.9
Define recession	65	50	15	1.9
What are first ten amendments called?	53	39	14	1.8
Size of federal budget	56	42	14	1.8
Federal budget: percent for defense	10	6	4	1.7
Who reviews constitutionality of laws?	72	60	12	1.7
U.S. supports El Salvadoran government	50	37	13	1.7
Percent poor in U.S.	23	15	8	1.7
Name Vice President	79	69	10	1.7
Percent with health insurance	11	7	4	1.6
Who declares war?	40	29	11	1.6
Describe one First Amendment right	43	32	11	1.6
Does U.S. have a budget deficit?	82	74	8	1.6
Party control of House	73	64	9	1.5
Name one of your U.S. Senators	60	50	10	1.5
Describe one Fifth Amendment right	56	46	10	1.5
Prior to *Roe*, was abortion illegal in all states?	63	54	9	1.5
Truman's party	63	54	9	1.5
FDR's party	67	59	8	1.4
Describe two First Amendment rights	21	16	5	1.4
Define effects of a tariff	56	48	8	1.4
Describe three First Amendment rights	9	7	2	1.3
Party control of Senate	58	52	6	1.3
Length of presidential term	96	95	1	1.3
Must students say pledge of allegiance?	78	74	4	1.2
Can states prohibit abortion?	75	71	4	1.2
Name U.S. Representative	31	27	4	1.2
Who appoints judges?	60	56	4	1.2
Date of women's suffrage	10	9	1	1.1
Nixon's party	76	76	0	1.0
Describe two Fifth Amendment rights	5	5	0	1.0
Did women always have suffrage?	89	90	−1	0.9
Date of New Deal	11	13	−2	0.8
Is there a right to counsel?	90	92	−2	0.8
Federal budget: percent for Social Security	4	6	−2	0.7

Table 2.2

Gender Differences in Knowledge of National Politics, 1996 National Election Study (percent correct)

	Men	Women	Difference	Odds ratio
Identify William Rehnquist	15.2	5.2	9.9	3.2
Candidates' positions on defense	60.3	42.7	17.6	2.0
Interviewer rated R above average in knowledge	51.6	35.6	16.0	1.9
Party control of Senate	79.0	67.0	12.0	1.9
Parties' positions on defense	57.8	42.8	14.9	1.8
Party control of House	81.4	71.0	10.3	1.8
Identify Boris Yeltsin	72.1	60.0	12.1	1.7
Knows deficit declined in past 4 years	35.4	25.1	10.3	1.6
Candidates' positions on spending	75.0	66.1	9.0	1.5
Identify Al Gore	90.6	86.4	4.2	1.5
Parties' ideological placement	73.1	64.7	8.3	1.5
Parties' positions on spending	69.5	60.6	8.8	1.5
Identify Newt Gingrich	64.0	54.9	9.1	1.5
Candidates' positions on health insurance	71.3	63.5	7.8	1.4
Candidates' positions on jobs	68.5	63.0	5.5	1.3
Candidates' ideological placement	72.6	67.7	4.9	1.3
Candidates' positions on abortion	60.2	59.6	0.6	1.0
Mean percentage correct	64.6	55.1	9.5	—

average difference across all items in the percentage correct for men and women was 9.8. On only four items did a higher percentage of women correctly answer the question. The differences between women and men were similar in the 1996 National Election Study (Table 2.2). The average percentage difference was 9.5, with the gap ranging from less than 1 percentage point (on knowledge of the candidates' relative positions on abortion) to nearly 18 points (on knowledge the candidates' relative positions on defense spending). In both surveys, the median score for men was approximately equal to the seventy-fifth percentile for women, meaning that about three-fourths of women scored at or below the average for men.[9]

Many legal, social, and cultural changes during the past fifty years in the United States have resulted in greater political integration of women. It is thus reasonable to expect that the gender gap in knowledge about politics has declined during that period as well. Available data suggest that the knowledge gap narrowed very little over the period from the 1940s to the 1980s, although there is slight and inconsistent evidence of greater parity between women and men beginning in the 1990s (Jennings 1996).

We have two bases for making comparisons over time. Part of our 1989 national survey was devoted to the replication of several questions asked by the Gallup Organization during the 1940s and 1950s.[10] The other data source is the set of National Election Study surveys, which date back to 1952. While there are only a few knowledge items in the time series, the study methodology for each of the surveys was nearly identical, providing some reassurance that differences (or lack thereof) reflect the underlying phenomenon rather than differences in measurement or measurement error itself. Table 2.3 shows comparisons between men and women for the Gallup and 1989 political knowledge surveys, while Figure 2.1 displays trends from the NES data.

Across eight Gallup questions for which comparisons can be made with the 1989 survey, the gender gap in knowledge was smaller in five and larger in three. For questions with a smaller gap in 1989, the decline varied from 2 to 9 percentage points, with a mean change of 4.5 percent. The other three questions showed increases of 5 to 8 percentage points in the knowledge gap. The median change across all eight items was a modest decline of between 2 and 3 percentage points in the gender gap.

The NES data also suggest that there was little narrowing of the gap during this period. All four of the items depicted in Figure 2.1 do show some evidence of greater parity in 1996 than in 1992. However this slight decline in the disparity between men and women does not appear to carry over into 2000, at least for three of the four items for which we have data.[11]

Explaining the Gender Gap in Knowledge

The existence of *some* gender differences in political knowledge is not surprising, given the history of women's exclusion from national politics in the United States and the continuing inequality between women and men in access to many of the resources that contribute to political integration. However, its size and persistence over a period during which other indicators showed increased political engagement by women, raises questions about the genesis of the gap and the factors that contribute to its maintenance.

Most theories regarding gender differences in political orientation are rooted in structural and situational explanations: females know less about politics than males do because of differences in how the sexes are socialized and because of the different opportunities afforded them to engage the political world. But how, specifically, do structural and situational inequities translate into differences in political knowledge? The simplest argument is that they act as a barrier, preventing women who have the motivation to learn about politics from having the opportunity or ability to do so. Except among the youngest cohort of citizens, women have less formal education than men (and education is related to political knowledge). A smaller percentage of women than men is in the labor force (and employment outside the home provides politically relevant experiences). Women in the labor force are also likely to work in less "politically impinged" jobs than men (Luskin 1990). Unmarried women have lower incomes than unmarried men (and income is associated with political knowledge). Because of child care responsibilities, women have much less time for political activity and spend less of their time in contact with adults—who are more likely than children to talk about politics (Sapiro 1983; Jennings and Niemi 1981). According to this argument, if women had the same incomes, educational attainment,

Table 2.3

Gender Differences over Time, Gallup Surveys and 1989 Political Knowledge Survey

| | Gallup surveys | | | | Difference (men minus women) | | 1989 Political Knowledge Survey | | | |
| | Men | | Women | | | | Men | | Women | |
	%	Number	%	Number	%	%	%	Number	%	Number
Name your U.S. Representative (1947)	49	(1479)	36	(1497)	13	4	31	(279)	27	(331)
Name both U.S. Senators (1954)	37	(653)	20	(712)	17	12	31	(279)	19	(331)
What does Fifth Amendment mean to you? (1957)	50	(792)	35	(851)	15	10	56	(279)	46	(331)
What is a presidential veto? (1947)	86	(1455)	74	(1498)	12	9	94	(279)	85	(331)
Length of President's term (1952)	94	(666)	91	(652)	3	1	96	(279)	95	(331)
Name the Vice President (1952)	71	(666)	66	(652)	5	10	79	(279)	69	(331)
First ten amendments are called "Bill of Rights" (1954)	34	(653)	27	(711)	7	14	53	(279)	39	(331)
2/3 vote required to override presidential veto (1947)	54	(1455)	33	(1498)	21	29	50	(279)	21	(331)

Sources: USAIPO 52–0491; USAIPO 47–0401; USAIPO 47–0392; USAIPO 57–0581; USAIPO 47–0396; USAIPO 54–0526.
Note: Numbers in parentheses are numbers of cases.

28

Figure 2.1 **Over-Time Trends in the Knowledge Gap**

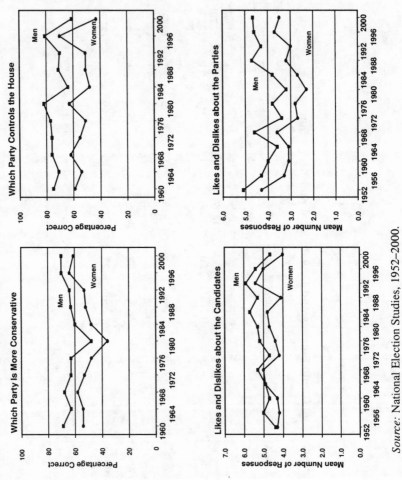

Source: National Election Studies, 1952–2000.

types of employment, free time, and social and work-related contacts as men, their levels of political knowledge would be similar to men's. Yet even if these factors do not constitute barriers in the strict sense of the word, they may nevertheless act as negative reinforcement, discouraging women who have the ability and opportunity to learn about politics from doing so. Socioeconomic disadvantages simply make it more difficult for women to be politically engaged.

We designed a multivariate model to examine the ways in which structural-situational and attitudinal factors mediate gender's effect on knowledge.[12] The full model (for the NES data) includes twenty-one such variables, selected on the basis of theoretical considerations, the findings of other researchers in this area (Bennett and Bennett 1989; Luskin 1990), and extensive testing of the model with several different sets of data.[13] The simple correlation between gender and political knowledge (using the eighteen-item index in the 1996 National Election Study) was −.20, but controlling for theoretically relevant variables reduces this to −.04 (standardized beta), indicating that most of the relationship between gender and knowledge can be explained by demographic, structural-situational, and attitudinal differences between men and women.

In order to test the specific relationships between structural-situational factors and attitudinal ones, we prepared a simplified version of the model. Latent variables representing the structural and attitudinal elements of the model were created and then included in a path analysis along with gender, race, age, and region, which are treated as intercorrelated, but causally exogenous. The model performed well, explaining an estimated 62 percent of the variance in the political knowledge scale. Figure 2.2 shows the path coefficients for the simplified model.

The path model allows us to decompose the simple bivariate relationship between gender and knowledge into four specific pathways. Consistent with the notion of structural barriers, about a third of the original relationship is explained by the path from gender through structure to knowledge. A somewhat smaller portion (about one-fifth) is explained by the negative reinforcement argument, defined here as the path from gender through structure and attitudes to knowledge. Taken together, the two structure-based arguments account for about half of the original relationship.

The path model also provides some insight into what is missed by the structural arguments. Over one-fourth of the original relationship is accounted for by the path from gender through attitudes to knowledge, suggesting that even while in nominally equal socioeconomic circumstances, women are less psychologically engaged in politics, and thus less likely to be politically informed. And the direct path from gender to knowledge remains statistically significant, accounting for about one-fifth of the original relationship.

Socialization and Motivation

Undoubtedly some of the strength of these last two pathways results from measurement error and a failure to account for all of the relevant structural and situational

Figure 2.2 **A Simplified Path Model of Political Knowledge**

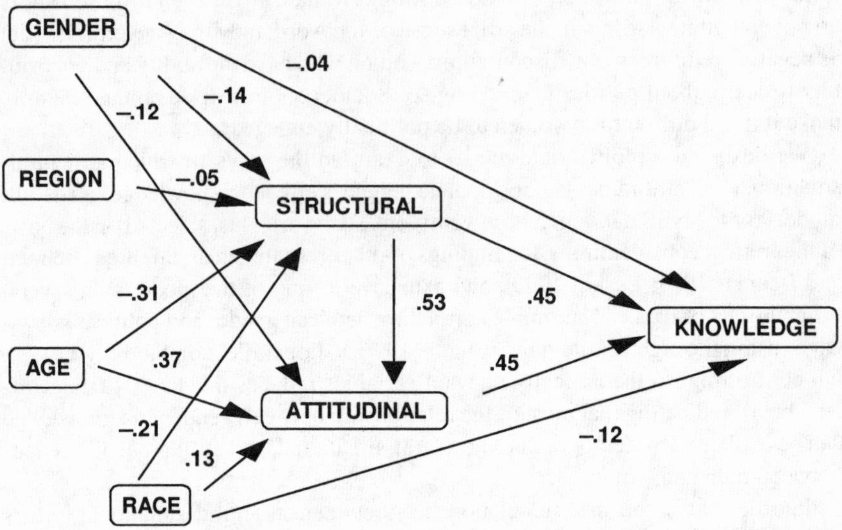

GENDER

REGION

AGE

RACE

STRUCTURAL

ATTITUDINAL

KNOWLEDGE

−.04
−.14
−.12
−.05
−.31
.37
−.21
.13
.53
.45
.45
−.12

Source: 1996 National Election Study.

factors that depress women's knowledge of politics.[14] However, it also seems likely that some is due to more deep-seated differences in socialization that are not erased by adult circumstances and a more nominally equal playing field. Most obviously relevant here is explicitly *political* socialization, which may be different for many females as a result of the legacy of de jure gender discrimination and attendant societal views of the "proper" (i.e., nonpolitical) role of women. Although few women alive today were ever prohibited by law from voting or taking part in politics, many were socialized to politics by mothers who were (and by fathers who directly experienced the pre-suffrage period). Traditional views of the "appropriate" role for women in politics have not vanished. While only a small minority of survey respondents express such views, they are found in younger as well as older cohorts (Bennett and Bennett 1989, 1992). Even when conservative norms were not explicitly transmitted to the next generation, the example of nonparticipation by mothers would still have a significant impact on daughters (and, in a different way, on sons).[15] Evidence to support a socialization theory of the gender gap in knowledge can be found in the civics knowledge and attitudes of school students. Niemi's and Junn's (1993) analysis of data from the National Assessment of Educational Progress (a large national survey of school-age children) found that males were more likely than were females "to say that government is their favorite subject, or that they enjoy civics classes more than their other classes" (p. 6). Male students were significantly more politically knowledgeable than females, even after controlling for a number of background and curriculum variables.

Theories of *gender role socialization* that are not explicitly political in nature may also have significant political implications. The nature of—even the very existence of—many of these differences is controversial. As summarized by scholars such as Gilligan (1982) and Tannen (1990), girls from an early age are less interested in the "rules of the game" and notions of "abstract justice" than are boys. Their games tend to be less conflictual than boys' games, and more likely to founder if disputes arise (Lever 1976, 483; Lever 1978, 476). In addition, girls (and women) are more interested in and more likely to talk about personal, immediate, consensual issues in their conversations, while boys and men turn to more conflictual, abstract, and less personal topics. To the extent that these generalizations apply to the political world, we would expect women to be less knowledgeable and concerned than men about much of mainstream national politics, given its conflictual, rules-driven, abstract, and physically and psychologically distant nature.

These socialization explanations are difficult to assess directly with the data we have available, though the path in Figure 2.2 from gender through attitudes to knowledge provides some circumstantial support for the political socialization argument, and the direct path from gender to knowledge is consistent with a gender socialization explanation. Beyond this, testing the socialization explanations necessarily consists of deriving plausible propositions that follow from them, and then looking for data that support or contradict these propositions.

One such proposition is that socialization away from mainstream politics would affect the motivation to learn about politics, rather than the ability or opportunity to do so. If this is the case, then we would expect women to exhibit greater levels of knowledge on issues of national politics that are perceived as more relevant to them. This was precisely the pattern we observed in a range of different surveys: topics of potentially special relevance to women showed smaller or nonexistent gender gaps. For example, a 1994 *Times Mirror* national survey found women to be 22 percentage points less able than men to name Boris Yeltsin as the president of Russia, and 18 points less able to name the Serbs as the group besieging Sarajevo; however, on the issue of health care, which is a central concern in the "private sphere," women in the same survey were only 4 points less likely than men to know that President Clinton's proposed reform program mandated employers to provide coverage to their workers. There were also trivial or nonexistent gender gaps in knowledge of presidential candidate positions on abortion in the 1992 and 1996 National Election Studies (see Table 2.2), as well as in knowledge of gubernatorial candidate positions in two 1989 Virginia election surveys we conducted.[16]

As a somewhat more systematic test of this hypothesis, we placed five potentially gender-relevant knowledge items on a 1991 statewide Virginia survey ($N = 804$), along with five questions that measured knowledge of national politics more broadly. The gender-relevant items included two questions about the Supreme Court decision in the case of *Rust v. Sullivan*, one on Clarence Thomas's stand on quotas, one on the position of the political parties regarding abortion, and one asking if there were a woman on the U.S. Supreme Court (and if so, to

Table 2.4

Gender-relevant Items Compared with Others (Virginia Survey)

Subject	Males % correct	Females % correct	% Difference	Odds ratio
Percent needed to override a veto	48	25	−23	2.8
Government benefits are not guaranteed in Bill of Rights	71	57	−14	1.8
Consumer protection not guaranteed in Bill of Rights	54	42	−12	1.6
Length of senator's term	30	22	−8	1.5
Free speech guaranteed in Bill of Rights	95	93	−2	1.4
Clarence Thomas opposes quotas	38	30	−8	1.4
Which party more opposed to abortion?	59	51	−8	1.4
What was *Rust v. Sullivan* about?	21	17	−4	1.3
Can Congress do anything about *Rust* decision?	62	55	−7	1.3
Name woman on Supreme Court	38	33	−5	1.2
Median Difference: Gender neutral			−12	
Median Difference: Gender relevant			−7	
Gender-neutral Scale (0–5) (Mean Score)	2.98	2.39	−0.59	
Gender-relevant Scale (0–5) (Mean Score)	2.37	2.05	−0.32	

Note: Questions in the shaded area are gender-neutral. Questions in the white area are potentially gender-relevant.

name her). Table 2.4 presents the percentage correct for men and women on these ten items. As with other data we have reviewed, men were generally more informed than women. However, gender differences were much less substantial for the "gender-relevant" questions: 5 of the 6 smallest differences were on these items. And while the correlation between gender and knowledge was significant for both scales, it was smaller for the "gender-relevant" (−.11) than the "gender-neutral" (−.21) one. Finally, in a multivariate model controlling for structural variables, the beta for gender's direct effect on "gender-neutral" knowledge was .17, compared with .07 for "gender-relevant" knowledge.

Equalizing Opportunity, Ability, and Motivation: The Case of Local Politics

An important implication of both the structural and socialization arguments is that women "opt out" of national politics because of some combination of their exclusion from it and its perceived irrelevance to them, relative to the costs of engagement. Thus, within more hospitable arenas for women's political activities, gender differences in knowledge should be smaller or nonexistent. Local politics may provide one such setting. Local government is the arena where issues that directly affect family, schooling, and community are most often and most tangibly debated. Given this physical and symbolic closeness to the "private sphere" of women, their participation in local politics has always been viewed as more acceptable, and so this arena has been more accessible than state or national politics. This access is reflected in the relatively high percentage of female representation in city and county leadership positions as compared with state and national legislative or executive positions (Darcy, Welch, and Clark 1987). If historical exclusion and a sense of issue-irrelevance are partly responsible for women's relatively lower levels of knowledge about national politics, then gender differences in knowledge should be muted at the local level.

Several surveys confirmed this expectation. Women in the Richmond, Virginia, metropolitan area were at least as knowledgeable as men on such topics as how the mayor and city council are selected, which party controlled the county board of supervisors, and the names of elected and appointed officials. Women were quite a bit *more* likely than men to know the name of the head of the local school system, a finding confirmed nationally by the General Social Survey. Table 2.5 shows the gender differences for all of these items.[17]

Two of our local surveys also included questions on national politics, providing a basis of comparison. As can be seen, the gender differences were much more pronounced for national than local politics. For all of the questions examined, the median gender difference on local politics items was −3 percentage points; for national (and state) items it was −11 points. Taking account of structural and situational differences between the women and the men in the local surveys (via multiple regression analyses), the gender gap in knowledge of local politics actually shows a small—though statistically nonsignificant—*female* advantage.

Our exploration of the sources of the gender gap in political knowledge highlights the complex, interactive effects of structural, attitudinal, and environmental factors, as well as the difficulty in capturing these processes with standard measures of political engagement and structural opportunity. The absence of legal barriers to participation in politics for women is no guarantee that the opportunities are, in fact, the same as for men.[18]

The lack of a gender gap on gender-relevant issues and matters of local politics also provides a vivid example of the situational nature of political knowledge and reinforces our earlier caveat regarding the dimensionality of knowledge (note 5). Political knowledge is mostly, but not entirely, unidimensional. Some types of issues are of special relevance to certain groups, and some arenas of politics are more accessible than others to them. Where this is true, the groups will be more motivated to learn and better able to do so.

Table 2.5

Knowledge of Local Politics

Survey and Subject	Males % correct	Females % correct	% Difference	Odds ratio
Richmond City survey (1991) N = 800				
Who is Boris Yeltsin?	43	23	−20	2.5
Percent needed to override a veto	45	26	−19	2.3
Party control of U.S. House	60	41	−19	2.2
Who reviews constitutionality of laws?	72	61	−11	1.6
How is city council elected?	60	53	−7	1.3
How is mayor selected?	62	59	−3	1.1
Name the city manager	60	60	0	1.0
Name the school superintendent	11	18	+7	0.6
Richmond City survey (1990) N = 409				
Who is the current mayor?	31	28	−3	1.2
How is mayor selected?	62	59	−3	1.1
Heard or read about historic designation controversy	81	84	+3	0.8
Chesterfield County survey (1991) N = 329				
National unemployment rate	55	31	−24	2.7
Does U.S. have a trade deficit?	92	81	−11	2.7
First 10 amendments are the "Bill of Rights"	74	63	−11	1.7
Is there a county impact fee?	34	26	−8	1.5
Harry Truman's party affiliation	65	60	−5	1.2
Name the local U.S. Representative	35	31	−4	1.2
Which party has most seats on county Board of Supervisors?	33	32	−1	1.1
Name the school superintendent	30	40	+10	0.6
General social survey (1987) N = 1,819				
Name governor	82	71	−11	1.9
Name U.S. Representative	38	31	−7	1.4
Name head of local school system	28	33	+5	0.8

Source: Richmond and Chesterfield County surveys conducted by the authors. General Social Survey conducted by the National Opinion Research Center at the University of Chicago.

Note: Shaded rows contain national or state knowledge items for comparison.

The Consequences of the Gender Gap in Political Knowledge

The significance of the gender gap in knowledge ultimately depends upon the impact of political information on the formation and expression of citizens' individual and collective opinions. Elsewhere we have shown that more-informed citizens are more supportive of democratic norms, more likely to participate in politics, more likely to hold opinions, and more likely to hold opinions that are consistent with each other and that are stable over time (Delli Carpini and Keeter 1996, 220–38). Here we focus on two additional effects of political knowledge: enlightened self-interest and issue-consistent voting.

Political Knowledge and Enlightened Self-Interest

A healthy democracy requires a citizenry capable of knowing and expressing its interests, and doing so in the context of the broader public interest. Philosophers and theorists have long wrestled with the question of what is a citizen's political interest. Rightly enough, there is great reluctance to impute interests to individuals. At the same time, citizens clearly differ in the accuracy of their perceptions about the political world and about the likely impact of current or proposed government policies on them, on important groups to which they belong, and on the polity more generally. Where perceptions on these matters are incomplete or inaccurate, we would question whether a citizen had fully comprehended his or her interest. The lack of sufficient information is one barrier to knowing one's interest. Another is incorrect information. While political observers may debate the extent of "false consciousness" among the public, and few will offer an operational definition of it, most would agree that some citizens, on some issues, don't know their own interest because they have been manipulated by others who, in Hamilton's words, "flatter their prejudices to betray their interests . . ." (Hamilton, Madison, and Jay 1787–88, #71).

A common theoretical approach to the identification of interests is through the notion of "enlightened preferences." In this context, "enlightened" refers not to some absolute standard of what is right or just but rather to the conditions under which the individual chooses among alternatives available to him or her. For example, Dahl (1989, 180–81) writes, "A person's interest or good is whatever that person would choose with fullest attainable understanding of the experiences resulting from that choice and its most relevant alternatives." Similarly, Bartels's (1990) work on interests draws on three theorists across the political spectrum, whose common theme is information: what would an individual choose if she or he had perfect information and could experience the results of choosing each alternative (Mansbridge 1983; Connolly 1972), or "saw clearly, thought rationally, [and] acted disinterestedly and benevolently" (Lippmann 1955).

Of course, greater information does not assure that citizens will reach a consensus on important issues of the day. Ultimately, each individual brings a unique mix of personal experiences to his or her political calculus. Nonetheless, values, attitudes, and opinions do not develop in a vacuum, but rather are *socially* constructed out of material conditions and cultural norms. While some of these conditions and norms are likely to be similar for all members of a polity, many vary depending on one's particular socioeconomic location. Thus, for some issues at least, greater information is likely to lead to clearer and more consistent expressions of group interests.

The combined concepts of "enlightened preferences" and "socially constructed opinions" permit an empirical study of interests. If more informed citizens are better able to discern their interests, and if material interests differ across groups in the population, it should be possible to detect the influence of information by comparing the opinions of better and lesser informed members of different groups. We should reiterate that we do not see information or knowledge as the *only* determinant of a citizen's interest. One's view of "the good life" is based on norms and values that are rooted in belief systems only partially connected to the empirical world. In addition, the foundational issues of politics and society are inherently contestable (Connolly 1983) and so cannot be "solved" through the technical appraisal of facts. Nonetheless, as with the other aspects of opinion formation examined in this chapter, factual knowledge can help facilitate the process by which values, attitudes, and beliefs are combined into the expression of political interests. These interests may be defined narrowly (What is in *my* best interest?) or more broadly (What is in the best interest of people like me? Of the polity more broadly?), but to be meaningful, they must be based—at least partially—on an accurate understanding of the processes, people, and substance of politics.

Political Knowledge and the Expression of Gender-based Interests

Numerous studies have documented the emergence of a gender gap in public opinion over the past fifteen years. Much of this gap is attributable to the divergent financial and social situations of men and women and the way in which the parties have responded to issues affecting women.[19] Overlaid upon emerging gender differences in opinion are differences by marital status, which often reinforce the gender schism (Weisberg 1987). To the extent that political interests do in fact differ by gender and marital status, we would expect to see these differences reflected in the expressed opinions of married men, married women, single men, and single women. And to the extent that knowledge facilitates the connection between political interests and public opinion, we would also expect differences in the opinions between less and more informed members within each group. Whether the net effect of knowledge is to create greater polarization or greater consensus, however, depends on the specific way in which informed men and women define their group interests and/or the public interest more generally.

We used data from the 1992 National Election Study to examine how gender differences in opinions were affected by variations in political knowledge levels. In exploring the impact of political knowledge on group-level opinions, it is important to choose issues that are arguably relevant to the group characteristics in question—there is little a priori reason, for example, to expect men and women to differ systematically in their views regarding the trade or budget deficits. In the analysis presented here we looked at differences in opinions related to the proper scope of government in the area of social welfare, since theory and prior evidence suggest that women are more likely to draw on different values and experiences in evaluating such policies than are men (Shapiro and Mahajan 1986).[20] We also looked at gender differences in opinions about abortion—an issue of obvious relevance to women.

As a practical matter, the dearth of highly knowledgeable individuals in certain subgroups—for example, among poor and/or less educated women—imposes limits on what we can learn simply by looking at those individuals in a typical opinion survey. Further, because opinions are likely to be affected by a variety of personal and demographic factors other than political knowledge, and because these factors vary within groups, it is necessary to control for these potentially confounding effects. For each of the following analyses, we used multiple regression to estimate the impact of a set of twenty-two personal characteristics (for example, race, sex, age, education, income, and marital status) and political knowledge on the particular attitudes of interest. The regression model also included interaction terms for political knowledge and each of the personal characteristics. These interactions permit an estimation of how knowledge affects the relationship between personal characteristics and attitudes.[21] To simulate what the attitudes would be if all members of a group had a uniform level of knowledge, the regression coefficients from the model are used to compute an estimated attitude for each member of the group in the survey, using each person's actual data for all variables except political knowledge, which is imputed as either "uninformed" or "fully informed."[22]

For example, in the first analysis presented below, two sets of estimates were computed: one assumed that everyone scored 0 on the political knowledge scale, while the other assumed that everyone scored 28 (the highest possible score). Individuals were separated into four groups (married men, married women, single men, and single women). Each individual's scores on each variable were inserted into the equation, along with the appropriate imputed knowledge score (0 or 28, depending on which analysis was being conducted) and the corresponding interaction terms for knowledge with the other variables. This led to an estimated attitude score for each person. These estimates were aggregated (as means) for each group and then plotted on a graph. The opinion scale, arrayed along the vertical axis, is based on factor scores. Thus, the mean score for the sample is 0, and scores are based on their deviation from the sample mean (for example, a score of 1.0 is one standard deviation above the sample mean).[23]

The results of our first analysis are presented in Figure 2.3. Among the least informed citizens there are only modest differences in domestic political opinion among members of four groups (married men, married women, single men, single women). As knowledge increases, however, both single and married men become slightly more conservative, while married women move slightly in the liberal direction and single women become quite a bit more liberal. These changes lead to a clear gender and marriage gap on domestic welfare issues among knowledgeable citizens. Significantly, a "fully informed" citizenry would have collective consequences, resulting in a public opinion environment that is more ideologically diverse and slightly more liberal (a shift of $-.05$ on the standardized scale).

Figure 2.3 **Impact of Knowledge on Opinion, by Sex and Marital Status**

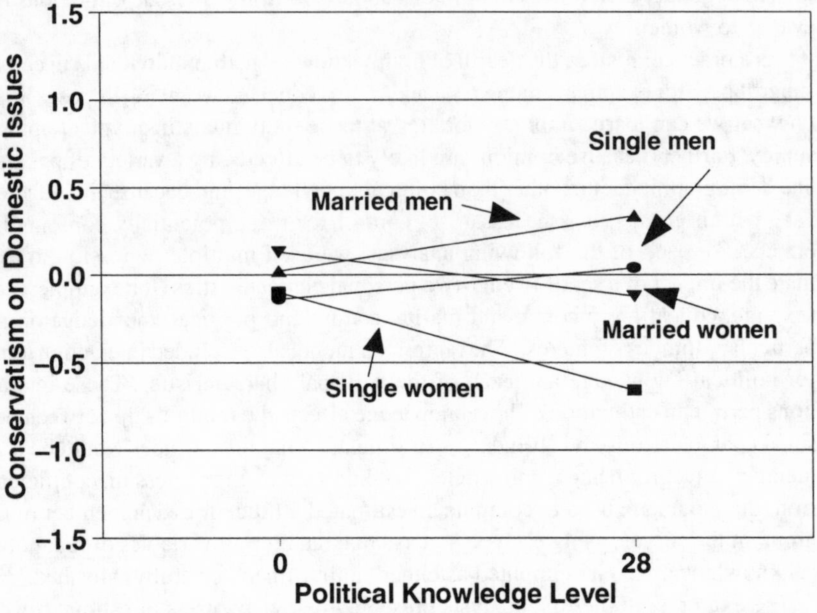

Knowledge also promoted greater gender differences on the issue of abortion (Figure 2.4). On a four-issue abortion index, the overall attitudes of men and women were about the same, but as women become more knowledgeable (other factors being equal) they also become more supportive of abortion rights. Significantly, knowledge also promotes greater support for abortion rights among men—a pattern that could result from more knowledgeable men believing that a woman's right to choose is also in their own interest, or believing that the right to choose is legal and/or just, regardless of their own interests. Although the effect for men is quite weak, it highlights the fact that increased knowledge need not always lead to movement in opposite directions among the groups in question. Nonetheless, because of the difference in the *rate* of change among women and men as knowledge rises, their *relative* position changes from one in which women are slightly more conservative than men to one in which women are considerably more liberal. The collective impact of a fully informed citizenry would be to shift the mean for attitudes on abortion in a liberal direction (from 0 to +.30) on our scale.

Gender, Knowledge, and Issue-consistent Voting

The formation of opinions based on an individual's (or group's) interests is only one step in the process by which citizens attempt to influence public policy. For opinions to result in real collective pressure on government, they must guide the

Figure 2.4   **Impact of Knowledge on Opinion, by Sex**

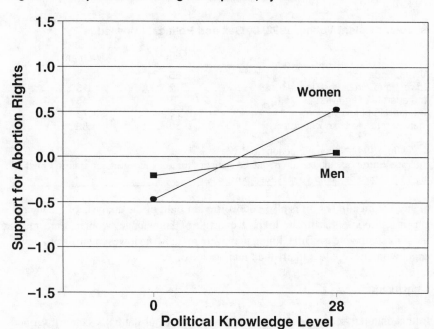

citizen's political behavior, most typically (and perhaps consequentially) through the evaluation and selection of public officials. Political knowledge is critical to this process, because voters must be aware both of their own interests and of what the candidates and parties stand for. In short, there must be consistency between citizens' opinions on issues and the votes they cast.[24]

To gauge the extent of issue-consistent voting among men and women, we regressed the two-party vote choice in 1992 (using logistic regression) on three issue scales: the domestic issue index used above, a comparable index for foreign and military issues, and self-identified political ideology. The extent to which these attitudes allow us to predict the vote—as measured by the pseudo r-squared of the regression (Hagle and Mitchell 1992)—is a simple measure of issue voting. The analysis was conducted separately for men and women, both for the whole sample and for individuals within each of four quartiles based on political knowledge level (Table 2.6).

The overall pseudo r-squared for men was 0.65; for women it was only 0.51. Thus, in the sample as a whole, men are somewhat more likely than women to use their political attitudes as a basis for choosing between candidates. But this difference is almost entirely a result of men's higher level of political knowledge: comparing men and women within each quartile of knowledge, the pseudo r-squares are much more similar. They are slightly higher for women in two quartiles, and

Table 2.6

Issue-consistent Voting, 1992, by Sex and Political Knowledge

	Men	Women
All respondents	.65	.51
Lowest quartile of knowledge	.12	.15
2nd quartile of knowledge	.51	.46
3rd quartile of knowledge	.78	.72
Highest quartile of knowledge	.80	.82

Source: 1992 National Election Study.
Note: Entries are the pseudo *r*-squared statistics for logistic regression analyses predicting vote choice based on voters' issue positions.

higher for men in two. It is also noteworthy, in light of the analysis of the gender gap in opinions, that in the highest quartile of knowledge, women were much more likely to vote for Bill Clinton than were men; in the lowest quartile of knowledge, women were less likely than men to do so.

Conclusion

In this chapter we have demonstrated that men are substantially better informed than women about national politics and government. This difference was seen in three national surveys covering a range of topics including civics, current issues, political leaders, and partisan alignments. In each of the surveys, the median score for men was near the seventy-fifth percentile for women. Furthermore, this gap has remained surprisingly consistent over time.

Controlling for variables known to be associated with political knowledge—education, income, type of employment, political efficacy and engagement, and the like—reduced the gender difference in knowledge, but did not eliminate it. Consistent with both political and gender socialization arguments, however, gender differences in knowledge are much smaller when the subject matter is arguably of special relevance to women. Perhaps most significantly, we found no evidence of a gender gap in knowledge of local politics, an arena in which both structural and psychological barriers to women are less formidable than at the national level, and in which the political agenda is likely to be seen as more relevant to women.

Finally, we presented evidence that political knowledge affects a citizen's ability to identify her—and his—interests. Equally important, knowledge is essential for citizens to connect their interests (in the form of their opinions) with their political participation. To the extent that women are less knowledgeable politically than are men, women will be less effective in pursuing their interests in the political system.

The application of political science's traditional criteria for political engagement to the matter of gender differences has occasioned considerable controversy

(Carroll and Zerilli 1993). Many feminist scholars argue that mainstream political science ignores women in politics, and when it does not ignore them, finds their behavior deficient in one or more aspects (Goot and Reid 1984; Welch 1977; Sapiro 1983; Jones 1988; Morgen and Bookman 1988). A common thread through these critiques of political science is the arbitrary distinction between the public and private spheres. According to this view, as long as activities conducted within the private sphere are not regarded as political, women will continue to be judged as less political (and less politically sophisticated) than men. In turn, such judgments raise issues that "have to do with changing women and adapting them to public life, rather than changing politics to accommodate the multiplicity and vitality of women's voices" (Jones 1988, 24).

This argument has obvious relevance to the analyses presented in this paper. Our findings regarding knowledge of gender-relevant issues and knowledge about local politics can be viewed as empirical confirmation for feminist critiques of how national politics is defined and conducted. Nonetheless, the bulk of our findings suggests many of the normative conclusions derided by the feminist scholars cited above. Without denying the legitimacy of much of this feminist critique, we would argue that there are real consequences of women's relatively lower levels of knowledge regarding national, mainstream politics. Jane Mansbridge has argued persuasively that some political issues can be settled only through formal, legalistic, and adversarial processes (Mansbridge 1983). For these issues, traditional political methods—and traditional political resources—are necessary for effective action. In her recent book, *Fire with Fire*, Naomi Wolf writes:

> The late feminist poet Audre Lorde wrote that the master's tools would never dismantle the master's house. But the electoral process, the press, and money are among the master's tools. . . . [I]t is *only* the master's tools that can dismantle the master's house. (1993, 54, emphasis in original)

Knowledge of politics is essential for the effective use of the master's tools.

Notes

1. Portions of this chapter were adapted from earlier work on gender and knowledge published in *What Americans Know About Politics and Why It Matters* (1996). The data and analyses have been updated.

2. It should be noted, however, that much of this "information-processing" literature uses measures of political knowledge as an indicator of cognitive ability rather than of stored knowledge that is recalled for use in subsequent political decision making (see Lodge, McGraw, and Stroh 1989). Our own approach is to conceptualize "political knowledge" as a substantive *resource* rather than a cognitive trait.

3. An extended discussion of issues in the measurement of political knowledge in general, and the development of our national survey in particular, can be found in Delli Carpini and Keeter 1993. The most appropriate way to measure political knowledge remains a matter of some controversy, centering on issues such as the dimensionality of knowledge (Zaller 1986; Bennett 1990; Iyengar 1990), the use of open- versus closed-question formats

(Kessel 1992; Mondak 2001), question ordering and placement (Kenski 2003), the number of response options (Kenski 2003), and the encouragement or discouragement of "don't know" responses (Anderson, Canache, and Mondak 2002). While in general, different approaches appear to result in similar substantive interpretations, Anderson, Canache, and Mondak (2002) find evidence that encouraging guessing diminishes the gender gap in knowledge by as much as 50 percent. They hypothesize that this is due to men's greater propensity to guess rather than admit that they do not know an answer, though it is also possible that it reflects women's greater unwillingness to talk about politics.

4. More specifically, these items tapped two important aspects of "the rules of the game" in the United States: political and economic processes (e.g., knowing how the veto process works, or knowing what a recession is); and individual rights (e.g., knowing what rights are protected by the First Amendment). They also tapped the two main components of "the substance of politics": domestic affairs (e.g., knowing what the "Superfund" is, or how much of the federal budget is spent on Social Security), and foreign affairs (e.g., knowing about the U.S.-Soviet arms agreement). And they tapped both the individual (e.g., knowing who your senators are) and the organizational (e.g., knowing which party controls the House) aspects of "the people and players" of national politics. In addition (and following Berelson, Lazarsfeld, and McPhee 1954), these items attempted to gauge citizens' knowledge of the past in each of these three domains (knowing when women were granted the right to vote, knowing what the New Deal was, knowing the party of Harry Truman, and so forth). Finally, the questions varied in both their degree of difficulty (as demonstrated by the marginal frequencies) and their format (e.g., multiple choice, open-ended, and so forth). In addition, questions asked about facts that were likely to be learned in the classroom or that required monitoring the changing political landscape.

5. The appropriateness of a simple additive index depends not only on the validity of the individual items from which the index is constructed, but also on the dimensionality of the construct to be measured. Elsewhere (Delli Carpini and Keeter 1992, 1993) we have reported on an extensive analysis of the dimensionality of political knowledge. Despite the reasonable assumption that citizens would manifest specialization in the types of political facts they know, our conclusion from examining several national surveys is that knowledge about national politics is a relatively undifferentiated and unidimensional phenomenon. While theoretically meaningful subdimensions of knowledge can be discerned (e.g., some citizens—principally partisans—are knowledgeable about matters relating to the political parties), a unidimensional model usually provides an adequate representation of the structure found in surveys of the mass public. The chief exception to this is knowledge of local politics, which, while related, appears to be relatively distinct from knowledge of national politics. This exception is of considerable importance to the study of gender and knowledge, as we discuss later in this paper. Zaller's (1986) analysis of knowledge items on the 1985 NES pilot survey also concluded that a unidimensional model of knowledge is appropriate. For somewhat different perspectives, see Iyengar (1990) and Bennett (1990).

6. We examined this measure for evidence of a gender-of-interviewer bias. In the aggregate, female respondents received comparable ratings from male and female interviewers in the pre-election survey, but received somewhat lower ratings from female than male interviewers in the post-election survey ($p < .05$). In any event, the potential magnitude of this bias would be small since only 13 percent of the interviews were conducted by males. However, the interviewer rating was very highly correlated with the rest of the knowledge scale (which was based on answers to factual questions).

7. Because the index uses items asked on both the pre-election and post-election waves of the survey, the actual sample size for our analysis is 1,534. There are 1,714 total cases in the data set, but some respondents were not reinterviewed in the post-election wave.

8. The items are sorted by the odds ratio, which shows the ratio of the odds that a man will correctly answer to the odds that a woman will do so. This statistic corrects for the

"floor" and "ceiling" effects that occur when comparing percentage differences in very difficult or very easy items.

9. Nearly identical distributions were found using knowledge indices constructed from the 1990 NES and 1991 NES pilot surveys (which included civics knowledge items), and from the 1992 NES survey.

10. See Delli Carpini and Keeter (1991) for a discussion of the data sets and the methodological issues involved in making these comparisons over time.

11. Kessel (1992) has used the open-ended questions as a knowledge measure, and provides a defense of such use. Elsewhere, we found the open-ended items to be fairly strongly correlated with a knowledge scale similar to the 1988 NES index (Delli Carpini and Keeter 1993).

12. The model is linear and recursive, although we recognize that political knowledge not only depends upon but also influences some of the attitudinal variables, and that the effects on knowledge may not be linear in all instances.

13. The independent variables drawn from the 1996 NES data included sex, race (coded as black and nonblack), region (coded as south and nonsouth), age, education, politically impinged occupation, income, strength of party identification, political trust, efficacy (five items), media use (four items), attention to politics (two items), discussion of politics. Details about coding are available from the authors.

14. Truly capturing "structural and situational" differences through surveys is obviously a difficult task. For example, women and men—even those in similar structural situations—often do different things with their time, and much of the difference results from the sexual division of labor. The 1991 Virginia survey on reading and viewing habits (referred to earlier) found that a similar proportion of women and men reported engaging in other activities while watching television news or reading the newspaper. *What* they were doing was highly gender-specific, however: 32 percent of women were cooking, cleaning, or caring for children while watching television news, compared with only 12 percent of men (who were more likely to be eating or reading). Such differences presumably have consequences for the comparative level of political engagement of women and men.

15. Doris Graber observed substantial gender differences in her subjects' reported childhood socialization to politics, with men able to recall far more specific politically relevant incidents than women (Graber 1988, 134; for a related argument and evidence see Rapoport 1982, 1985; also see Jennings and Niemi 1981; Orum et al. 1974). The "legacy" is not simply a matter of women's socialization, of course. Ample evidence exists that women continue to confront resistance from men when they take part in politics (e.g., Schumaker and Burns 1988; Winsky Mattei 1998). Such experiences also have socializing effects by lowering one's sense of efficacy.

16. We found similar patterns in other questions about abortion in the 1989 Survey of Political Knowledge.

17. We collected data from four surveys, including three we conducted in the Richmond, Virginia, metropolitan area. The most extensive of these was a 1991 survey of 804 residents in the city of Richmond. This survey included eight knowledge items, four on national and four on local politics. The local items included explaining how the city council and the mayor are selected, and naming the city manager and the superintendent of schools. Another Richmond city survey conducted in 1990 also included the item on how the mayor is selected, asked who was the incumbent, and asked about exposure to news of a dispute over the placement of a monument to civil rights leaders. A survey of suburban Chesterfield County (in the Richmond metro area) included four national knowledge items and four local items. The local items included naming the local U.S. representative and county school superintendent, stating whether the county imposes an environmental impact fee on developers, and stating which party has a majority on the county Board of Supervisors. In addition to these local surveys, the 1987 General Social Survey conducted by the National

Opinion Research Center at the University of Chicago asked respondents to name the head of their local school system, their U.S. representative, and their governor.

18. Given the similarities between women and African Americans in the obstacles each faced in achieving full rights of citizenship in the United States, much of what we have found about the gender gap in political knowledge may also apply to the race gap (Delli Carpini and Keeter 1996).

19. More controversially, these differences have also been attributed to socialization and even biological differences between men and women that lead the latter to be more "nurturing" in their approach to domestic social issues (see Tolleson Rinehart 1992, 1–17).

20. The domestic issues index was a factor score scale of support for or opposition to government spending and action on seven domestic issues including government services and spending, health insurance, government guarantee of a job and good standard of living, government spending on food stamps, assisting the unemployed, assisting blacks, and helping the public schools. Alpha for the scale was .65. The adjusted r-squared of the regression predicting attitudes with personal characteristics and knowledge was .27.

21. See Bartels (1994) for a similar analysis of voting behavior. Our list of demographic and personal variables is quite similar to his.

22. Because the estimates are derived from a linear model, it is necessary to compute only the endpoints; all intermediate points will fall on a straight line connecting the two endpoints.

23. For a fuller discussion of the methodology for this analysis, see Delli Carpini and Keeter 1996, Appendix Five.

24. We recognize that there are many definitions of "issue voting." But all of them have in common the notion that issue voting requires citizens to choose candidates primarily on the basis of issues rather than candidate personal qualities, generalized feelings about the status quo, or idiosyncratic factors. We also do not deny the importance of candidates' personal qualities as a criterion for casting a vote. We simply wish to demonstrate differences across groups in the extent to which vote choices are related to opinions on issues.

References

Anderson, Mary, Damarys Canache, and Jeffrey Mondak. 2002. "The Knowledge Gap: A Reexamination of Gender-based Differences in Political Knowledge." Paper delivered at the annual meeting of the American Association for Public Opinion Research, St. Petersburg.

Barber, James David. 1973. *Citizen Politics*. 2d ed. Chicago: Markham.

Bartels, Larry M. 1990. "Public Opinion and Political Interests." Paper delivered at the annual meeting of the Midwest Political Science Association, Chicago.

Bennett, Linda L.M., and Stephen Earl Bennett. 1989. "Enduring Gender Differences in Political Interest: The Impact of Socialization and Political Dispositions." *American Politics Quarterly* 17(1): 105–122.

Bennett, Stephen E. 1988. "'Know-Nothings' Revisited: The Meaning of Political Ignorance Today." *Social Science Quarterly* 69: 476–490.

———. 1990. "The Dimensions of Americans' Political Information." Paper delivered at the annual meeting of the American Political Science Association, San Francisco.

Bennett, Stephen Earl, and Linda L.M. Bennett. 1992. "From Traditional to Modern Conceptions of Gender Equality in Politics: Gradual Change and Lingering Doubts." *Western Political Quarterly*.

Berelson, Bernard R., Paul F. Lazarsfeld, and William N. McPhee. 1954. *Voting: A Study of Opinion Formation in a Presidential Campaign*. Chicago: University of Chicago Press.

Bourque, Susan, and Jean Grossholtz. 1984. "Politics an Unnatural Practice: Political Science Looks at Female Participation." In *Women and the Public Sphere: A Critique of Sociology and Politics*, ed. Janet Siltanen and Michelle Stanworth. London: Hutchinson.

Brady, Henry E., and Stephen Ansolabehere. 1989. "The Nature of Utility Functions in Mass Publics." *American Political Science Review* 83(1, March): 143–163.

Burns, Nancy, Donald R. Kinder, Steven J. Rosenstone, Virginia Sapiro, and the National Election Studies. 2001. *American National Elections Study, 2000: Pre- and Post-Election Survey*. Conducted by the Center for Political Studies of the Institute of Social Research, The University of Michigan. Ann Arbor: Inter-University Consortium for Political and Social Research.

Carroll, Susan J., and Linda M.G. Zerilli. 1993. "Feminist Challenges to Political Science." In *Political Science: The State of the Discipline II*, ed. Ada W. Finifter. Washington, DC: American Political Science Association.

Connolly, William E. 1972. "On 'Interests' in Politics." *Politics and Society* 2: 459–477.

———. 1983. *The Terms of Political Discourse*. 2d ed. Princeton: Princeton University Press.

Converse, Philip E. 1962. "Information Flow and the Stability of Partisan Attitudes." *Public Opinion Quarterly* 26, 4 (Winter): 578–599.

Darcy, R., Susan Welch, and Janet Clark. 1987. *Women, Elections, and Representation*. New York: Longman.

Dahl, Robert A. 1989. *Democracy and Its Critics*. New Haven: Yale University Press.

Delli Carpini, Michael X., and Esther Fuchs. 1993. "The Year of the Woman: Candidates, Voters, and the 1992 Elections." *Political Science Quarterly* 108: 29–36.

Delli Carpini, Michael X., and Scott Keeter. 1991. "Stability and Change in the U.S. Public's Knowledge of Politics." *Public Opinion Quarterly* 55: 583–612.

———. 1992. "An Analysis of Information Items on the 1990 and 1991 NES Surveys: A Report to the Board of Overseers for the National Election Studies."

———. 1993. "Measuring Political Knowledge: Putting First Things First." *American Journal of Political Science* 37: 1179–1206.

———. 1996. *What Americans Know About Politics and Why It Matters*. New Haven: Yale University Press.

Erikson, Robert S., and Kent L. Tedin. 1995. *American Public Opinion*. 5th ed. Boston: Allyn and Bacon.

Fiske, Susan T., Richard R. Lau, and Richard A. Smith. 1990. "On the Varieties and Utilities of Political Expertise." *Social Cognition* 8(1): 31–48.

Gilligan, Carol. 1982. *In a Different Voice: Psychological Theory and Women's Development*. Cambridge, MA: Harvard University Press.

Glenn, Norval. 1972. "The Distribution of Political Knowledge in the United States." In *Political Attitudes and Public Opinion*, ed. Dan Nimmo and Charles Bonjean. New York: McKay.

Goot, Murray, and Elizabeth Reid. 1984. "Women: If Not Apolitical Then Conservative." In *Women and the Public Sphere: A Critique of Sociology and Politics*, ed. Janet Siltanen and Michelle Stanworth. London: Hutchinson.

Graber, Doris. 1988. *Processing the News*. New York: Longman.

Hagle, Timothy M., and Glenn E. Mitchell, II. 1992. "Goodness of Fit Measures for Probit and Logit." *American Journal of Political Science* 36: 762–784.

Hamilton, Alexander, James Madison, and John Jay. [1787–88] 1961. *Federalist Papers*. Garden City, NY: Anchor Books.

Iyengar, Shanto. 1990. "Shortcuts to Political Knowledge: The Role of Selective Attention and Accessibility." In *Information and Democratic Processes*, ed. John A. Ferejohn and James H. Kuklinski. Champaign-Urbana: University of Illinois Press.

Jennings, M. Kent. 1996. "Political Knowledge Over Time and Across Generations." *Public Opinion Quarterly* 60 (June): 228–252.

Jennings, M. Kent, and Richard G. Niemi. 1981. *Generations and Politics: A Panel Study of Young Adults and Their Parents*. Princeton: Princeton University Press.

Jones, Kathleen B. 1988. "Towards the Revision of Politics." In *The Political Interests of Gender: Developing Theory and Research with a Feminist Face*, ed. Kathleen B. Jones and Anna G. Jonasdottir. Newbury Park, CA: Sage.

Junn, Jane. 1991. "Participation and Political Knowledge." In *Political Participation and American Democracy*, ed. William Crotty. New York: Greenwood Press.

Kathlene, Lyn. 1994. "Power and Influence in State Legislative Policymaking: The Interaction of Gender and Position in Committee Hearing Debates." *American Political Science Review* 88: 560–576.

Kenski, Kate. 2003. "Testing Political Knowledge: Should Knowledge Questions Use Two Response Categories or Four?" *International Journal of Public Opinion Research* 15: 192–200.

Kenski, Kate, and Kathleen Hall Jamieson. 2000. "The Gender Gap in Political Knowledge: Are Women Less Knowledgeable Than Men About Politics?" In *Everything You Think You Know About Politics . . . And Why You're Wrong*, ed. K.H. Jamieson. New York: Basic Books, 83–89.

Kessel, John. 1992. *Presidential Campaign Politics*. Pacific Grove, CA: Brooks/Cole.

Lanoue, David J. 1992. "One That Made a Difference: Cognitive Consistency, Political Knowledge, and the 1980 Presidential Debate." *Public Opinion Quarterly* 56 (Summer): 168–184.

Leighley, Jan E., and Jonthan Nagler. 1991. "Socioeconomic Class Bias in Turnout, 1972–1988: Institutions Come and Go, But the Voters Remain the Same." Presented at the annual meeting of the American Political Science Association, Washington, DC.

Lever, Janet. 1976. "Sex Differences in the Games Children Play." *Social Problems* 23: 478–487.

———. 1978. "Sex Differences in the Complexity of Children's Play and Games." *American Sociological Review* 43: 471–483.

Lippmann, Walter. 1955. *Essays in the Public Philosophy*. Boston: Little, Brown.

Lodge, Milton, Kathleen M. McGraw, and Patrick Stroh. 1989. "An Impression-driven Model of Candidate Evaluation." *American Political Science Review* 83: 399–419.

Luskin, Robert C. 1990. "Explaining Political Sophistication." *Political Behavior* 12: 331–361.

McGraw, Kathleen, and Neil Pinney. 1990. "The Effects of General and Domain-Specific Expertise on Political Memory and Judgment." *Social Cognition* 8: 9–30.

Mansbridge, Jane J. 1983. *Beyond Adversarial Democracy*. Chicago: University of Chicago Press.

Miller, Warren E., and the National Election Studies. 1988 and 1992. *American National Election Study, 1988; 1992: Pre- and Post-Election Survey*. Conducted by the Center for Political Studies of the Institute for Social Research, The University of Michigan. Ann Arbor: Inter-University Consortium for Political and Social Research.

Mondak, Jeffrey. 2001. "Developing Valid Knowledge Scales." *American Journal of Political Science* 45: 224–238.

Moon, David. 1990. "What You Use Depends on What You Have: Information Effects on the Determinants of Electoral Choice." *American Politics Quarterly* 18, 1 (January): 3–24.

Morgen, Sandra, and Ann Bookman. 1988. "Rethinking Women: An Introductory Essay." In *Women and the Politics of Empowerment*, ed. Sandra Morgen and Ann Bookman. Philadelphia: Temple University Press.

Neuman, W. Russell. 1986. *The Paradox of Mass Politics: Knowledge and Opinion in the American Electorate*. Cambridge, MA: Harvard University Press.

Niemi, Richard G., and Jane Junn. 1993. "Civics Courses and the Political Knowledge of High School Seniors." Paper presented at the annual meeting of the American Political Science Association, Washington, DC, September 2–5.

Orum, Anthony M., Roberta S. Cohen, Sherri Grasmuck, and Amy W. Orum. 1974. "Sex, Socialization and Politics." *American Sociological Review* 39: 197–209.

Palfrey, Thomas R., and Keith T. Poole. 1987. "The Relationship Between Information, Ideology, and Voting Behavior." *American Journal of Political Science* 31, 3 (August): 511–529.

Pew Research Center for the People and the Press. 2003. "Survey Report: U.S. Needs More International Backing." Washington, DC, February 20.

Rapoport, Ronald B. 1982. "Sex Differences in Attitude Expression: A Generational Explanation." *Public Opinion Quarterly* 46: 86–96.

———. 1985. "Like Mother, Like Daughter: Intergenerational Transmission of DK Response Rates." *Public Opinion Quarterly* 49: 198–208.

Sapiro, Virginia. 1983. *The Political Integration of Women.* Urbana: University of Illinois Press.

Schumaker, Paul, and Nancy Elizabeth Burns. 1988. "Gender Cleavages and the Resolution of Local Policy Issues." *American Journal of Political Science* 32: 1070–1095.

Shapiro, Robert Y., and Harpreet Mahajan. 1986. "Gender Differences in Policy Preferences: A Summary of Trends from the 1960s to the 1980s." *Public Opinion Quarterly* 50: 42–61.

Sigelman, Lee, and E. Yanarella. 1986. "Public Information on Public Issues." *Social Science Quarterly* 67: 402–410.

Sniderman, Paul M., Richard A. Brody, and Philip E. Tetlock. 1991. *Reasoning and Choice: Explorations in Political Psychology.* New York: Cambridge University Press.

Taeuber, Cynthia. 1991. *Statistical Handbook of Women in America.* Phoenix, AZ: Oryx Press.

Tannen, Deborah. 1990. *You Just Don't Understand: Women and Men in Conversation.* New York: Ballantine Books.

Tolleson-Rinehart, Sue. 1992. *Gender Consciousness and Politics.* New York: Routledge.

Verba, Sidney. 1990. "Women in American Politics." In *Women, Politics, and Change*, ed. Louise A. Tilly and Patricia Gurin. New York: Russell Sage Foundation.

Weisberg, Herbert F. 1987. "The Demographics of a New Voting Gap: Marital Differences in American Voting." *Public Opinion Quarterly* 51: 335–343.

Welch, Susan. 1977. "Women as Political Animals." *American Journal of Political Science* 21: 711–730.

Winsky Mattei, Laura R. 1998. "Gender and Power in American Legislative Discourse." *American Journal of Political Science* 60: 440–461.

Wolf, Naomi. 1993. *Fire with Fire.* New York: Random House.

Zaller, John. 1986. "Analysis of Information Items in the 1985 NES Pilot Study." A Report to the Board of Overseers for the National Election Studies.

———. 1991. "Information, Values, and Opinion." *American Political Science Review* 85: 1215–1237.

———. 1992. *The Nature and Origins of Mass Opinion.* New York: Cambridge University Press.

3

Gender and Political Participation

M. Margaret Conway

After two centuries of struggle to obtain equal rights, do women participate in politics at rates equal to men? To what extent do women's gender role orientations influence their patterns of political participation? To answer these questions this chapter first considers women's and men's patterns of political participation, then compares participation patterns among women on the basis of their gender role orientations. Lastly, it examines the impact of citizens' gender role orientations, beliefs and attitudes, political orientations, and the social context of their lives on their patterns of political participation.

A brief history of women's political participation provides background for this analysis. Until early in the twentieth century, women in the United States were denied political rights. The struggle for political rights for women began in America in the colonial period. One very early demand for political rights occurred in 1638, when Margaret Brent, a wealthy and very respected Maryland landowner, petitioned the Maryland colonial assembly for the right to vote. She requested not one vote, but two—one as a person who met the Maryland colony's property-owning requirements for the right to vote, and one as the administrator of the estate of Leonard Calvert, the recently deceased governor of the Maryland colony and the brother of Lord Baltimore, the colony's proprietor. The colonial assembly responded to her request for the right to vote with a resounding no. Lord Baltimore was furious that Margaret Brent had requested the right to vote, and she was so angry at being denied the right to vote that she moved to Virginia, where she became one of the wealthiest landowners in the American colonies. In some of the American colonies a few women did vote. However, as the colonies became states in the newly created United States of America, they drafted constitutions and laws that formalized the norms against political rights for women (Flexner and Fitzpatrick 1975).

Women's acquisition of political rights was a major focus of the first women's movement, which began with the women's rights convention held in Seneca Falls, New York, in 1848. A small group of women whose members included Elizabeth Cady Stanton and Lucretia Mott organized a local meeting to discuss the status of women and placed an announcement in the local paper inviting local residents to attend. The organizers drafted a Declaration of Sentiments and proposed twelve resolutions for adoption by the convention. The only controversial resolution asserted that women should have the right to vote. Stanton's husband considered the proposal so outrageous that the assembly and its supporters would be subject to public ridicule and their resolutions devalued as a consequence. Undeterred, Mrs. Stanton insisted that the right to vote must be included, as it was the key to obtaining all other rights. Also opposing the inclusion of the demand for political rights were Lucretia Mott and her husband James Mott; both believed that including political rights in the resolutions would be too controversial. The voting rights resolution was the only one with which the convention attendees did not agree unanimously, being passed by a small margin. Furthermore, many attending the meeting declined to sign the document containing the set of resolutions because that document contained the voting rights resolution (Flexner and Fitzpatrick 1975).

Prior to the ratification of the Nineteenth Amendment to the federal Constitution, which asserted that no state could deny women the right to vote in federal elections, several states enfranchised women to vote in some or all elections. The first was Kentucky in 1838, which granted widows who had school-age children and lived in rural areas the right to vote in school elections. By 1918, 15 states had enfranchised women for all elections, and by 1920, an additional 12 states had enfranchised women for presidential elections (Stucker 1977). The struggle for women's right to vote culminated in 1920 with the ratification of the Nineteenth Amendment to the United States Constitution by a sufficient number of states.

Patterns of Participation

There exist numerous different types of opportunities to participate in politics. Some are associated with elections, while others lie outside of the electoral context. Women participated in political activities before they had the right to vote. Many supported the revolt against England during the American Revolution. They were active in the abolitionist movement to end slavery, and from that social movement the first women's movement evolved, advocating equal rights for women in this country. After the Civil War, women actively supported the political movement seeking the establishment of pensions for the widows of Civil War soldiers.

After winning the eighty-year struggle to enact the woman suffrage amendment, its supporters were disheartened by women's low levels of voting participation. Those who had struggled for so many years to win women the right to vote could not understand why women's levels of participation in elections and in almost all other forms of political activity were lower than those of men.

Not until sixty years after the ratification of the Nineteenth Amendment did women vote in presidential elections at rates equal to men, and not until 1986 did women's voting turnout in the midterm congressional elections equal that of men (see Tables 3.1 and 3.2). In 2000, 58 percent of the men and 61 percent of women who were citizens reported voting in the presidential election. Although turnout is

Table 3.1

Patterns of Voting Turnout by Sex, Presidential Election Years
(percentage of eligible voters)

Year	Men	Women
1964	72	67
1968	70	66
1972	64	62
1976	60	59
1980	59	59
1984	59	61
1988	56	58
1992	60	62
1996	53	56
2000	58	61

Source: U.S. Department of Commerce, Bureau of the Census, Current Population Reports, *Voting and Registration in the Election of November 2000.* Series P20-552, February 2002, Table B.

Table 3.2

Patterns of Voting Turnout by Sex, Midterm Election Years
(percentage of eligible voters)

Year	Men	Women
1966	58	53
1970	57	53
1974	46	43
1978	47	45
1982	49	48
1986	46	46
1990	45	45
1994	45	45
1998	41	42

Source: U.S. Department of Commerce, Bureau of the Census, *Voting and Registration in the Election of November 1998.* Series P 20-523RV, August 2000.

lower in midterm elections than in presidential elections, since 1986 women's voting participation in midterm elections has equaled or exceeded that of men.[1] These patterns underestimate, however, the impact of women's electoral participation, as women outnumbered men in the voting age population by more than 8.9 million in 1980 and by 8.4 million in 2000. Even with equal rates of turnout, women's impact on electoral outcomes would be magnified by their larger share of the voting age population. Furthermore, women's and men's vote choices have diverged, with women being more likely to support Democratic party candidates

Table 3.3

Percentage Participating in at Least One Campaign Activity, Presidential Election Years

Year	Men	Women
1964	45.7	37.4
1968	47.7	35.4
1972	44.0	35.3
1976	47.3	37.3
1980	44.5	37.1
1984	41.1	36.5
1988	39.9	30.5
1992	49.3	38.2
1996	39.5	30.5
2000	44.7	36.6

Sources: Calculated from American National Election Studies Cumulative File, 1952–1992; American National Election Studies, 1996 File; American National Election Studies, 2000 File.

while men have been more likely to support Republican party candidates (Clark and Clark 1996, 1999).

In the 2004 presidential election, women were 54 percent of the electorate. The gender gap in vote choice persisted in 2004, with President George Bush receiving the votes of 55 percent of male voters and 48 percent of female voters. Bush increased his support among women from 2000 to 2004 by 5 percent (CNN exit poll, 2004).

Only citizens may vote in elections, but individuals may engage in a variety of campaign activities. These include attempting to persuade others how to vote, displaying campaign signs or wearing a campaign button, attending political meetings or campaign rallies, and working for a candidate or party. A greater proportion of men than of women report participating in at least one campaign activity. In 2000, for example, 44.7 percent of the men and 36.6 percent of the women participated in at least one campaign activity (see Table 3.3). A similar pattern existed in 2002. Men are also more likely than women to be involved in more than one type of campaign activity.

A different form of political activity is contributing money to a party, some other type of political organization, or a candidate, but only citizens may contribute to candidates or political parties for activities related to federal elections. Men are more likely to make political contributions.[2] Among both men and women, however, the proportion engaging in this type of political activity is low (see Table 3.4). In 2000, 16 percent of men and 9 percent of women reported making contributions to a party, another form of political organization, or a candidate. Of course, some individuals make contributions to more than one type of recipient. Of the men, 9 percent reported contributing to a political party, 8 percent to a candidate,

Table 3.4

Percentage Contributing Money During Presidential Election Campaigns

Year	Men	Women
1972	12	9
1976	21	14
1980	9	8
1984	9	7
1988	10	8
1992	9	6
1996	12	7
2000	16	9

Sources: American National Election Studies Cumulative File, 1952–1992; American National Election Studies, 1996; American National Election Studies, 2000 File.

and 7 percent to a political group. Of the women, 4 percent contributed to a political party, 5 percent to a candidate, while 3 percent gave money to a political group. In 2002, men were twice as likely as women to contribute money to a candidate, a party organization, or another type of political organization.

To summarize, for two of the three types of electoral activities (contributing money and engaging in campaign activities), men participate more than women. However, women are slightly more likely to vote.

Individuals have the opportunity to participate in a number of nonelectoral political activities. Are men and women equally likely to engage in those types of political activities? In 2000, about one-quarter of both men and women reported that during the past twelve months they had been active on a community issue. Men are more likely than women to report contacting a public official to express their views on an issue during the previous twelve months (24 percent of the men versus 18 percent of the women). Of the men, 29 percent compared with 26 percent of the women had attended a meeting about a community or school issue. More men than women reported being a member of some type of organization other than a church or synagogue (45 percent of the men versus 39 percent of the women). Slightly more than 3 percent of both men and women had participated in a protest, march, or demonstration on some national or local issue during the previous twelve months.[3]

Explanations for Patterns of Participation

What inhibits women's levels of political participation? A number of explanations have been examined in prior research (Conway 2000). Differences between men and women in patterns of participation may occur because of sex role socialization. Women may learn, perhaps as children, that "politics is a man's business." Indeed, research on the political socialization of children conducted in the 1960s suggests girls learned a passive orientation toward politics (Greenstein 1965; Hess and Torney 1967). However, the increasing number of women elected to public office and, especially to very visible offices such as U.S. senator, representative, governor, and mayor, provides an alternative pattern of role models. Life experiences as adults (observing women in leading political roles) could result in resocialization, with women learning that politics is also women's business (Burns, Schlozman, and Verba 2001; Verba, Burns, and Schlozman 1997; Sigel 1988).

A second explanation for patterns of participation focuses on resources available to support, either directly or indirectly, political participation. These resources include educational attainment. The cognitive skills acquired through education facilitate acquiring the information necessary to evaluate leadership alternatives and policy options. Educational attainment also structures placement in social networks, with those with higher levels of educational attainment tending to be more active in organizations in which political matters are discussed and formal and informal efforts at political mobilization occur (Burns, Schlozman, and Verba 2001; Brady, Schlozman, and Verba 1995; Verba, Schlozman, and Brady 1995; Rosenstone and Hansen 1993). Education has a stronger effect on women's participation in both community and campaign-related political activities than on men's participation. The effects of education remain after controlling for level of family income.

Two other resources that structure participation patterns are income and occupation. Income both directly and indirectly facilitates participation. Those who give money to political causes must have disposable income available. Those with higher incomes also have a higher probability of receiving requests to contribute to political campaigns. Some occupations enhance knowledge relevant to politics and government and facilitate the development and honing of skills useful in political activity. The general pattern is that women earn less than men in the same occupation. Among married couples, the husband generally has a higher income than the wife. Thus, to the extent that campaign contributions are based on the donor's income, women would be less likely to contribute money to political campaigns.

A third explanation for patterns of political participation emphasizes the social contexts within which individuals live and work. The workplace, the family, the neighborhood, and social and religious organizations influence communication patterns, peer pressure, and time demands (Conway 2000; Lake and Huckfeldt 1998; Verba, Schlozman, and Brady 1995; Burns, Schlozman, and Verba 2001). Another aspect of social context is place in the life cycle. Age differences exist in patterns of political participation, and the differences may be due to the time and task demands associated with the individual's position in the life cycle. For example, those who are just leaving college, starting new jobs, or caring for small children at home would probably have less time and money to be active in politics compared to those who are well established in their careers and whose children have completed college. Interest in politics and the resources necessary to participate vary with different stages of the life cycle.

Research also suggests that significant differences in political activity exist among generations (Bennett and Rademacher 1997; Miller and Shanks 1997). A generation is usually defined as people who were born during the same political and social era. Members of a generation are exposed to the same political and social events, although they may react to those political and social conditions in different ways. A study that traced patterns of voting turnout among three generations of the American electorate from 1952 to 1992 divided the electorate into the pre–New Deal generation (those who first became eligible to vote for the presidency before 1932), the New Deal generation (first eligible between 1932 and 1964), and the post–New Deal generation (those first eligible to vote for the presidency in 1992). The authors discovered significant differences in voting turnout among these three generations, with the New Deal generation having the highest rates of turnout after 1968. The differences remained after controlling for the effects of level of educational attainment, race, social connectedness, and several types of political beliefs (Miller and Shanks 1996).

Other research contrasts initial voting turnout rates in the first election for which Early Baby Boomers (those born between 1946 and 1954), Late Baby Boomers (those born between 1955 and 1964), and Generation X (those born after 1964) were eligible to vote (Bennett and Rademacher 1997). Initial turnout rates were substantially higher among the Early Baby Boomers in the first election for which they were eligible to vote than for the two subsequent generations in the first election for which they were eligible. Therefore, generational differences appear to exist at least in voting turnout.

Are there gender differences in patterns of participation among generations? For the purposes of analysis of differences among generations, the 2000 electorate has been divided into five generations. The generations, their ages, and the generation labels used in the discussion are as follows:

Birth cohort	Age in 2000	Generation label
1979–1982	18 to 21	Generation Y
1963–1978	22 to 37	Generation X
1948–1962	38 to 52	Baby Boomers
1925–1947	53 to 75	Silent Generation
1924 and earlier	76 or older	Oldest Generation

Analysis of survey data collected in 2000 indicates that in each generation, men tend to participate in political activities more than women do. Differences in voting turnout by generation existed in 2000, but only among the younger generations are the differences large enough to be statistically significant. With the exception of the Oldest Generation, significant differences exist between men and women in participation in campaign activities. Differences also exist in each generation between the proportion of men and women contributing money (see Table 3.5a).

Citizens can also participate in a variety of nonelectoral activities, such as contacting public officials, being active on community issues, attending local public

Table 3.5a

Generational and Gender Differences Among Participants in Three Types of Electoral Activities, 2000

Generation	Percent voting		Percent engaging in at least one campaign activity		Percent contributing money to a candidate, party, or political group	
	Men	Women	Men	Women	Men	Women
Generation Y	33	57	40	35	0	6
Generation X	71	65	41	36	7	5
Baby Boomers	81	77	45	37	18	9
Silent Generation	85	83	49	39	24	12
Oldest Generation	95	95	42	42	24	8

Source: American National Election Studies, 2000 File.

Table 3.5b

Generational and Gender Differences Among Participants in Nonelectoral Political Activities, 2000

Generation	Men	Women
Generation Y	21	32
Generation X	39	37
Baby Boomers	52	51
Silent Generation	49	39
Oldest Generation	39	39

Source: American National Election Studies, 2000.

meetings, and being a member of an organization that focuses some of its activities on policy issues. In 2000, only among Generation Y and the Silent Generation did significant differences exist between men and women in levels of participation in nonelectoral activities (see Table 3.5b).

To summarize, role socialization patterns, resources available to women, and the social contexts of their lives can facilitate or inhibit women's participation in both electoral and other forms of political activity. Generational differences also exist, with men in some generations participating more than women in some types of political activities. In 2000, Generation Y men and women differed significantly in participating in voting, other types of electoral activities, and in nonelectoral activities.

Gender Role Orientations and Political Participation

Another explanation for differences in political participation patterns among women is that the types and levels of participation activities in which they engage are influenced by their gender role orientations. The gender role orientations of women are influenced by their patterns of gender group consciousness. Many different varieties of gender group consciousness are possible. These result from differences in the group cultures in which women's lives are imbedded. For example, feminism is one type of gender consciousness; antifeminism is another.

How can women's gender role orientations be measured? One method uses a measure of gender consciousness, defined as "one's recognition that one's relationship to the political world is at least partly but nonetheless particularly shaped by being female or male. This recognition is followed by identification with others in the 'group' of one's sex, positive affect toward the group, and a feeling of interdependence with the group's fortunes" (Tolleson-Rinehart 1992, 32). If gender consciousness influences political orientations, political beliefs, attitudes, and activities would be expected to be different between women who operate within the context of this cognitive structure and those who do not. However, gender consciousness need not take one form. Different cognitive structuring may develop. Indeed, women who support a patriarchal culture and traditional definitions of women's roles would have a quite different set of gender role orientations than would women whose role orientations are more modern. Thus, while gender consciousness is one type of organizing schema, it can vary in its contents, depending on the beliefs and value structure of the individuals.

In their examination of subjective group identification, Gurin, Miller, and Gurin (1980) define four components of group consciousness. Those are a sense of belonging to a group; a preference for group members and dislike of nongroup members; evaluative assessments of the group's resources, power, and status relative to those of other groups; and attributions of responsibility for the status of the group (see also Miller et al. 1981; Gurin 1985). Gender consciousness could be manifested in the relationship between group identification and political beliefs, attitudes, and activities. Unfortunately, the measures needed to assess different types of gender consciousness among women rarely exist. However, it is possible to measure one type of gender consciousness, that which is generally referred to as feminist consciousness. Several different measures of feminist consciousness have been used.

One way to measure feminist consciousness is to evaluate responses to survey items assessing individuals' closeness to numerous groups in society, such as "women" or "environmentalists." The survey respondents are presented with a list of groups and asked to indicate whether or not they feel close to each group. The survey item asks if members of the group are "people who are most like you in their ideas and interests and feelings about things." In surveys prior to 1996, individuals were also asked to indicate to which group they felt closest. That permitted creating a scale of group closeness that ranged from 0 (not close at all) to 1 (close) to 2 (closest). Women's assessments of the extent to which they felt close to other women could be used as a measure of feminist consciousness (Tolleson-Rinehart 1992). However, the "closest" question was not included in the 2000 National

Election Study survey (Burns, Kinder, Rosenstone, Sapiro, and the NES 2000). Therefore that measure cannot be used to analyze patterns of feminist consciousness.

An alternative measure of feminist gender consciousness uses evaluations of feelings toward women as a group (Cook 1999). Because individuals vary in how positively they rate all groups, with some rating all groups very positively and others rating all groups more negatively, the scoring system must take into account differences in how individuals rate all groups. A mean rating score is created by summing the ratings given several groups, then dividing the summed score by number of groups. The four groups used were liberals, conservatives, big businesses, and labor unions. The average rating given to all groups is then subtracted from the rating given to women as a group. Those who score women 10 percent or more above their mean rating for all groups are evaluated as giving women a positive score and categorized as feminists. Those who score women 10 percent or more below the average score for the groups are scored as giving women a negative evaluation and labeled nonfeminists. Those rating women within 9.99 percent of their mean rating of comparison groups are scored as giving women a neutral rating and labeled as potential feminists.[4] Unfortunately, the group "women" was not included among the groups rated for closeness by those responding to the 2000 National Election Study survey.

Another measure of gender role orientations uses support for an equal role for women in society and politics. Are women who are more supportive of an equal role for women in society and politics more likely to participate in politics? Comparisons can be made among groups of women at one point in time, examining differences in participation levels by patterns of support for an equal role for women.

Whatever measure of gender role orientations is used, a pattern of changing support over time for the women's movement and for equal roles for women in politics and society is evident. Using an index based on three items in the national sample–based General Social Survey, Bennett and Bennett (1999) find such a trend present from 1974–75 through 1994–96. The same trend is evident using responses to the feeling close to women item and the thermometer scales rating of the women's movement in the biennial National Election Studies. Across time both men and women are increasingly positive in their assessments of the women's movement (Cook 1999; Conway, Steuernagel, and Ahern 1997). By 2000, only 14 percent of the women and 19 percent of the men surveyed evaluated the women's movement negatively.

An alternative measure of gender role orientations uses a survey item that asks individuals to place themselves on a five-point scale, with one end point of the scale being "women should have an equal role with men in running business, industry, and government," and the other being "women's place is in the home." On the basis of this measure, both men and women have become increasingly supportive of equal roles for men and women. By 2000, 78 percent of men and 83 percent of women endorsed equal roles for women, with only 6 percent of men and 5 percent of women opposing that idea, the rest being scored as neutral.

Table 3.6

Support or Opposition to Equal Role for Women by Generation and Gender, 2000 (percent)

Generation	Strongly support	Support	Neutral	Oppose	Strongly oppose
			Men[a]		
Generation Y	72	11	17	0	0
Generation X	68	11	16	1	4
Baby Boomer	69	10	17	1	3
Silent Generation	60	15	17	4	4
Oldest Generation	59	9	20	5	7
All Men	66	11.7	16.8	1.8	3.7

Generation	Strongly support	Support	Neutral	Oppose	Strongly oppose
			Women		
Generation Y	71	10	14	2	4
Generation X	76	10	11	2	1
Baby Boomer	79	9	10	1	1
Silent Generation	68	10	15	2	5
Oldest Generation	62	21	17	8	6
All Women	73.1	9.5	12.3	2.2	2.9

Source: National Election Studies, 2000.

Note: [a]Chi-squared tests indicate differences between men and women are significant for Generation X and the Baby Boomers, but not for the two older generations.

Given the high support for equal roles for women and high levels of positive evaluation of the women's movement, we might expect that gender role orientations would contribute little to explaining patterns of political participation. However, generational differences could exist in patterns of support for equal roles and approval of the women's movement, with those socialized when equal roles for women received less positive evaluation being less supportive. Examining first patterns of support for equal roles for women, among men the youngest generation is the most supportive, while among women Generation X and the Baby Boomers are the most supportive (see Table 3.6). In evaluations of the women's movement, Generation X and the Older Generation are more supportive among men, while among women the youngest generation is the most supportive (see Table 3.7).

Are patterns of support for an equal role for women and evaluations of the women's movement related to patterns of political participation? In 2000, women who were supportive of an equal role for women were more likely to engage in at least one type of campaign activity, but they were less likely to make a contribution to a political party, other type of political organization, or a candidate. Only

Table 3.7

Generational Differences in Percent Support for the Women's Movement, 1996

	Men			Women		
	Not feminist	Potential feminist	Feminist	Not feminist	Potential feminist	Feminist
Generation X	22	28	50	8	21	71
Baby Boomers	27	25	48	16	22	62
Silent Generation	27	23	50	21	28	51
Oldest Generation	18	32	49	26	27	48

Note: Entries based on computed scores.

those most supportive of an equal role for women were more likely to be active in nonelectoral political activities. Women who positively evaluated the women's movement in 2000 were less likely to participate in campaigns than were those who evaluated it negatively; they were also less likely to make a campaign contribution in 2000. Why? Those women who were more conservative in their ideology or who more strongly identified with the Republican party were also less likely to indicate support for the women's movement and for an equal role for women in politics and society. In 2000, those more conservative or more Republican in their political party support also tended to have higher levels of family income. Patterns of nonelectoral political participation did not vary with evaluations of the women's movement.

To summarize, both gender and generational differences exist in patterns of support for equal roles for women and for the women's movement. Men and women also differ in the number of types of campaign activities in which they engage and in their campaign contribution patterns. Gender role orientations as measured by the equal role indicator appear to have a limited impact on patterns of participation because of the overwhelming support for the idea that women should have an equal role in business, industry, and government. Those women who are less supportive of the women's movement participate more in both electoral and nonelectoral politics.

Do gender orientation and generation have an impact on these types of political participation when controls for other variables are included in the analysis? When measures of the social context, political context, and individuals' attitudes and beliefs are included in multivariate analyses, do gender role orientations and support for the women's movement affect patterns of political participation? The measures of social context included in the analyses are generation, level of educational attainment, marital status, employment status, level of family income, race, and membership in a secular organization. Political context variables include political mobilization contacts received by mail or telephone from political parties,

Table 3.8

Regression Analyses: Number of Types of Campaign Activities Performed and Types of Campaign Contributions Made, 2000

Independent Variables	Campaign activities	Campaign contributions
Social Context		
Gender	0.0178	−0.0462
Generation	−0.0175	0.0318*
Education	−0.0177	0.0549
Employed	0.145***	−0.0257
Married	−0.0095	−0.0432
Race	−0.0208	−0.0105
Family Income	0.0048	0.0217****
Organization member	0.141***	0.0813**
Political Context		
Political mobilization by political candidate, party, or organization	0.127****	0.0436****
Mobilization efforts by clergy	−0.0308	−0.0269
Strength of Democratic party identification	0.0443*	−0.0382
Strength of Republican party identification	0.0516*	0.0261
Care who wins election	0.127**	0.0606
Attitudes and Beliefs		
Equal Role for women	−0.0491**	0.0897
External efficacy	−0.0185**	−0.0288
Evaluation of the women's movement	0.0104	0.0109
Follow government and public affairs	0.176****	0.0798****
	Adj. $R^2 = 0.176$, $F = 14.349$, $p < .001$	Adj. $R^2 = 0.131$, $F = 10.472$, $p < .001$

Note: Entries are OLS regression coefficients. $* = p < .10$; $** = p < .05$; $*** = p < .01$; $**** = p < .001$.

candidates, and others, partisanship (with partisanship measured as strength of Democratic partisanship and strength of Republican partisanship), and efforts by clergy to influence participation. The attitudes and beliefs variables include a belief that elected officials will be responsive to people like oneself (external efficacy), following what goes on in government and public affairs, evaluation of the women's movement, and attitude toward an equal role for women.[5]

The campaign activities index sums the number of different types of activities in which the individual engaged during the campaign. The types of activities are trying to persuade someone how to vote, wearing a campaign button or displaying a campaign sign, attending a campaign meeting or rally, and engaging in some other form of campaign activity.

Examining the equations for level of participation in campaign activities, several variables are significant in explaining participation in campaign activities. Those who are employed and those who are members of at least one secular organization are more likely to participate in different types of campaign activities. As would be expected, those who follow what goes on in government and public affairs and who care about the outcome of the election are also more likely to be active. Individuals who are more partisan, whether Democrat or Republican, also are more active in campaigns. Individuals who are less likely to score high on an index of external efficacy are more active in campaigns. Those who receive more different types of mobilizing contacts from political parties, candidates, or issue groups are also more likely to participate in different types of campaign activities. Citizens who are more supportive of an equal role for women are less likely to engage in different types of campaign activities, and evaluation of the women's movement was not statistically significant.

Another form of campaign activity is contributing money to a candidate, party organization, or another type of political organization. The index of contributing money sums the number of different types of entities to which contributions have been made. Those who made no contributions are scored at 0 on this variable, while those who gave money to a candidate, a political party, and another type of political organization would have a score of 3.

Several variables are statistically significant in explaining patterns of contributing money during a campaign. These include generation, with members of older generations being more likely to contribute, having a higher level of family income, being a member of at least one secular organization, number of different sources of mobilizing contacts received, strength of Democratic party identification, strength of Republican party identification, and following what goes on in government and public affairs. (Table 3.8 illustrates the variables discussed above and their correlation with campaign activities and contributions.)

Should we conclude that gender role orientations do not influence campaign contribution patterns? The answer is no. Although two different measures of feminist gender consciousness are used that permit assessment of the direction of the attitude, both measures are limited in their ability to discriminate the intensity with which gender role orientations are held. Also lacking are direct measures of the connections the respondents draw between their gender role orientations and gender-related issue stands taken by political candidates, parties, or groups in the various electoral contests. Better measures of both gender role orientations and of the gender role–relevant perceptions of candidates, parties, groups, and issues are needed. Furthermore, measures of gender role orientation are needed that can assess a variety of orientations that exist and that could be activated to stimulate various types of political participation.

Notes

1. Data from U.S. Department of Commerce, Bureau of the Census, Current Population Reports, "Registration and Voting in the Election of November 2000." Series P20–552, February 2002, Table B.

2. Measures of giving both to political parties and to candidates are not available before 1964 in the National Election Studies.

3. Computed from variables in the 2000 National Election Study.

4. Unfortunately, the terms to indicate the women's movement have varied across time. In the National Election Studies from 1972 to 1984 the group label "women's liberation movement" was used. In the 1988 and 1992 surveys, the term "feminists" was used, and in 1992 and 1996 the reference group was the women's movement.

5. Because of their high correlation with several other variables, interest in the campaign and internal efficacy were not included in the multivariate analyses.

References

Bennett, L.L.M., and S.E. Bennett. 1999. "Changing Views About Gender Equality in Politics: Gradual Change and Lingering Doubts." In *Women in Politics: Outsiders or Insiders*, ed. L.D. Whitaker. Upper Saddle River, NJ: Prentice Hall.

Bennett, S.E., and E.W. Rademacher. 1997. "The 'Age of Indifference' Revisited: Patterns of Political Interest, Media Exposure, and Knowledge among Generation X." In *After the Boom*, ed. S.E. Craig and S.E. Bennett. Lanhan, MD: Rowman and Littlefield.

Brady, H., S. Verba, and K.L. Schlozman. 1995. "Beyond SES: A Resource Model of Political Participation." *American Political Science Review*, 89: 271–294.

Burns, Nancy, Donald R. Kinder, Steven J. Rosenstone, Virginia Sapiro, and the National Election Studies. *American National Election Study, 2000: Pre- and Post-Election Survey*. Conducted by the Center for Political Studies of the Institute of Social Research, The University of Michigan. Ann Arbor: Inter-University Consortium for Political and Social Research.

Burns, N., K.L. Schlozman, and S. Verba. 2001. *The Private Roots of Public Action*. Cambridge, MA: Harvard University Press.

Clark, C., and J. Clark. 1999. "The Gender Gap in 1996: More Meaning than a 'Revenge of the Soccer Moms.'" In *Women in Politics: Outsiders or Insiders*? ed. L.D. Whitaker. Upper Saddle River, NJ: Prentice Hall.

Clark, J., and C. Clark. 1996. "The Gender Gap: A Manifestation of Women's Dissatisfaction with the American Polity?" In *Broken Contract?* ed. S.C. Craig. Boulder, CO: Westview Press.

Conway, M.M. 2000. *Political Participation in the United States*. 3d ed. Washington, DC: CQ Press.

Conway, M.M., G.A. Steuernagel, and D.W. Ahern. 1997. *Women and Political Participation*. Washington, DC: CQ Press.

Cook, E.A. 1999. "The Generations of Feminism." In *Women in Politics: Outsiders or Insiders?* ed. L.D. Whitaker. Upper Saddle River, NJ: Prentice Hall.

Flexner, E., and E. Fitzpatrick. 1975. *Century of Struggle*. Cambridge, MA: Harvard University Press.

Greenstein, F. 1965. *Children and Politics*. New Haven: Yale University Press.

Gurin, P. 1985. "Women's Gender Consciousness." *Public Opinion Quarterly*, 49: 143–163.

Gurin, P., A.H. Miller, and G. Gurin. 1980. "Stratum Identification and Consciousness." *Social Psychological Quarterly*, 43: 30–47.

Hess, R.D., and J.V. Torney. 1967. *The Development of Political Attitudes in Children*. Chicago: Aldine.

Lake, R.L., and R. Huckfeldt. 1998. "Social Capital, Social Networks, and Political Participation." *Political Psychology*, 19: 567–565.

Miller, A.H., P. Gurin, G. Gurin, and O. Malanchuk. 1981. "Group Consciousness and Political Participation." *American Journal of Political Science*, 25: 494–511.

Miller, W.E., and J.M. Shanks. 1996. *The New American Voter*. Cambridge, MA: Harvard University Press.

Rosenstone, S.J., and J.M. Hansen. 1993. *Mobilization, Participation, and Democracy in America*. New York: Macmillan.

Sigel, Roberta, ed. 1988. *Political Learning in Adulthood*. Chicago: University of Chicago Press.

Stucker, J.J. 1977. "Women as Voters: Their Maturation as Political Persons in American Society." In *A Portrait of Marginality*, ed. Marianne Githens and Jewel L. Prestage. New York: David MacKay.

Tolleson-Rinehart, S. 1992. *Gender Consciousness and Politics*. New York: Routledge.

Verba, S., N. Burns, and K.L. Schlozman. 1997. "Knowing and Caring About Politics: Gender and Political Engagement." *Journal of Politics*, 59: 1051–1072.

Verba, S., K.L. Schlozman, and H.E. Brady. 1995. *Voice and Equality*. Cambridge, MA: Harvard University Press.

4

A Tougher Road for Women?
Assessing the Role of Gender in Congressional Elections

Pamela Fiber and Richard L. Fox

Throughout the 1990s, women made significant strides competing for and winning seats in the United States Congress. The 1992 elections, often referred to as the "Year of the Woman," resulted in an historic increase in the number of women in both the House of Representatives and the Senate.[1] These increases were an encouraging improvement in efforts to move toward some semblance of gender parity in our political institutions. After all, in the history of the House of Representatives, there have been roughly 11,500 male representatives, but fewer than 200 female representatives (CAWP 2003). Recent congressional elections, however, indicate that women's progress is beginning to stagnate. The 2002 elections marked the first time since 1994 that women did not increase their presence in Congress. Currently, 86 percent of the members of the U.S. Senate and 86 percent of the members of the U.S. House are male.[2] This places the United States fifty-ninth worldwide in terms of the number of women serving in the national legislature, a ranking far behind many other democratic governments (Inter-Parliamentary Union 2003).

The continued dearth of women members in Congress suggests that a "masculine" ethos still dominates the congressional electoral environment. A host of interrelated factors—money, familiarity with the political elite, political experience, and support from the political parties—all contribute to a winning campaign. Typically, traditional candidates are members of the political or economic elite. Most emerge from lower-level elected offices, or serve as successful lawyers or businessmen in the community. They are often encouraged to run for office by other community elites, party officials, or outgoing incumbents. And these same elites who encourage the candidacies also contribute money to the campaigns and hold fundraisers. This congressional candidate emergence process has been in place for most of the recent history of congressional candidacies (Thomas and Lamb 1965; Hibbing 1991; Loomis 1998).

For obvious reasons, this process has served men well and women very poorly.

Because they have been excluded from their communities' economic and political elite throughout much of the twentieth century, women's paths to Congress have often taken different forms. Widows of congressmen who died in office served as the first wave of successful female candidates. Between 1916 and 1964, 28 of the 32 widows nominated to fill their husbands' vacancies won their elections, for a victory rate of 88 percent. Across the same time period, only 32 of the 199 nonwidows who garnered their party's nomination were elected, for a 14 percent victory rate (Gertzog 1984, 18).

The 1960s and 1970s mark the second wave of women candidates, most of whom turned their attention from civic volunteerism to politics (Burrell 1994, 58). Some women involved in grassroots community politics rode this activism to Washington. Notable figures who pursued this path include Patsy Mink, elected in 1964; Shirley Chisholm, elected in 1968; and Pat Schroeder and Barbara Jordan, both elected in 1972.

We are currently in the midst of the third wave of women candidates. In this wave, the prevailing model of running for Congress has become far less rigid. As political parties have become less powerful and the media have become central to campaigns, more paths can lead to election to Congress. Women and men with more diverse backgrounds can now compete successfully for their party's nomination. Converging with this less rigid path is an increase in the number of women who now fit the profile of a traditional candidate. The number of women serving in the state legislature, a springboard to Congress, has increased almost sixfold since 1970 (CAWP 2003; Norrander and Wilcox 1998, 106).[3] Further, women's presence in the fields of business and law has dramatically increased. Together, these developments indicate that the eligibility pool of prospective women candidates grew substantially throughout the 1990s (Carroll 1994; Darcy, Welch, and Clark 1994).

Despite the small number of women in Congress, empirical examinations reveal that blatant sex discrimination does not account for women's numeric underrepresentation. Individual accounts of women who face overt gender discrimination once they enter the public arena are no longer commonplace (Woods 2000; Schroeder 1999; Witt, Paget, and Matthews 1994). In terms of vote totals and fundraising, investigators also find that women fare just as well as, if not better than, their male counterparts (Burrell 1998; Seltzer, Newman, and Leighton 1997; Chaney and Sinclair 1994). These researchers generally conclude that two barriers account for the small number of women serving in the House. First, simply too few women choose to run; second, the incumbency advantage translates into few good opportunities for women to gain congressional seats.

This is not to say, however, that gender is irrelevant in the political arena. In congressional elections, men and women candidates face an electorate, a press corps, and a political establishment that often rely on masculine and feminine stereotypes to assess candidates. Conover and Gray (1983, 2–3) define traditional assumptions about women's and men's proper place in society: "The role of a woman is defined by her reproductive, sexual, and child-rearing functions within the family, then there is a . . . division of activities into the public extra-familial jobs done by the male and the private intra-familial ones performed by the female." A number of researchers have found that substantial vestiges of these antiquated notions of "proper" gender roles usually disadvantage women candidates (Niven 1998; Fox 1997; Kahn 1996; Huddy and Terkildsen 1993a, 1993b).

Women congressional candidates' historical fortunes, coupled with recent academic research, suggest that men and women often have different experiences in the electoral process, and these different experiences are highly instructive of the gendered political dynamics that persist in American politics. In exploring the persistence of gender as a factor in congressional elections, we divide this chapter into two broad sections. Section one compares men and women candidates' levels of electoral performance and success in House elections from 1980 to 2002. Our results confirm previous research: the electoral playing field has become largely gender neutral. In the second section of the chapter, we turn to the more subtle ways in which gender might manifest itself in congressional elections. First, we find that the increased presence of women candidates and elected officials has not spread to all regions of the country. Next, when we turn to a focused examination of open-seat congressional races, we find important gender differences between the parties. We also find differences in the degree to which the presence of a woman candidate changes fundraising dynamics. Ultimately, our data and analysis encourage a number of areas of future research and suggest that broad empirical analyses declaring gender neutrality in the electoral process may be premature.

Men and Women Running for Congress: The General Indicators

The 1990s demonstrated a change in the gender dynamics of the congressional election process. Table 4.1 reveals substantial, albeit slow and steady, growth in the number of women seeking and winning congressional elections over the last thirty years. The only dramatic single-year jump occurred in 1992. Between 1996 and 2002, there have actually been an almost identical number of women general election House candidates. Nevertheless, the 2002 election set the record with 124 women candidates winning their party's nomination for a House seat. To put that in perspective, more than 650 male candidates garnered their party's nomination in 2002.

In addition to noting the increasing number of women running for Congress, Table 4.1 also illustrates a trend that pertains to the political parties. Since 1992, Democrats have been nearly twice as likely as Republicans to nominate women House candidates. This disparity is a subject to which we turn more fully later in this chapter.

Vote Totals

Recent work pertaining to the manner in which candidate sex has an impact on vote choice produces mixed results. Some experimental studies have found that

Table 4.1

Growth in the Number of Women Candidates Running for the U.S. House of Representatives

	1970	1980	1990	1992	1994	1996	1998	2000	2002
Democrats									
General Election Candidates	15	27	39	70	72	77	75	80	78
General Election Winners	10	11	19	35	30	35	39	41	38
Republicans									
General Election Candidates	11	25	30	36	40	43	46	42	46
General Election Winners	3	10	9	12	17	16	17	18	21
Total Women Candidates	26	52	69	106	112	120	121	122	124

Source: CAWP Fact Sheets, 2003.

Notes: Entries represent the raw number of women candidates and winners for each year. Four women won special elections between the 1996 and 1998 elections.

women continue to be disadvantaged in attracting votes (see Huddy and Terkildsen 1993a, 1993b; Fox and Smith 1998). Yet studies of actual vote totals do not provide evidence for this claim (Cook 1998; Dolan 1998; Darcy, Welch, and Clark 1994). Burrell (1994, 141), in a study of vote totals for House candidates from 1968 to 1992, concludes that candidate sex accounts for less than one percent of variation in the vote for men and women candidates. Dolan (2004), in a broad overview of gender and voting, concludes that gender is only a relevant factor in rare electoral instances.

If we turn to the performance of men and women in House elections between 1980 and 2002, we arrive at a similar conclusion. We divide the analysis into three categories: 1980–1990; 1992–2000; and 2002. We separate 2002 so as to update the performance of women candidates in the most recent House elections.

Table 4.2 confirms that, even in the most recent House races, women and men fared similarly in terms of raw vote totals. The only difference that approaches any threshold of statistical significance is women Republicans running in open seats in the first two time periods. Clearly, though, the results presented in Table 4.2 show that there is no widespread voter bias for or against women candidates.

Fundraising

Throughout much of the 1970s and 1980s, because so few women ran, many scholars assumed that women in electoral politics could simply not raise the amount of money necessary to mount a competitive campaign. Indeed, several anecdotal studies concluded that women ran campaigns with lower levels of funding than did

Table 4.2

Comparison of General Election Mean Vote Totals for Men and Women House Candidates, 1980–2002

	1980–1990		1992–2000		2002	
	Women	Men	Women	Men	Women	Men
Democrats						
Incumbents	73%	72%	67%	67%	69%	68%
	(59)	(1,384)	(149)	(830)	(38)	(138)
Challengers	35	34	38	35	33	32
	(80)	(763)	(157)	(633)	(32)	(118)
Open Seats	48	52	51	50	47	45
	(24)	(196)	(61)	(205)	(8)	(34)
Republicans						
Incumbents	68	68	65	67	63	68
	(52)	(911)	(64)	(859)	(12)	(169)
Challengers	33	33	31	34	35	31
	(98)	(1,023)	(92)	(791)	(19)	(134)
Open Seats	41	49	44	49	50	53
	(16)	(193)	(30)	(222)	(8)	(34)

Sources: 1980–2000 compiled from FEC reports; 2002 results drawn from *Congressional Quarterly Almanac*.

Notes: Candidates running unopposed are omitted from these results. Entries indicate vote share won. Parentheses indicate the sample size for each category. None of the comparisons between women and men achieves even borderline statistical significance.

men (Mandel 1981; Baxter and Lansing 1980). More systematic examinations of campaign receipts, however, uncover little evidence of sex differences in fundraising. Burrell (1985), in a study of congressional candidates from 1972 to 1982, found only a "very weak" relationship between gender and the ability to raise campaign funds. More recently, she found that, by the 1988 House elections, the disparity between men and women in campaign fundraising had completely disappeared (Burrell 1994, 105; see also Burrell 1998). Uhlaner and Schlozman (1986) determined that women House candidates did tend to raise less money than did men, but they account for the difference by noting that male incumbents generally held positions of greater political power; accordingly, they attracted larger contributions.

Table 4.3, which presents the fundraising totals of men and women general election candidates between 1980 and 2002, tends to confirm other recent studies. While there are some sizable discrepancies in the comparisons of women and men, most are not significant. In fact, the discrepancies actually reveal an advantage for women candidates in a number of instances. The conclusion to draw from Table 4.3 is that women and men perform roughly equally well in fundraising.

Table 4.3

Comparison of Mean Campaign Receipts for Men and Women General Election House Candidates, 1980–2002

	1980–1990		1992–2000		2002	
	Women	Men	Women	Men	Women	Men
Democrats						
Incumbents	$573,608 (59)	$526,148 (1,384)	$720,182 (149)	$745,155 (830)	$841,913 (38)	$1,002,492 (136)
Challengers	257,962* (80)	189,379 (763)	403,676* (157)	249,329 (633)	354,576 (31)	471,656 (82)
Open Seats	630,211 (24)	576,502 (196)	808,326 (61)	719,076 (205)	1,326,667 (8)	1,078,387 (34)
Republicans						
Incumbents	599,976 (52)	566,213 (911)	913,748 (64)	796,776 (859)	1,330,750 (11)	975,888 (167)
Challengers	237,188 (98)	206,037 (1,023)	278,845 (92)	266,938 (791)	453,196 (16)	354,576 (102)
Open Seats	625,569 (16)	628,873 (193)	733,134 (30)	720,351 (222)	1,131,347 (8)	1,270,492 (34)

Sources: 1980–2000 compiled from FEC reports; 2002 results drawn from *Congressional Quarterly Almanac.*

Notes: Candidates running unopposed are omitted from these results. Entries indicate total money raised. Parentheses indicate the sample size for each category. Significance levels: * = $p < .01$ in difference of means test for Democratic challengers in 1980–1990 and 1992–2000.

Based on general indicators, we see what appears to be a gender-neutral electoral environment. Women are steadily increasing their numbers in Congress, and men and women perform similarly in terms of vote totals and fundraising. The data certainly suggest that men have lost their stranglehold over the congressional election process and that there are now excellent opportunities for women seeking a seat in the House of Representatives. But these indicators tell only part of the story.

Are Women Making Gains Everywhere? State and Regional Variation

If we examine the prevalence of men and women House candidates by region and state, we see that the broader inclusion of women in high-level politics has not transcended to all regions of the country. Table 4.4 tracks women's electoral success to the House since 1970. Before 1990, the Northeast had two and three times as many women candidates as any other region in the country. Things changed dramatically with the Year of the Woman elections in 1992. The number of women winning election to Congress from western states more than doubled, and in the South, the number more than tripled. The Midwest's numbers stagnated until 1998, and there were only modest gains in the Northeast. Since the late 1990s, only the West continues to show clear gains for women. This geographic breakdown puts the 1992 elections, as well as the modest increases of women's elections to Congress since that time, into perspective. The Year of the Woman gains were strictly in the West and South; only the West has maintained progress toward increasing the number of women heading to Congress.

More specific than region, there are also several striking differences among individual states. Consider, for instance, that heading into the 2004 elections, 20 states have no women representatives in Washington. While a record 141 women were general election candidates, only 7 women won open seats and 1 woman successfully challenged an incumbent and won (in Illinois); 57 women won re-election as incumbents. Further, 29 states have never been represented by a woman in the U.S. Senate, and only 14 states have ever elected a woman to a full Senate term (CAWP 2003). Table 4.5 indicates which states have had the best and worst records in terms of sending women to serve in the House of Representatives between 1992 and 2002. Sixteen states never sent a woman to serve in the House during this time period. Several states with relatively large House delegations, such as New Jersey (with 13 members) and Massachusetts (with 10 members), currently have no women representatives. Only 1 of Pennsylvania's 21 members is a woman; and only 2 of the 20 members from Illinois are women. Following the 2004 elections, Pennsylvania and Illinois each gained one woman.

The table also demonstrates that women congressional candidates have been very successful in a number of states, such as the larger states of California, Florida, and New York, and the smaller states of Connecticut and Missouri. Why have women done well in these states and not others? Three of these states—California,

Table 4.4

Regional Differences in the Percentage of Women House Candidates, 1970–2002

	West	South	Midwest	Northeast
1970	3.9%	0.0%	2.5%	4.9%
1980	2.6	1.6	3.3	8.1
1990	8.2	2.3	6.2	9.6
1992	17.2	7.9	6.7	12.4
2000	25.8	9.2	10.9	11.3
2002	25.5	8.7	11.5	9.8
Net Change	+21.6	+8.7	+9.0	+4.9

Source: CAWP Fact Sheets.

Notes: Percentages are based on the size of each region's House delegation. The sizes of the delegations differ because of redistricting.

Table 4.5

States with the Highest and Lowest Percentages of Women in the House, 1992–2002

States with No Women Representatives	States with Low Percentage of Women Representatives		States with High Percentage of Women Representatives	
Massachusetts (10)	Pennsylvania (21)	2%	Connecticut (6)	43%
Minnesota (8)	Tennessee (9)	2	Missouri (9)	23
Alabama (7)	Wisconsin (9)	2	California (52)	22
Louisiana (7)	Virginia (11)	4	Florida (23)	21
Oklahoma (6)	Illinois (20)	4	New York (31)	19
Mississippi (5)	Georgia (11)	7	Washington (9)	18
Iowa (5)	Texas (30)	8	Colorado (6)	17
Nebraska (3)	Indiana (10)	8	Maryland (8)	15
Rhode Island (2)	New Jersey (13)	8		
New Hampshire (2)				
Montana (1)				
North Dakota (1)				
Delaware (1)				
South Dakota (1)				
Vermont (1)				
Alaska (1)				

Notes: Entries indicate the total percentage of years women served as representatives for each state over the course of the election cycles between 1992 and 2002. For instance, Wisconsin had a total of 90 years (9 seats x 10 years), of which a woman served for only 2 years. Thus, the percentage is roughly 2 percent. Parentheses indicate the number of House seats in the state.

New York, and Florida—are among those with the biggest delegations, so perhaps we can assume that many more opportunities for women exist. This would not, however, explain the lack of success among women candidates in the large states of Texas and Pennsylvania. What explains success in states like Missouri, though? Missouri borders Iowa, which has never elected a woman House candidate, and

Oklahoma, which elected its only woman House member (to one term) in 1921. By the same token, why has Connecticut elected so many more women than neighboring Massachusetts?

Clearly, there are some important gender dynamics at work in various state political cultures. Hill (1981) argues that state political culture serves as an important determinant of women's ability to win elective office. Norrander and Wilcox (1998) find considerable disparities in the progress of women's election to state legislatures across various states and regions. They explain the disparities by pointing to differences in state ideology and state culture (116). States with a conservative ideology and "traditionalist or moralist" cultures (Elazar 1984) are less likely to elect women (see also Sanbonmatsu 2002a, 2002b). A strong correlation between the percentage of women in the state legislature and the number of women in Congress, however, does not always exist. Wisconsin, Minnesota, and Massachusetts, for example, are above average in terms of the number of women serving in the state legislature, yet each has a very poor record of electing women to the House of Representatives. Diagnosing the specific causes of regional and state differences in electing women House members is beyond the scope of this chapter. Our findings, however, suggest that the interaction of gender and state culture requires more extensive exploration.

Gender and Open-Seat Contests

Political scientists often identify the incumbency advantage as one of the leading explanations for women's slow entry into electoral politics. Low turnover, a direct result of incumbency, results in few opportunities for women to increase their numbers in male-dominated legislative bodies (Burrell 1994; Carroll and Jenkins 2001; Darcy, Welch, and Clark 1994). Since 1990, fewer than 7 percent of all challengers successfully defeated incumbent members of the U.S. House of Representatives.[4] In most of these races, the average incumbent received roughly 68 percent of the vote-share.[5] Accordingly, as Gaddie and Bullock (2000, 1) note, "Open seats, not the defeat of incumbents, are the portal through which most legislators enter Congress."

Although open-seat elections serve as the venue through which many new members come to Congress, these elections differ from other congressional contests in several notable ways. First, these races tend to attract the largest number of qualified and experienced candidates, particularly those with experience serving in local and state government offices. Second, candidates in open-seat contests are better funded, which facilitates more voter contact and media exposure. Open-seat races also tend to receive a great deal of attention from political parties, political action committees (PACs), and large contributors (Herrnson 2000). As a result, the average winning open-seat candidate's receipts in the 2000 election exceeded the average winning incumbent's receipts by almost $200,000 and the average challenger's by over $750,000.

Table 4.6

Percentage of Women General Election Candidates, by Type of Seat, Party, and Electoral Era

	1980–1990		1992–2000	
	Democrat	Republican	Democrat	Republican
Type of Seat				
Open Seat	11%	8%	23%	12%
	(24)	(16)	(61)	(30)
Challengers	10	9	20	10
	(80)	(98)	(157)	(92)
Incumbents	4	5	12	7
	(59)	(52)	(149)	(64)
Type of Open Seat				
Democrat Leaning	12	11	21	11
	(9)	(7)	(15)	(8)
Republican Leaning	13	4	22	9
	(10)	(3)	(17)	(7)
Toss-up	7	4	24	15
	(3)	(2)	(22)	(13)

Note: Entries indicate the percentage of women general election candidates for each category. The number of elections for each category is in parentheses.

In order to measure the electoral arena's levels of gender neutrality and assess prospects for gender parity in Congress, therefore, it is critical to focus on open-seat races and provide a more nuanced examination of the dynamics involved in them. This is our focus for the remainder of this chapter.

Party and the Presence of Women Candidates in Open-seat Contests

We begin our analysis with a general examination of the presence and performance of women in open-seat House races. As the atmosphere for women candidates has changed dramatically since the early 1990s, we divide our analysis into two distinct periods: 1980–90, and 1992–2000 (see Thomas and Wilcox 1998). The top half of Table 4.6 compares women's presence in House elections by time period, party affiliation, and type of seat. As expected, we uncover differences across the two time periods, with significantly more women candidates in the later era. The increase in women candidates is not constant across parties, though. Between the first and second time period, the number of women Democrats running in all types of races more than doubled, whereas the increases among Republicans were much smaller. Regardless of party, however, in the second time period, the highest percentage of women candidates sought open seats.

We know that candidates are most likely to win elections when the voters in the district lean toward the candidate's party; this is especially true in open-seat races, since incumbency status cannot serve as a mitigating factor. The bottom half of Table 4.6 breaks down the type of open seat by the congressional district's partisan demographics.[6] Although the number of open-seat races with women candidates is small, it is important to emphasize that the data include *every* race with a woman candidate. There are a very limited number of cases from which we can attempt to discern patterns. If we focus on the period between 1992 and 2000, we see that Democrats are roughly equally likely to nominate women in all types of open seats, although they are least likely to nominate women to Democratic-leaning seats. In a similar vein, Republicans are least likely to nominate women for Republican-leaning seats, but the spread of women across all types of open seats is much less constant for Republicans. This finding may explain, at least in part, the difference in the numbers of women Republican and Democrat general election winners shown in Table 4.1.

In order to understand more fully the gap between Democratic and Republican women candidates, we need to begin to focus on what the parties do to recruit and promote women's candidacies. No systematic, empirical analyses shed light on the parties' recruitment practices at the state and local levels (see Fox and Oxley 2003). We also know very little about who chooses to get involved in politics. Research clearly identifies a gender gap within the American populace, with women favoring the Democrats and men the Republicans. But no research examines whether this is also the case among individuals who are in the pipeline to be candidates for public office.

Fundraising and Competition in Open-Seat Races

Considering that in the last five election cycles, women candidates have been most likely to emerge in open-seat contests, it is important to turn our attention to the fundraising dynamics of these races. As previously documented, women and men perform equally well in terms of fundraising. But does this mean that there is no interaction between gender and campaign finance (see Herrick 1996)?

Table 4.7 provides an in-depth analysis of Federal Election Commission (FEC) reports for general election House candidates between 1980 and 2000.[7] We examine campaign contributions of all women candidates, all men candidates, and men candidates who ran against women in the general election. Not only do our results offer a fresh perspective on the interaction of gender and campaign finance, but we also demonstrate that the presence of a woman in the race appears to affect men's campaign contributions.

The first row in Table 4.7 presents total campaign receipts. Women, on average, raise about $100,000 more than men. This type of comparison obscures an important gender difference, though. If we hone in on the races in which men faced women opponents, we see that men raised roughly $100,000 more than the women

Table 4.7

Performance of Open-Seat Candidates, by Sex and Opponent Sex, 1980–2000 (in $US)

	Women Candidates (All)	Men Candidates (All)	Men Running Against Women
Total Receipts	$634,659 *	$528,684	$730,597
Individual Contributions	375,653***	297,042	348,809
$200–499	58,983***	48,447	54,666
$500–749	54,168***	45,576	58,152
$750–1,000	101,282	91,856	126,677
Percent Out-of-State Contributions	23%	14%	15%
PAC Contributions	183,430*	140,685	177,902
Labor	64,186***	37,494	29,582
Corporations	32,002	35,910	54,926
Nonconnected	40,204***	23,993	33,868
Trade, Health	43,572	39,871	55,055
Candidate Contributions	71,470	105,784	205,084
Party Contributions	9,325	10,173	10,589
Percent Vote Share	48%	50%	49%
Percent Elections Won	44**	53	57
Sample Size	130	784	113

Source: Compiled from FEC reports.
Note: Significance levels: * = $p < .10$, ** = $p < .05$, *** = $p < .01$ in difference of means test. Significance tests compare all women with all men.

against whom they ran.[8] At the very least, this suggests that women run in more competitive races, since money signifies the participation of a wider range of political actors. Perhaps more importantly, the findings reveal that the fundraising playing field is not as equitable as aggregate fundraising totals often suggest.

Sources of campaign funding further illuminate some gender differences in open-seat races. When we compare all women to all men, we see that women tend to raise more money than men from individuals, labor, nonconnected PACs, and out-of-state individuals. Several of these differences are expected. Unions and labor organizations, for instance, contribute significantly more to Democrats than to Republicans. Because the majority of female candidates in open-seat races are Democrats, they receive a higher percentage of money from labor.[9] That women receive more money than men from nonconnected PACs may represent the efforts of EMILY's List, a group organized to assist female candidates. The work of EMILY's List might also explain the gender difference in out-of-state contributions. They "bundle" funds from contributors across the country and send contributions to individual candidates.

Once again, though, a comparison of the full population of women and men candidates blurs some of the differences that emerge when we focus on men running against women. In most categories, men running against women raise more money than the women they seek to defeat. Women remain more likely to receive out-of-state funding, but men receive more than women from corporations. Men also tend to receive larger individual contributions and use more of their own financial resources to assist their campaigns. The question of self-financing deserves further examination. Anecdotal evidence and FEC listings of candidates who contributed to their own campaigns suggest that men are more likely than women to commit substantial resources toward their campaigns. This makes sense as men still control the vast majority of wealth in the United States. The degree to which this impacts the electoral arena is a subject worthy of further investigation.

Although most recent research suggests that women and men compete evenly for campaign funds, our analyses indicate gendered funding differences in open-seat races in which women run against men. Men raise higher amounts of money when they run against a woman than when they run against a man. Regardless of the reasons, the increase indicates that gender considerations continue to play a substantial role in the electoral environment.

Candidate Gender, Campaign Receipts, and Multivariate Analysis

Aggregate level differences in campaign contributions provide important insights into the gender dynamics of campaign finance, but we can employ regression analysis to explore further gender's role in open-seat races. We employ three dependent variables to assess potential ways that gender might affect an open-seat contest: whether a woman wins the race, the candidate's vote share, and the candidate's total campaign receipts. The independent variables of substantive interest are the candidate's sex and the opponent's sex. Our analyses control for candidate party, whether the candidate has prior electoral experience, whether the opponent has prior electoral experience, and the party leaning of the seat.

In the first two equations—likelihood of winning and vote share—neither of the gender variables is significant (results not shown). This finding confirms the general conclusion that the sex of the candidate does not affect the electoral outcome (e.g., Seltzer, Newmann, and Leighton 1997). Women fare as well as men, both in terms of electoral success and margin of victory.

When we turn to campaign receipts, we find that gender does emerge as significant. Table 4.8 presents two ordinary least squares (OLS) regression equations, both of which have the total fundraising receipts as the dependent variable. The first equation includes all open-seat races; the second equation includes only male–female races. Focusing first on the coefficients in the first equation, we see that holding prior elected office and running in a toss-up district significantly increase total receipts. A candidate's receipts also increase as the opponent's receipts increase. These findings are to be expected, since these are the criteria that make a race more competitive. Most important for our purposes, however, is the fact that a candidate's receipts are significantly higher when the opponent is a woman.

Table 4.8

Gender and Total Receipts: OLS Regression Coefficients (and Standard Errors) Predicting Total Campaign Receipts in Open-Seat Races, 1980–2000

	All Open-Seat Races	Male–Female Races
Sex	−42,955.00	210,177.69**
	(48,931.29)	(97,326.61)
Ran Against a Woman	192,126.23***	
	(47,934.48)	
Party	6,860.96	164,849.15*
	(33,249.14)	(97,316.41)
Previously Held Elected Office	92,696.40***	142,969.35
	(34,272.68)	(95,470.20)
Opponent Previously Held Elected Office	−126,391.68***	−51,555.79
	(33,931.47)	(94,993.00)
Opponent's Expenditures	0.35***	0.41**
	(0.03)*	(0.07)
Toss-up	85,565.16**	104,024.01
	(40,029.64)	(109,379.73)
Democratic District	−14,960.39	−11,197.45
	(39,690.67)	(109,869.67)
Constant	377,760.63	140,973.23
	(68,776.86)	(147,534.47)
R^2	0.177	0.198
N	809	208

Note: Significance levels: * = $p < .10$; ** = $p < .05$; *** = $p < .01$ in difference of means test.

Turning to male–female races, we see that many of the variables lose their significance. Receipts are influenced by party (Democrats raise more money) and by opponent expenditures. The sex variable remains significant and positive, further corroborating the claim that men raise substantially more money than women in male–female open-seat races. Overall, our multivariate analyses confirm the cross-tabulated data presented in Table 4.7.

Our finding that women raise less money than men when they compete against each other in open-seat contests contradicts the research that concludes there is no funding gap between women and men candidates. Women may not be on equal footing in the races that are most important. Even if women are not less likely than men to win open-seat contests, the exorbitant campaign expenditures devoted to these races indicate that women are forced to compete in particularly intense electoral environments. Our results also indicate the importance of more nuanced approaches to data analysis and broader conceptualizations of the manner in which the presence of a woman candidate might change the dynamics of the race.

Conclusion and Discussion

When political scientists in the late 1970s and early 1980s began to study the role of gender in electoral politics, their investigations tended to be motivated by concerns about representation and democratic legitimacy. These concerns are as pertinent today as they were more than twenty years later. An expansive, impressive body of empirical work finds that a political system that does not allow for women's full inclusion in positions of political power increases the possibility that gender-salient issues will be overlooked (Dodson 1998; Rosenthal 1998; Kathlene 1995). Evidence based on the behavior of public officials clearly demonstrates, for example, that women are more likely than men to promote legislation geared to ameliorate women's economic and social status, especially concerning issues of health care, poverty, education, and gender equity (Swers 2002; Thomas 1994; Flammang 1997). From a normative perspective, a political system that produces governing bodies overwhelmingly dominated by men offends our sense of "simple justice" (Tolleson-Rinehart 1994). In this vein, some researchers argue that the reality of a male-dominated government may suggest to women citizens that the political system is not fully open to them (see Lawless 2004).

Despite the substantive and symbolic importance of women's full inclusion in the electoral arena, the number of women serving in elected bodies remains quite low. This chapter's overview of women's performance in congressional elections makes it clear that we need to take a more nuanced approach to understanding gender's evolving role in the electoral arena, as well as assessing the prospects for increasing the number of women serving in high-level elective office.

To summarize briefly, two broad findings emerge from our analysis. First, women are competing in House races more successfully now than at any time in history; there are few gender differences in terms of the major indicators of electoral success. While these findings might lead some to conclude that the electoral environment is gender neutral, our second broad finding, based on a more in-depth analysis of gender dynamics in elections, indicates that gender continues to play an important role in the electoral arena. Notably, there are sharp state and regional differences in electing men and women to Congress. Acceptance and support of women candidates does not appear to have been achieved at equal levels throughout the United States. Further, our examination of open-seat candidates' experiences reveals that the electoral environment continues to treat women and men differently.

Our analysis opens the door to several directions for future research. First, because women's electoral opportunities appear so promising, we need to understand why there continue to be so few women candidates. Very little research examines the initial decision to run for office. Perhaps our focus should be not on what happens in elections, but rather, on what factors lead to the candidacies in the first place (see Fox and Lawless 2004). Second, we must gain a better understanding of sharp geographic differences in support for women's candidacies. We can speculate about differences in political culture, or the varying practices of state and local party organizations, but these areas have not been sufficiently explored. Third, we must turn our attention to the manner in which the presence of a woman candidate has an impact on other actors in the public sphere. Now that we know that men raise more money when they run against women than when they run against men, we need to investigate more broadly the effects of having a woman candidate enter a race. Put simply, our results point to the importance of moving beyond aggregate analyses of vote shares and campaign receipts as general indicators of electoral success. Gender permeates the electoral environment in subtle and nuanced ways that broad empirical analyses may overlook.

Notes

1. One might note that 1974, 1984, and 1990 were also dubbed the Year of the Woman. But these elections resulted in only minor electoral gains for women. The recognition that 1992 was indeed a major breakthrough year for women candidates continues to be regarded as accurate.

2. Shortly after the 2002 elections, Alaska governor Frank Murkowski appointed his daughter to fill the Senate seat vacated when he was elected governor. This raises the number of women senators to an all-time high of fourteen, but Lisa Murkowski was not popularly elected.

3. It is important to note that women's presence in the state legislatures has also stalled in recent elections.

4. Research by congressional scholars consistently demonstrates that incumbency remains the best predictor of success in House races (Jacobson 2001).

5. These percentages are compiled from FEC 2000 data. House races in which the winner garners less than 60 percent of the vote are usually considered competitive.

6. District type is based on the incumbent's previous election vote share. If the Democratic vote was 60 percent or more, we consider the district Democratic. If the Democratic vote was 40 percent or less, we consider the district Republican. And if the previous winner had a vote share of 41 to 59 percent, we consider the district a toss-up.

7. When we break down the data by the two time periods (1980–90 and 1992–2000), the results are very similar.

8. In our data set, there are 113 male–female contests, 7 female–female races, and 330 male–male races.

9. There are 39 female Republicans and 74 female Democrats in the male–female contests.

References

Baxter, Sandra, and Majorie Lansing. 1980. *Women and Politics: The Invisible Majority*. Ann Arbor: University of Michigan Press.

Burrell, Barbara. 1985. "Women's and Men's Campaigns for the U.S. House of Representatives, 1972–1982: A Finance Gap?" *American Political Quarterly* 13: 251–272.

———. 1994. *A Woman's Place Is in the House*. Ann Arbor: University of Michigan Press.

———. 1998. "Campaign Finance: Women's Experience in the Modern Era." In *Women and Elective Office*, ed. Sue Thomas and Clyde Wilcox. New York: Oxford University Press.

Carroll, Susan J. 1994. *Women as Candidates in American Politics*. 2d ed. Bloomington: Indiana University Press.

Carroll, Susan J., and Krista Jenkins. 2001. "Increasing Diversity or More of the Same? Term Limits and the Representation of Women, Minorities, and Minority Women in the State Legislatures." Paper presented at the annual meeting of the American Political Science Association, San Francisco, August 30–September 2.

CAWP Fact Sheets. 2003. "Women in Elective Office 2003." New Brunswick, NJ: Center for the American Woman and Politics.

Chaney, Carole, and Barbara Sinclair. 1994. "Women and the 1992 House Elections." In *The Year of the Woman*, ed. Elizabeth Adell Cook, Sue Thomas, and Clyde Wilcox. Boulder, CO: Westview.

Conover, Pamela Johnston, and Virginia Gray. 1983. *Feminism and the New Right: Conflict over the American Family*. New York: Praeger.

Cook, Elizabeth Adell. 1998. "Voter Reaction to Women Candidates." In *Women and Elective Office*, ed. Sue Thomas and Clyde Wilcox. New York: Oxford University Press.

Darcy, Robert, Susan Welch, and Janet Clark. 1994. *Women, Elections, and Representation*. Lincoln: University of Nebraska Press.

Dodson, Debra L. 1998. "Representing Women's Interests in the U.S. House of Representatives." In *Women and Elective Office*, ed. Sue Thomas and Clyde Wilcox. New York: Oxford University Press.

Dolan, Kathleen A. 1998. "Voting for Women in the 'Year of the Woman.'" *American Journal of Political Science* 42: 272–293.

———. 2004. *Voting for Women*. Boulder, CO: Westview.

Elazar, Daniel. 1984. *American Federalism: A View from the States*. 3d ed. New York: Harper and Row.

Flammang, Janet. 1997. *Women's Political Voice: How Women Are Transforming the Practice and Study of Politics*. Philadelphia: Temple University Press.

Fox, Richard L. 1997. *Gender Dynamics in Congressional Elections*. Thousand Oaks, CA: Sage.

Fox, Richard L., and Jennifer L. Lawless. 2004. "Entering the Arena? Gender and the Decision to Run for Office." *American Journal of Political Science* 48 (2): 264–280.

Fox, Richard L., and Zoe Oxley. 2003. "Gender Stereotyping in State Executive Elections: Candidate Selection and Success." *Journal of Politics* 65: 833–850.

Fox, Richard L., and Eric R.A.N. Smith. 1998. "The Role of Candidate Sex in Voter Decision-Making." *Political Psychology* 19: 405–419.

Gaddie, Ronald K., and Charles S. Bullock. 2000. *Elections to Open Seats in the U.S. House*. Lanham, MA: Rowman and Littlefield.

Gertzog, Irwin. 1984. *Congressional Women*. New York: Praeger.

Herrick, Rebekah. 1996. "Is There a Gender Gap in the Value of Campaign Resources?" *American Politics Quarterly* 24: 68–80.

Herrnson, Paul S. 2000. *Congressional Elections*. Washington, DC: Congressional Quarterly Press.

Hibbing, John. 1991. *Congressional Careers*. Chapel Hill, NC: University of North Carolina Press.

Hill, D. 1981. "Political Culture and Female Political Representation." *Journal of Politics* 43: 159–168.

Huddy, L., and N. Terkildsen. 1993a. "Gender Stereotypes and the Perception of Male and Female Candidates." *American Journal of Political Science* 37: 119–147.

————. 1993b. "The Consequences of Gender Stereotypes for Women Candidates at Different Levels and Types of Office." *Political Research Quarterly* 46: 503–525.

Inter-Parliamentary Union. 2003. "Women in National Parliaments." See www.ipu.org/wmn-e/classif.htm.

Jacobson, Gary. 2001. *The Politics of Congressional Elections*. 5th ed. New York: Longman.

Kahn, Kim Fridkin. 1996. *The Political Consequences of Being a Woman*. New York: Columbia University Press.

Kathlene, Lyn. 1995. "Alternative Views of Crime: Legislative Policymaking in Gendered Terms." *Journal of Politics* 57: 696–723.

Lawless, Jennifer L. 2004. "Politics of Presence? Congresswomen and Symbolic Representation." *Political Research Quarterly*, March 53(1): 81–99.

Leeper, Mark. 1991. "The Impact of Prejudice on Female Candidates: An Experimental Look at Voter Inference." *American Politics Quarterly* 19: 248–261.

Loomis, Burdett A. 1998. *The Contemporary Congress*. 2d ed. New York: St. Martin's.

Mandel, Ruth B. 1981. *In the Running: The New Woman Candidate*. New York: Ticknor and Fields.

Niven, David. 1998. "Party Elites and Women Candidates: The Shape of Bias." *Women and Politics* 19: 57–80.

Norrander, Barbara, and Clyde Wilcox. 1998. "The Geography of Gender Power: Women in State Legislatures." In *Women and Elective Office*, ed. Sue Thomas and Clyde Wilcox. New York: Oxford University Press.

Rosenthal, Cindy Simon. 1998. *When Women Lead*. New York: Oxford University Press.

Sanbonmatsu, Kira. 2002a. "Political Parties and the Recruitment of Women to State Legislatures." *Journal of Politics* 64(3): 791–809.

————. 2002b. "Women's Election to the State Legislature." Paper presented at the annual meeting of the American Political Science Association, Boston, MA, August 28–September 1.

Schroeder, Pat. 1999. *24 Years of House Work . . . and the Place Is Still a Mess*. Kansas City, MO: Andrews McMeel.

Seltzer, Richard A., Jody Newman, and M. Voorhees Leighton. 1997. *Sex as a Political Variable*. Boulder, CO: Lynne Reinner.

Swers, Michele L. 2002. *The Difference Women Make*. Chicago: University of Chicago.

Thomas, Norman C., and Karl A. Lamb. 1965. *Congress: Politics and Practice*. New York: Random House.

Thomas, Sue. 1994. *How Women Legislate*. New York: Oxford University Press.

Thomas, Sue, and Clyde Wilcox. 1998. *Women and Elective Office: Past, Present, and Future*. New York: Oxford University Press.

Tolleson-Rinehart, Sue. 1994. "The California Senate Races: A Case Study in the Gendered Paradoxes of Politics." In *The Year of the Woman: Myths and Realities*, ed. E.A. Cook, Sue Thomas, and Clyde Wilcox. Boulder, CO: Westview.

Uhlaner, Carole Jean, and Kay Lehman Schlozman. 1986. "Candidate Gender and Congressional Campaign Receipts." *Journal of Politics* 52: 391–409.

Witt, Linda, Karen M. Paget, and Glenna Matthews. 1994. *Running as a Woman*. New York: Free Press.

Woods, Harriet. 2000. *Stepping Up to Power: The Political Journey of American Women*. Boulder, CO: Westview.

5

Are Moral Voices Gendered?
Care, Rights, and Autonomy in Reproductive Decision Making

Eric Plutzer

> If men were angels, no government would be necessary. If angels were to govern men, neither external nor internal controls would be necessary. In framing a government which is to be administered by men over men, the great difficulty lies in this: you must first enable the government to control the governed; and in the next place oblige it to control itself.
>
> —James Madison, *Federalist 51*

James Madison's skepticism, especially that concerning the competency of citizens to govern themselves, was shared by the other founders and is an enduring dimension of U.S. political culture. As a result, a core component of American political thought is the belief that citizens require a structure of incentives and punishments—codified into law—in order not only to protect the fruits of their labor and pursue happiness but also to make wise personal choices and contribute to the collective good.

In spite of its influential pedigree, however, this pessimistic strain in American political thought has never held complete sway. The belief in human perfectibility and the potential for self-governance, as reflected in early Puritan efforts (e.g., Winthrop's sermon on Christian charity, the Mayflower Compact, New England town meetings) provide a continuing counterpoint to skepticism and lingering fears about self-governance. Indeed, writers from Tocqueville to the present have observed that voluntary civic behavior is a distinguishing characteristic, and a strength, of the American political system.

As a result, much debate about public policy in the United States is really an argument about the competency and capacity of citizens and political actors to make unregulated choices. For the most fundamental political choice, the vote, we are all familiar with the struggles to extend the franchise to African Americans (Fifteenth Amendment), women (Nineteenth Amendment), and those as young as eighteen years old (Twenty-sixth Amendment). In each instance, the debate concerned the competency of a specific group of citizens to choose wisely and responsibly. In each case, skeptics relied on stereotypes and biases to conclude that extending the franchise would have negative—even disastrous—consequences for American democracy.

Likewise, in the realm of public policy we ask if citizens can make competent and moral judgments in virtually any imaginable context. In some cases, such as laws that deter insider stock trading, false advertising, or environmental pollution, the regulations seek to eliminate the worst effects of unprincipled self-interest. In many others, especially those concerning alcohol, drugs, and sexuality, we debate whether citizens can make mature and sensible choices in the absence of laws and sanctions. Most laws are compromises that divide the citizenry into "competent" and "incompetent" groups—as when states restrict alcohol consumption and availability for those under twenty-one years of age but assume that older adults can make wise choices unfettered by the government.

In no policy area has the judgment of citizens been more scrutinized than in the case of abortion. Indeed, the forces fighting for unlimited freedom to abortion characterize the issue in terms of the competency of women (in consultation with their physicians) to make appropriate, moral choices without any interference from the government. Abortion opponents, in contrast, view the availability of legal abortion as a temptation to morally questionable women (and men) to engage in behaviors that are not merely wrong but which also poison the collective culture (see Luker 1984; Ginsburg 1984).

The abortion controversy also taps into longstanding debates about women's competency as citizens, echoing concerns voiced during the decades-long struggle for women's voting rights. Not only politicians, but (as Flammang 1997 documents) political scientists until well into the 1960s viewed women as less competent than men to act responsibly in the civic arena—whether as voters or officeholders. Indeed, the entire field of women and politics emerged partly as a challenge to political scientists who assumed women were less able to make responsible choices. Although the pro-life movement would like to entirely eliminate the possibility of choice, most regulations enacted by states have been intended by lawmakers to help women make "better" choices by requiring that they consult with others, take more time to think over their decision, or demonstrate to a judge their competence to choose.

Seen in this light, current abortion controversies raise a series of related questions—questions that ultimately take us to core assumptions about the concepts of sex and gender, and their impact on the U.S. political system.

- When faced with an unwanted or unexpected pregnancy, how do women (and men) actually think about the choices facing them?
- In what sense do moral considerations come into play when an individual makes an abortion choice? And what might this suggest about women's capacities for autonomy and the need for laws that regulate the availability of abortion in the United States?

- Is personal morality gendered? Here I raise the possibility that women hear a different "moral voice" than men. The assertion of multiple "moral voices" by Carol Gilligan in her landmark *In a Different Voice* has influenced the field of gender and politics since its publication in 1982. Yet this influence has been quite superficial in empirical political research. I argue that the full implications of Gilligan's work for political science, and especially for gender and politics, have often been misunderstood and applied inappropriately.
- If the notion of a male (or masculine) and a female (or feminine) moral voice is valid, what implications should this have for the study of the gender gap, of women as political leaders, and for democratic theory?

In this chapter, I provide a preliminary answer to each of these questions. I begin by briefly reviewing Gilligan's theory of a *Different Voice*. I then report on a study that provides a window on how women approached a specific moral dilemma—whether or not to tell their partner or husband about their pregnancy and their consideration of abortion.

This study's unique data provide a more complex picture about gender and moral reasoning than most students of politics appreciate. I argue that this more complex picture provides an opportunity to enrich the field of gender and politics, and I discuss implications for several key research areas. In particular, the results speak to the ways in which we think about "gender gaps" of various kinds—differences in voting, differences in the legislative and leadership behaviors of men and women, differences in policy preferences.

Carol Gilligan's *In a Different Voice*

The 1982 publication of *In a Different Voice* was a watershed in gender politics. In order to understand why, it is essential to understand how developmental psychologists studied moral reasoning in the 1970s and 1980s. Psychologists would pose a hypothetical moral dilemma for each subject participating in a study. A typical (and the most famous) protocol is described by Gilligan as follows:

> A man named Heinz considers whether or not to steal a drug which he cannot afford to buy in order to save the life of his wife. . . . [T]he description of the dilemma itself—Heinz's predicament, the wife's disease, the druggist's refusal to lower his prices—is followed by the question, "Should Heinz steal the drug?" The reasons for and against stealing the drug are then explored through a series of questions . . . designed to reveal the underlying structure of moral thought. (Gilligan 1982, 25–26)

Subjects' detailed answers are then carefully examined—usually by two or more coders—and scored on a six-point developmental scale developed by Lawrence Kohlberg. Gilligan reports that girls and women tended to score lower on measures of moral development than boys and men. Rather than try to "explain away" this "gender gap" (for example, by multivariate analyses that consider factors such as education, demographic variables, and the like) Gilligan shook up not only developmental psychology but all of the social sciences and humanities by arguing that the theory of moral development then in fashion, and Kohlberg's six-point development scale, were systematically biased against women and girls.

She argued that boys tended to be given higher scores on Kohlberg's scale because they were more likely than girls to use abstract reasoning and appeal to impersonal laws and rights as they tried to deal with hypothetical moral dilemmas. Girls, in comparison, tended to focus on how various solutions to ethical dilemmas would affect the lives and relationships of the people involved. Even quite intelligent girls would not follow the series of probing questions to what was regarded as the "best" and most mature way to reason through moral choices.

Gilligan argued that women tend to hear a different "moral voice," one that emphasizes care, attachments, and personal relationships. Moral reasoning is *gendered*, Gilligan explained, because of the different socialization patterns of men and women. Drawing on the work of Nancy Chodorow (1978), Gilligan argued that boys have an especially strong drive for separation from their primary care giver because this is usually the mother, and this sets the stage for a more abstract way of approaching personal and moral dilemmas. Girls, in contrast, develop a moral voice that emphasizes an ethic of care and the nurture of relationships. Gilligan argued that this feminine mode of reasoning was as valid as the more masculine abstract reasoning and appeals to impersonal rules, laws, and norms of justice.

In essence, Gilligan argued that there were two equally valid ways that you might think about real-life moral dilemmas. On the one hand, you might view the dilemma through the lens of empathy with a primary concern about how your own personal choice might affect the lives, feelings, and important relationships of others. Such an "ethic of care" highlights the consequences of personal choices. On the other hand, you could look at general rules of justice and try to apply them consistently across a range of circumstances without any regard for the personal circumstances of the people involved. Gilligan acknowledged that women and girls were far more likely to use the ethic of care in making moral decisions while boys were more likely to use the "ethic of justice." However, Gilligan challenged established scholars by questioning why the ethic of care was characterized as developmentally immature. This resonated with many other cultural observers who pointed out that gender stereotypes often painted women as less mature and more childlike than their male counterparts. Gilligan urged that scholars recognize the value of both approaches to moral dilemmas.

It would be difficult to overstate the influence that Gilligan had on gender studies. Even in 2002, twenty years after initial publication, the Social Science Citation Index shows 260 published articles citing Gilligan's 1982 book in that single year alone. For comparison, the *combined* citations to *The American Voter, The*

Civic Culture, and *An Economic Theory of Democracy* was 275 in 2002. Since publication, *In a Different Voice* has been cited more than 6,000 times.

Different aspects of Gilligan's efforts have resonated with different scholars. Perhaps most important among these was the charge that models and standards based on men and devised by male social scientists were invalid models to apply uncritically to women (Steurnagel 1987 develops this argument extensively in the context of political science). Second, the idea that men's and women's thinking could be fundamentally different seemed to provide one compelling explanation for a variety of sex differences observed in daily life. As a result, Gilligan's theory was invoked as a potential explanation for almost every imaginable sex difference—everything from sex differences in corporate management styles to sex differences in the reasoning of judges (an extensive literature summarized by Susan Mezey's contribution to this volume). Third, many social scientists were inspired by the idea that by listening to women speak—and listening without an implicit male standard in mind—new and exciting ways of looking at the world could be developed.

The influence on political scientists who study gender and politics has been substantial. Reviewing every article published in the journal *Women and Politics* from 1984 to 1998, we find at least 37 citing *In a Different Voice* (more than two every year). A similar number of articles citing Gilligan's work has appeared in political science's general journals as well.

However, the "use" of Gilligan by political scientists has been controversial. More than a decade ago, Virginia Sapiro observed that "Gilligan's name now seems to be invoked whenever anyone makes note of any gender difference in thinking" (1987, p. 22; a similar point is made by Tronto 1987, p. 88). If anything, a review of recent articles in political science's leading journals suggests an acceleration of this uncritical invocation of Gilligan's research.

In addition, Sapiro pointed to a fundamental misreading of Gilligan: the confusion between "modes of reasoning and the conclusions people reach as a result of their reasoning" (1987, 23). Sapiro recognized that, like the psychologists she criticized, Gilligan was unconcerned whether her subjects determined that Heinz should steal the drug or not. Either choice could be justified by an ethic of care, by an appeal to universal rights and justice norms, or even by less mature forms of moral reasoning.

By analogy, political scientists seeking to build on Gilligan's work should be unconcerned with sex differences in party identification or presidential voting (the "gender gap"), with differences in roll-call votes of male and female legislators, or other discrete outcomes. Rather, the potential for enriching empirical political research lies in the observation that citizens might employ different moral paths to reach the *same* conclusions. I am not aware of any political scientists who have deliberately attempted to explore moral choices in this way. Moreover, it is *possible* that in some circumstances one mode of moral reasoning would lead to different choices than the other. But we currently have little basis for developing a systematic theory of when and where this might occur.

Yet these are exactly the types of studies that can integrate the study of gender and politics with questions of citizen competence that are so central to democratic theory. One "traditional" assumption is that women tend to be more emotional and less rational than men. If rationality is equated with "better" (at least in some circumstances) then this conclusion can be used to justify additional laws and regulations in domains of special relevance to women—such as reproductive choices and job discrimination.

In the remainder of this chapter, I report on a study completed in the mid-1980s that, although designed to answer specific policy questions, provides an opportunity to explore the modes of reasoning that women employ in a non-hypothetical context. This study was motivated by proposed laws that would have denied women the right to choose an abortion unless they had notified the man who shared responsibility for the pregnancy. For many women, the choice to tell their partner was an easy one. But many others struggled with this choice and described their reasoning to counselor-interviewers who collected the data. These women's accounts provide an unusual window on difficult choices that many citizens and government officials believe should be strictly regulated.

"Did You Tell Your Partner?": The Hope Clinic Study

In the early 1980s, many state legislatures were debating laws that would place restrictions on women's reproductive decisions. Women seeking abortions might have to get permission from their husband (if married), or their mother or father (if under eighteen) before terminating a pregnancy. Less stringent versions of these laws required only "consultation" or "notification," although some critics argued that in abusive relationships and other coercive settings consultation might be little different from getting permission. Outside of state legislatures, pro-life attorneys were offering "Father's Rights Litigation Kits" to men intent on preventing their wives, girlfriends, or acquaintances from terminating their pregnancies. Articles in popular magazines ranging from *Glamour* (Weiss 1989) to the *New York Times Magazine* (Black 1982) focusing on men's rights and men's perspective in the abortion choice were popular at the time. Sociologists Arthur Shostak and Gary McClouth wrote a book (1984) documenting the dynamics and emotions of men's abortion experiences, and the authors were invited to appear on major talk shows.

It was in this context that Barbara Ryan, Anne Baker, and I undertook a large study of women who had chosen abortion as their desired outcome. The study was carried out with the cooperation of the management and staff of the Hope Clinic for Women, a full-service family planning center in Granite City, Illinois. Granite City is a medium-sized industrial city ten miles east of St. Louis. A majority of the clients of the clinic came from towns and cities within the St. Louis metropolitan area. For a variety of reasons, including limited abortion services in bordering states (especially second-trimester procedures), clients also traveled from Indiana, Iowa, Kentucky, and Tennessee.

A three-part survey was administered to patients at the clinic from January through August 1984. The first part of the survey was a brief self-administered questionnaire, which 2,337 patients completed in the waiting room. This part of the questionnaire contained most of the basic background and demographic questions and did not include any sensitive questions.

The second part of the questionnaire was administered by clinic counselors during the routine pre-procedure counseling session. The purpose of this counseling session, on the day of the planned procedure, is to ensure that the woman has no second thoughts, that she is psychologically prepared, and to make sure that she is not being coerced by anybody into a decision she opposes. As a result, this counseling session would normally include questions about the co-conceiver and the woman's discussions and interactions with him. This made it possible to incorporate our survey questions into the normal flow of discussion without lengthening the 15- to 40-minute counseling sessions by more than a few minutes. This portion of the survey ascertained information concerning the interaction between the client and the co-conceiver, and her perceptions of that interaction. The third part of the questionnaire was self-administered at the close of the counseling session and asked a series of attitude questions that were deemed too sensitive to be completed in the waiting room in the company of close friends or relatives.

More than 2,000 women completed the first part of the survey, while a sample of 506 was selected to complete the latter two parts. For the purpose of this chapter, we can treat that data as two subsamples: one including *every* woman who did not tell the co-conceiver ($N = 243$) and a second subsample ($N = 263$) that includes approximately one in every nine women who did inform the co-conceiver about the pregnancy (for details on the sampling procedures and other aspects of the methodology, see Ryan and Plutzer 1989).

In reporting on the study, we use the term *co-conceiver* because, as I will show shortly, the men who shared responsibility for the pregnancy are so diverse that they cannot be easily subsumed by terms like "partner," "lover" or "significant other."

The data I report here are based primarily on open-ended questions that allowed multiple responses. The answers were not recorded verbatim but rather through the use of a long list of pre-coded answers, which were anticipated on the basis of two extensive pre-tests and lengthy discussions with the counseling staff of the clinic. While open-ended questions entail certain limitations, we preferred them because they permitted the women we studied to speak for themselves without having to conform to choices given to them by the researchers. The method of coding, however, permits us to meaningfully classify the large number of responses.

All participants were provided with study information in writing when they arrived and then again orally as the counseling session began. All women were told that participation was voluntary, but only 4 percent declined to participate. The 96 percent response rate is high—perhaps too high, indicating that in a clinical setting patients do not feel they have the power to decline—but consistent with response rates approaching 100 percent in similar studies (e.g., McCormick 1975; Zimmerman 1984).

Study Participants and Their Choices

On most important background characteristics, the larger sample of 2,337 women closely resembles estimates of the national profile of abortion patients. About two-thirds of the Hope Clinic's clients had never been married, while a little more than one-fifth were divorced or separated (see Table 5.1). Only 12 percent of the clinic clients were married at the time of their abortion. Among those who were unmarried, most were in fairly close relationships, including those engaged to be married (8.3 percent), living together (9 percent), or "going steady" (41.3 percent). A smaller group of about 13 percent had recently broken up with the man involved. This group includes those who divorced after conception, those with broken engagements, those who had moved apart after living together, and those who had previously "gone steady" but had since broken up. Only 14.2 percent described their relationship as casual and consensual (about half of these had broken up). An extended portion of the interview concerned the decision whether or not to tell the partner or "co-conceiver" about the pregnancy. We also asked about any discussion of the abortion or abortion alternatives. In all, 89.5 percent of the women told the co-conceiver of the pregnancy and 82.5 percent of the men knew of the woman's decision to have an abortion. The small discrepancy between the two figures arises because some women did not tell the co-conceiver about the abortion (at least not until after the procedure) and because for some women, men ended the relationship after learning of the pregnancy.

The nature of the relationship was a crucial factor in determining the likelihood of confiding. Table 5.2 reports the percentage of women who told their partner, broken down by a detailed classification of relationships. The categories are ordered from most to least likely to tell, and this reveals that women who were no longer involved and those in casual relationships were least likely to inform the man involved. Even so, most women in every category confided and discussed the situation with the co-conceiver. We then asked women a series of questions about why they made the choice they did and whether they had mixed feelings along the way. These questions only scratch the surface of the ethical considerations that characterized these women's choices. As in all studies that are carried out in a clinical setting, our main concern was for the well-being of the patients. As a result, we felt that probes to elicit longer responses and more detailed recollections would place an unreasonable burden on the women who participated in the study. Nevertheless, the answers provide a rich description of the variety of moral points of view that women considered during the decision-making process.

Women Who Told the Man Involved

Regardless of the choice made, we were interested in learning the reasons for that decision. We asked those who did tell, "What were your main reasons for telling him?" We allowed women to give multiple answers, and the percentages of women mentioning each response are contained in Table 5.3.

Table 5.1

Describing the Marital Status and Current Relationships of the Women in the Sample

I. Marital status (weighted $N = 505$)

Never married	65.5%
Divorced/Separated	22.3
Married	12.0
Widowed	0.3
	100.0

II. Current relationship with co-conceiver (weighted $N = 497$)

Going steady	41.3%
Married	11.3
Living together	9.0
Engaged	8.3
Casual relationship; no longer seeing one another	8.1
Had gone steady; no longer seeing one another	7.6
Casual/dating and still seeing one another	6.1
Living together; no longer seeing one another	2.0
Ex-husband	1.8
Had been engaged; no longer seeing one another	1.4
Divorced after conception	1.2
Raped (those not classified in other categories)	0.9
Extra-marital affair	0.8
	100.0

Table 5.2

How the Nature of the Relationship with the Co-conceiver Is Associated with the Decision to Tell About the Pregnancy (weighted $N = 497$)

Living together	98.6%
Engaged	97.4
Going steady	95.5
Married (told husband)	95.4
Ex-husband	95.2
Had been engaged; no longer seeing one another	87.4
Living together; no longer seeing one another	85.1
Divorced after conception	82.2
Casual/dating and still seeing one another	80.1
Had gone steady; no longer seeing one another	77.0
Casual relationship; no longer seeing one another	70.9
Extra-marital affair (told husband)	—
Raped (excluding those counted in above categories)	—
All rapes (includes cases counted in above categories)	73.9

Note: Percentages for cells with five or fewer cases are not reported.

Table 5.3

Why Women Decided to Tell the Co-conceiver
(women who told co-conceiver, $N = 261$)

His right to know	58.6%
It's his responsibility also	34.9
Why not? Why wouldn't I? I tell him everything	24.5
Needed his emotional support	19.5
Needed his financial support	16.5
Wanted to know how he felt	15.7
Needed somebody to talk to	11.9
He'd find out anyway	4.2
Hoped he would help with abortion arrangements	3.4
He knew first; was certain I was pregnant	2.7
Angry at him	2.3
Wanted him to know (to feel guilty, etc.)	1.1
Impulse	1.1
Other responses	6.9

What we find here is evidence of both "moral voices" and corresponding ethics. Over half (58.6 percent) of the women couched their answer in terms of the co-conceiver's "right to know." In addition, over one-third said they felt it was "his responsibility also." These answers, focusing on rights and responsibilities, would seem to correspond most closely with Kohlberg's notion of high moral reasoning—which Gilligan claims is more characteristic of masculine thought and derives from the need for separation that characterizes male socialization.

On the other hand, almost 20 percent of the women mentioned their need for his emotional support as one reason they told the co-conceiver. In addition, over 15 percent of the women reported that one of the reasons they told was they wanted to know how the co-conceiver felt; approximately 12 percent needed someone to talk to. These responses (about 30 percent of all confiders mentioned at least one of them) evoke Gilligan's description of an ethic of care and nurturance deriving from socialization patterns that emphasize interpersonal attachments.

Women Who Told but Had Mixed Feelings

Among those who told, 61 women, or 23 percent, reported having some mixed feelings about the decision. Counselors asked these women, "What reasons did you think of for not telling him?" As in all open-ended questions, interviewers were instructed to check all responses that were mentioned. The answers are reported in Table 5.4. The most frequent response was an unqualified "I was afraid" (26.2 percent). Often, women clarified this by describing their fear of the co-conceiver's anger or verbal abuse (14.8 percent), fear of his physical abuse (8.2 percent), fear that he would blame her for the pregnancy (11.5 percent), fear that he would leave and the relationship would end (6.6 percent), or that he would seek legal revenge (3.3 percent).

Table 5.4

Reasons Considered for Not Telling the Co-conceiver
(women who did tell but had mixed feelings, $N = 61$)

Fear of unknown; general fear	26.2%
He'd want her to have the baby	21.3
Protecting him from crisis	21.3
Fear of his anger/verbal abuse	14.8
He didn't need to know	14.8
Fear he wouldn't care	11.5
Fear he'd blame her for pregnancy	11.5
Fear of his physical abuse	8.2
Fear he'd leave; relationship would break up	6.6
Broke up since conception	4.9
Man raped her	4.9
He would deny paternity	4.9
To avoid his influence	4.9
He'd want to get married	3.3
Felt ashamed	3.3
Fear legal revenge (e.g., custody problems)	3.3
Fear he would tell others (or use info against her)	1.6
Wants to reconcile with husband or boyfriend (not co-conceiver)	1.6
He is married (to somebody else)	1.6
Other responses	8.2

Together, these can be seen as motivations for self-preservation, and at least one of these was mentioned by 45 percent of the women who confided despite mixed feelings. In the few cases in which women mentioned the possibility of physical abuse, self-preservation is quite literal. In others, women are concerned with their psychological well-being and the emotional stability of the relationship. Such concerns are also reported by some of Gilligan's subjects too, but Gilligan is not entirely clear on where this type of thought might fit in either her conception or the more traditional conception of moral development. Nevertheless, these answers provide evidence of a third voice, a voice of self-preservation and survival.

The second most common type of response involved concern for the well-being of the partner. Twenty percent of the ambivalent confiders recounted a concern to protect their partner from a crisis of some kind. For example, in one case a woman's husband was struggling through a difficult stint in medical school and she considered sparing him the additional burden of dealing with an unplanned pregnancy. In almost all of these cases, the women were swayed by the man's right to know—seeing this as outweighing any harm that might result. Thus, these sixty-one ambivalent women overcame their fears about their own well-being or concerns about their partner and responded to the voice of rights and responsibility.

Table 5.5

Why Women Decided Not to Tell the Co-conceiver
(women who did not tell, $N = 242$)

He'd want her to have the baby	35.5%
He didn't need to know	31.0
Broke up since conception	25.2
He'd want to get married	17.4
Fear he would tell others (or use info against her)	16.1
Protecting him from crisis	14.9
Fear of his anger/verbal abuse	13.3
Fear of unknown; general fear	9.1
Fear of his physical abuse	6.6
Fear he'd blame her for pregnancy	6.6
Fear he wouldn't care	6.2
Felt ashamed	4.5
Man raped her	4.5
Fear he'd leave; relationship would break up	4.1
Couldn't tell (e.g., co-conceiver unknown)	2.5
Wants to reconcile with husband or boyfriend (not co-conceiver)	1.7
Fear legal revenge (e.g., custody problems)	1.2
One-night stand	1.2
To avoid his influence	1.2
Other responses	3.7

Women Who Chose Not to Tell

When clinic clients indicated that they did not tell the co-conceiver about the pregnancy, counselors asked, "What were your main reasons for not telling him?" Responses are reported in Table 5.5, and here we see a greater variety of rationales than for women who chose to confide.

The dominant concern expressed by these women seems to be maintaining autonomy and self-preservation. Over one-third of the women mentioned, as at least one of the reasons for not telling, their assumption that the co-conceiver would want her to have the baby. In addition, the belief that the male would want to get married was mentioned by over 17 percent of the women. In addition, we again see a wide range of fears and concerns, including for physical abuse (6.6 percent), verbal abuse (13.3 percent), and the fear he would tell others or somehow use the information against her (16.1 percent). Overall, 36 percent of the women who did not tell mentioned at least one of these fears as a reason for not telling—providing additional evidence of a third voice concerned with self-preservation.

The second major explanation invokes the context of the relationship. Breaking up since conception accounted for one-fourth of the responses clients gave as a reason for not telling; nearly one-third of the women felt that the co-conceiver "did not need to know." Here we see evidence that women regarded the "right to know" as being conditional not only on shared responsibility for the pregnancy but on the closeness of the relationship. It is important, however, to remind ourselves of the general pattern of responses reported earlier in Table 5.2: that even in the most casual relationships and in all categories of broken relationships, roughly 80 percent of women confided anyway. We also see among this group of women a small group, 15 percent, who did not tell in order to protect the male from crisis—the clearest evidence of Gilligan's ethic of care.

Women Who Did Not Tell but Had Mixed Feelings

Of those women who did not inform the man about the pregnancy, 37 percent expressed mixed feelings. Counselors asked these clients, "What were some of the main reasons you thought of for telling him?" These data are reported in Table 5.6.

The most frequent response, mentioned by more than half the women with mixed feelings, was "his right to know." That it was "the male's responsibility also" was a response almost one-fourth of the women gave for having mixed feelings about not telling. Thus, the voice or rights and responsibilities played a major role in the dilemma faced by these women.

On the other hand, a substantial number of these women were tempted to tell because of concerns related to the quality of the relationship. Nearly one-fourth of the women with mixed feelings about their decision to tell reported a desire to know how the co-conceiver felt. Needing his emotional support was reported by almost 14 percent of the women, and 11.5 percent felt a need for somebody to talk to. Here we see reasons that appear similar to those characteristic of the ethic of care—except that these women could be accused of being selfish.

What About Men?

The Hope Clinic Study was limited to women and therefore cannot speak directly to gender differences. It shows that women do not rely exclusively on the voice of nurture and relationships, but frequently invoke the "masculine" voice of impersonal rules and, less often, invoke an ethic of survival. This raises the question of whether men hear a similar chorus of voices or whether men rely more or less exclusively on the "masculine" voice of rights and responsibility.

There is no study examining a representative sample of co-conceivers. There have, however, been a small number of studies of "waiting room men"—men who accompany women to their physician's office on the day of a scheduled abortion procedure. These samples are not representative because waiting room men are presumably those who are most supportive. Indeed, it would be very difficult to identify and interview a sample of men that were unsupportive of their partner's decision to terminate a pregnancy and whose behavior and personality elicited the strong fears described by many of the women.

Table 5.6

Reasons Considered for Telling the Co-conceiver
(women who did not tell co-conceiver but had mixed feelings, $N = 87$)

His right to know	55.1%
It's his responsibility also	23.0
Wanted to know how he felt	23.0
Needed his financial support	18.4
Needed his emotional support	13.8
Needed somebody to talk to	11.5
He'd find out anyway	4.6
Hoped he would marry me	3.4
Hoped he would help with abortion arrangements	2.3
Other responses	9.0

Nevertheless, the waiting room studies are useful in that they show that men also hear multiple ethical voices when confronting an unexpected pregnancy. Shostak and McLouth's (1984) *Men and Abortion* reports that most waiting room males tacitly accepted that it was women's *right* to have the final say about the pregnancy. But many of these men also indicated that their interactions were guided by concern about the relationship, or concern about the physical and emotional health hazards involved. In explaining why they came to the clinic that day, some men reported it was their "duty" while others said they were there to provide emotional support. Of course, men and women are situated differently with respect to an unplanned pregnancy—the implications for personal autonomy, for continuing one's education or career, and the social expectations from society are fundamentally different. Most fundamentally, while men's autonomy is influenced by an unplanned child (men might drop out of school to take a job and meet immediate financial obligations), they do not face the burden of pregnancy, childbirth, and care of newborns that women do. They also have much better financial and career prospects than their partners should the relationship end in breakup or divorce. Even so, the limited evidence on men in similar circumstances also reinforces the conclusion that men and women confronting ethical dilemmas hear multiple moral voices when trying to make the right decision.

Summary and Implications

The women who took part in the Hope Clinic Study are representative of the roughly 1.1 to 1.4 million who have terminated a pregnancy each year since the early 1980s (Centers for Disease Control 1996). For many of these women—most especially those who were married, engaged, or living with the partner—the decision to discuss the pregnancy was hardly a dilemma at all. But for many other women, the decision to bring the man involved into the discussion is a moral choice. The

man's right to know or the man's responsibility for the consequences of his actions
—abstract principles that can be applied to many moral dilemmas and across a
wide range of circumstances—weigh heavily on the minds of most of these women.
That is, in this particular context the voice of rights and responsibilities speaks
quite loudly and most often decisively.

Even women who kept their partners in the dark were pulled by the voice of
rights and principles. Unlike the carefully crafted hypothetical dilemma of Heinz,
his wife, and the pharmacist, real-life dilemmas may invoke one mode of reasoning more than others. As Sapiro observed, "People do not reason similarly in all
situations, and some of the context-driven patterns [in reasoning mode] are gender
relevant" (1987, p. 23). Ironically, this particular context of reproductive decision
making may be inherently structured in a way that enhances the salience or "volume" of the ethic of rights and responsibilities—which Gilligan and others associate with men and masculinity.

It therefore seems likely that men and women each carry with them the ability
to reason in all ethical modes, and the particular mode invoked may be subject to
manipulation and socialization. Indeed, many women concerned with control of
their bodies and self-preservation nevertheless were persuaded by the idea that the
co-conceiver had a right to know. This suggests that any analysis of ethical reasoning must be placed in the context of politics and culture. There are many rights that
citizens do not claim (e.g., many citizens eligible for Food Stamps do not take
advantage of this opportunity). And there are other rights, such as the right to have
an attorney present during questioning by police, that were once so rarely understood that the Supreme Court required that they be explained in every instance in
which they might be applicable. Today, more people are cognizant of this right and
so we might expect it to be invoked routinely by those in police custody. This is
also true in reproductive dilemmas. I have shown that women more frequently
give answers invoking the voice of justice than the voices of care or self-preservation.
Yet this may say more about U.S. culture than it does about the reasoning style or
gender of the individual facing a difficult choice.

Although a concern with rights and responsibilities is prevalent, we see that
the mode of thinking is nevertheless varied. Many women heard both of
Gilligan's moral voices. Closer analysis of the data shows, for example, that
among the women who did not tell and had mixed feelings, about 25 percent
simultaneously invoked the ethic of care (e.g., "sparing him from crisis") *and*
the ethic of rights and responsibilities in explaining their thinking. Similarly,
about one-fifth of all women who told their partner gave multiple answers that
reflected both modes of reasoning. These percentages almost surely under-
state the true proportion of women hearing both moral voices, because the
survey did not include explicit probes to encourage lengthy answers and multiple responses. This substantial degree of overlap should lead us to be skeptical of theories that posit essential differences between men and women. And it
speaks for efforts such as Tronto's (1993) to consider how normative political

theory might derive from Gilligan's ethic of care and nurturance without asso- ciating that ethic with women and femininity.

We also see in this analysis that the mode of thinking is loosely linked with the choice made—the invocation of a rights-based explanation is more associated with telling than for withholding information. In this sense, the dilemma is fundamen- tally different from that confronting Heinz because the decision to steal the drug (or not) can be reached through either mode of reasoning. The association be- tween mode of reasoning and outcome is an empirical question, and the answer is likely to differ from one situation to the next.

This should lead us to eschew hypothesizing *specific* gender gaps simply on the basis of an assumption of different modes of reasoning. It also suggests that struc- tures of power, law, and tradition may be crucial in determining both the dominant mode of reasoning for some dilemmas, and the association between mode and outcome in others.

Indeed, the data reveal that the way in which women reason through ethical choices depends on context. In close relationships, the "rights" of the man loom larger—but so also does the consideration that telling the man might not be the "caring" thing to do. Indeed, this suggests that the original dilemma faced by Heinz is not a neutral story but may contain elements that specifically evoke the ethic of care. We can ask ourselves how the responses of Gilligan's subjects might have differed if the person needing the expensive drug was not Heinz's wife but his girlfriend, neighbor, co- worker, or simply a stranger who confided her illness to Heinz.

The loose connection between mode of reasoning and outcome also helps place other research in context. The literature on judicial decision making reviewed by Mezey in her contribution to this book serves as a good example. Many of the studies of judges were inspired by Gilligan's insights, but the scholars then used a variety of different indicators for gender differences. These ranged from the actual vote (with or opposed to a particular majority), the likelihood of dissent, or the type of representation. None of these indicators is very similar to the central phe- nomena in Gilligan's own research: personal accounts that explain moral choices. When the mode of reasoning is highly correlated with the choice made, then look- ing at choices (e.g., voting with the liberal majority on a particular court) may tell us something about the moral reasoning that preceded the choice. For example, if we know that a woman told her partner, we can be fairly confident that she was guided by an ethic of rights and responsibilities. But when situations are such that different modes can be used to get to the same outcome—as in the recom- mendation that Heinz steal the drug—we are unable to guess about the specific reasoning used. Or, to take a more political example, we simply do not know whether women disproportionately support the Democratic party because they hear the voice of justice or the voice of care. Attributing the gender gap to pre- sumed differences in ethical thought is purely speculative. This is why it is so important to *ask* why people made specific choices—as Barbara Ryan and I did when we designed the study.

The Hope Clinic Study also shows us that strictly moral reasoning is often complicated by imperatives toward self-preservation. This suggests an important place for discussions of *power* in discussions of different modes of moral reasoning. Such concerns may not manifest themselves in the types of hypothetical scenarios on which much psychological research is based (although they are quite prominent in Gilligan's study of women who confronted an abortion dilemma). In the case of abortion restrictions in particular, a sensitivity to women's autonomy is crucial because proposed legislation may be couched in terms of rights (the rights of husbands or parents, for example) yet the effect of the law may be to reduce women's autonomy with respect to actions they might take to preserve their physical or mental health, or the quality of their intimate and familial relationships. In relationships characterized by physical or verbal abuse, these laws would have the affect of increasing the power that abusive men hold over women.

Finally, the data from this study speak to the policy questions that introduced the chapter. These data were collected in a time and place completely free of government regulations intended to promote consultation and better decision making. Had the married women been subject to a law requiring spousal notification, we see that 93 percent were in complete compliance; in research reported previously, Ryan and I show that most of the married women who did not tell their husband provided reasons that would have required a judge to waive the spousal notification requirement (the so-called "judicial bypass," Plutzer and Ryan 1987). For women in other types of long-term relationships (engaged, living together, going steady), who comprise more than 60 percent of the single women seeking abortions, we see similarly high rates of confiding.

The reasons given by these women are again frequently of the type that would make them exempt from most proposed laws. Yet even when the reasons might be deemed questionable by some, we see evidence of considerable thought and the weighing of rationales that derive from different ethical perspectives. In this sense, and given the fundamental legality of abortion, the data weigh in favor of considerable autonomy for women since they invoke the same types of concerns that would be considered by a judge who was asked to authorize an exemption from a notification requirement.

It is of course true that the strong proponents of abortion regulation support any laws that hinder abortion access and increase the costs to women to obtain and physicians to provide abortion services. But most of these laws could only pass with assistance of "moderate" legislators who see the laws as providing prudent reforms that help women and physicians to make better choices. Indeed, McBride's chapter in this volume points to key changes in rhetoric that have changed the legislative landscape in the United States. These changes are dramatic in outcome but only involve small shifts of legislators positioned near the middle of the political spectrum. As a result, the conclusion that women appear to reason through these choices carefully and use the same considerations relevant to the so-called judicial bypass may persuade some centrists that such regulations are unnecessary or even harmful.

In a more general sense, examining the way that men and women reason through real decisions could make a substantial contribution to the way we evaluate regulations of various kinds. Similarly, such a mode of inquiry can be especially useful whenever it is claimed that one group, such as women, are somehow less able to act responsibly and carry out political and personal choices in a free society.

* * *

The Hope Clinic Study would not have been possible without the efforts of my collaborator, Barbara Ryan and Hope Clinic director Anne Baker. Julie Adams, Sarah Boswell, Joyce Glasgow, Allison Hile, and Doris Westfall conducted the interviews while Sara Delashmutt, Paul Mosley, Steve Gelinas, and Ann Wimsat all served as able research assistants. I also thank the members of the Penn State gender and politics reading group for helpful comments on an earlier draft, and the editors and their students for showing me how the first edition of this chapter could be improved to better connect with students. Even for a short chapter it takes a village, and I am thankful for all the help along the way.

References

Black, Pamela. 1982. "Abortion Affects Men, Too." *New York Times Magazine*, March 28, Sec. 6, Pt. 1.

Centers for Disease Control and Prevention. 1996. "Abortion Surveillance, 1992." *Morbidity and Mortality Weekly Report* 45 (May 17, No. SS-3). Washington, DC: U.S. Government Printing Office.

Chodorow, Nancy. 1978. *The Reproduction of Mothering*. Berkeley: University of California Press.

Flammang, Janet A. 1997. *Women's Political Voice: How Women Are Transforming the Practice and Study of Politics*. Philadelphia: Temple University Press

Gilligan, Carol. 1982. *In a Different Voice*. Cambridge, MA: Harvard University Press.

Ginsburg, Faye. 1984. "The Body Politic: The Defense of Sexual Restriction by Anti-Abortion Activists." In *Pleasure and Danger: Exploring Female Sexuality*, ed. Carole S. Vance, pp. 173–188. Boston: Routledge and Kegan Paul.

Luker, Kristen. 1984. *Abortion and the Politics of Motherhood*. Berkeley: University of California Press.

McCormick, E. Patricia. 1975. *Attitudes Toward Abortion: Experiences of Selected Black and White Women*. Lexington, MA: Lexington Books.

Plutzer, Eric, and Barbara E. Ryan. 1987. "Telling Husbands About an Abortion: An Empirical Look at Constitutional and Policy Dilemmas." *Sociology and Social Research* 71 (April): 183–189.

Ryan, Barbara, and Eric Plutzer. 1989. "When Married Women Have Abortions: Spousal Notification and Marital Interaction." *Journal of Marriage and the Family* 50 (February): 41–50.

Sapiro, Virginia. 1987. "Reflections on Reflections: Personal Ruminations." *Women and Politics* 7 (Winter): 24–25.

Shostak, Arthur B., and Gary McLouth, with Lynn Seng. 1984. *Men and Abortion: Lessons, Losses, and Love*. New York: Praeger.

Steurnagel, Gertrude A. 1987. "Reflections on Women and Political Participation." *Women and Politics* 7 (Winter): 3–13.

Tronto, Joan. 1993. *Moral Boundaries: A Political Argument for an Ethic of Care*. New York: Routledge.

——. 1987. "Political Science and Caring: Or, The Perils of Balkanized Social Science." *Women and Politics* 7 (Fall): 85–97.

Weiss, Michael J. 1989. "Equal Rights: Not for Women Only." *Glamour*, March, pp. 276–277 and 317–322.

Zimmerman, Mary K. 1984. "'It Takes Two': An Examination of Contraceptive Risk Taking and the Role of the Male Partner." Paper presented at the annual meeting of the Midwest Sociological Society, April. Chicago.

Part Two
Public Policy

6

Gender and U.S. Foreign Policy

Hegemonic Masculinity, the War in Iraq, and the UN-Doing of World Order

Janie Leatherman

The U.S.–led war against Iraq has rocked the foundations of the international political system. The Bush administration took upon itself the task of enforcing UN Security Council Resolution 1441, which the Security Council passed in October 2002, requiring full cooperation of the Iraqi government with weapons inspections. However, the resolution did not include clear guidelines for triggering enforcement. When it became clear to the Bush administration in January and February 2003 that there would be no Security Council consensus on a new resolution to mandate enforcement of 1441, the Bush team worked around the United Nations. For critics of the U.S. administration, the action was the first clear-cut example of the implementation of the Bush national strategic doctrine that the White House announced in September 2002. This doctrine calls for preemptive action against potential threats to U.S. national security in the present, and to U.S. domination in world politics in perpetuity. Hence, the Iraq War pitted two conflicting visions of U.S. foreign policy against each other. On the one hand were claims that the United States was saving the UN Security Council from its own inadequacies and political ineptitude. On the other hand were visions of the role of the United States as the sole remaining superpower.

The exercise of such arrogance by the United States, with the aim of imposing its own will on the world while stripping the United Nations of its role and legitimacy in international affairs, is a clear display of hegemonic masculinity. Such a socially constructed role draws from an aggressive, nationalist orientation in foreign policy that prioritizes national interest, aggrandizement, and domination over the pursuit of common interests and the global public good (Richardson 2003). The United Nations is *the* universal body charged with safeguarding and promoting humanitarianism and development, as well as peace and social justice. But the U.S. policy of hegemonic masculinity puts the United Nations in a subordinate, feminized position, discrediting its efforts to preserve a space for consensus building and multilateral decision making. In this chapter, I will conceptualize the elements of a hegemonic masculinist foreign policy. The analysis develops two dimensions of hegemonic masculinity. The first dimension is that of the hegemonic masculinist state itself as an actor in international relations. I develop a framework for understanding how hegemonic masculinity is articulated in U.S. foreign policy by focusing on aggressive nationalism and the doctrine of superiority. But I am also interested in showing how hegemonic masculinity plays out in real policymaking. Here the playing field is interactive. How does the hegemonic masculinist state construct other states and international organizations, react to these constructions, and further justify its own acts of superiority and aggression? Understanding these dynamics of policymaking is the focus of the second dimension of the analysis. Here I will show how the rhetorical and policy initiatives of hegemonic masculinity are used to feminize foreign policy strategies of other states and international organizations that emphasize consensus building and multilateralism.

The September 2002 National Security Strategy of the United States (NSS) provides the key template for understanding the ideology and rhetoric of aggressive nationalism and the doctrine of superiority. I draw from this doctrine to illustrate the first dimension of my analysis of hegemonic masculinity. To illustrate the second dimension, and its connection to policymaking, I will show how this strategic doctrine provides the key tenets for the Bush administration's policy toward the United Nations and other key member-states in the context of the war on Iraq. The conclusions will weigh in on the matter of the new imperialism that this hegemonic masculinity espouses. I agree with Richardson, who argues that "enhancing the universal authority of UN Charter–anchored international law comprises an independent imperative for the world community" (2003, 1). Even the United States needs to have an effective, internationally accepted, authoritative system of international law to advance its own purposes and protect its own people (3). The atrocities at the Abu Ghraib prison and perhaps other locales underscore the self-defeating dangers of a U.S. policy of calling for others to uphold international law such as the Geneva conventions, when the United States is seen clearly to fail to apply these standards to detainees in its own custody.

My own view is that imperialism, at least as we have traditionally known it—the conquering of other people's land and their colonization—is dead. We live in a globalized world. People are educated and connected to global events today as never before. Global media, communications through the Internet, phones, faxes, as well as flow of people mean that no country can dominate others without scrutiny (Leatherman and Webber forthcoming). An open environment dooms such attempts to failure. The creation of the United Nations was itself part and parcel of efforts to undo imperial politics. This was the bitter pill that Churchill and other European imperialists had to swallow when they signed on to the UN Charter, the provisions of which were most strongly advanced by then U.S. president Franklin Roosevelt. Of the great allied leaders, it was Roosevelt who led the call for decolonization, and it was the work of such international civil servants as Ralph

Bunche that ensured decolonization would not just be an aim of the United Nations, but a realizable goal with the institutional machinery and practices to make it happen (Henry 1999). The U.S. military presence in Iraq, assisted by British troops—themselves once familiar colonial rulers in the Middle East—smacks, nonetheless, of the rebirth of imperialism. It also suggests that the United Nations plays second fiddle to the most powerful country in the world. Has the United Nations outlived its mission, or is it still relevant and able to respond effectively to new challenges to international peace and security? At the core of this debate is the question of whether collective security, as envisioned by the framers of the United Nations Charter, can still serve the needs of the world community in an era defined, on the one hand, by new demands for the pursuit of the *global interest*, and on the other, the political reality of the unparalleled *dominance of the United States* on the world scene today.

Hegemonic Masculinity

Bringing gender to the study of international relations is not a matter of "add women to foreign policy and stir." The point of making a gendered analysis explicit is to highlight different social expectations and consequences that attend from the gendered roles of masculinity versus femininity. As Cynthia Enloe reminds us, patriarchy is not natural. It requires great effort to reproduce it and sustain it every day (Cohn and Enloe 2003, 1192). I argue here, as do many feminist scholars of international relations, that masculinity is not a monolithic, universal phenomenon. Rather, the social construction of gender roles produces various masculinities that are always in competition and constantly being restructured as historical circumstances change (Enloe 1990, 2000, 2002). To understand masculinity, we have to see it as an open-ended process, in constant flux and reconstitution (Hooper 2001, 39). Gendered relationships, like all international relationships, are about power and resistance (Hooper 2001; Enloe 1990, 2–3).

Hooper helps us understand these social expectations by developing a model of "masculinism," which term she prefers to "partriarchy" to convey the privileging of masculinity. Thus, she argues that it is not men as such who give rise to a male-centered order. Instead, she puts the emphasis on access to power and privilege. Men gain this "not by virtue of their anatomy but through their cultural association with masculinity. It is the qualities of masculinity that are closely associated with power, rather than men per se, and the term *masculinism*, which implies a privileging of masculinity, best captures this relationship" (Hooper 2001, 41). Hooper also argues for differentiating various types of masculinity. One type that she develops, following the work of R.W. Connell (1987), is "hegemonic masculinity." As Connell points out, "mass culture generally assumes there is a fixed, true masculinity" (1995, 45). The concept of masculinity is typically thought to emanate from the male body itself. However, masculinity does not exist in and of itself. It is a relational term, and thus what is key is how it is socially constructed in relation to

those who are in competition with or subordinated to it. Connell makes an historical argument about the emergence of hegemonic masculinity as a function of the
development of a Western bourgeois ideology in the nineteenth century (Connell
1995, 68). Hooper also argues that hegemonic masculinity developed in the West
as "a global, racialized hierarchy of masculinities." These were "created as part of
the institutionalization of a complex set of race and gender identities sustaining
European imperialism—identities that still have a cultural legacy today" (Hooper
2001, 55). Enloe also invokes this colonial theme. She reminds us that women
played a role in the imperial expansion in their capacity as wives of military men,
or colonial administrators, for example. Thus, we should not leave out of the picture how international affairs has depended on the ways both sexes relate to issues
of dominance (1990, 4; UN Security Council 2000).

The construct of hegemonic masculinity enables us to see the dominant patterns of masculinity that function "at the level of the whole society and shore up
male power and advantage" (Hooper 2001, 54). This leads us to important questions: How does hegemonic masculinity subordinate other masculinities (e.g., non-
whites, racialized Others, members of different social classes, or gay men)? How
does it function to subordinate women (Hooper 2001, 54)? What are the historic
origins of the models for hegemonic masculinity, and how are they repackaged
and reconstructed over time?

Hooper answers these questions by identifying four models of hegemonic masculinity in the Western tradition: the Greek citizen-warrior; the partriarchal Judeo-
Christian model; the aristocratic honor/patronage model; and a Protestant,
bourgeois-rationalist model. These four categories are just heuristic devices, not
distinct types. In practice, hegemonic masculinity is constructed by drawing on
various components of these ideal types.

Theorists of international relations draw from these categories in the way they
analyze the role of the state in foreign policy. In effect, they "reify" or personalize
the nation-state itself. The state becomes embodied as a (male) actor. Thus, the
United States is treated as though it is a single, purposeful player on the international stage, when in reality we know that there are many policymakers involved
in designing the plans and actions that the United States carries out, and even
opponents of those plans and actions within the state. But personifying the state
also makes it possible to imbue it with the qualities of hegemonic masculinity, just
as we might the heads of state who represent that country. These kinds of maneuvers and the assumptions of hegemonic masculinity they subsume, can be found in
both realist and liberal approaches to the study of foreign policy. Realism tends to
make assumptions about the inherently conflictual nature of international relations, drawing from such political philosophers as Hobbes and Machiavelli. Liberals, in contrast, hold on to the possibility of good in human nature, and the benefits
of facilitating communication and understanding. They often look to Locke, Kant,
or Grotius for inspiration, for example. Liberalism tends to emphasize more the
Protestant, bourgeois-rationalist model of hegemonic masculinity. But the realist

perspective is probably the most predominant both in the practice and the study of international relations and foreign policy.

Perhaps what makes realism so powerful is that it draws from all four ideal types and uses them in different combinations as changing political and historical circumstances warrant (Hooper 2001, 66). The spread of realism around the world as the model for statesmanship has been supported in no small measure by its intellectual ascendancy. New adherents are literally schooled into this approach through their studies in leading university centers (notably in the global North), that continue to attract students from all parts of the globe. Centers of higher education in the United States have played a central role in the socialization of elites into hegemonic masculinity by virtue of the ascendancy of American scholarship on international relations that has lasted from the end of World War II through at least the early 1990s (Friedrichs 2004). The United States has also played the leading role in world politics throughout much of the twentieth and into the twenty-first century. Being a "winner" in wars and the game of international politics in general, and enjoying the extraordinary influence of a superpower role in the Cold War period that pitted the United States against a competing Soviet Union, and then in a post–Cold War context that has left the United States as the sole, uncontested superpower, has amply fed U.S. leaders and policymakers who desire to be hegemonic masculinists. If U.S. history had been different, hegemonic masculinity might not have come to dominant foreign policymaking in this way. Thus, hegemonic masculinity is an especially powerful conceptual lens for understanding U.S. foreign policy. The United States has waged wars in Latin America, Vietnam, and, via proxy, in much of the rest of the third world in an effort to secure its hegemonic role and preserve it against the communist threat. Since the end of the Cold War and the demise of the Soviet Union, no other single state can challenge U.S. dominance in the world. The United States draws from vast resources in economic, technological, intellectual, sociocultural, and military spheres. To date, neither the European Union, China, India, Japan, nor any other country in the world can compete on these expansive terms. Indeed, the United States has more military capability that all the rest of the countries in the world combined. Thus, we need to think critically about the U.S. role as global hegemon and how we can understand the reasons behind its reliance on an often aggressive, militarist approach to domination (Boggs 2003).

Although the United States historically has relied on coercive force along with more consensual forms of hegemony (Brilmayer 1994), since the 1990s, the United States has increasingly imposed force without explicit endorsement from the United Nations (Lobel and Ratner 1999). The concept of hegemonic masculinity gives us one lens through which to develop a critique of this action, gain new insights, and think about ways that leadership can be employed differently. One question this exercise poses is, "Where are the women?" How might including women systematically in positions of leadership change the conduct of U.S. foreign policy? Does it have to be aggressive in order to be effective? Indeed, does hegemonic masculinity impose certain costs on U.S. standing in the world? And what are the costs that it imposes on us as Americans at home? Are these acceptable? Are there better, more effective ways of leading?

Mechanisms of Dominance

International relations is a grand, strategic arena for the deployment of hegemonic masculinity. Many mechanisms of dominance, such as military service, colonialism, or the management of the national security state, shore it up. Some of these mechanisms have become highly ritualized. For example, Memorial Day celebrations ritualize the institutionalized practices, customs, and expectations of the military and a militarized society. Language itself can become ritualized and masculinized. This has happened with the rational language used to justify nuclear deterrence. Strategies were debated about weapons that could destroy civilization without thinking about the real human terms of what was at stake. And much of the rhetoric was highly sexualized. Defense intellectuals talked about missile "throw weight," or its circular error of probability for landing at its intended target, as well as its "penetrating capacity." They also used sexy acronyms for missiles, like SLCMs and GLCMs—Sea Launched Cruise Missiles or Ground Launched Cruise Missiles (pronounced slick'ems and glick'ems) (Cohn 1987). Similarly, the concept of surgical strikes sanitizes war—almost turning it into a healthy endeavor, while precluding the expression of any emotion and recognition of the deadly stakes involved.

The imagery and rhetoric of colonialism that defined hegemonic masculinity for many generations also persists in new forms as a postcolonial legacy. For example, strategic studies and international security are steeped in the rhetoric of "mature" and "immature" anarchies, or zones of peace and zones of war that echo the language used to justify colonial rule in the eighteenth and nineteenth centuries (Tickner 2001, 56). Today European and especially Anglo-Saxon values of hegemonic masculinity still set international standards in foreign policy, even if the male actor is of a different cultural origin (Hooper 2001, 85–6).

The role expectations of hegemonic masculinity may also be placed on women heads of state. As Enloe notes, "elite men may let in a woman here or a woman there, but these women aren't randomly selected." Indeed, Enloe tells us that Margaret Thatcher served one of her most useful functions by "break[ing] through our numbness." Seeing her in photos at head of state functions forced us to recognize that all the other players were male (1990, 6).

Hegemonic masculinity is also at stake in advancing and protecting the institutions and ideology of national security. One of the rituals of such foreign policymaking in the United States is the development of a presidential strategic doctrine that sets the parameters of threat assessments. The focus of these doctrines has shifted over time, but the functions of hegemonic masculinity remain the same. For example, U.S. foreign policymakers used the war against communism to justify both the U.S. military buildup and a nuclear arms race against the

Soviet Union. In this instance hegemonic masculinity operated on two fronts. First, U.S. foreign policymakers projected the United States to the international audience as on guard, at the ready, all-powerful, and determined to dominate its Soviet opponent, or at least to maintain a precarious balance of mutual assured destruction (MAD). But domestically, the war on communism was also used as a tool to police and thwart internal dissent. Thus, liberal critics were emasculated and feminized as "pinkos" (Hooper 2001, 86).

The precepts of political realism are deeply invested in hegemonic masculinity. They have prevailed in the United States and around much of the world since the end of World War II. As Hooper explains,

> realism, largely developed in a cold war climate, had an affinity with the type of cold war masculinity discussed above—the masculinity of tough-talking presidents and of John Wayne and James Bond. Its ascendancy over prewar liberalism was in part achieved through a successful "emasculation" of liberalism and of liberals as "failed men" who had sought to domesticate international politics with Enlightenment reasons but had ended up appeasing Hitler. (2001, 103)

The post–World War II triumph of realism cast liberals in a subordinate role. The implication was that liberals were at risk of aiding communists, or at the very least, of going soft on the struggle against communism. This also meant that liberal strategies for international politics—communication, negotiation, consensus building, multilateralism, and institution building among nations—were suspect. Such soft approaches to power were discounted as feminine. Thus, the national security of the United States could not be trusted to liberals. That this is still an issue is evidenced by the press discussion in the run-up to the 2004 presidential election on the Democrats' dilemma on foreign policy (Brooks 2004, 23).

The threat of the emasculation of U.S. power was further reinforced by the outcome of the war in Vietnam, coupled with the collapse of the imperial presidency with the Watergate scandal (Schlesinger, Jr. 1973), the resignation of Nixon, and the election of Jimmy Carter, who promised disarmament and raised human rights to the pinnacle of foreign policy. It fell to Reagan, as well as to George H.W. Bush, and later his son, George W. Bush, to erase the Vietnam legacy, the liberalism of Carter, and reestablish U.S. military dominance. Reagan did this by playing up the communist threat and outracing the Soviet Union with new generations of actual and proposed nuclear weapons, and a program for "star wars" defense (Wittner 2003). With the collapse of communism, George H.W. Bush developed a strategic doctrine based on a "new world order" and the threat of rogue states (Klare 1995). Thus, the Gulf War, started in 1991 by Bush to drive Saddam Hussein back into Iraq from his illegal domination of Kuwait, was the first great test of the Bush doctrine of promoting a new world order against threats from the periphery (Hermann 1991). This doctrinal approach, which emphasizes the dominant role the United States plays in the world as the key state in the "core," versus the subordinated position of third world states in the "periphery," has been continued under the presidential term of George W. Bush. Indeed, he has organized his foreign policy around the war on terrorism specifically in the context of threats from the periphery, from mostly poor, developing countries like Libya, North Korea, or Iran (i.e., the "axis of evil").

Women are largely absent from the "war on terrorism." Indeed, they are mostly absent from the formal settings where power and politics meet (Tickner 1999). Hegemonic masculinity works very effectively to erase the concerns of domestic and civil life from the international agenda (Hooper 2001, 92). Yet in the late 1990s and early twenty-first century, we see a new ideal type of masculinity emerge, the "New Man." Hooper suggests this ideal type has emerged in part because of the end of mandatory military conscription and the growing importance of activities previously considered feminine that are now being incorporated into the global economy. The softening of hegemonic masculinity has legitimized the show of emotion by men, and their participation in household responsibilities—like assisting in the rearing of children (2001, 73–74). However, as Hooper notes,

> in the struggle to transform hegemonic masculinity, there is a rivalry between New Men and a backlash masculinity supported by disaffected blue collar males who have lost both their job security and their patriarchal positions in the family. In the United States these are the "angry white males" who disciplined Bill Clinton, the "new style" president, forcing him to reinvent himself as an "all American man's man" who would keep Hillary, "the wicked witch of the West," out of public eye, at least until the latter part of his presidency (2001, 157, citing an article from the *Independent on Sunday*).

To mobilize public support for the war on terror, the Bush administration plays on the cultural politics of this backlash. Thus, in tough guy mode, the president donned a flight suit and landed an F-16 top-gun style on the deck of an Air Force carrier to announce (as it turned out, prematurely) the end of hostilities in Iraq. (If his pronouncement had been correct, the image would have become the centerpiece of his reelection campaign.)

The Bush rhetoric also works to subordinate and racialize terrorists for cowardly acts of violence: their uncivilized behavior, their low-tech, crude strategies of shock and awe that rely on the beheading of captives. The often-run videotaped image of Saddam in captivity, unshaven, hair wild, eyes unfocused and confused, and above all, submissive before a male U.S. officer probing his oral cavity with a tongue depresser, speaks volumes of the effort to render the (Arab) terrorist threat docile and subordinate. This imaging seems to stand in contrast to earlier portrayals of Arabs. Norton argues that those images tended to conflate "sexuality with violence." Saddam himself was often depicted as a "figure of phallic danger" (the first President Bush typically mispronounced Saddam as "Sodom") (Norton 1991, 27–28). Thus, the masculinity of the Arab has often been emphasized, in contrast to other colonial representations, which play up the Other as feminine, passionate, irrational, weak, and cowardly (Norton 1991, 26). Yet the recent media coverage of Saddam and the insurgents and terrorists in Iraq, as well as the Bush rhetoric, have emphasized feminine rather than hypermasculine qualities. Even the White House's attempts to play up Saddam's weapons of mass destruction (WMD) were framed less in the context of hypermasculinism than as cowardly acts of deception waged against the (impotent) United Nations.

The War on Terror and the Bush Strategic Doctrine

On September 17, 2002, the White House issued the "National Security Strategy of the United States" (NSS), its first comprehensive rationale for pursuing an aggressive and preemptive national security strategy against hostile threats, especially from rogue states and terrorists. The document, the origins of which can be traced to a 1992 Defense Planning Guidance draft report by Paul Wolfowitz, maps out the Bush administration's approach to foreign policy across a number of issue areas. These include dealing with terrorist threats, regional conflicts, working with allies, economic growth, development assistance and trade, and promoting democracy. It is partly triumphalist in tone—heralding the end of the Cold War and the "victory of the forces of freedom," and also partly a warning about new threats on the horizon from terrorists and rogue states who are "enemies of civilization" (NSS 2002, 1). The NSS also points repeatedly to the danger of renewed great power aggression. I will focus my attention on a gendered analysis of the document's threat assessments and responses. As we shall see, the NSS encompasses a number of principles that provide the rationale for the Bush-led war against Iraq and justification for sidestepping the United Nations in the process. The Bush NSS is premised on a doctrine of ensuring the perpetuity of U.S. power and enforcing it through unilateral and proactive measures, including preemptive war, or anticipatory self-defense. Balance of power in this case means U.S. preeminence—"a balance of power that favors freedom" (2002, 3). One might even read this to mean freedom for the Bush administration to impose its will as it wishes. Indeed, the document later says, "while the United States will constantly strive to enlist the support of the international community, we will not hesitate to act alone, if necessary, to exercise our right of self defense by acting preemptively against such terrorists, to prevent them from doing harm" (2002, 5). This policy is extended not only to terrorists, but to "those who knowingly harbor or provide aid to them." Thus, the Bush administration determined that "America will act against such emerging threats before they are fully formed" (2002, 1). The word "multilateral" appears in the document just nine times. The great majority of these utterances are in the context of economic relations. Where multilateral cooperation is required on security issues, the NSS is vague. In fact, all it states is, "the United States is committed to lasting institutions like the United Nations, the World Trade Organization, the Organization of American States, and NATO as well as other long-standing alliances." But even this meager indication of support is undermined in the next sentence, which argues, "coalitions of the willing can augment these permanent institutions" (2002, 2). In other words, if multilateralism does not work, the United States will lead on its own. Hence the document makes clear that multilateralism is subordinate to the unilateral exercise of U.S. power. The NSS also foresees U.S. dominance in perpetuity. These claims to enduring superiority are stated repeatedly. For example, the NSS claims that the United States "must build and maintain our defenses beyond challenge" (2002, 18). Later it continues:

> [T]he United States must and will maintain the capability to defeat any attempt by an enemy—whether a state or non-state actor—to impose its will on the United States, our allies, or our friends. We will maintain the forces sufficient to support our obligations, and to defend freedom. Our forces will be strong enough to dissuade potential adversaries from pursuing a military build-up in hopes of surpassing, or equaling, the power of the United States. (NSS 2002, 18)

The Bush doctrine is cloaked in the rhetoric and practices of hegemonic masculinity. First, it feminizes and discounts multilateralism for its failures of the past and naïve faith in the goodness of the human community. Here an implicit link is drawn between failure to act and liberalism, echoing realists' critiques of the failure of liberals in the run-up to World War II. Thus, the NSS states, "we cannot defend America and our friends by hoping for the best. So we must be prepared to defeat our enemies' plans, using the best intelligence and proceeding with deliberation. History will judge harshly those who saw this coming danger but failed to act" (2002, 1). It equates passivity with liberalism and implicitly with the feminine qualities of powerlessness, vulnerability, and victimization. Such a feminine posture, says the Bush doctrine, is destined to fail in the international arena as well as in protecting domestic interests (and the home front). This is reiterated later when the NSS argues that "our best defense is a good offense" (2002, 6). The best offense puts the battle outside the United States, but the Bush doctrine also calls for an offensive strategy in the guise of homeland security. Thus, the hegemonic masculinity of the NSS sets up mechanisms of dominance and subordination for U.S. rule internationally and also domestically. Second, the doctrine is steeped in patriarchal attitudes of dominance and subordination. One means of subordinating the "Other," including third world governments that are would-be recipients of U.S. aid, is to make subtle threats of the costs of noncompliance with U.S. security actions. Thus, the NSS makes clear that "nations that seek international aid must govern themselves wisely, so that aid is well spent. For freedom to thrive, accountability must be expected and required" (2002, 2). One element of the patriarchal maneuver here is to leave silent the identification of the party that is doing the judging, but it should be clear to the reader that the United States both issues the standards and alone delivers the judgments. Third, the NSS invokes patriarchal dominance to dehumanize and subordinate the enemy. The principal threat is seen as coming from rogue states. The language of the war against terror is thus cloaked in the language of the civilized fighting against the uncivilized. This racialist rhetoric is neocolonialist and illustrates how hegemonic masculinity draws on historical models, and particularly Western, colonialist, and Anglo-Saxon models of superiority to justify the aggressive postures pursued under the rubric of national security. In the NSS document, rogue states—which is code for small, poor states that are very Other, very different from the West, and part of the global south—are said to share such attributes as brutality against their own people, greed, disregard for international law, insatiable appetite for acquiring weapons of mass destruction and advanced military technology, active sponsorship of terrorism around the world, and the rejection of basic human values. Finally, they are said to "hate the United States and everything for which it stands" (2002, 8–9). The enemy soldiers are feminized for their cowardly fighting strategies, as much as for their desire to attain a masculine status of parity that is not to be theirs. We see such rhetorical moves in the NSS's claims that "traditional concepts of deterrence will not work against a terrorist enemy whose avowed tactics are wanton destruction and the targeting of innocents; whose *so-called soldiers* [emphasis added] seek martyrdom in death and whose most potent protection is statelessness." Moreover, the document emphasizes that these so-called soldiers act in secretive, elusive ways—again feminizing them as playing dirty, using trickery, acting like a deceptive whore. Because these so-called soldiers do not play fair, the United States is justified in its own interpretations of international law that lead it to generously claim rights to act preemptively (NSS 2002, 9).

The NSS also calls the United States to a military role that is global in its patriarchal reach. It admonishes other great powers not to test its resolve. It calls for building and maintaining U.S. defenses on a scale that is "beyond challenge." The deployment of U.S. force encompasses allies and friends, thus casting a large protective umbrella. The maintenance of armed forces overseas is a profound symbol of U.S. commitment. These claims invoke the Judeo-Christian model of patriarchy, the aristocratic codes of honor and patronage, as well as the Greek warrior-citizen. We are prepared to spend our treasure, and to sacrifice our blood for the greater good. "Through our willingness to use force in our own defense and in defense of others, the United States demonstrates its resolve to maintain a balance of power that favors freedom" (NSS 2002, 18). Finally, the NSS is characterized by hegemonic masculinity in its duplicity and hypocritical approach. Double standards, or the ability of the hegemon to act outside of any set standards, is another mechanism for promoting U.S. superiority, and simultaneously the subordination and feminization of Others. We see this in the NSS aims to deny rogue states and terrorists access to weapons of mass destruction and advanced military technology, while the NSS simultaneously outlines an aggressive policy of military expansionism for the United States in bases around the globe, and an ongoing commitment to the technological superiority of U.S. forces. This policy line was further elaborated in a classified version of the NSS document, a six-page version of which was released in December 2002. It takes the United States a step closer to the limited use of nuclear weapons. The release of the document was timed to serve as a warning to Saddam Hussein. While U.S. officials denied that the administration was lowering the threshold for the use of nuclear weapons,

> they also argue that the strategic calculations necessary for combating terrorism and hostile nations must inherently be different from those used during the Cold War, when deterrence meant simply convincing the Soviets that the United States, if attacked, could and would wipe them out. Against today's new enemies, the administration has argued, it may be necessary to strike preemptively and with nuclear weapons that would keep fallout to a minimum. (Allen and Gellman 2002, 1)

Such weapons include low-yield nuclear weapons that can burrow deep into the earth and destroy underground bunkers or warehouses of biological or chemical weapons (Allen and Gellman 2002, 1). Similarly hypocritical, the NSS derides rogue states and terrorists for a failure to adhere to human rights and international law, while it explicitly calls for exemptions for the United States—especially immunity from the International Criminal Court.

In the next section, I investigate how this doctrine, steeped in hegemonic masculinity, plays itself out in the Bush administration's relationship with the United Nations and the policymaking that led to the war on Iraq. I begin this discussion with a brief overview of the UN's mission, and how the Bush policies of domination have threatened the historical viability of this universal institution.

The UN's Historical Mission

The United Nations' historical mission is to prevent future generations from suffering the scourge of war. What the founders of the United Nations had most immediately in mind was the prevention of another world war, having already witnessed two in little more than a generation. However, they also spelled out other goals: to reaffirm fundamental human rights, and promote the equal rights of men and women and of all nations of the world—large and small; to establish conditions for justice and support for international law; to practice tolerance and live in peace; to ensure that the resort to the use of armed force was only for the common interest; and to promote the economic and social development of all peoples. These ideals are announced in the preamble to the United Nations Charter and are developed throughout the Charter and in subsequent UN resolutions, treaties, and agreements that add to the body of international law and customary practices. To further these aims, the United Nations was established with a General Assembly (GA) to represent equally the voices of all the independent countries in the world; a World Court, to solve disputes between them through adjudication; an Economic and Social Council to promote development and human security; a secretary general to lead symbolically and to a limited degree politically with respect to the aims and interests of the world's peoples; a Trusteeship Council to oversee decolonization; and of course, a Security Council to maintain international peace and security. Of these bodies, only one has clearly outlived its purposes: the Trusteeship Council. It has overseen perhaps the most extraordinary of political transformations of the twentieth century—decolonization. This is often little noted, but of momentous historic significance. The work of the Trusteeship Council tells us that it is possible for the world community to come together with common purposes for the restructuring of international politics and the uplifting of human rights and equality among all peoples. Decolonization was a change that was both political and mental—a transformation of both people's minds and lives. It challenged and sought to transform the practices of Western hegemonic masculinity. While the Trusteeship Council has outlived its mandate, we have not yet seen the end of the work to be done when it comes to thinking about the long-term effects of colonialism.

We assumed that once decolonization was abolished, all nations became equal. Instead, we have witnessed the emergence of new forms of hegemonic masculinity and new expressions and policies of oppression. As we have seen above, we still have to check our mindsets: the Bush administration casts the war on terrorism as a war between the civilized and uncivilized worlds. This echoes of colonialism and imperial disregard. The cruel, trophy photos of prisoner abuse at Abu Ghraib prison in Iraq disturb us partly because of their historical insinuation. Susan Sontag (2004) develops a comparison between these photos and the photos made at the turn of the last century of black victims of lynching here in the United States. Sontag argues that the white people first committed the lynchings, then triumphantly photographed their trophies. She says the Abu Ghraib photographs are a part of the same phenomenon. These photos are also symbolic statements of how the U.S. treats "rogue states." They are to be disciplined, punished, and tortured or killed by shock and awe techniques. Even though the world has moved past the organizational structures of colonialism, hegemonic masculinity continues to thrive and to promulgate a motif of racialized Others to motivate the design and implementation of foreign policy whether on the individual prisoner or countries as a whole.

What may be most striking about the UN's historic mission is the great mismatch between its design for dealing with issues of international peace and security, and the real problems it has faced since its founding in 1945. The UN was established with the idea of ensuring security between states—averting *international war*. But the bulk of threats to security have come from internal conflicts— civil wars and their spillover effects regionally. The United Nations has been hampered in responding to these problems for several reasons. The Charter enshrines the sovereign equality of nation-states, and it calls for the nonintervention in the internal affairs of states. These bedrock principles mean that the internal threats to security are—formally speaking—out of bounds.

In practice, the United Nations has evolved slowly since 1945 to deal with these challenges. Three developments can be highlighted. First, the creation of a body of human rights law has undermined the principle of nonintervention. Most recently these provisions have been extended to the notion of aiding internally displaced persons (IDPs), and not just refugees; and the international community has moved toward upholding the principles that any people targeted for mass extermination or harm should be rescued by the international community. It is not enough to condemn genocide in the aftermath. Intervention in such cases is fully warranted. Somalia underscored this notion, as did Rwanda, albeit in vain. Second, peace-keeping missions have been established in the post–Cold War period in the absence of signed consent by the warring parties. Thus, contrary to Cold War practices, in the 1990s the United Nations has been prepared to move into failed states and provide assistance, as was done in Somalia or East Timor. Third, Secretary General Boutros Boutros-Ghali, in his landmark 1992 report, *An Agenda for Peace*, called on the United Nations not only to have conflict early warning and prevention, but also peace enforcement and postconflict reconstruction (Boutros-Ghali 1992). So the United Nations has been in the business of rebuilding countries and aiding with their democratic development. It has come a long way from prohibitions on nonintervention, in spite of the fact that many third world countries still eye such activities with distrust and disapproval, including China.

A second basic problem with the original conception of the United Nations' mission lies in the formation of a Security Council with five permanent members (the P-5). Through the presence of these states—the United States, Britain, France, Russia, and China—the legacies of World War II still echo in the Security Council chambers. Here we see the partriarchal and masculinist privileges of the five permanent members of the Security Council come head to head with the pillar of liberalism on which much of the United Nations is built. What is still more problematic is the Permanent Five's exclusive right to the veto. This sets up a mechanism for dominance and subordination in the core of the United Nations' institutional machinery for collective security. In practice, this prerogative obviates the possibility of universal enforcement of international peace and security if it does not suit one of the P-5. Any of the P-5 can veto a resolution that threatens its own interests. The United States has done this on many occasions with respect to the Israeli-Palestinian conflict, an important reason why this dispute is resistant to resolution.

Another basic problem is that the composition of the Security Council does not reflect the world's opinions. The P-5 tend to work with their own interests in mind, not global interests. Collective security is undermined by these developments—we have seen such failures in Vietnam, Panama, Rwanda, Somalia, Sierra Leone, and Congo, among others. Such self-interested participation is amply demonstrated by the U.S. Presidential Decision Directive 25 (PDD 25, February 1996), a document signed by President Clinton in the aftermath of the Somalia crisis. Its provisions for peacekeeping were so restrictive that the United States practically shut down UN peacekeeping efforts in the mid-1990s. Only the General Assembly can overcome a deadlock in the Security Council. GA resolutions may speak to the conscience of the world community—as a 2003 GA resolution condemning the Israeli airstrikes against Syria did. However, even with an overwhelmingly favorable vote—in that case the United States was joined by only a couple of micro states in opposition—the GA resolution is not legally binding. It is merely a symbolic statement with no teeth. Consensus building and multilateralism in this context are feminized under the doctrines of hegemonic masculinity. Indeed, Carol Cohn tells us that in her research at the United Nations, she "heard the Third Committee of the General Assembly—that's the committee that works on social, humanitarian, and cultural issues—referred to in-house as the 'ladies' committee. On the other hand, the Security Council remains an overwhelmingly male and masculinized preserve" (Cohn and Enloe 2003, 1189–90). The great range of UN peace operations in the 1990s has stretched the United Nations thin. Meanwhile, the United Nations has faced massive budget shortfalls as the United States and some other countries following suit have repeatedly failed to pay their UN dues and arrears to the special funds for UN peacekeeping. The United Nations is itself chronically underfunded; its operating budget is about $1 billion dollars a year—what the United States spends in Iraq in just one week's time. And these limited funds have to be stretched to cover the needs of all the countries of the world, not just for humanitarian needs but also for health, education, development, climate, and disaster relief. The United Nations' effectiveness thus suffers from some inherent weaknesses. Some of these, as we have seen, stem from the founding structures and principles of the UN, while others are a function of the overwhelming tasks it faces and the limited resources it has with which to address them.

Beyond these internal and external problems, the Security Council has been particularly stymied by the rise of the United States as the sole superpower. Throughout the 1990s the United States has used multilateralism when it has served its purposes, and if not, then unilateralism. Under the second Bush administration, unilateralism has predominated at the expense of the UN's legitimacy. Boutros Boutros-Ghali's memoir, *Unvanquished*, is essentially a treatise, as he puts it, on "the loss of an opportunity to construct an agreed-upon post–Cold War structure for international peace and security." He writes somewhat bitterly that it was his fate, as the secretary general of the United Nations following the end of the Cold War, to create a post–Cold War structure and to do so with the United States as the sole remaining superpower. Yet, the opportune moment for transformation was lost, and the United Nations emerged instead from the 1990s "seriously damaged" (Boutros-Ghali 1999, 336–337).

This period has been bracketed by the U.S.-led coalition that forced Iraq out of Kuwait and the current U.S.-led coalition occupying Iraq. During this period, Iraq has been one of the driving concerns of the UN Security Council. Following Iraq's invasion of Kuwait in August 1990, the Security Council unanimously adopted Resolution 678 authorizing the use of force under Chapter VII of the UN Charter to secure Iraq's withdrawal. This action followed eleven other Security Council resolutions already passed in 1990 that sought Iraqi compliance. From 1991 to 2002, the Security Council passed twelve more resolutions that imposed on Iraq comprehensive sanctions and numerous requirements for disarming (Browne 2003). On September 12, 2002, Iraq was again the center of attention as President Bush made enforcement of UN resolutions and the disarmament of Iraq weapons of mass destruction a key foreign policy objective of the United States in his statement before the United Nations General Assembly in its opening session.

Bush used the occasion of his address to the GA to bring together key strands of his September 17, 2002, NSS and to characterize the Iraqi regime as a rogue state, deceitful and conspiring to develop and produce weapons of mass destruction, including biological, chemical, and nuclear arms. He placed Iraq in the category of a grave threat that the world community faced from "outlaw groups and regimes and that accept no law of morality and have no limit to their violent ambitions" (Bush 2002, 1). The greatest concern, he made clear, was that "terrorists will find a shortcut to their mad ambitions when an outlaw regime supplies them with the technologies to kill on a massive scale." According to Bush, Iraq was the one place where all these dangers converged "in their most lethal and aggressive forms, exactly the kind of aggressive threat the United Nations was born to confront" (Bush 2002, 1).

Similar to the NSS doctrine, Bush warned other UN member states that they could not afford to place their confidence in the good faith of the Iraqi regime. The speech, like the NSS, lays out the logic for preemptive action. The justification for doing so against Iraq is mapped out extensively by Bush in the context of Saddam's repeated acts of defiance towards UN Security Council resolutions. But Bush's speech goes further than just mapping out a justification for war against Iraq to thwart any possibility of Saddam equipping terrorists with WMD. What Bush aims to put at stake is the viability of the United Nations and the system of collective security in place since the UN's founding in the aftermath of World War II. As Bush states, "the conduct of the Iraqi regime is a threat to the authority of the United Nations, and a threat to peace. Iraq has answered a decade of UN demands with a decade of defiance. *All the world now faces a test, and the United Nations a difficult and defining moment.* Are Security Council resolutions to be honored and enforced, or cast aside without consequence? *Will the United Nations serve the purpose of its founding, or will it be irrelevant?*" (Bush 2002, 3, emphasis added).

This speech constitutes the Bush administration's bid for imperial power. It casts the United States in the role of the lone ranger—prepared to go to the rescue when no other legal instruments provide redress, when the rest of the world fails to attend to the "urgent duty of protecting other lives, without illusion and without fear" (Bush 2002, 1). Bush assures his audience that "by heritage and by choice, the United States of America will make that stand" (2002, 4). He makes it clear that "the purposes of the United States should not be doubted. The Security Council resolutions will be enforced—the just demands of peace and security will be met—or action will be unavoidable. And a regime that has lost its legitimacy will also lose its power" (2002, 4).

Bush's approach to liberating Iraq, as heralded in his GA speech, also intones the kinds of patriarchal claims to protection and the neocolonialist forms of hegemonic masculinity that we reviewed above in the NSS document. Among the justifications for the aggressive U.S. policy, Bush cites the long suffering of the Iraqi people in "silent captivity. Liberty for the Iraqi people is a great moral cause, and a great strategic goal" (Bush 2002, 4). The remainder of this paragraph hints at the

U.S. strategy of liberating Iraq to occupy it and turn it into a free, democratic society in the American mold. However, there is no recognition here that the long suffering of the Iraqi people has come at the hands of U.S. and Security Council policies of imposing indiscriminate sanctions on the Iraqi people (Arnove and Abunimah 2002). Responsibility and accountability for the U.S. role in this suffering is erased from the text.

Bush's speech to the GA stands in sharp contrast to the address given by Secretary General Kofi Annan. He, too, understood that the Bush strategic doctrine put the viability of the United Nations at risk. Speaking to the GA shortly before George Bush, Annan used the podium as an opportunity to draw sharp lines between the unilateralist, preemptive doctrine emerging from the U.S. administration, and the multilateralism and rule of law that the United Nations stands for. He called for the full use of multilateral institutions to deal with the threat of terrorism. And he insisted "every government that is committed to the rule of law at home must be committed also to the rule of law abroad" (Annan 2002, 1). Recalling the founding principles of the United Nations, and also alluding to the historical legacy of colonialism, he reminded the member states gathered that "international security is not a zero-sum game. Peace, security, and freedom are not finite commodities like land, oil, or gold that one state can acquire at another's expense. On the contrary, the more peace, security and freedom that any one state has, the more its neighbors are likely to have" (2002, 1). In sum, Annan warned that following or rejecting a multilateral course of action "must not be a simple matter of political convenience. It has consequences far beyond the immediate context" (2). On November 8, 2002, the Security Council finally adopted Resolution 1441 after two months of laborious consultations and negotiations among the fifteen members of the chamber. As Henry Richardson notes, this process

> illustrated a new constitutive problem for the international community. For the first time, the United States publicly approached the Security Council as a hegemon to threaten the organization with "global irrelevance" and to demand, rather than negotiate, a certain result from the Council, accompanied by the threat of military action against Iraq outside of and against Council authority if its wishes were not met. Washington did so in spite of the common knowledge of deep suspicions, questions, and opposition throughout the world community against attacking Iraq at that time (2003, 6).

What is perhaps most significant about the Council's efforts was the role it played as a "fourth branch of the U.S. government." While the Congress effectively abandoned its role in the U.S. system of checks and balances, giving the Bush administration a Congressional Resolution that amounted to a blank check to go to war, the Security Council, backed by world public opinion, put the breaks on (Richardson 2003, 6). The UN Security Council Resolution 1441 did give the Bush administration much of what it sought. It notified Iraq that it "has been and remains in material breach of its obligations under relevant resolutions," and that it has "a final opportunity to comply with its disarmament obligations" and "set up an enhanced inspection regime" to complete the disarmament process established by Resolution 687. It also committed the Security Council to "convene immediately upon receipt of a report" to consider false statements or omissions and to seek full compliance, and "in that context, that the Council has repeatedly warned Iraq that it will face serious consequences as a result of its continued violations of its obligations" (UN Security Council 2002).

But for the United States a key shortcoming of the resolution was the lack of any automaticity regarding enforcement action in the absence of Iraqi compliance. The United States did not want to seek a second UN resolution to authorize the use of force, but other Council members, and notably France, refused to accept any automaticity in the resolution (Murphy 2003; de Villepin 2003a, 1). During the months that followed leading up to the March 19, 2003, U.S.-led coalition attack on Iraq, the Security Council remained seized of the Iraqi crisis. It continued to review reports from such bodies as the UN Monitoring, Verification and Inspection Commission (UNMOVIC) and the International Atomic Energy Agency (IAEA). The United States mounted its own efforts to provide the Security Council with evidence of Iraqi programs of WMD in order to gain support for a second resolution authorizing the use of force for noncompliance. However, the United States failed in this endeavor. In an unprecedented show of public concern, the Security Council was showered with hundreds of thousands of e-mails from individuals across the globe urging the Council to stand firm against U.S. imperialist ambitions. French foreign minister Dominique de Villepin spoke to these concerns in the chambers of the Security Council on March 19, 2003, on the eve of war, and to unprecedented applause following his speech. He warned:

> Make no mistake about it: the choice is indeed between two visions of the world. To those who choose to use force and think they can resolve the world's complexity through swift and preventive action, we offer in contrast determined action over time. For today, to ensure our security, all the dimensions of the problem must be taken into account: both the manifold crises and their many facets, including cultural and religious. Nothing lasting in international relations can be built therefore without dialogue and respect for the other, without exigency and abiding by principles, especially for the democracies that must set the example. To ignore this is to run the risk of misunderstanding, radicalization and spiraling violence (de Villepin 2003b, 1).

In the absence of Security Council endorsement, the Bush administration assembled its own coalition of the willing. The Bush team claimed prior authority for enforcement action, pointing to earlier UN Security Council resolutions on Iraq. In so doing, the White House was following a trend already established in the 1990s by the first Bush White House, and later by President Clinton, in reference to enforcement action against Iraq. Already in a 1999 article published in the *American Journal of International Law*, Lobel and Ratner warned that "the tendency to bypass the requirements for explicit Security Council authorization, in favor of more ambiguous sources of international authority, will probably escalate in the coming years" (1999, 125). Thus, failing to achieve a new UN Security Council Resolution to endorse enforcement action against Iraq, the United States essentially carried out an end-run operation around the UN. The United States launched offensive operations against Iraq in a "shock and awe campaign," which it had widely advertised in advance of the attack, and thus took into its own hands key prerogatives of the United Nations Security Council under the provisions of collective security: namely, strict control over the initiation, duration, and objectives for the use of force (Lobel and Ratner 1999, 125). As Farer (2002, 360) also argues, "the Bush Doctrine, *to the extent it implies unilateral action*, cannot be contained within the UN Charter norms that have served as the framework of international relations for the past half century."

In fall 2003, the Bush administration sought a new UN resolution in an effort to secure additional troops and funding for the reconstruction efforts in Iraq. As with other UN resolutions, the Bush administration resisted negotiations on the draft it presented. But it is indeed interesting that the United States returned to the United Nations in another effort to gain that legitimacy. The result in this instance was Resolution 1511. It transferred some limited authority to the United Nations—a bare-boned mandate to delimit and oversee the U.S. occupation. For example, 1511 acknowledged that the Security Council would deploy UN personnel but only "as circumstances permit." It committed the United States to providing the Security Council with a timetable for the drafting of a new constitution for Iraq and holding democratic elections. It required the United States to report back to the Security Council on these developments at least every six months (UN Security Council 2003). But it did not commit troops or funding by other countries to the efforts in Iraq. It did not go very far in committing UN legitimacy to the initiative. Yet it opened the door to this process by investing oversight in the Security Council for the U.S. occupation of Iraq and transfer of sovereignty to the Iraqi people. In so doing, Resolution 1511 raised the question of whether the dog is wagging the tail or it is the other way around.

Even if the United States gained the consent of the Security Council members for Resolution 1511—did it gain legitimacy for the U.S. occupation of Iraq, for U.S. dominance, for a U.S. doctrine of preemptive action? I doubt this. What the members of the Security Council were signaling was the imperative of forging a global interest, of working as an international community in the common interests of the Iraqi people, including for the reconstruction of Iraq and finding the common means to do this: for example, establishing as a priority the International Advisory and Monitoring Board, and using the Development Fund for Iraq in a transparent manner. It takes real multilateralism to work for the global interest, not virtual multilateralism. Coerced cooperation is not cooperation; it is capitulation.

The real essence of the Security Council negotiations in New York has not been about the future of Iraq, but the future of the United Nations, of international law, and of political legitimacy—not just at the national, but at the global level. Paradoxically, as the United States has sought to sideline the United Nations, yet return to it for the cloak of legitimacy, the Bush administration has stoked the fires of an international debate of the greatest import. As Richardson notes, "this global dialogue has reaffirmed the Council under the Charter as a major prescriber of global legal authority about the use of force against Iraq, in restraint of a demand by Washington for recognition of global U.S. hegemony" (2003, 2).

Concluding Thoughts

I began this chapter asking questions about how and why it matters to analyze foreign policy through a gendered lens. Throughout this critique of the Bush doctrine of the war on terrorism and U.S. policy on the United Nations and Iraq, we have approached the challenge of a gendered analysis using the concept of hegemonic masculinity. One of the important challenges we are left with is to think creatively about the costs that such a foreign policy imposes. Also, what kinds of issues might come to the forefront if we had a different gendered lens on foreign policymaking than a masculinist one?

At the time of this writing (summer 2004), elites in Washington have a growing sense of unease that the occupation of Iraq has undermined the Bush doctrine. Many of its pillars have been called into question. The preemptive strategy, as well as the pillar of unilateralism (also known as "go-it-alone with a coalition of the willing"), and the proposition that bringing democracy by force, from the top down, to Iraq could transform that country in short order, as well as provide a stimulus for democratic change throughout the region—all these tenets are now in question. Robin Wright of the *Washington Post* reports that "the Bush doctrine could become the biggest casualty of U.S. intervention in Iraq" (Wright 2004). U.S. credibility and integrity have been thrown into doubt. The pretexts for invading Iraq have not held up to scrutiny—the WMD were never found; the claimed ties between Iraq and al-Qaeda have not materialized; and the war on Iraq has destabilized the region, making it more prone to terrorism and violence, not less. Many critics point out that the Bush approach to the war on terror, exemplified by occupying Iraq, plays directly into the hands of Osama bin Laden, and fuels, not dampens, the fires for recruiting new terrorists members. The claims to moral superiority behind the Bush policy of proactive defense are also in tatters. In spite of evidence of U.S. forces and subcontractors torturing prisoners in Iraq, administration officials have tried to direct the horror at the photos themselves—as though they are the problem. And they have tried to frame the treatment of prisoners as humiliation or abuse, not torture. As Susan Sontag points out, "even when the President was finally compelled, as the damage to America's reputation everywhere in the world widened and deepened, to use the 'sorry' word, the focus of regret still seemed the damage to America's claim to moral superiority" (2004, 1). Sontag sees no retreat on the horizon from such horrors as long as the United States is committed to an endless, perpetual war on terror. The history of the annals of war is a history of the corruption of the human spirit that violence invites. She is right to tell us that this "inevitably leads to the demonizing and dehumanizing of anyone declared by the Bush administration to be a possible terrorist." The torture at Abu Ghraib prison and "the extralegal American penal empire" (Sontag's phrase) should shock Americans into questioning the failures of a "pseudo-religious doctrine of war, endless war" (Sontag 2004, 3). Trophy photos of torture are, however, not so frequently found in the annals of war. These pictures may be so disturbing to us in part because they remind us of the racialized nature of the U.S. war on terror, and its connections with the country's own racial history. As Sontag writes (2004, 26),

> if there is something comparable to what these pictures show it would be some of the photographs of black victims of lynching taken between the 1880s and 1930s, which show Americans grinning beneath the naked mutilated body of a black man or woman hanging behind them from a tree. The lynching photographs were souvenirs of a collective action whose participants felt perfectly justified in what they had done. So are the pictures from Abu Ghraib.

The policy of going it alone may have its benefits from a military strategic perspective—the United States could keep strict control over command and operational objectives and means of achieving them—but these are short-term gains at the expense of longer-term costs. The international community has been reluctant to provide assistance in the reconstruction of Iraq and forces to shore up internal security. In essence, the United States has been told, "If you want to do it your way, you can do it your way all the way. Don't come running to us to bail you out." Is a muscular policy of preemption and unilateralism dead? Many neoconservatives still say no. The war on terror will continue; the threat of WMD is still present; the need for preemptive action has been neither exhausted nor discredited. They see no alternative (Wright 2004).

This chapter's analysis warns us to count carefully the costs of hegemonic masculine policies, and to look for alternatives. To find the alternatives, we need to think about the impact that hegemonic masculinity has on real lives. This means on the lives of the victims of our policies—like the prisoners in Abu Ghraib or elsewhere who were tortured or killed in captivity—as well as what these policies are doing to us as Americans. What makes us seek such trophies as the photos of Abu Ghraib? We need to look long and hard at the answers. For these photos are really there for us as a mirror to see ourselves. This is what happens to those in the role of implementing a policy of domination cloaked in moral superiority. There are signs that the international community is beginning to look at the consequences of war and violence in a new light and in ways that signal the first significant challenge to hegemonic masculinity in the chambers of the Security Council itself. In October 2000, the fifteen member states took up for the first time in history a detailed discussion of the impact of war and conflict on women, and also the imperative for women to be involved in peace negotiations, conflict early warning and prevention, demobilization, disarmament, reconstruction, and decision making. The results of that discussion led to the unanimous adoption of Resolution 1325, a landmark document that treats women and the girl child not just as victims of war and targets of systematic rape, but as active agents who play many roles in war and also are essential to the pursuit of peace. Resolution 1325 underscores that including women in the framing of international relations puts into perspective the kinds of gendered violence that hegemonic masculinity perpetuates, and its high social costs. Keeping women in the picture brings forward new questions, and also new possibilities for the resolution of conflict.

Keeping an eye on the gendered dimensions of foreign policy also alerts us to the costs of policies justified under the guise of hegemonic masculinity. A *New York Times* article by Somini Sengupta about the life of Iraqi girls in the aftermath of the U.S.-led invasion and occupation brings this story home to us (2004). She tells us that "even though the last years of Saddam Hussein's rule had brought new restrictions on women's freedoms, the simultaneous collapse of the police state that had kept public order and the new leeway for religious clerics to demand stricter compliance with Islamic law have increasingly narrowed girls' lives." One of them, fifteen-year-old Mariam Saeed, said, "It's as if you are in prison." Girls and women live in virtual lockdown in their own homes—for fear of being raped or kidnapped if they step outside. The violence and economic turmoil are robbing them of their future, as they sit at home watching their chance at schooling and a meaningful life slip past their reach (Sengupta 2004). These are some of the real costs of hegemonic masculinity that are obscured when the first line of action is the pursuit of narrow, national interests rather than the global interest, the common human interest. There are other signs that the United States must start counting the costs of hegemonic masculinity, as the international community grows wary of the United States' special role. In a telling move, Secretary General Kofi Annan urged the Security Council not to grant U.S. troops in peacekeeping operations any exemption from prosecution under the provisions of the International Criminal Court. Alluding to the atrocities at Abu Ghraib, he said that "it would be unwise to press for an exemption, and it would be even more unwise on the part of the Security Council to grant it. It would discredit the Council and the United Nations that stands for the rule of law" (Lynch 2004). Indeed, the United States determined by late June that it did not have the support to gain the adoption of the resolution for the third year in a row, and thus decided not to pursue the matter further in the Council. This defeat can be taken as a very significant measure, along with the steady determination of the Council over the last year and a half not to legitimize the U.S.-led invasion of Iraq, that hegemonic masculinity has its costs—and its time of accounting. This analysis also reminds us that there are alternative approaches to foreign policy, and that thinking through a gendered lens can lead us to self-criticism, self-awareness, empathy for others, and new creative ways to evaluate the old approaches and formulate new ideas.

References

Allen, Mike, and Barton Gellman. 2002. "Going Backwards. Preemptive Strikes Part of U.S. Strategic Doctrine." *Washington Post*, December 11, pp. 1–3. www.commondreams .org/cgi-bin/print.cgi?file=/headlines02/1211–02.htm.
Annan, Kofi. 2002. "Global Interest Is Our National Interest." *Presidents and Prime Ministers* 11, no. 6 (November–December): 26–27.
Arnove, Anthony, and Ali Abunimah, eds. 2002. *Iraq Under Siege: The Deadly Impact of Sanctions and War*. Cambridge, MA: South End Press.
Boggs, Carl, ed. 2003. *Masters of War: Militarism and Blowback in the Era of American Empire*. New York: Routledge.
Boutros-Ghali, Boutros. 1992. *An Agenda for Peace: Preventive Diplomacy, Peacemaking and Peacekeeping*. New York: United Nations.
———. 1999. *Unvanquished*. New York: Random House.
Brilmayer, Lea. 1994. *American Hegemony: Political Morality in a One-Superpower World*. New Haven, CT: Yale University Press.
Brooks, David. 2004. "The Party of Kennedy, or Carter?" *The New York Times*, February 17, p. A23.
Browne, Marjorie Ann. 2003. "The United Nations Security Council—Its Role in the Iraq Crisis: A Brief Overview." CRS Report for Congress. Received through the CRS Web.
Bush, George W. 2002. "President's Remarks at the United Nations General Assembly." September 12. www.whitehouse.gov/news/releases/2002/09/print/20020912–1.html.
Cohn, Carol. 1987. "Sex and Death in the Rational World of Defense Intellectuals." *Signs* 12, no. 4: 687–718.
Cohn, Carol, and Cynthia Enloe. 2003. "A Conversation with Cynthia Enloe: Feminists Look at Masculinity and the Men Who Wage War." *Signs* 28, no. 4 (Summer): 1187–1207.
Connell, R.W. 1987. *Gender and Power*. Oxford: Polity/Basil Blackwell.
———. 1995. *Masculinities*. Berkeley: University of California Press.
de Villepin, Dominique. 2003a. "Question and Answer Session Following the Speech Given by Dominique de Villepin, Minister of Foreign Affairs, at the International Institute for Strategic Studies." London, March 27. www.info-france-usa.org/news/statements/2003/villepin_iiss032703.asp.
———. 2003b. "Address by Dominique de Villepin, French Foreign Minister, Before the United Nations Security Council." March 19. www.info-france-usa.org/news/ statements/2003/villepin_uno031903.asp.
Enloe, Cynthia. 1990. *Bananas, Beaches and Bases*. Berkeley: University of California Press.
———. 2000. *Manuevers*. Berkeley: University of California Press.
———. 2002. "Demilitarization—or More of the Same? Feminist Questions to Ask in the Postwar Moment." In *The Postwar Moment*, ed. Cynthia Cockburn and Dubravka Zarkov, pp. 22–31. London: Lawrence and Wishart.
Farer, Tom. 2002. "Beyond the Charter Frame: Unilateralism or Condominium?" *American Journal of International Law* 96, no. 2 (April): 359–364.
Friedrichs, Jörg. 2004. *European Approaches to International Relations Theory: A House with Many Mansions*. New York: Routledge.
Henry, Charles. P. 1999. *Ralph Bunche. Model Negro or American Other?* New York: New York University Press.
Hermann, Richard K. 1991. "The Middle East and the New World Order." *International Security* 16, no. 2 (Fall): 42–75.
Hooper, Charlotte. 2001. *Manly States*. New York: Columbia University Press.
Klare, Michael. 1995. *Rogue States and Nuclear Outlaws*. New York: Hill and Wang.

Leatherman, Janie, and Julie Webber. 2005, forthcoming. *Beyond Global Arrogance: Charting Transnational Democracy* (working title). New York: Palgrave Macmillan.

Lobel, Jules, and Michael Ratner. 1999. "Bypassing the Security Council: Ambiguous Authorizations to Use Force, Cease-Fires and the Iraqi Inspection Regime." *American Journal of International Law* 93: 124–154.

Lynch, Colum. 2004. "Annan Opposes Exempting U.S. from Court." *Washington Post*, June 18, A24. www.truthout.org/docs_04/061904E.shtml.

Murphy, Sean, ed. 2003. "Contemporary Practice of the United States Relating to International Law." *American Journal of International Law* 97, no. 2 (April): 419–432.

National Security Strategy of the United States of America (NSS). 2002. The White House. September 17. www.whitehouse.gov/nsc/nssall.html.

Norton, Anne. 1991. "Gender, Sexuality and the Iraq of Our Imagination." *Middle East Report* no. 173 (November–December): 26–28.

PDD 25. 1996. Clinton Administration Policy on Reforming Multilateral Peace Operations (PDD 25). Bureau of International Organizational Affairs. U.S. Department of State, February 22, 1996. www.fas.org/irp/offdocs/pdd25.htm.

Richardson, Henry J. III. 2003. "U.S. Hegemony, Race, and Oil in Deciding United Nations Security Council Resolution 1441 on Iraq." *Temple International and Comparative Law Journal* 17, no. 1 (Spring): 27–83.

Schlesinger, Arthur M., Jr. 1973. *The Imperial Presidency*. Boston: Houghton Mifflin.

Sengupta, Somini. 2004. "For Iraqi Girls, Changing Land Narrows Lives. *The New York Times*. June 27, p. A1.

Sontag, Susan. 2004. "Regarding the Torture of Others." *The New York Times*, May 23, p. 25.

Tickner, J. Ann. 2001. *Gendering World Politics*. New York: Columbia University Press.

———. 1999. "Why Women Can't Run the World: International Politics According to Francis Fukuymama." *International Studies Review* 1, no. 3: 3–11.

United Nations Security Council. 2000. Resolution 1325. Adopted October 31, 2000.

———. 2002. Resolution 1441. Adopted October 8, 2002.

———. 2003. Resolution 1511. Adopted October 16, 2003.

Wittner, Lawrence S. 2003. *Toward Nuclear Abolition. A History of the World Nuclear Disarmament Movement 1971 to the Present*. Vol. 3, *The Struggle Against the Bomb*. Stanford, CA: Stanford University Press.

Wright, Robin. 2004. "Iraq Occupation Erodes Bush Doctrine." *Washington Post*, June 28, p. A01.

7

Gendering Policy Debates
Welfare Reform, Abortion Regulation, and Trafficking

Dorothy E. McBride

For over thirty years, organizations and individuals in the feminist movement in the United States have sought to influence government. By the 1990s, the movement activists had formed a number of strong, professional organizations with close ties to each other and to feminists inside the legislature and government agencies (Costain 1992; Spalter-Roth and Schreiber 1995). What has been the impact of this women's policy network on politics and policymaking? There are various ways to try to assess the impact of social movements on government (Gamson 1975). One is to look at the *content* of laws passed. Another is to see if government leaders recognize and receive movement leaders as legitimate representatives of a constituency, a *procedural* response. This chapter focuses on a third type of response that is an important link between movement actors' demands on the one hand and policy content and procedural responses on the other: *substantive representation* of movement demands in the policymaking process. Substantive representation is the inclusion of a group's policy preferences and issues in the agenda of government (Pitkin 1967). For the feminist movement, such representation involves more than just putting their issues on the agenda; it means the inclusion of their gender ideas in the framework of the debates on these issues.

This chapter is organized in three parts. First is a discussion of how the framing of policy debates may lead to substantive representation of feminist goals through gendering. A description follows of three policy debates in Congress: on welfare reform, abortion regulation, and trafficking of women and girls.[1] Finally, there is an assessment of the effect of framing in these debates on policy content and procedural responses.

Substantive Representation and Framing Policy Debates

This research is based on a conception of the policymaking process in the American government as a conflict of ideas about what policy actions the government should take. In fact, conflict persists in regular patterns that develop around policy issues and become institutionalized. Policy actors—in Congress, the executive branch, interest groups, and the courts—participate in these structured patterns of controversy and are part of a policy community. Consideration of specific issues takes place in the context of a *frame* or mode of defining policy problems. The dominant frame of an issue is the accepted understanding in the policy community of what the conflict is about. For example, in considering a question of regulating pornography, whether on the street or the Internet, the problem is typically defined as a conflict over what the limits of government regulation of free speech should be. Although there are many points of view about problems raised by pornography other than free speech—for example, concerns about the exploitation of women, morality and decency, and literary merit—these are secondary topics that policy actors consider only as they pertain to the overall dominant frame of the issue.

Knowing the frame of the debate is especially important to social movement activists and any others who are seeking to influence the content of policy. Gelb and Palley (1982) produced evidence of this in their study of the feminist movement lobbying activities on a series of women's rights issues in the 1970s. They found that feminist activists had a better chance of success if they defined their demands in terms of achieving equality between the sexes—role equity—rather than in terms of recasting traditional roles of men and women—role change. Role change issues were considered to be too threatening and radical. In other words, they did not fit the dominant frame—the institutionalized definition of policy issues relating to gender.

The way debates are framed or defined also affects who gets access to public discussions, that is, the procedural aspect of policymaking. "To define an issue is to make an assertion about what is at stake and who is affected, and therefore, to define interests and the constitution of alliances" (Stone 1997, 231). The frame, therefore, sets forth which social interests should have a say when specific bills are considered by Congress. Issues defined as health concerns invite doctors and other health professionals into the political arena. Issues that are about role equity bring liberal feminist advocates to the congressional hearings. Of course, there are no formal regulations that bar others from trying to press their point of view. Getting the attention of the powerful, however, is problematic for those not considered to be affected by a particular policy discussion.

Taken together, the conceptual frameworks of all debates on public issues constitute a guide to what and who matter in a democracy. The public agenda consists of a set of issue conflicts that concern political leaders. There is a hierarchy of such conflicts: those at the top of the agenda, their dominant frames, and the people considered to be affected by them are close to centers of power—they are *heard*. Those at the bottom are on the *margins* of the policy scope. And, conflicts not on the agenda and the people they affect are *unheard*. The vital conflict in policymaking in democracy, therefore, is less over the issues themselves and more about the way the conflicts about the issues are framed and thus the priority given to some groups over others (Schattschneider 1960; Przeworksi 1991).

Feminist advocates seek to gender policy debates, that is, to insert references to their conceptions of gender into the frame of the debate. *Gender* refers to ideas about men and women in relation to each other and ideas about women or men as a group distinct from each other. Gendering means policy actors explicitly and intentionally portray the policy problem under consideration in terms of its relation to people in their gender roles, that is, as women and not men or men and not women. To be a success for the feminist movement, the gendered terms must coincide with feminist perspectives, usually in terms that advance the status of women in relation to men and that challenge gender hierarchies.[2] It is important to remember, at this point, that feminist activists do not always agree among themselves on precisely what actions will best accomplish this goal.

To be successful in the democratic policy process, feminist activists must be concerned with more than simply presenting petitions relaying the demands and interests of their constituents in the hope that Congress will act. They must push their priority conflicts higher on the agenda of government. They must influence the institutionalized or dominant frame of debate on important issues in feminist terms, so that the questions policymakers will consider concern whether or not to enact policy provisions that will improve the status of women in relation to men. If both goals are achieved, then they are in a position to present their list of demands and interests and call upon their political resources to promote them. Their long-term goal is to institutionalize their definition of the issue in the policy community. In short, women's rights activists want government to take women's situation into account and to make it and its relation to men's situation the business of government. Of course, it is not enough that policies be defined as gender questions; feminists want to see that the debate presents congressional representatives with one choice: whether to act for or against improving women's rights and status.

What do feminists hope to gain by such a strategy? They want legislation that advances the feminist agenda, or in other words, success for their movement in influencing the content of policy. Then, as a matter of course, statutes enacted by Congress would include provisions to advance women's status in relation to men. But there are other rewards, possibly more important in the long run. By defining policy issues in terms of women and their status, feminists, as representatives of women's groups and as advocates for a particular agenda, would be considered important spokespeople for a particular constituency and experts in a policy area, and become regular participants in the policy process. Thus, whenever a proposal arises within this—let's call it a feminist—frame, then feminist organizations would be called upon to participate. And their views would be taken into account.[3]

Goal and Approach

This chapter examines debates on welfare reform, abortion regulation, and trafficking for the sex industry, three issues before Congress in the 1990s. These policy areas represent three different types of gender issues in the public arena in the

1990s. Welfare involves cash transfers to needy persons and is a distributive policy question: conflicts pertain primarily to cost of the programs and whether those who receive the support are deserving of it. If there are adequate funds, conflict is often minimal; in times of budget restraint, recipient groups scramble to maintain their piece of the pie. Welfare is also an issue that pertains to gender roles in the family and at work; the vast majority of adult clients are women with children. Other issues in this area are childcare, job training, labor rights, education, and equal opportunity laws. Abortion policy is an example of an emotive-symbolic issue. Conflicts over emotive-symbolic issues pertain primarily to basic values such as the beginning of life and fundamental human rights. They do not lend themselves easily to compromise, because people feel so strongly about such values. Abortion regulation also represents a group of issues that involve gender roles in reproduction. Other issues in this area include contraception, sterilization, and new reproductive technologies. Trafficking is a regulatory issue: the conflicts involve using the authority of government to set standards and punish those who do not comply. It also pertains to female and male sexuality. Other issues in this area include rape, pornography, homosexuality, sexual harassment, and prostitution.

The welfare reform debate of the 1990s resulted in a major overhaul of welfare policy in the United States. The sixty-year-old entitlement program, Aid to Families with Dependent Children (AFDC) was abolished and replaced with Temporary Assistance to Needy Families (TANF) through the Personal Responsibility and Work Opportunity Act (PRWORA) of 1996. The abortion controversy revolved around the debates over the Partial-Birth Abortion Ban Act (PBAB) of 1995 and their aftermath. Finally, traffic in women and girls occupied Congress from 1998 to 2000 when it enacted the Trafficking Victims Protection Act.

Welfare reform, abortion regulation, and trafficking are gender issues in that they affect men and women differently. But each can be discussed without reference to ideas about men and women. The task here is to find the gendered references, if any, and compare them to demands of feminist movement individuals and organizations. The policy debates over each of the bills studied in this chapter will be presented according to the following outline. First, I will describe how the policy proposals came to the congressional agenda, the dominant frame of the debate, and the positions of proponents and opponents in relation to it. Then I will discuss the gendered ideas in the debate—images of women and men as presented by the proponents and opponents—including a judgment on the centrality of gender to the overall frame of the issue. Finally, I will draw conclusions regarding the extent to which the gendering coincides with goals and demands of feminist organizations and the impact on policy content and procedures.

Welfare Reform

Aid to Families with Dependent Children (AFDC), commonly referred to as *welfare*, lasted sixty years—from 1935, when it was enacted as part of the Social

Security Act, until 1996, when it was replaced by TANF (for full discussion of the policy process leading to the Act see Weaver 2000). For most of that time *welfare reform* was on the congressional agenda. AFDC was a program funded by both the federal government and the states to provide income to parents (mostly single) with children under eighteen in families with no wage earners. Along with a modest monthly stipend, the family was eligible for food stamps and Medicaid health care. In the early years of debate, reform proposals were intended to improve the program's record in reducing poverty, especially among children. From the late 1970s onward, however, there was increasing emphasis on reducing welfare expenditures themselves. The solution was to find some way to get parents off welfare and into jobs and to require both parents to support their children.

This goal to reduce federal spending coincided with ideas of "new federalism," which envisioned moving most federal programs to the states. Many national leaders looked to the states as sites of experimentation and innovation in solving policy problems. Governors, for the most part, welcomed this trend because it promised more unfettered *block grants* from the federal government. Thus, there was widespread support in 1988 for the Family Support Act (FSA), which required states to provide a range of services to the poor to promote their self-sufficiency: jobs, job training, education, childcare assistance. What turned out to be the most significant part of FSA, however, was authorizing states to experiment with the policy, especially in finding ways of reducing the welfare rolls through placement of clients in jobs. FSA was so successful that governors and many in Congress wanted to expand it. One of these was Bill Clinton, governor of Arkansas, who was elected president in 1992. When he ran, one of his campaign promises was to "end welfare as we know it." The means would be to "make work pay."

Neither Clinton nor the Democrats were able to maintain control of the definition of the welfare issue. Conservative ideas, especially relating to social programs such as welfare, had become more and more popular in the 1980s (Bashevkin 1998; O'Connor 2001). Energized by the presidential terms of Ronald Reagan and George H.W. Bush, they gradually replaced entrenched liberal notions from the New Deal. Clinton's approach to welfare reform was part of his effort to present himself as a "new Democrat," someone in the center of the political spectrum. Nevertheless, critics saw his proposals for more training and childcare to be more of the same failed welfare policy. To make matters worse, between 1988 and 1992 there were dramatic increases in AFDC cases, out-of-wedlock births, and teen pregnancies. For Conservatives, these trends reinforced their resolve: something drastic had to be done.

By 1992, there was widespread agreement among policymakers on the dominant frame of the issue of *welfare reform*: the problem was AFDC itself and the resulting cycle of welfare dependency. AFDC was extremely unpopular with the public, so there were votes to be won by proposing to abolish it. Clinton had campaigned to "end" it in 1992. When he finally proposed a bill in late 1994, it did not abolish the program, but sought to provide services to move recipients into jobs. The Republicans, led by Representative Newt Gingrich, drafted a Contract with America, promising to introduce ten specific pieces of legislation within the first one hundred days of the legislative session and were successful in winning votes in the 1994 elections. One of their pledges was to abolish the AFDC *entitlement* (anyone who qualified could receive cash assistance) and replace it with an entirely new program. During this time, there was a contest between Republicans and Democrats over the frame that would shape the inevitable reform.

The victory of the Republicans in the House of Representatives in 1994 (the 104th Congress) pushed aside the Clinton Democrats' plan to make work pay through programs of job training and childcare while retaining a modest entitlement for the poor. Influenced by conservative public intellectuals (Murray 1984; Rector and Lauber 1995) the Gingrich Republicans' issue frame became dominant, shaping subsequent policy action. This frame runs as follows: AFDC/entitlements reward *behavioral poverty*, that is, out-of-wedlock births, avoiding or rejecting marriage, delinquent child support, absent fathers, crime, drug use. All of these behaviors are possible, they reasoned, because people can expect to receive money from the government for having children, no matter what the circumstances. The solution is to cut off the government dole: force poor adults to work and establish penalties for immoral and irresponsible behavior. The means would be through block grants to the states (thus making the powerful National Governors Association lobby happy) and holding the states responsible for reducing both welfare rolls and out-of-wedlock births (by whatever means, but without increasing abortion rates).

Despite the fact that the vast majority (90 percent) of welfare recipients were lone mothers with children, there were few explicit gender references in the congressional debates on PRWORA.[4] The best idea we can get of these policy actors' views of women and men comes from their descriptions of welfare mothers and the men in their lives. There were two images: One might be called "she's doing the best she can." According to this representation, a single mother is forced to seek AFDC services for her children because she is poor. For most this is temporary and they are able to move quickly off welfare. However, for the very poor, there are few choices. A woman in severe poverty does not have adequate education and work experience to get a job. The men in her life, especially her own father and the father of her children, have walked away from their responsibilities, leaving her to cope on her own. She is likely to have suffered violent abuse in her relationships. Her children are the central part of her life, and she worries that if forced to take a job, they will not be cared for.

The other view might be called "she's perpetuating poverty and immorality." According to this perception, poor young women act irresponsibly and give birth outside of marriage because they know they will get money from the government. They have serial relationships with men, none of which provide a stable parental environment for their children. Their sons turn to drugs and crime, launching a reign of terror in poor neighborhoods. Their daughters get pregnant in their early teens, quit school, and perpetuate the welfare dependency cycle.

Women's advocacy organizations interested in the welfare reform debate ranged from the Women's Committee of 100 to the Women's Freedom Network (Mink 1998; Abramowitz 1996; Kornbluh 1996). They articulated similar images of the welfare mother, but had different policy solutions. The Committee wanted to retain AFDC to give poor mothers the means to stay at home to care for their children and opposed the work requirements in PRWORA. The Women's Freedom Network, on the contrary, advocated work requirements that would bring, in their view, dignity and self-sufficiency to welfare mothers.

Most of the feminist activists took a middle position, lining up behind the leadership of the National Organization for Women (NOW). They urged Congress not to repeal the AFDC entitlement while at the same time supporting programs for finding good jobs for welfare mothers. They advocated programs to provide education, childcare, and other support for welfare mothers to take jobs that would pay enough to support their families. They supported improved child support enforcement. They opposed the Republican plan in PRWORA, especially the penalties of lifetime limits, family caps, forced identity of fathers, and cutting off teenage mothers. While urging President Clinton to veto the Act, they supported adding protections for victims of domestic violence.

Outcome

The "she's perpetuating crime and immorality" view of welfare mothers prevailed in the dominant frame of the welfare reform issue. The Act retained most of the punitive provisions envisioned by the Contract with America. This was a defeat on all fronts for feminists who had argued "she's doing the best she can." After the Republicans gained full control of Congress and their frame became dominant, women's rights advocates found themselves on the margins of the policy arena, relying on sympathetic Republican women in the House and Senate to push their demands (Casey and Carroll 2001). They enjoyed only limited success with respect to policy content as well. Of the thirteen major components of PRWORA, only three received the positive support of the feminist lobby: improving child support enforcement, some funding for childcare, and exemptions to work requirements for victims of domestic violence.

The Partial-Birth Abortion Ban Act of 1995

From 1973 until 1992, the pro-life movement in the United States waged a campaign against legalized abortion. They had three goals: to reduce the number of abortions; to make abortions difficult to get; and, the ultimate goal, to overturn *Roe v. Wade* (410 U.S. 113. 1973), the Supreme Court decision that prohibited state regulation of abortion in the first trimester of pregnancy. In those twenty years there had been some pro-life victories: the Hyde Amendment restricted use of federal funds to pay for abortions for poor women; President Ronald Reagan had appointed many sympathetic justices to the federal courts, even the Supreme Court; and those courts ruled that states could enact requirements that would make it more difficult for women to obtain abortions. But the hopes raised in 1989 in the case of *Webster v. Reproductive Services* (492 U.S. 490. 1989) that the Court would reverse the *Roe* ruling were dashed in 1992. In *Planned Parenthood of Southeastern Pennsylvania v. Casey* (505 U.S. 833. 1992), the justices struck a compromise that upheld women's liberty to choose abortion while at the same time allowing states to set limits on the procedures as long as they did not overly burden that liberty.

After the *Casey* ruling, pro-life activists shifted their campaigns to legislatures, vowing to test the limits of the "undue burden" test. When they read the description of something called "dilation and extraction," a procedure used in clinics for second- and third-trimester abortion, it seemed especially barbaric and a candidate for criminal sanction.[5] They called this procedure "partial-birth abortion," claiming that the practitioner killed a partially delivered fetus. To them it seemed like infanticide. A full-scale effort was launched to criminalize this procedure through state laws. In 1994, the Republican party, comprising many ardent opponents of legal abortion, gained majorities in both houses of Congress. The pro-life campaign against "partial-birth abortion" moved to the federal level. Despite twenty years of campaigns, *Roe v. Wade* continued to be in force with no change in the dominant frame of abortion debates. Although administrative hurdles and declining services hampered many women seeking abortions, it was still legal. With the PBAB Act, the proponents of abortion regulation took a bold new tack: to change the frame of the debate on abortion, making the issue the procedure itself.

The PBAB Act of 1995 proposed a nationwide ban on the procedure the proponents of the bill called "partial birth." They let their definition of this procedure stand as representative of the public policy problem they hoped to address: "An abortion in which the person performing the abortion partially vaginally delivers a living fetus before killing the fetus and completing the delivery" (United States Congress, House of Representatives 1995, H.R. 1833, 2). They offered both clinical and emotional elaborations of the procedure to complete their definition of the issue at hand: this procedure is gruesome. Because the fetus is killed while its head is still in the uterus, they claimed, it is "3 inches" away from an act that could be called murder.

Opponents of the ban sought to turn the discussion away from baby-killing and the proponents' emotion-laden version of the procedure, but they were not united in their definition of the issue. Some said that partial birth didn't exist as named. A few assumed there was a medical procedure involved but wanted to make the issue the question of the federal government's prohibiting a medical procedure—an unprecedented extension of federal power, they said. Another opposition argument pleaded for an exception to the ban to protect a woman's life and health. Some Senate Democrats confronted this bill as a tactic in the pro-life agenda to outlaw all abortions and saw the bill, while not affecting many people who seek abortions, as an assault on the basic right to have an abortion. In this they hoped to bring the debate back to right-to-choose/right-to-life terms.

Despite such efforts, during the PBAB hearings Congress was arguing less over women's rights and more over physicians' rights to use a particular medical procedure. There were gendered ideas in the debate, to be sure, but they were not central to the conflict. In fact, the fetus took center stage in the discussions as the "partial birth" procedure was characterized as an assault on human life: "This is a method that takes that life as the baby emerges from the mother's womb and while the baby is in the birth canal" (U.S. Congress, House, 1995, 1). In the depiction of the procedure there were no gender representations, except to the extent that body parts that were depicted were parts of a woman's body: the uterus (womb) and the vagina (birth canal). There was no explicit recognition that the procedure portrayed involved a woman. Body parts were in the background and important only in reference to the placement of the fetus during the procedure. When whole women were discussed, they were either talked about as pregnant women, "the natural protector of her child in the womb," or, if a doctor performed an abortion, "her child's deadly adversary." One participant described women as victims of abortion, casting physicians in the role of villains and putting women on the margins of the issue.

Opponents of the ban sought to place gender in a more central position in the debate. They charged that the proponents were trying to cast women, along with doctors, as demons, even witches, by making the procedure sound so terrible. They tried to discuss women as responsible citizens seeking health care. The bill would interfere with a medical decision between a woman and her doctor, they claimed. Women must have the right to decide when and where to bear children and government should place no limits on the doctor's choices. Many also focused on the question of federal government power, trying to shift attention toward a question of federalism—and saying that the government should not tell the "women of America and their families" what medical procedures they should have.

The debate on the PBAB Act is noteworthy because it represents a change in the dominant frame of the abortion regulation issue, which had been institutionalized since *Roe v. Wade*. That decision defined the abortion issue as a matter of women's privacy and rights balanced against the interests of the state in protecting the fetus. The PBAB debate degendered the conflict and put feminist advocates outside the policy process. The proponents of the ban were successful in shifting the frame away from the gendered issues of rights of women to make the issue under consideration a gruesome depiction of an abortion procedure. Opponents of the ban tried, unsuccessfully, to bring gendered ideas of women's rights, self-determination, and health into the discussion. They made their points, but they were not successful in casting the proposal in gendered terms. These points were consistent, as before, with mainstream feminist organizations. So, a failure for them can be seen as a failure for the feminists regardless of whether the ban went into effect or not. Further, this new definition of the abortion issue undercut the legitimacy of feminist groups—and their friends in Congress—jeopardizing their membership in the policy community.

But enacting the PBAB Act in 1995 did not signal the end of the debate. President Clinton, with assistance of his White House Office on Women's Initiatives and Outreach, staged a veto ceremony that brought women's interests back into the debate. This Act was wrong, he contended, because it did not allow doctors to select the procedure to protect a woman's health. To drive home the point, he introduced several women who claimed that without the procedure they would not have been able to have more children. Sometimes, it was medically necessary. This action brought the issue of women's health back into the dominant frame of the debate. Subsequent hearings, in 1996 and 1997, addressed the health issue, and congressional committees received testimony from women's rights advocates on this subject. It was the basis for the Supreme Court's ruling in *Stenberg v. Carhart* (530 U.S. 914. 2000) declaring many of the state partial-birth ban acts unconstitutional in 2000. Then in 2003, encouraged by President George W. Bush's promise to sign the Act, the House of Representatives devoted the bulk of its report on the bill to arguing that partial-birth abortion procedures were dangerous to women's health and were never considered "medically necessary."

Outcome

The PBAB Act passed both houses of Congress in 1995 but was vetoed by President Clinton. In 1997, advocates again successfully pushed the bill through Congress followed by a presidential veto. Efforts to override the veto succeeded in the House of Representatives but failed by three votes, in 1998, in the Senate. The Act passed both houses of Congress again in 2003.[6] The dominant frame of the abortion debate involved whether or not a particular procedure was ever necessary to protect women's health. With that, feminists had gained access to the conflict, but in narrow terms. At the same time, congressional policy actors no longer entertained questions of women's reproductive rights and freedoms.

Traffic in Women and Children

Until the late 1990s, the issue of trafficking in women and children had not been on the national agenda since the Mann Act was passed in 1910 (Langum 1994). Bringing women and children illegally into the United States to work in the sex industry occurred, but when traffickers were caught, they were punished under immigration laws and their victims were deported as illegal aliens (sometimes deporting the primary witnesses in the process). Things changed when the United Nations and other international organizations began to draw attention to the increase in the practice of trafficking, especially from Asia and countries of the former

Soviet Union. Media ran stories of women, many from Russia and Eastern Europe, held captive in brothels in Europe and even the United States.

In 1998, President Bill Clinton responded to international prodding and issued a directive, placing the issue on the national policy agenda and assigning the President's Interagency Council on Women (IAC) responsibility for developing policy initiatives to address the problem. The IAC, composed of secretaries of State, Health and Human Services, and the attorney general (all women) had been established to implement the UN Plan of Action developed at the Beijing World Conference for Women in 1995. The IAC was housed administratively in the Department of State and chaired by Secretary of State Madeleine Albright. The honorary chair was the first lady, Hillary Rodham Clinton. Both Albright and the first lady brought attention to the problem of trafficking of women and girls in speeches and interviews.

Simultaneously, the issue attracted the attention of some Republicans in Congress, specifically Representative Chris Smith (R-NJ). He chaired a subcommittee on human rights and was a delegate to meetings of the Organization for Security and Cooperation in Europe (OSCE). In this capacity, he was part of a group of policy actors who wanted to see the United States use its power for good in the world. They were fresh from successfully sponsoring the Religious Freedom Act, which empowered the president to levy punitive sanctions on countries who abused religious minorities. Smith, who had been moved by the testimony of oppression and exploitation of women lured into bondage by traffickers, envisioned using U.S. power similarly to punish countries that tolerated this abuse against women and girls.

Both the IAC and Representative Smith prepared anti-trafficking bills. Since the Republicans had the majority in both houses of Congress, Smith's bill had the better chance of coming to the floor. Both bills conformed to a policy definition that considered trafficking a problem of human rights, not immigration. Many policy actors linked the practice to slavery and used terms like *involuntary servitude, devastating brutalization*, and *evil*. Victims were degraded, used as chattel to be bought and sold, denied their essential humanity. Most thought that victims were vulnerable to this treatment because of dire economic conditions in their countries: impoverishment of the former communist countries and chronic underdevelopment in the Third World. Those who took advantage of this situation were portrayed as villains: organized crime rings based in Russia or a variety of Asian countries. Their crimes were considered to be a dark by-product of globalization. Both bills proposed that U.S. laws be changed to accomplish three goals. First was *prevention*, through providing economic assistance to the source countries and aid to the victims. Second was *prosecution*, through stronger penalties for traffickers and better training of immigration and law enforcement officials. Finally, third was *protection*, through granting victims special visas, shelter, and rehabilitation.

The dominant frame of the debate was gendered at the beginning. The problem the bills were to address was sexual exploitation and victimization of *women and girls* perpetrated by *men* in international organized crime. Policy actors portrayed these women and girls as victims—naive, coerced, isolated, powerless, vulnerable, exploited, duped, degraded, prostituted, and abused. It might thus come as a surprise that the Clinton administration and the IAC made a concerted effort during consideration of the trafficking bills in Congress to *degender* the frame of the debate, in other words, to make the debate not about women and girls, but about *persons*. Theresa Loar, Senior Coordinator for Women's Issues, admitted to having a mandate to promote women's human rights within U.S. foreign policy. She was responsible for the IAC's anti-trafficking initiative. Nevertheless, in testimony before Smith's Human Rights Subcommittee, she stated: "Although this is sometimes characterized as a women's issue, it is, in fact, a global issue involving human rights, economics, migration, transnational crime, labor, and public health" (U.S. Congress, House of Representatives 1999, 14). She went on to say that the sex industry was "merely one component of trafficking," inseparable from trafficking for slave labor. She argued that the problem was best treated as a matter of labor human rights, not as a women's issue. In this she was supported by the testimony of Harold Koh, assistant secretary of state for Human Rights, who testified that trafficking takes many forms: "from forced prostitution to bonded domestic servitude; from coerced sweatshop work to child soldiers. It involves women and children, yes, but also men, victims from every walk of life, culture, and religion" (9). Assuming that a bill "only about women" would be considered too narrow, the IAC adopted this degendering strategy to win allies among labor interests in support of the legislation (Botti 2000). This degendering did not include men as victims of sex trafficking. Rather, they expanded the scope of the stated purpose of trafficking to include men for sweatshop labor. They were partially successful in this effort; eventually the bill became gender neutral—the Traffic in Persons Protection Act of 2000.

The dominant frame of the debate did not explore the gendered aspects of prostitution itself, but the feminist debate over the relationship of women's rights to the sex business was an undercurrent in the policy process over trafficking. There is among feminists worldwide a fundamental division over whether selling sex can be a valid choice for women. Some women's rights activists believe strongly that women should have the right to make free choices about their sexuality and that, if left alone by government rules and regulations, they should be able to choose prostitution as a way to earn money, even as a form of legitimate work. These feminists thus oppose any form of coercion related to sexuality, whether by pimps and traffickers or by the police. Other women's rights activists are just as strongly convinced that prostitution is part of an integrated system of exploitation of women through masculinist institutions that protect male prerogatives to use women sexually. Although women may *think* they have freely chosen to prostitute themselves, the sex trade is exploitation. All prostitution is coerced, according to this view.

In the debate over the trafficking issue in the United States there was an active coalition of women's rights organizations who lobbied Congress and the Clinton administration. Composed of thirteen organizations, the coalition subscribed to the idea that all prostitution was exploitation.[7] Thus, they wanted the new law to define trafficking accordingly and punish anyone who brought women into the United States for the purposes of prostitution, regardless of their consent. The first lady, Secretary Albright, IAC, and the congressional Democrats considered it possible that some women might choose prostitution and wanted the new law to apply only to circumstances of force, fraud, and coercion. Let's recap the conflicts that arose between the feminist lobby and the IAC during the debate.

1. Should coercion be required to prove sex trafficking? The IAC said yes, the feminist lobby said no.
2. Should sex trafficking be considered a form of coerced labor under a common definition or should sex trafficking be treated as a separate and special offense? The IAC said treat it all as coerced labor, the feminists wanted sex trafficking to be treated separately.
3. Should the U.S. issue sanctions against countries that don't fight sex trafficking? The IAC said no, while the feminists supported sanctions.

Outcome

As with so many policy debates in the United States, the outcome of the debate over trafficking was a compromise; the feminist lobby had some success, as did the IAC. The dominant issue frame was gendered although the title and authoritative provisions of the act were gender neutral, pertaining to "Trafficking Victims." The "purposes and findings" section of the Act made it clear that the victims are "predominately women and children trafficked into the international sex trade, often by force, fraud, or coercion." The reference to the use of force, fraud, and coercion as occurring "often" instead of "always" signaled a small feminist victory over the IAC. Frustrated that neither the IAC nor the congressional Democrats would accept their definition of prostitution as always involving exploitation, they had turned to an unlikely feminist ally, Representative Chris Smith. Smith, a staunch opponent of legalized abortion, was an adversary of NOW and other groups in the anti-trafficking feminist coalition. However, he agreed with them that sex trafficking was a serious violation of women's human rights and that prostitution represented the worst kind of exploitation and victimization. Thus, he and his supporters accepted a two-tier definition of sex trafficking in the Act:

Sex trafficking means the recruitment, harboring, transportation, provision, or obtaining of a person for the purpose of a commercial sex act.

Severe sex trafficking means sex trafficking in which a commercial sex act is induced by force, fraud, or coercion, or in which the person induced to perform such act has not attained 18 years of age (114 STAT.1470).

This compromise had little effect on the operation of the Act, because the prevention, protection, and prosecution provisions applied only to severe forms of trafficking. And although sex trafficking was separated as a special form of trafficking, the Act lumped all trafficking together in its provisions. In the end, trafficking in women became a degendered issue and a gender-neutral policy. But this occurred after feminists had gained procedural access to the policy arenas.

Conclusion

In this chapter we have been able to review three policy debates on issues of interest to the feminist movement in the United States. These cases represent only a small number of the many efforts by feminist activists to influence Congress. Yet they show that encounters between the movement and the government are dynamic, and they reinforce the conclusion that assessing the impact of the feminist movement is a complex undertaking. They also illustrate the significance of the conflict over the frame of the debate for policy content and process for movement activists.

When welfare reform, abortion regulation, and trafficking reached Congress's agenda in the 1990s, they were defined as matters of women's status and rights. Nevertheless, as debates unfolded, women's rights advocates faced adversaries who opposed any explicit gender references. In the discussion of welfare reform, there were competing images of welfare mothers. During the debate, it was the feminist version that was removed from the dominant frame in place of a punitive one. In the abortion controversy over partial-birth abortion, the pro-life activists were very nearly successful in changing the dominant definition of the abortion issue in a way that would remove any mention of women from discussion. Only President Clinton's intervention reincorporated a limited reference to women's health as a matter of debate. At the same time it was President Clinton's agency that worked to degender the trafficking debate, and the issue frame that had been initially gendered to promote women's rights wound up being largely gender neutral.

The pattern of policy content, that is, *substantive* representation, for the feminist movement followed from successes and defeats in gendering the issue frames. Feminist activists won only minor concessions from the Republicans in the Welfare Reform Act of 1996. Their victory in stopping the partial-birth abortion bill was short-lived. With respect to trafficking, the statute went in the feminist direction, but its gender-neutral provisions and limited scope fell short of a direct attack on the criminal exploitation of women. These three debates represent three classes of gender issues: work and family, reproduction, and sexuality. There seems to be little variation in the feminist substantive representation among them, suggesting that these modest successes may represent the pattern of women's movement influence across a number of debates in the 1990s.

The procedural access of women's policy activists followed the fate of their influence on gendering the frames as well. In the issues of welfare reform and abortion, feminists had enjoyed routine access to policy arenas in the 1970s,

1980s, and early 1990s. When the dominant frames became degendered in the late 1990s, women's rights activists found themselves on the margins of the debate. This link between gendering and access is especially visible in the partial-birth debate. The partial-birth issue frame was nongendered from the outset with no participation by feminists. When President Clinton succeeded in making women's health a part of the debate, feminists reappeared at the congressional hearings. The trafficking issue was a new one in 1998 for women's policy activists in Washington. Prostitution and trafficking had rarely come to the congressional agenda, and feminists had not developed a pattern of participation on that issue (Stetson 2004). Coming from the international arena, trafficking began as a gendered issue promoting women's rights. The IAC, a government women's policy agency, assumed policy leadership, promising to open channels of communication and, feminists hoped, increase influence of the women's rights lobbies. When the IAC was successful in degendering the issue frame in Congress, far from direct procedural access, women's rights activists moved to the margins of the debate.

These findings are important to consider in making assessments of the political status of the women's movement today. Most studies of the history of feminist activism in the United States show that, similar to the women's movements in many Western democracies, the patterns of organization and activism have shifted from the autonomous, unconventional, and radical forms that characterized the 1970s to consolidation of formal organizations with national leadership. Today, these activists have resources to sustain policy coalitions over many years, working to influence national policymakers whenever their issues are on the agenda (see, for example, Ferree and Hess 2000). This Women's Lobby, composed of over 150 women's advocacy groups based in Washington, has developed regular and some might say institutionalized channels of access to sympathetic congressional representatives and Senators. Since 1978, the Congressional Caucus on Women's Issues (CCWI) helped by providing a direct link between movement leaders and women members of both Houses.[8] Thus, when policy proposals reached the congressional agenda, these activists were inside the policy system to present their feminist claims.

The debates on welfare reform, partial-birth abortion, and trafficking in the 1990s, however, illustrate the limits of such consolidation in maintaining influence in the policymaking process. The victory of the Republican party in 1994 gave conservatives in that party control of many aspects of the agenda, including the access to committee hearings and deliberations. The Women's Lobby still had their allies on Capitol Hill, but they were much diminished in influence. The CCWI lost its organizational support in Congress. While feminist activists were present in the important policymaking arenas and continued to take positions on proposals that have gendered impacts, their ability to maintain effective access depended on maintaining the gendered frame of the debate. To maintain such frames requires allies, either through the women's policy agencies, in the case of the partial-birth abortion debate, or with the Republican leaders in the case of trafficking. Welfare reform debate reveals that the Women's Lobby, without such allies, is likely to remain on the margins of the process. Even when the dominant frame of a debate, such as abortion, becomes gendered in terms of women's choice and privacy, as occurred in the 1970s, there is no guarantee that it will remain so when the political ground shifts. This was the lesson learned when the Republican party assumed the majority in Congress.

The information in this chapter illustrates a way of using the concept of gender to study change in the policymaking process and the impact of social movements. The debates studied here demonstrate the significance of the use of language and ideas in securing access to power and resources. It is not just the provisions of policy proposals that matter; the meaning of these provisions to policy actors is just as important. To be successful, movement activists must recognize what is at stake and struggle to retain a place for their ideas in the dominant frame of policy issues high on the public agenda. It is also clear that the Republican dominance in the 1990s made this goal difficult to meet. Nevertheless, depending on the issue, allies can and must be found in both political parties.

Notes

Most of the research for this chapter was part of my work in the Research Network on Gender, Politics, and the State (RNGS) and made possible by a grant from the National Science Foundation (SES 008450) (Stetson 2001; 2004).

1. The sources of information on these debates are transcripts of congressional hearings: U.S. Congress, House: 1992, 1994, 1995, 1996, 1999, 2003. Senate: 1994, 1995, 1996. See the list of hearings examined for this chapter below. These are an excellent source of information about the range of debates because the practice is to include a variety of policy actors—members of Congress, bureaucrats, interest group spokespeople, experts, and personal testimony of individuals. Newspapers would be another source. Often these depend heavily on information found in the hearings.

2. For various studies of U.S. feminism, its origins and impact on politics see, for example, Offen 1988; Ferree and Martin 1995; Gelb 1989; Katzenstein and Mueller 1987; Katzenstein 1998; Ryan 1992; Whittier 1999; Mazur 2002.

3. Rochon and Mazmanian (1993) refer to these movement successes in terms of *process change*. They argue that process change may prove to have a more long-lasting impact than changes in policy content.

4. Two-thirds of welfare recipients were either black or Hispanic, but race and ethnicity remained undertones in the debate, with no explicit references to either.

5. We trace this to a paper given by Dr. Martin Haskell, an abortion provider, at a conference of the National Abortion Federation. The procedure was developed for later-term abortions because it could be performed in out-patient clinics. Other procedures for such abortions had to be performed in hospitals, and due to pervious pro-life campaigns, many hospitals, both public and private, would not allow abortions. This was considered to be a safe alternative by those who used it.

6. President George W. Bush signed the 2003 Act in October 2003. Its constitutionality was immediately challenged.

7. Equality Now!; Planned Parenthood Federation of America; International Women's Health coalition; NOW; Women's Environment and Development Organizations; Catholics

for a Free Choice; Protection Project; Coalition Against Trafficking in Women; Sisterhood Is Global Institute; National Black Women's Health Project; Feminist Majority; Gloria Steinem; Center for Women Policy Studies.

8. The Congressional Caucus on Women's Issues was composed of all female members of Congress as well as many men who supported its goals. Congress provided some financial support for a staff, which worked developing consensus positions on policies related to the status of women (Hammond 1998).

References

Abramovitz, Mimi. 1996. *Under Attack, Fighting Back: Women and Welfare in the United States.* New York: Monthly Review Press.

Bashevkin, Sylvia. 1998. *Women on the Defensive: Living Through Conservative Times.* Chicago: University of Chicago Press.

Botti, Anita. 2000. Interview. August 29.

Casey, Kathleen J., and Susan J. Carroll. 2001. "Welfare Reform in the 104th Congress: Institutional Position and the Role of Women." In *Women and Welfare: Theory and Practice in the United States and Europe,* ed. Nancy J. Hirschmann and Ulrike Liebert, pp. 111–32. New Brunswick, NJ: Rutgers University Press.

Costain, Anne N. 1992. *Inviting Women's Rebellion: A Political Process Interpretation of the Women's Movement.* Baltimore, MD: Johns Hopkins University Press.

Ferree, Myra Marx, and Beth B. Hess. 2000. *Controversy and Coalition: The New Feminist Movement Across Four Decades of Change.* 3d ed. New York: Routledge.

Ferree, Myra Marx, and Patricia Yancey Martin, eds. 1995. *Feminist Organizations.* Philadelphia: Temple University Press.

Gamson, William A. 1975. *The Strategy of Social Protest.* Homewood, IL: The Dorsey Press.

Gelb, Joyce. 1989. *Feminism and Politics.* Berkeley: University of California Press.

Gelb, Joyce, and Marian Lief Palley. 1982. *Women and Public Policies.* Princeton, NJ: Princeton University Press.

Hammond, Susan Webb. 1998. *Congressional Caucuses in National Policymaking.* Baltimore, MD: Johns Hopkins University Press.

Katzenstein, Mary Fainsod. 1998. *Faithful and Fearless: Moving Feminist Protest Inside the Church and the Military.* Princeton, NJ: Princeton University Press.

Katzenstein, Mary Fainsod, and Carol Mueller, eds. 1987. *The Women's Movements of the United States and Western Europe.* Philadelphia: Temple University Press.

Kornbluh, Felicia. 1996. "Feminists in the Welfare Debate: Too Little? Too Late?" *Dollars and Sense.* November–December 24–25, pp. 39–40.

Langum, David J. 1994. *Crossing over the Line: Legislating Morality and the Mann Act.* Chicago: University of Chicago Press.

Mazur, Amy G. 2002. *Theorizing Feminist Policy.* Oxford: Oxford University Press.

Mink, Gwendolyn. 1998. *Welfare's End.* Ithaca, NY: Cornell University Press.

Murray, Charles. 1984. *Losing Ground.* New York: Basic Books.

O'Connor, Alice. 2001. *Poverty Knowledge: Social Science, Social Policy and the Poor in Twentieth-Century U.S. History.* Princeton, NJ: Princeton University Press.

Offen, Karen. 1988. "Defining Feminism: A Comparative Historical Approach." *Signs,* 14: 119–57.

Pitkin, Hanna Fenichel. 1967. *The Concept of Representation.* Berkeley: University of California Press.

Przeworski, Adam. 1991. *Democracy and the Market: Political and Economic Reforms in Eastern Europe and Latin America.* Cambridge: Cambridge University Press.

Rector, Robert E., and W.F. Lauber. 1995. *America's Failed $5.4 Trillion War on Poverty.* Washington, DC: Heritage Foundation.

Rochon, Thomas R., and Daniel A. Mazmanian. 1993. "Social Movements and the Policy Process." *Annals of the American Academy of Political Social Science,* 528: 75–87.

Ryan, Barbara. 1992. *Feminism and the Women's Movement: Dynamics of Change in Social Movement Ideology and Activism.* New York: Routledge.

Schattschneider, E.E. 1960. *The Semisovereign People: A Realist's View of Democracy in America.* New York: Holt, Rinehart and Winston.

Spalter-Roth, Roberta, and Ronnee Schreiber. 1995. "Outside Issues and Insider Tactics: Strategic Tensions in the Women's Policy Network During the 1980s." In *Feminist Organizations,* ed. Myra Marx Ferree and Patricia Yancey Martin, pp. 105–27. Philadelphia: Temple University Press.

Stetson, Dorothy McBride. 2001. "U.S. Abortion Debates 1959–1998: The Women's Movement Holds On." In *Abortion Politics, Women's Movements, and the Democratic State: A Comparative Study of State Feminism,* ed. Dorothy McBride Stetson, pp. 247–66. Oxford: Oxford University Press.

———. 2004. "The Invisible Issue: Prostitution and Trafficking of Women and Girls in the United States." In *The Politics of Prostitution: Women's Movements, Democratic States, and the Globalisation of Sex Commerce,* ed. Joyce Outshoorn, pp. 245–64. Cambridge: Cambridge University Press.

Stone, Deborah. 1997. *Policy Paradox: The Art of Decision Making.* New York: Norton.

United States Congress. House of Representatives. 1995. The Partial Birth Abortion Act of 1995. H.R. 1833. 104th Congress, first session.

Weaver, R. Kent. 2000. *Ending Welfare as We Know It.* Washington, DC: Brookings Institution Press.

Hearings

United States Congress. House of Representatives. 1992. Beyond Public Assistance: Where Do We Go From Here? Hearing before the Select Committee on Hunger. March 25.

United States Congress. House of Representatives. 1992. Federal Policy Perspectives on Welfare Reform: Rhetoric Reality and Opportunities. Hearing before the Domestic Task Force of the Select Committee on Hunger. April 9.

United States Congress. House of Representatives. 1992. State and Local Perspectives on Welfare Reform: Rhetoric, Reality and Opportunities. Hearing before the Domestic Task Force of the Select Committee on Hunger. June 4.

United States Congress. House of Representatives. 1992. Rethinking Poverty Policy. Hearing before the Select Committee on Hunger. October 2.

United States Congress. House of Representatives. 1994. Ending Welfare as We Know It: Progress or Paralysis? Hearing before the Human Resources and Intergovernmental Relations Subcommittee of the Committee on Government Operations. March 10.

United States Congress. House of Representatives. 1994. Hearing on H.R. 4605, Work and Responsibility Act of 1994. Hearing before the Committee on Education and Labor. August 2.

United States Congress. House of Representatives. 1994. Hearing Regarding the Impact of Welfare Reform on Child Care Providers and the Working Poor. Hearing before the Subcommittee on Human Resources of the Committee on Education and Labor. September 20.

United States Congress. House of Representatives. 1995. Contract with America—Overview. Hearings before the Committee on Ways and Means. January 5, 10, 11, 12.

United States Congress. House of Representatives. 1995. Contract with America—Welfare Reform. Hearings before the Committee on Ways and Means. January 13, 20, 23, 27, 30, February 2.

United States Congress. House of Representatives. 1995. Child Care and Child Welfare. Joint Hearing before the Subcommittee on Human Resources of the Committee on Ways and Means and the Subcommittee on Early Childhood, Youth, and Families of the Committee on Economic and Educational Opportunities. February 3.

United States Congress. House of Representatives. 1995. Subcommittee on the Constitution of the Committee on the Judiciary. "Partial-Birth Abortion Ban Act of 1995." June 15.

United States Congress. House of Representatives. 1996. Welfare Reform. Hearing before the Subcommittee on Human Resources of the Committee on Ways and Means. May 22, 23.

United States Congress. House of Representatives. 1996. The Personal Responsibility and Work Opportunity Act of 1996. Hearing before the Committee on Commerce. June 11.

United States Congress. House of Representatives. 1996. Causes of Poverty, with a Focus on Out of Wedlock Births. Hearing before the Subcommittee on Human Resources of the Committee on Ways and Means. March 5.

United States Congress. House of Representatives. 1999. Trafficking of Women and Children in the International Sex Trade. Hearing before the Subcommittee on International Operations and Human Rights of the Committee on International Relations. September 14.

United States Congress. House of Representatives. 2003. Partial-Birth Abortion Ban Act of 2003: Report of the Committee. Washington, DC. April 3.

United States Congress. Senate. 1992. Administration's Welfare Reform Proposal. Hearing before the Subcommittee on Social Security and Family Policy of the Committee on Finance. August 4.

United States Congress. Senate. 1994. Welfare Reform. Hearings before the Subcommittee on Social Security and Family Policy of the Committee on Finance. January 18, February 25.

United States Congress. Senate. 1995. Broad Policy Goals of Welfare Reform. Hearing before the Committee on Finance. March 9.

United States Congress. Senate. 1995. Teen Parents and Welfare Reform. Hearing before the Committee on Finance. March 14.

United States Congress. Senate. 1995. Welfare Reform—Views of Interested Organizations. Hearing before the Committee on Finance. March 29.

United States Congress. Senate. 1995. States' Perspective on Welfare Reform. Hearing before the Committee on Finance. March 8.

United States Congress. Senate. 1995. Child Support Enforcement. Hearing before the Committee on Finance. March 28.

United States Congress. Senate. 1995. Committee on the Judiciary. "The Partial-Birth Abortion Ban Act of 1995." November 17.

United States Congress. Senate. 1996. Welfare and Medicaid Reform. Hearings before the Committee on Finance. June 13, 19.

8

Gender, Social Construction, and Policies for Low-Income Men and Women

Jyl J. Josephson

Scholars of public policy have long observed that much of the policy process, from agenda setting to policy implementation and evaluation, is not rational. Often, public policies are contradictory, have unclear goals, and bear little relation to the empirical findings of policy analysts (Stone 1997). As a result of this long-standing observation, scholars have been paying increasing attention to the nonrational aspects of policy formulation and implementation.

One aspect of this new arena in the study of public policy is the study of the interaction between policies and the groups to which public policies are targeted. As Schneider and Ingram have observed, policymakers target policy to specific groups (Ingram and Schneider 1991). Because of their ultimate goal of reelection, elected officials will target policy goals and benefits or costs in ways that will provide them with the greatest "political value: votes to be gained, co-optation of potential opponents, possible campaign contributions, and/or favorable press reactions" (Ingram and Schneider 1991, 340). In a subsequent essay, the same authors argue that the social construction of target populations will shape the nature of the policy process as well as the type of policy (Schneider and Ingram 1993). These arguments are developed more extensively in their book on the same subject (Schneider and Ingram 1997). Public policy scholars have found Schneider and Ingram's theoretical framework useful in application to a variety of policies (Donovan 1997; Goetz and Sidney 1997; Hogan 1997; Sidney 2003). Here, the theoretical framework will be extended by adding the interactive roles of gender, race, and class in the social construction of target populations. This framework will be applied to several examples from contemporary social policymaking.

Feminist scholarship on social policy in the United States has very much attended to the role of policymakers' perceptions regarding gender, race, and class, and the appropriate roles for men and for women based on their social location with respect to these characteristics. Feminist scholars have shown that men's and women's actual gender roles, as well as perceptions about appropriate gender roles for men and women of different race and class status, have played a significant role in the formation of social policy in the United States. Some programs, such as unemployment compensation and worker's compensation, were designed primarily with male wage earners in mind; other policies, such as the Aid to Dependent Children program (ADC, later renamed), were designed specifically for women who were single mothers (Nelson 1990). Scholarship on the formation of the welfare state in the United States has clearly outlined the role that race and gender played in the design of these and other social policies (Gordon 1990, 1994; Lieberman 1998; Mink 1995; Orloff 1991). Contemporary social policy, however, is focused more on program retrenchment and termination than on the formation of new social policies and programs. Thus, this essay will examine the role that gender plays in the process of public policymaking involving program termination or restructuring. Because much of the focus of termination has been on moving those recipients of public benefits who are seen as capable of working for wages off of social programs, the gender analysis will focus especially on gender, race, and wage labor, comparing the actual characteristics of target populations to the ways that they were depicted in the policy debates.

The Model

Schneider and Ingram provide a useful way to analyze the role that perceptions and descriptions of populations targeted by social policy play in policy formulation and implementation. They argue that both the relative power of groups who are the targets of specific public policies, and the positive or negative public perceptions of these groups, affect the kind of policies that are implemented. As they put it,

> The social construction of target populations refers to the cultural characterizations of the persons or groups whose behavior and well-being are affected by public policy. These characterizations are normative and evaluative, portraying groups in positive or negative terms through symbolic language, metaphors, and stories. (Schneider and Ingram 1993, 334)

Schneider and Ingram argue that both agenda setting in public policy and the design of policies themselves are shaped by the social construction of the populations targeted. To explain how the public perception and the relative power of target groups shapes public policy, they construct a simple two-by-two table, one dimension of which is the political power of the groups targeted by a public policy, and the other of which is the social construction of the population targeted. This typology provides four different categories in which target populations are categorized: the advantaged, contenders, dependents, and deviants.

In this model, public policies are seen as instruments that distribute both benefits and costs (or burdens) to the affected target population. Different categories

Table 8.1

Social Constructions of Target Populations

| | Constructions | |
Power	Positive	Negative
Strong	*Advantaged*	*Contenders*
	Veterans	The Wealthy
	The Elderly	Labor Unions
Weak	*Dependents*	*Deviants*
	Children	Criminals
	People with Disabilities	Gangs
		Drug Addicts

Source: Adapted by the author from Schneider and Ingram 1993. Reprinted with the permission of Cambridge University Press.

of target populations will be treated in different ways through public policy. Groups constructed positively, and with relatively greater political power, such as the elderly, veterans, and business leaders and interests, are likely to be targeted by public policies that will be beneficial to them. Schneider and Ingram term this group the "advantaged." On the other hand, groups with relatively little political power who are perceived in negative terms are likely to be the objects of punitive public policies. Schneider and Ingram term this group "deviants," including such categories as drug addicts, communists, and flag burners. The group termed "contenders," who are negatively constructed but have political power, will have some control over the agenda-setting process, are likely to receive burdens that are more symbolic than actual, and are provided benefits in less visible ways than the advantaged groups. Examples include wealthy individuals and labor unions. The group identified as "dependents" will have little control over the agenda-setting process and will tend to receive more burdens than benefits, although they will receive more benefits than the "deviant" target populations. People with disabilities are generally seen as dependents, in need of public provision through no fault of their own. This categorization is summarized in Table 8.1.

Schneider and Ingram argue that elected officials will concentrate most of their efforts in the policymaking process toward two cells of this table: the "advantaged" and the "deviant." Such policies provide the greatest rewards in terms of public approval and translate into benefits in the electoral process (Schneider and Ingram 1993, 337). Thus, advantaged groups will receive more benefits than would be warranted by either their size or policy effectiveness considerations. Similarly, groups constructed as deviants will receive more burdens than would be warranted by their size or the scope of the perceived social problem that they represent.

Although they only briefly develop this point, Schneider and Ingram suggest that social policy is one arena in which it is particularly useful to examine the distinction between "dependents" and "deviants" (Schneider and Ingram 1997, 124). They note in particular that the termination of Aid to Families with Dependent Children (AFDC) results in part from the negative construction of its recipients as deviants, given

> increasingly negative constructions of the target groups as undisciplined persons unwilling to work or immoral mothers who have illegitimate children to garner the increase in their welfare checks. When dependent populations who have not done anything overtly deviant are, nevertheless, socially constructed in a negative manner, public officials want to enjoy the political benefits of appearing to be tough while avoiding the pitfalls of seeming to be mean. (1997, 124)

The "dependent" category is especially noteworthy because benefits provided to these groups must be justified, in part, by showing that those who receive benefits are deserving of them and by carefully constructing the policies so as to separate the deserving from the undeserving (Schneider and Ingram 1997, 138–40). Thus, public officials are more likely to write legislation that requires strict eligibility determinations for social policies targeted toward dependent populations, to ensure that deviants, or the undeserving, do not receive these benefits. The policies examined below show a shift in the construction of target populations from dependent to deviant status.

Another way to see the importance of the social construction of a target population for the nature of the public policies targeted toward them is in terms of what scholars who study the media call "framing." According to Nelson, Clawson, and Oxley, "frames act like plot or story lines, lending coherence to otherwise discrete pieces of information. . . . Frames organize the presentation of facts and opinion within a newspaper article or television news story" (1997, 568). Such framing has been especially important in the recent devolutions and terminations of social programs, especially in the two social programs discussed below. The "story line" or "plot" of program termination is that the program creates and sustains the deviancy of the recipients. Thus, the story goes, to treat the deviant target population in a way that is appropriate through public policy, the program must be terminated. In the policies examined below, the framing of these target populations was pervasive in the statements of public officials justifying policy termination, as well as in media reports on the policy areas involved. In addition, as will be illustrated below, gender and race play an important role in the framing of target populations (Daniels 1997; Mettler 1998; Mink 2003). We now turn to an application of the Schneider and Ingram model to policymaking in the social policy arena.

The Social Construction of Social Policy Target Populations

Social policy in the United States consists of two types of programs: social insurance programs and public assistance programs. Social insurance programs, such

Table 8.2

Social Constructions and Political Power in Social Policy

	Constructions	
Power	Positive	Negative
Strong:	*Advantaged*	*Contenders*
Social	Elderly:	Work-Based beneficiaries:
Insurance	Social security recipients	Worker's compensation
	Medicare	Unemployment insurance
	Medicaid—Long-term care	
	Widows (survivor's benefits)	
Weak:	*Dependents*	*Deviants*
Public	Children:	"Welfare" mothers
Assistance	School lunch	Teenage mothers
	Medicaid/health care	Jobless adults
	Food stamps	Unmarried low-income mothers
	Widows (under ADC)	and fathers
	Persons with disabilities	Racial/ethnic minorities

as Old Age Survivors and Disability Insurance (commonly known as social security), Medicare, and unemployment and worker's compensation, provide benefits for recipients based upon payments made into the program by the beneficiary or on his or her behalf. For example, both employers and employees pay social security taxes; recipients of social security are eligible for benefits upon retirement (or on the basis of a disabling condition) based upon these payments. On the other hand, public assistance programs, such as Temporary Assistance to Needy Families (TANF, formerly AFDC), Medicaid, Food Stamps, and General Assistance, are funded through general tax revenues.

Because of this difference in the funding mechanism for these two types of programs, the recipients of social insurance have generally been viewed very differently from the recipients of public assistance (Mettler 1998; Nelson 1990). People who receive social insurance benefits such as unemployment compensation or Medicare are seen as deserving of assistance and are relatively politically powerful among groups targeted by social policies. People receiving food stamps or TANF, on the other hand, are perceived as undeserving. Thus, the structure of the programs themselves provides the basis for very different levels of political power and influence among the target populations of these two types of programs. People who receive public assistance benefits consequently have very little political power, and are constructed at best as dependents and at worst as deviants. These differences in political power are reflected in Table 8.2, which provides a typology of political power and social construction of target populations in the arena of social policy.

However, it is not only the type of benefits that target populations receive that determines their placement in the Schneider and Ingram schematic; gender and race also play a significant role. Feminist scholars have argued that gender roles are socially constructed through a variety of mechanisms, including the socialization of children in families and by society, the structure of economic and political institutions, and the deployment of symbols (Scott 1986). Through these many mechanisms, children learn very early on what types of behavior are considered appropriate for their gender. Gender roles, in turn, have historically shaped the institutional structure of social policy in significant ways: social policies intended primarily for women have historically been structured to address the perceived needs of women in their gender role as mothers, whereas social policies designed primarily for men have focused on their attachment to wage labor through social insurance, unemployment, and pension programs (Abramovitz 1988; Gordon 1990, 1994; Mettler 1998; Mink 1995). Here, race and marital status have also been significant factors; advocates of the AFDC program passed in 1936 depicted recipients as white widowed mothers, in need of assistance through no fault of their own (Gordon 1994; Mink 1995). This differs greatly from the depiction of recipients during the debates over the 1996 welfare law, as well as in the proposed reauthorization bill, as we will see below.

Social policy takes gender into account by providing services in different forms for different gender roles, which in turn reinforces those roles. Programs intended to address men in their gender-appropriate roles generally relate benefits to working for wages and do not consider any family-related responsibilities that a worker may have. For example, in order to collect unemployment, one cannot have left employment for such reasons as conflicts with childcare, or caring for a sick or disabled child, since these reasons are considered a matter of personal choice. On the other hand, the program now called Temporary Assistance for Needy Families (TANF) was originally called Aid to Dependent Children (ADC) and later, AFDC, and was designed for single-mother families with minor children—that is, for (white) women in their traditional gender roles. The program was designed to provide support for mothers to care for children without working for wages, though the benefits were always so low that families generally could not survive on the benefit alone.

Indeed, there is some evidence that, as a result of the type of unemployment compensation rules noted, many women have utilized AFDC/TANF as a form of unemployment compensation (Mettler 1998, 150–57). Even before the 1996 welfare law more than 40 percent of women receiving AFDC had earnings from wages during the same year that they received benefits (Spalter-Roth et al. 1995). Further evidence for this claim is supported by another study, which found that of those women receiving AFDC who had substantial work hours, only 11 percent worked in jobs that were covered by unemployment insurance (Spalter-Roth, Burr, and Hartman 1994; see also Williams 1999). Of course, since the adoption of civil rights laws, men who are single parents and are otherwise eligible for AFDC/TANF do qualify and receive benefits; women who work for wages and are otherwise eligible receive unemployment insurance and social security on the same basis as eligible men. The point is that the structure of these programs was designed with assumptions about gender roles in mind.

In the social construction of gender-appropriate roles, race and class are important factors. For example, behavior that is perceived as gender-appropriate for white middle-class men will not be the same as behavior that is perceived as gender-appropriate for black working-class men. Think, for example, of the common scene in U.S. airports of one man shining another man's shoes, and try reversing the standard race and class markers of shiner and shinee. Social policies that are intended to target specific groups will be based on these perceptions about appropriate gender, race, and class roles. For example, it has been fairly clearly established that the exclusion of agricultural and domestic workers from eligibility for social security intended and resulted in the exclusion of most African American workers, especially in the South, from eligibility for social security benefits (Lieberman 1998; Mettler 1998; Quadagno 1988).

In times of policy devolution and termination, it is the contention here that public officials will construct target populations who are seen as failing to comply with appropriate gender/race/class roles as "deviants," and that consequently policy decisions will place greater burdens on these groups. Groups that are already marginalized in terms of political power, and who are constructed as "dependents" through public assistance programs, may move from that category to the category of "deviants" if the target population can be successfully depicted as "deviant" by policymakers. Thus, previously positive social constructions of politically powerless groups will be transformed in public discourse, in media presentations, and in agenda setting and policy formulation into negative constructions of these groups as "deviants" who deserve whatever burdens are placed upon them. These social constructions, in turn, will serve as justification for program termination. Such was the case in both of the policy changes examined here: the termination of General Assistance programs in Michigan in 1991, and, at the federal level, the end of the AFDC program in 1996.

The TANF program, established in 1996 to replace AFDC, was due to be reauthorized by Congress in 2002. At the time of this writing, however, no reauthorization bill has been finalized. Although in 2002 the Republican-controlled House passed a reauthorization bill, the Democrat-controlled Senate did not, and the existing program was extended through September of 2003. In February of 2003, the House passed a revised version of the bill it had passed the previous year. In September 2003, Congress extended the existing program through the end of March 2004. As of October, the Senate Finance Committee has approved a version of the legislation, but the full Senate chose to take no action until after the 2004 election. Thus, what is analyzed below is the legislation proposed during the 108th Congress; the sections relevant to the analysis were fairly similar in both versions.

Social construction can occur through many mechanisms. For present purposes,

we will consider the social construction of target populations in the policy termination cases through depictions of the population by political leaders and through
analysis of the deployment of cultural stereotypes regarding these populations in
the form that the policy itself takes, as contrasted with empirical data regarding the
actual demographic and other characteristics of the target population. For the proposed revisions to TANF, we will consider the legislation itself and the assumptions embedded in two sections of the proposed legislation.

Ending General Assistance in Michigan

Background

Prior to the New Deal, assistance was provided to impoverished people through
state and local governments. One of the reasons that federal social programs were
created during the New Deal was that state and local governments could not address the burden of providing assistance when unemployment rates skyrocketed
during the Great Depression. But, despite the programs created during the New
Deal period, and the expansion of social assistance through the Great Society programs of the 1960s, some impoverished people are not covered by federally funded
programs. Many state and local governments thus continue to provide assistance
to people who are not eligible for federal aid, through programs termed General
Assistance. Generally, General Assistance programs provide assistance for impoverished adults who do not have minor children living with them. These programs vary a great deal from state to state; in some states they are completely
locally administered, whereas in other states it is the state that administers the
program. The type of assistance also varies greatly from one state or local program
to the next: some provide only in-kind assistance or emergency aid, while others
provide ongoing monthly cash assistance based on eligibility.

Although a number of states were making major changes to their General Assistance programs in the late 1980s and early 1990s, Michigan was the only state
to completely terminate its program in that period (Begala and Bethel 1992). This
is what makes it a useful case for present purposes. In Michigan, the state-level
General Assistance program was created in the late 1970s, replacing previous county-
level programs. The program provided cash assistance. Most persons eligible for
this program were also eligible for other forms of assistance, such as food stamps
and housing assistance. At the time that the program was terminated in 1991, General Assistance required recipients to earn less than $262 monthly, to have total as-
sets of less than $250, and if the recipient owned a vehicle, its value could be no
more than $1,500. Total expenditures by the state for this program increased steadily
from its inception until 1985, when an improving economy led to decreasing numbers of recipients and thus declining expenditures (Thompson 1995, 82).

Opposition to the General Assistance (GA) program in Michigan grew during
the 1980s, and Republican representatives and senators made repeated attempts to

both curtail and eliminate the program (Thompson 1995, 85). In the 1980s, the Democratic party controlled both the House and the governorship, but this changed with the 1990 election of John Engler as governor. Engler's determination to end the program, and the political failings of his Democratic predecessor, Jim Blanchard, were important components in the demise of General Assistance. Another important factor was the fiscal crisis facing Michigan in the 1990–91 budget cycle. The termination of GA was part of an effort to reduce expenditures, given that the state had a budget shortfall. But the choice of termination of this particular program, rather than other possible solutions, such as across-the-board budget cuts, was related to the relative ease with which program termination could be justified for General Assistance. This in turn is related to the social construction of the population targeted by this program, who were depicted by public officials as able-bodied minority men who were unwilling to work, that is, "deviants."

Crucial to termination of the program was not only the reality of who received General Assistance in Michigan, but the public rhetoric that moved this group from the category of "dependent," and thus deserving of minimal support, to the category of "deviant." The realities of business cycles and capital mobility in capitalist economies mean that there will be cycles of unemployment, and that when capital exits a geographic area, workers will be displaced. This is the justification for programs such as unemployment insurance. General Assistance also provided assistance to persons displaced by these cyclical functions of a capitalist economy: many Michigan General Assistance recipients had received unemployment benefits in the past but were no longer eligible. A program such as General Assistance that is perceived as providing temporary support for workers displaced through no fault of their own constructs the target population in sympathetic terms, although they are relatively politically powerless. Therefore, at the time that the program was created, General Assistance recipients were originally constructed as "dependents" in Schneider and Ingram's typology.

Over the course of the 1980s, however, Michigan's economy was changing. De-industrialization, especially cutbacks in the auto industry, meant that unemployment rates remained very high throughout the 1980s in the state, and even higher in Detroit, where most of the GA recipients lived. In addition, real incomes were falling in Michigan in the 1980s, as they were in the rest of the country (Thompson 1995, 86). As a result, though many GA recipients worked for wages, many others were chronically unemployed. Given that unemployment rates among African American men have continued to be higher than rates among white men, even in times of economic prosperity, it is not surprising that a disproportionate number of GA recipients were African American men.

Gender and the Justification for Policy Termination

The justification for termination of the GA program involved, in part, constructing GA recipients as deviants. The demographic characteristics of recipients highlighted ways that the target population could be characterized in this way. In March of 1991, prior to the termination of the program, the Michigan Department of Social Services profiled the characteristics of recipients. Recipients were majority male (59 percent), predominantly African American (56 percent), and nearly half (49 percent) of the recipients lived in Detroit (Wayne County). Since the majority were also between the ages of sixteen and forty (60 percent), recipients were generally seen as able-bodied minority men who were able to work (Thompson 1995, 84). Those opposed to continuation of the program pictured recipients as "slackers" who were capable of working, but were not doing so because of an over-generous public program. Because men's appropriate gender role is to work for wages, and because urban minority men especially are seen as workers who should take any available job, it was fairly easy to depict GA recipients as deviants rather than dependents.

This perception was heightened by the way in which GA was terminated. Prior to termination, Governor Engler initiated the creation of two new programs to address the needs of subgroups of GA recipients who were still pictured as "dependents": families with children, who constituted 11.5 percent of recipients in March 1991, and recipients who were elderly or disabled, who constituted about 1 percent of recipients. These new programs were created with the intention of serving the "deserving" recipients of General Assistance. This isolation of the deserving recipients of GA made it possible to depict those who would lose their General Assistance benefits as "deviants." Moved from being seen as temporarily out of work (and therefore deserving dependents) to being seen as chronically unemployed despite being able-bodied adult men and capable of work, GA recipients could be depicted as deserving of the policy burden of benefits termination. Indeed, public officials argued that former recipients would be forced into the work force through policy termination and that they would thus benefit from termination of the program.

Through Engler's strategizing on budget cuts, the GA program was also set off and compared to other programs. In the spring of 1991, a standoff developed between the governor and the Democratic-controlled house. Engler wanted to terminate General Assistance to save costs; the Democrats favored other approaches to cost savings. As the standoff continued, the governor invoked the seldom-used State Administrative Board and transferred funds from the GA program to other social services programs. Legislators immediately filed suit, claiming that the funds transfer exceeded the authority of the Board, given that budget allocations are legislative, not executive, functions.[1] While the legislators eventually won in court, a legislative solution was eventually reached. Engler essentially presented the legislature with the choice of accepting across-the-board budget cuts to all social service programs, including Medicaid, or accepting the termination of GA (Thompson 1995). Thus, Engler provided legislators with explicit trade-offs between funding GA and funding other social services programs. Required to choose between target populations that had successfully been depicted as "deviants" and those still in the "dependent" category, the choice was simple. Enough Democrats crossed party lines to secure a vote for the termination of General Assistance, which ended in October of 1991.

Empirical Evidence Regarding the Target Population

How did this characterization of GA recipients as able-bodied male slackers, or deviants, compare with their actual ability to work? The Michigan Department of Social Services study conducted in 1991 indicated that only half of the recipients had a high school diploma, limiting the job opportunities available to them. Further, given that studies of GA programs indicate that receipt rates generally correspond with the unemployment rate—as unemployment rates go up, so does GA receipt (Halter 1996)—it is significant that most recipients lived in Wayne County, with the highest rates of unemployment, and of minority poverty, in the state of Michigan (Danziger and Kossoudji 1994/5). In a survey conducted two years after the policy was terminated, researchers found that large numbers of former recipients had health problems that interfered with their ability to work (Danziger and Kossoudji, 1994/5). In this study, 58 percent of all former recipients (all of whom had been classified as able-bodied by the state) reported chronic health problems that required medical attention. Of those respondents over forty, 77 percent had chronic health problems. By June of 1993, 15 percent of those studied were enrolled in a state or federal disability program—an indication that they were not able-bodied, given the stringency of disability program requirements (Danziger and Kossoudji 1994/5).

This study also indicated that most former GA recipients did not find permanent employment; although 38 percent had some work in 1992, only 5 percent worked in all four quarters of that year. Those who did find work did not earn enough to become self-sufficient; average wages were $650 per month. Only 12 percent had health insurance. Generally, the jobs and benefits that recipients had were worse than those that they had held while they received GA (Danziger and Kossoudji 1994/5).

The studies also indicate that public costs for providing assistance to this target population may not have been reduced, but rather shifted to different entities. For example, 25 percent of former GA recipients reported experiencing homelessness within seven months after the program was terminated. In addition, utilization of emergency rooms for medical services increased significantly after the end of GA. Since local public hospitals are required to provide services regardless of ability to pay, costs for the medical care provided to these former recipients were simply shifted to a different public entity (Hauser 1994, 1458–59). As Hauser puts it:

> [I]t is unclear whether costs are saved in the long run or are simply shifted to different agencies or arms of government, such as publicly funded shelters, public hospitals, other publicly funded service providers, and the criminal justice system. (Hauser 1994, 1459)

There is little evidence that GA recipients belong to a subculture that does not share mainstream American values regarding work. For example, respondents in a study by Kathleen Kost all indicated that they would prefer working for wages to receiving GA. This sentiment is made clear by the quote that forms the title of her study, from a statement made by one of the respondents: "A man without a job is a dead man." All of the recipients in this study had been employed, most in many different, short-term jobs, and all indicated that they preferred working to receiving GA; most indicated that they had used it only as a last resort (Kost 1996).

Thus, the depiction of GA recipients as deviants, able-bodied but unwilling to work, and likely to find employment if forced off of public assistance is not in accord with the empirical evidence. In this instance, it would seem that policymaking was driven more by budget constraints and the social construction of the target population than by empirical reality.

The 1996 Welfare Law: Ending Entitlement to Assistance

Background

When the program originally known as Aid to Dependent Children (ADC) was included in the Social Security Act of 1935, it was as a result of vigorous lobbying by women's groups that had been involved in the development of the state-based programs on which ADC was modeled. These programs, termed "mothers' pensions," were intended to provide financial assistance to women who were single mothers. At the state level, these programs were adopted beginning in 1911; by 1920, most states had such programs, although they were small in comparison to the need, and were intended not only to support children but to supervise women who were single mothers (Gordon 1994, 37–64). The ADC program was based on these mothers' pensions, and was added to the Social Security Act in a last-minute compromise (Gordon 1994, 253–85).

Crucial to the adoption of ADC was the framing of recipients in the category of deserving dependents by picturing the single-mother families that would benefit from the program as those of widows. The reformers who advocated for ADC knew that many single mothers who might benefit from the program had become so as a result of desertion or divorce, but chose not to emphasize this fact, fearing that this would erode support for the program (Gordon 1994, 281). Thus, ADC was depicted as a program that benefited the children of widows, and the legacy of moral supervision by social workers under the mothers' pensions was implicitly endorsed in the enactment of ADC. However, just four years after the adoption of the program, Old Age Survivors and Disability Insurance (commonly known as social security) was expanded so that widows and their children were eligible for survivors' benefits if the deceased spouse was an eligible worker (Orloff 1991, 272–73). These benefits were much more generous, and were offered through a national program, not the state-based discretionary programs of ADC. Thus, since

1939, most widows and their dependent children apply for and receive social security benefits.

As Gordon shows, the women reformers who drafted ADC legislation intended it to be a small and temporary program, hoping for more universal programs for families with children, which never materialized (Gordon 1994, 253–85). What happened instead was that this program was altered and expanded, until by the 1960s it had become one of the principal programs for children available in the partial, decentralized social welfare programs of the U.S. welfare state. As a result, instead of expanding social supports for all families with children, the programs developed in the New Deal divided citizens along gender lines and according to family structure, offering expansive benefits for beneficiaries of social insurance programs while limiting and restricting the inclusion of public assistance recipients as citizens (Mettler 1998). Despite the establishment of ADC as an entitlement program, meaning that all families who were eligible were entitled to receive benefits, it was still a state and locally implemented program, which meant that states were provided a great deal of discretion regarding whether and to what extent to implement the program. States utilized a variety of means, including moral supervision through the so-called "man in the house" rules—which required case workers to determine whether single-mother recipients were involved with a man, making them ineligible for benefits—as well as administrative exclusions, to keep the program relatively small in relation to the level of need.

Changes to the AFDC Program

The limited availability of ADC, now renamed Aid to Families with Dependent Children (AFDC), began to change in the 1960s due to several court decisions, as well as the advocacy of the welfare rights movement. The National Welfare Rights Organization (NWRO) was a grassroots movement in the late 1960s and early 1970s of poor women advocating for the rights of women receiving welfare. Among other things, the NWRO advocated for the enforcement of the entitlement status of welfare, insisting that everyone who requested an application for benefits had a right to apply, and that eligibility rules must be made clear to applicants. The NWRO also conducted public information campaigns, ensuring that people who might be eligible for public assistance benefits were aware of the programs. In part as a result of the work of the NWRO, the number of people receiving AFDC benefits expanded rapidly in the late 1960s and early 1970s (Amott 1990, 288–89).

As a result of this expansion of participation in the program, Congress enacted a series of changes to federal AFDC policy beginning in the 1960s. These changes increasingly encouraged participation in work and education programs, and introduced a number of cost-saving or cost-recovery measures, including the implementation of a program to collect child support from absent parents as a reimbursement for AFDC payments (Josephson 1997). States also were permitted to let their benefit levels fall in relation to inflation, so that the value of benefits decreased markedly from the early 1970s through 1996. The most extensive change prior to the 1996 law was the Family Support Act of 1988, a bipartisan effort that reformed a number of aspects of the AFDC program and created Job Opportunities and Basic Skills (JOBS), which was intended to provide support for recipients seeking work as well as work training through post-secondary education. JOBS provided assistance with expenses such as childcare and transportation for recipients who were working or were in school, as well as transitional assistance (such as continued health benefits) for those recipients who obtained paid employment. The services provided by JOBS were very popular with recipients, and many states had long waiting lists of those eligible for these services, which were chronically underfunded in most instances.

The effort to reform welfare in the 1990s began with President Clinton's campaign promise to "end welfare as we know it." The rhetoric called for extensive changes, including time limits and work requirements, despite the fact that in 1992, many provisions of the 1988 Family Support Act were only beginning to be implemented by the states. Upon election, Clinton promised to reform health care first, and only introduced his welfare reform proposal in the summer of 1994, after his health care proposal had died a very public death. The proposal, though watered down from the original proposal of Clinton's Domestic Policy Council, would have provided *more* funding for the JOBS program, expanding the number of eligible recipients, with the intention of providing them a path to education and training, and then to jobs that would offer wages that could support their families. The Domestic Policy Council argued that this was the only way to have effective welfare reform that would lead to self-sufficiency for former recipients. However, the proposed legislation died in committee in both Houses.

Campaigning in the 1994 mid-term election based on the Contract with America, the Republican party came to power in the House and the Senate promising, in part, to reform the welfare system. One of the ten items in the Contract was the Personal Responsibility Act (PRA), introduced as H.R. 4. This legislation, which was eventually passed by Congress but vetoed by the president in January of 1996, had many provisions that ended up in the Personal Responsibility and Work Opportunity Reconciliation Act (PRWORA) of 1996, which the president did sign. However, as originally introduced, it also would have changed entitlement and funding for the school lunch program and supplemental security income for disabled children, which provided part of the justification for Clinton's veto (Edelman 1997; U.S. House of Representatives 1996).

Perhaps most significant among the changes enacted with the elimination of AFDC and the creation of TANF through the 1996 law is the end of the entitlement status of AFDC through the creation of a block grant system of providing TANF benefits. Under an entitlement program, persons who are eligible for benefits are entitled to receive them, regardless of how many other people are receiving benefits. Entitlement programs are responsive to cyclical fluctuations in the economy: when there is an economic downturn, more persons will be eligible to receive benefits. In times of economic prosperity, on the other hand, more people will have earned income in amounts that make them ineligible for benefits, which are means-tested. With the new block grant system, the federal government provides a block grant to the states, but states may choose to limit the amount that they spend on the program, as long as they maintain at least 80 percent of their historic expenditures. Thus, persons otherwise eligible for benefits may be denied them on the basis of state limitations on the amount it will spend on the program, making the program less responsive to both individual circumstances and economic fluctuations.

More familiar changes in the 1996 law are the addition of work requirements and lifetime time limits. Many states had such provisions in their AFDC programs prior to the 1996 law, and states were given the option of continuing to follow their pre-existing programs. However, the federal law mandates that states require all recipients to work after two years of receipt of benefits and require community service work of beneficiaries after two months of assistance. The law also changes what is defined as work or work-related activity. Under previous law, recipients could participate in postsecondary education, including two- and four-year degree programs; such activities were defined as training, given that they were more likely to lead to higher-wage jobs and the ability to be self-sufficient in supporting one's family. The 1996 law eliminated postsecondary education as a work-related activity, limiting eligible training programs to those lasting twelve months or less, thus providing states with incentives to emphasize work first, regardless of the recipients' education or skill level. Recipients not meeting the work requirement may be sanctioned and/or terminated from the program. The time limits include a lifetime sixty-month (five-year) limit on receipt of benefits for any family including an adult recipient. Benefits will be terminated for all family members after five years total time receiving benefits. States are permitted to grant limited exemptions to the time limits.

These provisions are based on a set of perceptions of the target population of AFDC that see recipients as capable of working, but unwilling to do so. The incentives of time limits, work requirements, and the end of entitlement are based on the idea that recipients do not work for wages (which, as we will see below, is not accurate) and that they simply need the incentive to work in order to do so. The provisions also assume that recipients will be better off working for wages, regardless of their employment skills or educational backgrounds, than they would be receiving public benefits. As we will see, these perceptions differ in rather significant ways from both the actual characteristics and work experiences and opportunities of women receiving AFDC. However, first we will examine the role that the perception of women on AFDC as deviants played in the justification for the termination of this program.

It is important to note as well that the strategy of isolating the target population constructed as "deviant" occurred in the case of federal welfare reform as it did in the termination of General Assistance in Michigan. As noted, the original welfare legislation, the Personal Responsibility Act of 1995, called for block grants of the school lunch program and of supplemental security income. However, the school lunch program proved difficult to terminate, given that the federal aid provided through the program supplements the provision of hot lunches to all schoolchildren and benefits middle-class children as well. It is difficult to construct all school-age children in a negative light, and this proposal did not survive the legislative process. The early versions of PRWORA also included block grants for the Medicaid program (Edeleman 1997). However, President Clinton indicated early on that he would veto any effort to create block grants for the Medicaid program. This program actually benefits middle- and working-class voters, since most Medicaid expenditures go to long-term care recipients, especially elderly persons in nursing home care, because Medicare does not pay for long-term care. The beneficiaries are, for the most part, the parents and elderly relatives of middle- and working-class voters, and a block grant program that might have reduced these benefits would have been particularly unpopular with these groups (Edelman 1997, 46). The removal of block grant programs for Medicaid and for school lunches left AFDC as the primary program targeted for termination. Thus, AFDC recipients were isolated from other beneficiaries of social programs, constructed as deviant, and therefore deserving of policy burdens, regardless of the empirical evidence regarding this population.[2]

Gender and the Justification of Policy Termination

Negative constructions of recipients of AFDC were not new to the welfare debates of the 1990s. Indeed, when the first work requirements were added to the AFDC program in 1967, the debate focused on a characterization of AFDC recipients as "unmarried illiterate women with a massive number of children and a lack of appropriate parenting skills" (Williams 1997, 5). Racial imagery was prominent in the depictions of AFDC recipients as bad mothers, such as in Senator Jacob Javits's statement that the children whose families received AFDC were "from Harlem. That is what creates the problem. Forty-six percent of the people in Harlem are from broken homes" (Williams 1997, fn 101). Members of Congress, in 1967 and in 1996, argued that women who were single parents should be in the work force, and that they were using their children as an excuse not to work. Williams points out the contrast drawn during the debates between these irresponsible mothers on AFDC and responsible mothers who, if they are single parents, work for wages, or who are properly married to husbands who earn wages high enough that they are able to stay home and care for their children.

One significant factor in the changing perceptions of women on AFDC beginning in the 1960s is the changes that have occurred in women's roles, such that, by the 1990s, most women with young children worked for wages. These changes with respect to women's gender roles in relation to wage labor have been especially significant for middle-class white women: while 33.6 percent of white women participated in the labor force in 1960, 56.4 percent did so in 1988 (Ortiz 1994). African American women and Asian American women had higher rates of labor force participation than did white women in 1960, and continued to participate in the labor force at slightly higher rates in 1988. Latina women's labor force participation rates for this same period were relatively comparable to the labor force participation rates of white women, although this varies by subgroup (Ortiz 1994). As women's roles with respect to employment have changed, there has in turn been a change in perceptions of appropriate roles for women receiving AFDC. While the dominant perception of women's proper roles in 1935 when the legislation was first passed was that women, even single mothers, should stay at home with their children, by the 1990s, most women were working for wages, either full or part time. These changes in gender roles have been reflected in legislation regarding AFDC since the 1967 legislation noted above, as work requirements were increasingly added to the program until its termination in 1996.

As a result of these changes in gender roles in relation to work, as well as negative depictions of women who received AFDC in the media, by public officials, and by opponents of AFDC, the target population of AFDC moved from being seen as widows or single mothers through no fault of their own, who should be provided with public support to stay home and care for their children—that is, in terms of Schneider and Ingram's typology, from deserving dependents requiring support—to being seen as bad mothers, taking advantage of society through the AFDC program, passing their status as welfare recipients on to their children. Thus, despite being able-bodied and capable of work, these women refuse to do so. Public officials thus characterized recipients as able-bodied; capable of work, and therefore lazy; urban, minority, and sexually deviant females; addicted to public benefits and to their dependent status; and bad mothers, passing their dependency status on to their children. All of these characteristics added up to "deviant" status, since minority women's appropriate gender role is seen as being obligated to work for wages, not staying home and caring for their own children (Dill 1994).

The negative depictions of women on AFDC were particularly clear in the debates over the Personal Responsibility Act of 1995. During floor debates in the House, Representative John L. Mica of Florida compared welfare recipients to alligators. Noting signs posted in Florida that read "Do Not Feed the Alligators," he stated:

> [W]e post these warnings because unnatural feeding and artificial care creates dependency. When dependency sets in, these otherwise able-bodied alligators can no longer survive on their own. Now, I know that people are not alligators, but I submit to you that with our current handout, nonwork welfare system, we have upset the natural order. . . . We have created a system of dependency. (Congressional Record 1995, H3766)

In a similar vein, Representative Barbara Cubin of Wyoming compared welfare recipients to wolves:

[R]ecently the Federal Government introduced wolves into the state of Wyoming, and they put them in pens and they brought elk and venison to them every day. This is what I call the wolf welfare program. The Federal Government introduced them and they have since then provided shelter and they have provided food, they have provided everything that the wolves need for their existence. Guess what? They opened the gate to let the wolves out and now the wolves will not go. They are cutting the fence down to make the wolves go out and the wolves will not go. What has happened with the wolves, just like what happens with human beings, when you take away their incentives, when you take away their freedom, when you take away their dignity, they have to be provided for. . . . Just like any animal in the species, any mammal, when you take away their freedom and their dignity and their ability, they cannot provide for themselves. (Congressional Record 1995, H3772)

Other members objected to the imagery, and these references were widely reported in the press. Although clearly all members of Congress did not agree with these depictions, the fact that some members felt free to characterize welfare recipients as animals on the floor of the House makes very clear that the target population of AFDC was being pegged as deviants. The justification for terminating AFDC, and for the policy burdens of lifetime time limits for both parents and children, work requirements even for mothers with very young children, and the elimination of funding for educational programs, was based on this construction of AFDC recipients as deviant single mothers who are able-bodied and simply unwilling to work.

Empirical Evidence Regarding the Target Population

How did the characterization described above compare to actual characteristics of recipients? First, it is crucial to note that the above depictions focus almost exclusively on adult recipients of AFDC, although two-thirds of recipients in 1996 were children (under eighteen) and half of those children were under the age of six. In addition, the characterization that AFDC recipients are unwilling to work is an inaccurate depiction of their actual behavior, as has been documented in numerous scholarly studies. For example, in a study of a nationally representative sample utilizing data from the Survey of Income and Program Participation, Spalter-Roth and colleagues found that 43 percent of the women in their sample either worked while they were receiving AFDC or cycled from work to AFDC and back to work (Spalter-Roth et al. 1995). They also found that more than half of those who did not work spent substantial amounts of time looking for work. Thus, most of the women (about 70 percent) in this study demonstrated their willingness to work either by working or by looking for work. This does not accord with the image presented of women unwilling to work for wages. However, most of the women in the sample worked in jobs at or near the minimum wage, and often were not able to obtain full-time employment. Thus, they were unable to lift their families out of poverty through their work, despite their willingness to work.

Another study, by Kathryn Edin and Laura Lein, involved interviews with women on welfare and women in low-wage work in four U.S. cities. The study found that, because the benefits that they received through AFDC and food stamps were simply not enough to cover their families' basic needs, most AFDC recipients supplemented benefits with other income from wages, contributions from family members, or from other sources. In addition, about half of all the welfare recipients in this study had worked in the formal economy during the previous year (Edin and Lein 1997, 221). Sixty percent of the wage-reliant women in the study had used AFDC recently. Therefore, Edin and Lein argue, women in low-wage jobs and women receiving welfare should be seen as "two overlapping populations on a single continuum" (1997, 220). In general, they found that women in low-wage jobs were often worse off than their counterparts on welfare, given the added expenditures for childcare, medical care, and transportation that go with working for wages.

Edin and Lein also utilized their study to test the thesis that women who receive AFDC are part of a deviant "culture of poverty." They looked at differences among the women based on welfare status, marital status, family background, neighborhood, and race and ethnicity to see what effect these factors had on their abilities to manage their meager funds, whether they engaged in work, what kinds of social networks they utilized to obtain additional economic support, and whether they utilized the assistance of charitable agencies to supplement their resources. They found that women on welfare were actually more frugal and more capable of managing their resources than were the women who worked for wages. They found that African American and Mexican American mothers spent significantly less, on average, than did white mothers. They found that the vast majority of the women in their sample wanted to work for wages and had fairly realistic ideas about the amount that they would need to earn (at least eight dollars an hour) to provide minimal support for their families. Overall, their data contradicted in many ways the thesis that women on AFDC are somehow part of a "deviant" subgroup, with values different than those of the mainstream culture (Edin and Lein 1997, 192–217).

Perhaps most significantly, the Edin and Lein study, which involved repeated in-depth interviews with 379 women, found that the consistent theme of these mothers, whether wage-reliant or welfare-reliant, was that they were trying to provide the economic support necessary to ensure their children's well-being. The series of economic choices that these women made, based on the fact that their monthly expenditures for basic needs exceeded their monthly income, whether from wages or AFDC or a combination thereof, were based on their efforts to protect and provide for their children. As the authors put it, "our data . . . strongly suggest that most women usually behaved in ways that reflected reasoned calculations of which alternatives would be likely to expose their children to the least harm" (Edin and Lein 1997, 221).

The contrast between the empirical evidence regarding women receiving AFDC in 1996 and the description offered by political leaders and policy entrepreneurs provides compelling evidence of the way in which the target population of public policy is socially constructed in a way very different from the reality of actual policy targets. Once again, policymaking was driven by the social construction of a dehumanized, deviant female subject rather than by empirical evidence regarding the characteristics of the target population and the means by which their poverty might be alleviated.

Reauthorization of TANF: Gender, Race, and Marital Parenthood

As noted above, TANF has not yet been reauthorized, so the 1996 version is still in place. Several proposed revisions are particularly significant to the above analysis, however, and are fairly similar in bills proposed in both the House and Senate. Particularly relevant to a gender analysis of welfare law, both versions add designated funding streams for marriage-promotion and family formation, and for fatherhood programs. Although the 1996 TANF legislation permitted state use of funds for marriage promotion, it did not provide any specific federal funding for these programs. In addition, both proposed bills alter the stated purposes of the TANF program and explicitly add language that states that one purpose is to "encourage the formation and maintenance of healthy, two-parent married families and encourage responsible fatherhood." The existing TANF program states this purpose as "encourage the formation and maintenance of two-parent families." Thus, the new legislation specifically states that desirable two-parent families are "married" and that "responsible fatherhood" is part of the purpose of the program. The term "healthy" was not in the originally proposed legislation, but was added due to concerns regarding domestic violence, to ensure that states would not be required to promote marriage regardless of the presence of domestic violence in parental relationships (United States Congress 2003).

These proposals are clearly intended to promote one particular form of familial life: the gendered, heterosexual, marital family (Josephson and Burack 1998). Further, the type of assistance provided indicates the nature of the perceived deviancy of low-income families, as well as some rather interesting assumptions about the types of assistance that these families require in order to come into compliance with this ideal. The Senate and House versions of the bill provide different amounts of funding for the "Fatherhood Program," but both provide most of their funds for "demonstration projects" aimed at promoting responsible fatherhood.

What is meant by responsible fatherhood? Although the goals differ somewhat in the House and Senate versions of the proposed legislation, the focus is not on providing services to fathers to, for example, improve their job skills or educational attainment, but rather to, for example, improve "fathers' family business management skills through education and counseling" (H.R. 4). Clearly, what low-income fathers need in the congressional imaginary is not better jobs skills, or even more income, but rather better money management skills. Further, in both versions of the bill, the majority of these demonstration projects will be conducted not by state agencies but by nonprofits, including religious organizations. In addition, the Senate bill would provide $25 million annually for state and federal "responsible fatherhood" media campaigns.

The marriage-promotion activities divide funding between Health and Human Services (HHS) and the states, and list similar activities eligible for grant funding. Interestingly, the only place where "financial management" is mentioned as a service provided to mothers is in services to "unmarried pregnant women and expectant fathers." Obviously, if a man is present in the family, Congress assumes that he is the one who should manage the family's finances. Both bills also permit spending on public advertising campaigns promoting marriage, and on marriage education programs in high schools. Both bills also permit provision of these services to individuals and couples who are not eligible for TANF benefits—in other words, to families who are not low-income families. At the same time, both versions require significant increases in the work participation rates required of recipients and of states' overall caseloads, without increasing federal funding for childcare. Thus, states will need to either come up with additional money for childcare or cut childcare services even while requiring more work. States will also have increased incentives to remove recipients who are unable to work from their caseloads to avoid federal sanctions. While the overall impact of these provisions will depend, of course, on the details of implementation, what is clear is that this legislation sees low-income families as requiring assistance in developing proper attitudes toward marriage and fatherhood, and in complying with proper gender roles, but not in receiving additional resources to facilitate work, such as funding to pay for childcare or transportation. Clearly, program recipients are viewed as deviants deserving of policy burdens, and marriage is viewed as the optimum solution to their problems.

This proposal for marriage promotion was proposed by the Bush administration in part to satisfy the concerns of Bush's conservative base in an election year (Pear and Kirkpatrick 2004). The proposal to spend $1.5 billion over a five-year period on this initiative is seen as a way to satisfy conservative concerns about traditional marriage and help Bush present himself as a "compassionate conservative" (Pear and Kirkpatrick 2004, A1). Since conservatives see not only contemporary trends among heterosexuals with respect to marriage, but also the prospect of same-sex marriage as threatening to their conception of the institution of marriage, the promotion of this policy could prove very useful to the Bush administration in shoring up its base, regardless of whether the policies actually work.

Empirical Evidence

The marriage promotion provisions of the proposed reauthorization bill assume that low-income parents need to be encouraged to be interested in marriage, and that marriage will in fact be desirable in the vast majority of low-income families. The legislation also assumes that these types of services will be more helpful to low-income families than would additional funding for childcare or for job skills acquisition. But none of these assumptions bear up under scrutiny. Further, feminists, and others concerned with privacy, may wonder whether the state should be in the business of promoting marriage for low-income couples who receive public benefits.

With respect to the assumption that marriage is a desirable goal for low-income families, there is a great deal of research indicating that family formation patterns and patterns with respect to parental support of and contact with children is a good deal more complex than this one-size-fits-all model assumes (Coontz 1992, 1998; Josephson 2001; Mincy 2002; Stacey 1997). For example, even Ronald Mincy, who is neither a feminist nor a critic of marriage, argues that policies that encourage marriage for low-income families without taking into account the variety of situations of these families and racial and ethnic variations in family formation may in fact harm low-income fathers in particular (Mincy 2002). There is also evidence from a number of studies, including the study of "fragile families" conducted jointly by Princeton and Columbia universities, that low-income men and women do value and respect marriage, but that economic factors are key in decisions with respect to when and whether to marry (Edin 2000; Jones-DeWeever 2002). Indeed, among those advocates who work with low-income fathers, the prospect of promoting marriage as the primary solution to help these fathers connect with and support their children is not seen favorably (Gavanas 2002; Mincy 2002).

Part of the problem here is a problem of social science evidence and a question of the direction of the causal arrow. Conservatives see differences between poverty levels in married families and in single-parent and cohabiting families and conclude that marriage causes economic well-being. More nuanced interpretations of the existing evidence, however, seem to indicate that the causal arrow points the other direction: economic well-being may cause marriage. Thus, to improve the economic well-being of low-income children, it may be better to provide more job training and educational opportunities for low-income mothers and fathers.

Conclusion

As noted at the outset of this chapter, much policymaking is not about rational choices based on empirical evidence, but rather is the result of a series of political calculations regarding the populations targeted by public policies. This chapter has argued that, in times of austerity, when social programs are being cut, target populations are constructed as deviant by policymakers through a use of their perceived compliance with appropriate gender-, race-, and class-based social roles, irrespective of empirical evidence regarding the characteristics of target populations. In the two programs examined, these depictions differed by gender: although both AFDC and GA recipients were characterized as deviant for not having earnings from wage labor (despite the fact that, as noted, many in both populations actually did have such earnings), women on AFDC were also characterized as deviant for being "bad mothers." Their deviancy derived from the circumstances that made them eligible for the program itself: their status as single mothers. In these two cases, both groups were characterized as deviant for failing to comply with gender role expectations. These evaluations were used by policymakers to construct the target population as deviant, and therefore deserving of public policy burdens through termination of public programs. These negative constructions were in turn used to justify policy terminations to the public, and to those opposed to policy termination.

Budget shortfalls and changes in political ideology and perceptions of public assistance programs certainly help to explain why budget cuts in social policy were on the political agenda in each of these cases. However, the model utilized here helps explain why programs with politically weaker target populations were proposed for termination. It also helps to explain why the programs that were actually terminated were those whose target population was successfully constructed by policymakers as deviant. And, as I have shown, this deviancy had much to do with the perceived failure of the target population to conform with the role expectations suited to their gender, race, and class status.

Notes

1. See *Dodak et al. v. Miller et al.* 191 Mich. App. 689; 479 N.W.2d 361 [1991].
2. It should be noted that this same legislation imposed policy burdens on immigrants as well, which is beyond the scope of this chapter, but could be subjected to a similar analysis.

References

Abramovitz, Mimi. 1988. *Regulating the Lives of Women: Social Welfare Policy from Colonial Times to the Present.* Boston: South End Press.
Amott, Teresa L. 1990. "Black Women and AFDC: Making Entitlement out of Necessity." In *Women, the State, and Welfare*, ed. Linda Gordon, pp. 280–298. Madison: University of Wisconsin Press.
Begala, John A., and Carol Bethel. 1992. "A Transformation Within the Welfare State." *Journal of State Government* 65, 1 (January): 25–30.
Congressional Record, 104th Congress, 1st session, 1995, Vol. 141. March 24.
Coontz, Stephanie. 1992. *The Way We Never Were: American Families and the Nostalgia Trap.* New York: Basic Books.
———. 1998. *The Way We Really Are: Coming to Terms with America's Changing Families.* New York: Basic Books.
Daniels, Cynthia. 1997. "Between Fathers and Fetuses: The Social Construction of Male Reproduction and the Politics of Fetal Harm." *Signs* 22(3): 579–616.
Danziger, Sandra K., and Sherrie A Kossoudji. 1994/5. "What Happened to General Assistance Recipients in Michigan?" www.irp.wisc.edu/publications/focus.htm.
Dill, Bonnie Thornton. 1994. "Fictive Kin, Paper Sons, and Compadrazgo: Women of Color and the Struggle for Family Survival." In *Women of Color in U.S. Society*, ed. Maxine Baca Zinn and Bonnie Thornton Dill. Philadelphia: Temple University Press.

Donovan, Mark C. 1997. "The Problem with Making AIDS Comfortable: Federal Policy Making and the Rhetoric of Innocence." *Journal of Homosexuality* 32(3/4): 115–144.

Edelman, Peter. 1997. "The Worst Thing Bill Clinton Has Done." *The Atlantic Monthly* 279(3): 43–58.

Edin, Kathryn. 2000. "Few Good Men: Why Poor Mothers Don't Marry or Remarry." *The American Prospect* 28, January 3: 26–31.

Edin, Kathryn, and Laura Lein. 1997. *Making Ends Meet: How Single Mothers Survive Welfare and Low-Wage Work.* New York: Russell Sage Foundation.

Gavanas, Anna. 2002. "The Fatherhood Responsibility Movement: The Centrality of Marriage, Work and Male Sexuality in Reconstructions of Masculinity and Fatherhood." In *Making Men into Fathers: Men, Masculinities, and the Social Politics of Fatherhood*, ed. Barbara Hobson, pp. 213–242. New York: Cambridge University Press.

Goetz, Edward G., and Mara S. Sidney. 1997. "Local Policy Subsystems and Issue Definition: An Analysis of Community Development Policy Change." *Urban Affairs Review* 32, 4 (March): 490–512.

Gordon, Linda. 1990. *Women, the State, and Welfare.* Madison: University of Wisconsin Press.

———. 1994. *Pitied But Not Entitled: Single Mothers and the History of Welfare.* New York: The Free Press.

Halter, Anthony P. 1996. "State Welfare Reform for Employable General Assistance Recipients: The Facts Behind the Assumptions." *Social Work* 41, 1 (January): 106–110.

Hauser, Sandra. 1994. "Jobless, Penniless, Often Homeless: State General Assistance Cuts Leave 'Employables' Struggling for Survival." *Clearinghouse Review* (April): 1456–1459.

Hogan, Nancy Lynne. 1997. "The Social Construction of Target Populations and the Transformation of Prison-based AIDS Policy: A Descriptive Case Study." *Journal of Homosexuality* 32(3/4): 77–114.

Ingram, Helen, and Anne Schneider. 1991. "The Choice of Target Populations." *Administration & Society* 23(3): 333–356.

Jones-DeWeever, Avis. June 2002. "Marriage Promotion and Low-Income Communities: An Examination of Real Needs and Real Solutions." Institute for Women's Policy Research Briefing Paper #D450. Washington, DC: Institute for Women's Policy Research.

Josephson, Jyl J. 1997. *Gender, Families, and State: Child Support Policy in the United States.* Lanham, MD: Rowman & Littlefield.

———. 2001. "Liberal Justice and the Political Economy of Children's Well-Being." *New Political Science* 23(3): 389–406.

Josephson, Jyl J., and Cynthia Burack. 1998. "The Political Ideology of the Neo-Traditional Family." *Political Ideologies* 3(2): 213–231.

Kost, Kathleen A. 1996. "'A Man Without a Job Is a Dead Man': The Meaning of Work and Welfare in the Lives of Young Men." Madison, WI: Institute for Research on Poverty, Discussion Paper no. 1112–96.

Lieberman, Robert. 1998. *Shifting the Color Line: Race and the American Welfare State.* Cambridge: Harvard University Press.

Mettler, Suzanne. 1998. *Dividing Citizens: Gender and Federalism in New Deal Public Policy.* Ithaca, NY: Cornell University Press.

Mincy, Ronald B. 2002. "What About Black Fathers?" *The American Prospect* 13(7), April 8: 56–58.

Mink, Gwendolyn. 1995. *The Wages of Motherhood: Inequality in the Welfare State, 1917–1942.* Ithaca, NY: Cornell University Press.

———. 2003. "From Welfare to Wedlock: Marriage Promotion and Poor Mothers' Inequality." pp. 207–218. In *Fundamental Differences: Feminists Talk Back to Social Conservatives*, ed. Cynthia Burack and Jyl Josephson. Lanham, MD: Rowman and Littlefield.

Nelson, Barbara. 1990. "The Origins of the Two-Channel Welfare State: Workmen's Compensation and Mother's Aid." In *Women, the State, and Welfare*, ed. Linda Gordon, pp. 123–151. Madison: University of Wisconsin Press.

Nelson, Thomas E., Rosalee A. Clawson, and Zoe M. Oxley. 1997. "Media Framing of a Civil Liberties Conflict and Its Effect on Tolerance." *American Political Science Review* 91(3): 567–598.

Orloff, Ann Shola. 1991, "Gender in Early U.S. Social Policy." *Journal of Policy History* 3(3): 249–281.

Ortiz, Vilma. 1994. "Women of Color: A Demographic Overview." In *Women of Color in U.S. Society*, ed. Maxine Baca Zinn and Bonnie Thornton Dill, pp. 13–40. Philadelphia: Temple University Press.

Pear, Robert, and David D. Kirkpatrick. 2004. "Bush Plans $1.5 Billion Drive for Promotion of Marriage: Officials Try to Address Conservatives' Concerns." *The New York Times*, January 14, 2004, A1.

Quadagno, Jill. 1988. "From Old-Age Assistance to Supplemental Security Income: The Political Economy of Relief in the South, 1935–1972." In *The Politics of Social Policy in the United States*, ed. Margaret Weir, Ann Shola Orloff, and Theda Skocpol. Princeton: Princeton University Press.

Schneider, Anne, and Helen Ingram. 1993. "Social Construction of Target Populations: Implications for Politics and Policy." *American Political Science Review* 87(2): 334–347.

———. 1997. *Policy Design for Democracy*. Lawrence: University Press of Kansas.

Scott, Joan. 1986. "Gender: A Useful Category for Historical Analysis." *American Historical Review* 91: 1053–75.

Sidney, Mara S. 2003. *Unfair Housing: How National Policy Shapes Community Action*. Lawrence: University Press of Kansas.

Spalter-Roth, Robert, Beverly Burr, and Heidi Hartman. 1994. *Income Insecurity: The Failure of Unemployment Insurance to Reach Working AFDC Mothers*. Washington, DC: Institute for Women's Policy Research.

Spalter-Roth, Robert, Beverly Burr, Heidi Hartman, and Lois Shaw. 1995. "Welfare that Works: The Working Lives of AFDC Recipients." *Focus* 17, 2 (Fall/Winter): 10–12.

Stacey, Judith. 1997. *In the Name of the Family: Rethinking Family Values in the Postmodern Age*. Boston: Beacon.

Stone, Deborah. 1997. *Policy Paradox*. New York: W.W. Norton.

Thompson, Lyke. 1995. "The Death of General Assistance in Michigan." In *The Politics of Welfare Reform*, ed. Donald F. Norris and Lyke Thompson, pp. 79–108. Thousand Oaks, CA: Sage Publications.

U.S. Congress. House of Representatives. 1996. Personal Responsibility and Work Opportunity Act of 1995—Veto Message from the President of the United States. (House Document No. 104–164), p. H342.

———. 2003. Personal Responsibility, Work, and Family Promotion Act of 2003. H.R. 4. 104th Congress, first session.

Williams, Lucy. 1997. "Decades of Distortion: The Right's 30-Year Assault on Welfare." Somerville, MA: Political Research Associates.

———. 1999. "Unemployment Insurance and Low-Wage Work." In *Hard Labor: Women and Work in the Post-Welfare Era*, ed. Joel F. Handler and Lucie White, pp. 158–174. Armonk, NY: M.E. Sharpe.

9

"Women Get Sicker; Men Die Quicker"
Gender, Health Politics, and Health Policy

Sue Tolleson-Rinehart

Sex: The classification of living things, generally as male or female, according to their reproductive organs and functions assigned by chromosomal complement. (Institute of Medicine 2001, 17)

Gender: A person's self-representation as male or female, or how that person is responded to by social institutions based on the individual's gender presentation. Gender is rooted in biology and shaped by environment and experience. (Institute of Medicine 2001, 17)

"Women get sicker, men die quicker" was once the dismissive rubric about sex differences taught to medical students; except with regard to fertility and child-birth, the health care system paid little attention to "men's health" or "women's health." In this chapter, I argue that underlying beliefs about gender have affected health care and, potentially, women's health, by making women at least secondary, and at most invisible, to the medical establishment, *except* in terms of reproduction.

The odd consequence of the *gendering* of health care and health research is that it has obscured the system's ability to engage in a truly rigorous evaluation of the conditions under which *sex*, as biology, does and does not matter to health and health care (quite apart from reproduction). Uncritical acceptance of gender role attitudes has helped to perpetuate a paradoxical approach to women's health, and the very fact that the paradox has persisted, unchallenged by those trained to think critically as "scientists," shows the power of gender as an organizing principle.

The paradox is this: On the one hand, women have been seen as *not* different enough from men, or important enough in their own right, to warrant research on their health. On the other hand, women have been seen as *so* different from men that the scientific community has often "defined" women's health almost entirely in terms of women's reproductive roles. The health care system has behaved as if men have "health" and women have "women's health"—but "women's health" is only about reproduction. The paradox produces an environment in which we have access to considerable information on women's reproductive and breast ailments,

but we know much less about the other ways in which women and men may meaningfully differ. We have too little information on the myriad *non*-sex-related health
challenges women face, and too much confusion about when biology and/or gender may, or may not, influence men's and women's health and response to illness.

The political culture of gender is powerful enough to have imbued the entire
health system—from researchers and policymakers to providers and patients, including women themselves, with an assumption that there is "health" and "women's
health." Recent changes have brought new attention to gender, biology, health
politics, and health policy, but that attention has not always resulted in good policy.
In this chapter, I provide a brief review of U.S. health care and gender ideology,
after which I examine the history of medical research (or lack thereof) on women.
I then illustrate the chapter's points with the example of controversies over breast
cancer screening. I conclude with a discussion of some of the consequences of
viewing health through a gendered lens. The entire discussion is guided by three
questions:

- Does two decades of "women's health" policy activity mean that we have
  succeeded in breaking the constraints imposed by a gendered view of women's
  health?
- Should reproduction be the sine qua non of women's health?
- In the words of the subtitle of a recent Institute of Medicine (IOM) study,
  "Does Sex Matter?" (IOM 2001).

The Practice of Medicine

In most human cultures over time, the practice of medicine has been a matter of
tradition, the passing of the current state of knowledge from one generation to the
next. Most "knowledge" has accrued from anecdotal experience that was experimental in spirit, but was essentially the result of individual attempts to link cause
and effect through case-by-case observations. Today, much of what physicians,
surgeons, nurses, pharmacists, and other caregivers do continues to be the result of
the same kind of iterative process—these practitioners administer treatments or
use techniques that they have learned from their own teachers and textbooks, or
that they judge to be effective based on observations of the health outcomes of
patients in their care. The health care establishment, perhaps understandably, seldom pauses to consider whether this concatenation of biomedical knowledge has
been influenced by other phenomena, like perceptions of gender.

The body of medical knowledge, moreover, is now transmitted and applied in
the context of an extraordinarily large, complex, and costly system. The contemporary politics of health care finance and delivery is Byzantine. Debates over the
form our health care system-should take are bitter, and the stakes, in money and
human well-being, are huge. This space is not adequate to describe the workings
of the entire system, but some examples will suffice. In the United States, we spent

$5,440 per person for health care in 2002, making our system the costliest in the world. Our aggregate health care spending is a mind-boggling $1.6 trillion per year, or 14.9 percent of our GDP (Levit, Smith, Cowan et al. 2004). Our mixed public–private system of health coverage relies significantly on employer-sponsored premiums (note "sponsored," not paid; it is well accepted that employees themselves pay for their own premiums, in the form of lower wages). That cost now exceeds $7,000 per year for family coverage. Although this system delivers some level of health care to about 176 million people, 14 percent of the population is uninsured—and over half of that group is in the workforce.

Another 80 million or so Americans are a part of the public health insurance system. The public insurance system covers those age sixty-five and older, and some nonelderly persons under certain conditions, through Medicare; it covers some poor people through Medicaid (and some poor elderly people are eligible for both forms of assistance); it covers some children through the State Children's Health Insurance Programs; and it covers those who are serving or have served in the military through the Department of Defense's TriCare system (for active military) and through the Department of Veterans' Affairs' VA health system (Carroll 2003; Cubanski and Kline 2003).

Whether this state of affairs is good or bad, whether we should have a nationalized health system or leave health care to the private, for-profit sector, and whether our health system is the "best in the world" or is facing a "quality chasm," are strongly, and perpetually, argued. But, best or worst, a bargain or horrifyingly expensive, the health care system's orientation to women has been reflexive, rather than reflective. By that, I mean that the system has been *reflexive* in its narrow, and virtually automatic, view of women as reproductive systems and women's health as reproductive health. One might also say that the system has been almost as narrow in its view of men as virtually "sexless," in the sense that it has not recognized the role sex might play in men's health, except for attention to some disorders of the Y chromosome and a couple of male reproductive ailments. A *reflective* view, on the other hand, is one that is prepared to explore meaningful sex differences *and* their absences, beyond chromosomes and reproduction, as both more illuminating and more accurate. This more reflective view would also alert us to unsupportably gendered approaches to health as well.

To take one simple example, "gender-rating" in health insurance—that is, the practice of charging women higher premiums than men are charged, may once again be on the rise (Kaiser Daily Health Report 2004). This controversial practice, challenged by feminists in the 1980s and outlawed in some states, is grounded in the assumption that women use more health services because of childbearing and longer life expectancy, and thus should pay more for health insurance—that is, that "women get sicker and men die quicker"—without a more detailed analysis of health care costs and expenditures by sex and through the life cycle. Such an analysis, for example, would reveal that the total "national bill" for women's hospitalizations in 2001 was indeed higher than was the "national bill" for men's hospitalizations, but that men's average hospital stays were consistently more expensive than were women's, across every age group (statistics from author query of HCUPNet, the Healthcare Cost and Utilization Project interactive database; HCUPNet 2003). Further analysis would show that, while women consume more health services than do men as young adults—including more preventive care that may lead to lower long-run health care costs—men begin to outpace women in the amount and cost of medical care by their mid to late fifties. Women are also more likely to be insured than are men—that is, they or their households are, in fact, already more likely to be contributing all or most of the cost of the care they consume. This more complex analysis, then, might suggest that simplistic "gender-rating" does not provide us with as accurate or detailed information to plan the workforce's health care needs and health care costs as we need, quite aside from simple questions of fairness.

Nor have we accumulated much scientific evidence to help us understand when we should be on the alert for meaningful sex differences in health and illness. Even in our highly complex modern health care system, the accumulation and use of biomedical knowledge has largely continued according to traditional beliefs about the practice of medicine. Startling, revolutionary breakthroughs in science and public health—the discovery of essential anatomical functions, the germ theory of disease, the ability to conduct surgery on patients who stood a chance of surviving the operation, or the discovery of antibiotics, for example—have been the exception rather than the rule of accumulated medical knowledge. Instead, medical research is more likely to proceed in small steps—and its agendas are no more immune than are others to being shaped by the forces of popular culture and politics.

In the best of all possible worlds, we would surely prefer that all health care be rooted in sound scientific evidence. In real-world medical practice, the majority of what caregivers do, however, is *not* "evidence-based." Research takes time and a great deal of money, and not every question attracts the interest or resources of researchers. Many other questions, even compelling ones, do not easily lend themselves to controlled research studies, whether for reasons of ethics, feasibility, or the limits of our capacity to investigate them. When evidence does exist, it is likely to be conflicting, inconclusive, and variable in its quality. Even the most rigorous development of measures of quality health care for women finds that only 40 percent of its indicators are backed up by "strong" scientific evidence (McGlynn, Kerr, Damberg, and Asch 2000).

The "Practice" of Gender in Health Policy and Health Politics

It should be no surprise that cultural preferences and political ideology play just as large a role today as they ever did in medicine's more traditional past—or larger, perhaps, for being less obviously recognized now. Because medical researchers and practitioners consider themselves to be "objective" scientists, they can be resistant to the idea that the parameters around the research questions they think important, or

the practice strategies they believe to be the best, are influenced by or at least suscep-
tible to cultural and political framing (Kinder 2003; Taber 2003) and the value structures underlying cultural and political orientations (Feldman 2003).

Nowhere is this framing more evident—and more challenging—than in the
case of gender, health politics, and health policy. In fact, except for research related to reproductive and breast health, what evidence we have seems to suggest
that women have been excluded from, or underrepresented in, a considerable amount
of biomedical research (Institute of Medicine 1994), most likely as a result of
strongly protectionist stances on the potential of research to cause fetal injury (in
the case of pregnant women research subjects), or because women have been seen
as "too difficult" to study, or for both reasons. Gender role ideology clearly frames—
or limits—both approaches.

Sapiro (2003, 602–603) notes four ways in which gender frames our thinking:
First, it is socially constructed and historically shaped. Second, some of its norms
have become "naturalized" or treated as fundamental facts of life. Third, gender has
been the source of differentiation of people into different tasks, activities, and institutional positions. Finally, gender has been the basis not just of differentiation but of
inequality: "research has yet to find a society," says Sapiro, "in which gender is
irrelevant to the division of power and authority" (2003, 603). The effect of all four
frames can be seen in health policy: gender role ideology is logically and historically
prior to the practice of modern medicine, and certainly, an assumption that reproduction is the sine qua non of women's health has been seen as "natural." In the past,
gender role ideology differentiated health care providers into different tasks and
statuses—physicians were men and nurses were women—as well as differentiating
assumptions about health status and the effect of health on other roles—for example,
by using childbearing as a justification for limiting women's participation in the
workforce. Gender role ideology has also contributed to inequity in health research,
not because we have not engaged in research into women's health, but because of the
limits we have placed on it. The system has been blind to the need to conduct research on some questions and has placed perhaps undue emphasis on certain others.

"Women's health" has seldom been viewed by the state as pressing enough to
force open a policy window (Kingdon 1995) *except* in terms of pronatalism—the
state requires some level of health in women of childbearing age if it is to assure
production of successive generations of citizens. Otherwise, until very recently,
studying sex differences was seen as tedious, expensive, and unnecessary. Traditional gender role stereotypes, overlaid on biological sex, combined to justify the
conclusion that it was "easier" to conduct studies using only men as research subjects and then, if necessary, merely apply the findings to women *except* in the case
of reproduction, as if nothing else about women's health has mattered. Such a
limited view has taken bizarre forms: a leading obstetrical textbook, for example,
says that "*women are physiologically ill-adapted to spend the greater part of their
reproductive lives in the nonpregnant state*. . . . Menstruation, therefore, is indis-
putable evidence of fertility failure, whether purposefully chosen or naturally

occurring" (Cunningham et al. 1993, 13–14; italics in the original). This is not a textbook of the nineteenth century, claiming that education would wither women's wombs. On the contrary, it presents itself as advocating strongly for the health and well-being of women (although the evidence on which it bases this extraordinary claim is questionable). Yet even this book, in its earliest pages, proceeds to reduce the health of the women it says it wishes to benefit to a single narrow dimension.

Serving State Interests by Privatizing Women

From the beginning, our political system, like most others, has sought its own interests in its treatment of women, and privatization has been an effective control strategy. The doctrine of *femme couverte* from early English Common Law, which indicates that a woman need not represent her own interests, because they are represented for her by her father or husband, effectively blocked most women's ability to own property or participate in public life. But at the same time that states embargoed women's citizenship, they needed women to produce citizens. The state of South Carolina, for instance, was established in no small part by single women who were given grants of land and cash in the new colony *providing* they married within a year of arriving there. The British West India Company and the British government were certain that the fastest way to create a stable, profitable colony was to get women to it, women who would marry, "tame" men, and create stable communities (Spruill [1938] 1972). Women who were unwilling or unable to marry within the year, of course, forfeited both land and money, because they had failed to fill the only function for which the state wanted them.

Pronatalist policies, however, have coexisted with extreme ambivalence about women's reproduction (Tolleson-Rinehart 1987). The notorious *Buck v. Bell*, 274 U.S. 200 (1927), upholding the sterilization of the "unfit," is the other side of policies that prevented "fit" women's use of contraception or choice to undergo sterilization. In both cases, the state is interested in women's reproduction to serve its own ends; in the United States, thirty-one states enacted such selective combinations of eugenics and pronatalism into law. In the first half of the twentieth century, the Comstock Laws made contraceptive information extremely difficult to obtain. Not until *Griswold v. Connecticut*, 381 U.S. 479 (1965) did women begin to have freer access to contraception and increasing control over their own reproduction. In this volume, Dorothy E. McBride's analysis of the framing of partial-birth abortion in terms of "women's health," however, illustrates how hard it still is for society to separate "women's health" from reproduction; no such connection vexes discussion of "men's health."

The Policy History of "Women's Health" Research

The paradox of simultaneously holding a view of research on women as unimportant or unnecessary, on the one hand, and as dangerous to their potential progeny, on the other, shows the ways in which both *gender* differences and *sex* differences have complicated the role of women as participants in biomedical research. As I have suggested above, the first element of the paradox has been to dismiss women as "too hard to study" because they have menstrual cycles (McDonald 1999). That is, menstrual cycles represent a real sex difference, but the willingness to reject women as research subjects on that score arises from sexist gender-role beliefs.

In fact, menstruating women's cyclical hormonal variation probably does cause some variation in their response to pharmaceuticals, for example—but we could argue that, far from wanting to "exclude" this from our research designs, we want to *understand* it in order to treat women most effectively. Surely we should be engaged in a rigorous evaluation of when sex differences might matter and when they do not. As the Institute of Medicine pointed out in its report on women as research subjects in 1994, it is not appropriate to "norm" men's gender as "neutral" and treat women as "deviant." On the contrary, to exclude women from clinical research for such reasons "promote[s] the misuse of scientific rationales [and] . . . it can also compromise subsequent clinical practice by leaving clinicians and patients uncertain about the applicability of research findings to women" (1994, 113).

The second element of the paradox is more complicated: it is the exclusion of women from research on the grounds of avoiding the ethical and legal problems associated with potential fetal injury. The interpretation and implementation of three policies in particular enforced women's exclusion from research for this reason. They are the Federal Policy for the Protection of Human Subjects of 1974 (45 CFR 46); the 1960 amendments to the Food and Drug Act; and the Food and Drug Administration's (FDA's) 1977 guideline, *General Considerations for the Clinical Evaluation of Drugs* (HEW/FDA-77-3040). Each of these federal policies had the effect of excluding women from almost all biomedical research, and in each case, the limiting factor on conducting research with women subjects became that of protection of the fetus.

The proscription on allowing women to choose to become research participants was an understandable, if not entirely rational, interpretation of policies arising in reaction to several events, including the birth of infants with devastating congenital malformations to women who had taken diethylstilbestrol (known familiarly as DES) or thallidomide, to the horrifying "research" abuses committed by Nazis in World War II, and to the shaming revelations of American research practices on black men in the infamous Tuskegee experiments. The intent of these policies was to *protect* human subjects from the unchecked power of science, and to respect autonomy of persons (Belmont Report 1979). The immediate and continuing problem these policies caused, however, was to further vitiate the autonomy of women as persons by subsuming it in concern for fetal injury. In "Part B: Basic Ethical Principles," the Belmont Report (1979) says that respect for persons requires two ethical standards: acceptance of persons' autonomy, and the recognition that some persons have diminished autonomy and require protection. The report calls an autonomous person one who can deliberate about and act on goals; it says that autonomy requires that we

> ... give weight to autonomous persons' considered opinions and choices while refraining from obstructing their actions unless they are clearly detrimental to others. To show lack of respect for an autonomous agent is to repudiate that person's considered judgments, to deny an individual the freedom to act ... or to withhold information necessary to make a considered judgment, when there are no compelling reasons to do so. . . . [A]n autonomous person is an individual capable of deliberation about personal goals and of acting under the direction of such deliberation.

To deny women the right to choose to participate in medical research, then, is to treat them as "persons with diminished autonomy" when there are no grounds, except for sexism, on which to deny women's autonomy. The system interpreted mandates to protect fetuses so broadly that the path of least resistance seemed to be just to exclude *all* women from many research studies, in order to preclude *any* woman research subject from becoming pregnant during the course of the research. Hence, women were "protected" out of virtually all systematic, controlled research into their health (Johnson and Fee 1997b; Baird 1999).

Women as autonomous individuals, capable of understanding and avoiding risks to the fetus and capable of providing informed consent, were nowhere to be found in these policies, or in the attitudes of the research community. In recent years, this severance of "woman as citizen" from "woman as reproductive system" is represented in the excruciating conflict engendered by the newly identified public problem of "fetal rights," the proposed solutions for which most often involve incarcerating or otherwise controlling women, even to the extent of invading women's bodies to perform state-sanctioned in utero surgery on the fetus (Daniels 1993). As with drug and other biomedical research, these solutions have also involved attempting to deny *all* women of childbearing age the right to work in certain occupations. While that policy initiative was ruled unconstitutional in *Automobile Workers v. Johnson Controls*, 499 U.S. 187 (1991), the question of fetal rights makes clear how terribly difficult it has been to think beyond women's reproductive functions. It might also be noted that discussions of men's health behavior are never advanced in terms of "fetal rights," even though men's health choices can affect the health of the children they may father (Schroedel and Peretz 1994).

The issue of fetal rights shows once again how deeply contradictory women's relation to the state remains. Indeed, women's health advocates themselves made deliberate choices in the early 1990s to take the first steps on the road to a women's health agenda by eschewing reproductive health. Florence Hazeltine (1997), then director of the Center for Population Health at the National Institutes of Health (NIH), and other high-ranking women in the federal health bureaucracy, proposed menopause as the first major NIH Women's Health Initiative Study research subject for two reasons. First, we had so little research evidence on menopause by the early 1990s that health care providers could not offer truly evidence-based care for menopausal women. Second, and possibly even more important, menopause was a safe subject, free of any taint of the politics of abortion.

Many serious people of good conscience can be harrowingly divided over questions of reproductive freedom and "fetal rights" versus women's rights. But feminists are particularly concerned about the conflicts because of their awareness of the long, and often disingenuous, history of using the language of morality or patriotism to control women, just as they are aware of the state's history of privatizing women. There are ways to protect fetuses both medically and legally that respect women's personhood—and, in fact, today we are more likely to recognize the importance of understanding the influence of disease and its treatment on *both* the pregnant woman and her fetus. The issues, however, remain challenging, and their profoundly difficult political history contributes to the current debates over the definition of "women's health" (Weisman 1997). As Dr. Hazeltine said,

> There has always been a vital tie between a woman's freedom over her sexual rights and her ability to control whether and when she will become pregnant. That is why it was so crucial to sever the link between women's sexual functioning and the new and important women's health research issues that were trying to emerge. Once that was accomplished, it became much more difficult to try and reconnect the two. (Hazeltine 1997, xv)

The Treatment of Preterm Labor as an Illustration of Rival Views of "Women's Health"

The severance Dr. Hazeltine and her colleagues sought is far less than complete, and women populate both sides of the ideological divide. Bitter arguments over how to manage preterm labor—which can lead to "premature" or "preterm" birth if it cannot be stopped—illustrate the dispute.

"Preterm labor" is the onset of labor before a pregnancy has reached thirty-seven weeks, which is close enough to full term to expect a good birth outcome. Preterm labor is the single most significant cause of the stillbirth, death, or resulting major illness or disability of newborns. Although it is a significant, emotionally wrenching and costly public health problem, its causes remain poorly understood, and we still have no "best practice" guideline for treating women who go into preterm labor (Berkowitz and Papiernik 1993). For this reason, physicians use a wide range of drugs and other techniques to try to stop preterm labor, in the hope that, if pregnancy can continue longer, the fetus might have a better chance of surviving. The FDA has approved only one drug, ritodrine, for the specific purpose of interrupting preterm labor. Every other drug that physicians use in preterm labor is used in what are called "off label" conditions—that is, the drug is neither specifically tested nor approved for use in preterm labor. One drug labeled for the treatment of asthma, terbutaline sulfate, is widely put to such "off label" use for the treatment of preterm labor. In 1996, after two pregnant women died, apparently from being given a form of terbutaline to treat their preterm labor, the National Women's Health Network (NWHN) petitioned the FDA to take action against such uses (NWHN Petition to the Food and Drug Administration, Docket No. 96P-0258, 1996). In response, the FDA conducted its own investigation and determined that terbutaline was potentially dangerous. It issued a so-called "dear colleague" letter, or a letter warning health professionals of unsafe medical practices. In this case, the letter warned physicians that the use of terbutaline in an infusion pump had not been tested for safety and efficacy in the treatment of preterm labor, and was potentially dangerous. The letter made clear that we lacked evidence of the safety of terbutaline for the fetus, but that the evidence of complications —including death—for pregnant women was strong enough to recommend against such use (FDA 1997). "Dear colleague" letters do not ban unsafe uses of drugs; they only warn against such practice. Many people, in fact, question whether "dear colleague" letters are effective strategies for improving patient safety. They do, however, put the health community on record that the FDA does not consider something to be safe or effective.

The most impassioned critics of the NWHN petition and the FDA "dear colleague" letter, however, were *other women*—specifically, members of multiple-gestation advocacy groups (groups representing women who are or have been pregnant with twins, triplets, or larger numbers of fetuses)—and the obstetricians who treat them. Preterm labor is common in a multigestational pregnancy. Multigestation advocacy groups give preterm labor treatments their highest priority, seeming to take the perspective that virtually any risk is worth it if there is any increased chance to continue the pregnancy long enough to deliver live, healthy babies. While the salience of this issue for multiple gestation groups is certainly understandable, as is their hope that terbutaline is an effective treatment (although the literature does not unequivocally demonstrate this), their rhetoric is telling. They accused the NWHN of *not* being advocates of women's health and of having suspect motives; they questioned why NWHN would "not reveal" its sponsors (it has none; it is solely supported by individual member dues) and called its action a "scare tactic" (Sidelines National Support Network 1997; Bleyl 2004; Newman 1997), illustrated by this comment from a terbutaline advocate:

> Why [asks the President of the Triplet Connection on her website] has this citizen's petition been filed? Who is behind this group of women, and for what reason? Could it possibly be that therapies which can be managed at home rather than in the hospital at savings of countless thousands of dollars could influence hospitals and physicians who could be benefiting financially by keeping women in the hospital rather than being able to safely maintain their pregnancies at home? Could self serving individuals and institutions have something at stake in the availability of such modes of therapy? (Bleyl 2004)

For multigestation advocacy groups, beliefs about women's health appear to be in largest part framed by women's reproductive roles, while the NWHN is attempting to address gender and health policy from the framework of evidence-based science and an avowedly feminist perspective. Both groups are concerned about quality of care—but they may define quality very differently. For the multigestation advocacy groups, the goal is live birth. For the National Women's Health Network, the goal is achieving evidence-based best practices in women's health care.

A review of multigestation advocacy groups' positions shows an understandable desire to do anything they think may prolong their much-desired pregnancies. They are eager for medical intervention and ready to accept anecdotes as evidence of a treatment's effectiveness. Since 1997, the evidence has continued to mount against such interventions—careful reviews of research findings to date suggest that most of the interventions to treat preterm labor, such as the use of terbutaline or Home Uterine Activity Monitors, cannot be shown to benefit the fetus or fetuses, but some of them *can* be shown to do potential harm to the pregnant woman (Berkman, Thorp, Lohr, et al. 2003; Sanchez-Ramos and Huddleston 2003; FDA 1997, 2001). Multigestation advocacy groups, however, are unwilling to accept those conclusions. For them, stopping preterm labor is a cause—almost an ideology —not a scientific or medical challenge. Their advocacy is part of a comparatively new phenomenon, but their orientation toward women's health is rooted in the old notions that "women's health" is about women's reproduction.

Changing Policy: Including Women in Research

The preterm labor example shows how "women's health" has been a growth industry. As the women's movement produced durable political interest groups in the 1970s and 1980s, and women policymakers' numbers increased in both the elective and bureaucratic arenas, policy activists seized new opportunities to reframe "women's health." Breast cancer became an early emphasis, at least partly because fear of breast cancer was such an effective source of mobilization; we consider breast cancer as the signature issue of the women's health movement in the pages to come. But women's health is a great deal more than an absence of breast cancer, and the paucity of research conducted with women as research participants has made it difficult to address questions other than those of reproduction. By the mid-1980s, the knowledge deficit arising as a consequence of excluding women from most biomedical research was attracting growing attention. For example, massive research efforts to improve cardiovascular health, such as the Harvard Physicians Health Study or the Multiple Risk Factor Intervention Trials (aptly named "MR. FIT"), drew results from studies on a combined 37,000 research subjects—not a single one of whom was female. How could we know whether any of the results applied to heart disease in women? The Baltimore Longitudinal Study on Aging, begun in 1958, included no women at all for its first twenty years, meaning that this enormous study would be useless for comparative analysis of men's and women's aging. By 1986, the NIH, the federal biomedical research juggernaut, tried to address this lacuna by issuing a statement encouraging—but not requiring—the inclusion of women in clinical research trials. Scientists were unmoved by the encouragement. In 1990, the General Accounting Office (GAO) published a report saying that little progress had been made and, in fact, our information was so poor that the GAO could not even determine how much of the total NIH budget had been spent on research questions relevant to women's health (Johnson and Fee 1997a; Baird 1999; Weisman 1997).

Women in Congress and at the higher levels of the federal bureaucracy were poised to use the 1990 GAO report for action. They stimulated the authorization of major research efforts. In 1993, legislation drafted by the Congressional Caucus for Women's Issues led to the creation of the NIH Office of Research on Women's Health, and moved from encouragement to a *requirement* that women be included as subjects in federally funded research unless there is scientific justification for excluding them. At the same time, the FDA issued new guidelines "strongly encouraging" the inclusion of women in clinical trials of new drugs (Johnson and Fee 1997b; Baird 1999). These two policies put public and private sector money behind the expectation that research would include women.

Simultaneously, the rapidly growing women's health network of women scholars, bureaucrats, and politicians set themselves the task of reconceptualizing women's health. At the most basic level, of course, we continue to recognize diseases found only in women—those that stem from reproductive roles (and, in fact, the increasing visibility of "women's health" gave rise to a similar approach to "men's health," with new attention, for example, to screening for prostate cancer). The newer conceptualization added levels of complexity: for example, in addition to diseases *unique* to women are those that "present" differently in women—that have a higher incidence in women, or exhibit different symptoms, or that have different risk factors for women (Hazeltine 1997; this is also the 1993 NIH definition of "women's health").

Note, though, that definitions devolving too tightly on women's reproductive roles, or focusing too much on disease, rather than health, or definitions that use what we know of men's health against which to measure women, harkened to the status quo women's health advocates were intent on changing. Some advocates labeled the 1993 NIH definition the "biomedical" model, and proposed an alternative "biopsychosocial" model, reconceptualizing women's health "in terms of the totality of women's experiences throughout the life span," including their social, economic, cultural, and psychological roles, and the environments in which they live (Weisman 1997, 182).

That definition, too, attracted criticism, especially for seeming to be everything and, thus, nothing—for taking on so much that it would achieve little, while missing less grand but more achievable opportunities to improve women's health. In the meantime, breast cancer screening became the first real popular women's health policy success, and it, like every policy success, came with its own unintended consequences.

Breast Cancer Case Study: To Screen or Not to Screen?

Breast cancer is the second most common cancer after skin cancer and the second leading cause of cancer death among women (a vanishingly small number of men is also diagnosed with breast cancer each year). The risk of having breast cancer increases with age, and women older than sixty are at the greatest risk. In the recent past, breast cancer, as was true of other cancers, was not publicly discussed and was even treated as something shameful. This general attitude probably led to more late or missed diagnoses. The screening techniques with which we are most familiar today—the *breast self-exam* performed by the woman herself, the *clinical breast exam* performed by a health care provider, and the *screening mammogram*, or x-ray examination of breast tissue—were not commonly used until recently, and the treatment for breast cancer was drastic, usually taking the form of the *radical mastectomy*, which included removal of the entire breast, the chest wall muscles underneath it, and the surrounding lymph nodes. In recent years, so-called "breast-conserving" surgery has been favored over radical mastectomies, because women who have had the less drastic surgery have had equally good rates of cancer-free survival after treatment.

Because an American woman's lifetime risk of getting breast cancer is one in eight (with several known risk factors altering those odds), because early detection is associated with better prognosis, and because research and technology offered hope for improved treatment, breast cancer was ideally positioned to become an obvious target for the newly invigorated women's health policy movement. The issue took on exceptional visibility when notable women like First Lady Betty Ford and others "went public" about their breast cancer, and Nancy Brinker started the Susan G. Komen Foundation in memory of her sister, Suzy Komen, who had died of breast cancer at age thirty-six. Very quickly, American women became avid seekers of information about the disease.

The emerging "breast cancer lobby" capitalized on Congress and the NIH's new interest in research on women, assisted by canny women members of Congress such as Patricia Schroeder (D-CO), who used her position on the House Armed Services Committee for the purpose of adding money to the Defense Department's budget for breast cancer research as a matter of national security. The National Cancer Institute (NCI) increased the funds devoted to breast cancer research by more than 300 percent in a decade from the early 1980s to the early 1990s, and the level of research funding went from $81 million in the early 1990s to over $548 million in fiscal 2003—an increase of more than 650 percent since 1992 (National Cancer Institute 2004). Private foundations such as the Komen Foundation and the American Cancer Society have contributed millions more in research funds.

The vastly heightened attention to breast cancer, with everything from pink ribbon jewelry to "Races for the Cure," is a probable reason for an apparent increase in its incidence. The diagnosis rate for breast cancer has increased since

1980, but the mortality rate has dropped (National Cancer Institute 2004). In 1999, the breast cancer mortality rate reached the lowest age-adjusted level (27 deaths per 100,000 population) since 1973 (Fletcher and Elmore 2003).

> [Meanwhile,] . . . 71 percent of women in the United States who were 40 years of age or older reported having undergone mammography during the previous two years. . . . Ironically, just as screening (or better treatment or both) seemed to be lowering mortality from breast cancer nationally, questions were raised about the validity of the studies that had led to widespread screening. (Fletcher and Elmore 2003, 1672)

The latest questions about whether screening mammography saves lives, raised by a pair of Danish researchers (Gotzsche and Olsen 2000; Olsen and Gotzsche 2001), ignited another breast cancer firestorm, and demonstrate the politicization of breast cancer. The success of the breast cancer lobby at raising awareness of breast cancer has created an enormous treatment and research infrastructure, as well as a public composed of women who are frightened by the prospect of getting the disease. The most recent controversy follows an earlier contretemps in 1997 over the value of screening mammography for women in their forties (almost no one disputes the value of mammography as a screening tool for older women).

Screening mammography has come to be seen as the most important tool for preventing deaths from breast cancer. Although their likelihood of getting, and dying from, breast cancer remains quite small, even when they are older, as Table 9.1 shows, women are intensely interested in breast cancer and contribute considerably to the general current enthusiasm for cancer screening (Schwartz, Woloshin, Fowler, and Welch 2004). Younger women and, indeed, the entire health system, may well be prone to overestimating the benefits of screening, and underestimating its risks (Salzman 1998; Berry 1998; Black, Nease, and Tosteson 1995), at least partly because media portrayals of screening do a poor job of balancing benefit with risk, and are particularly unidimensional in their "pro-screening" message when they are targeting less educated women (Dobias 2001; Burke et al. 2001). Belief in mammography screening, for women and for many health professionals, has gone beyond an evaluation of the science to something akin to a religious conviction.

As Fletcher and Elmore note, the vast majority of women over forty years of age have had mammograms. Mammograms, however, are not free of risk to the women who have them, or to the health care system. The health system's main risk is that mammography may not be cost-effective, either in terms of cost per life-year saved (Salzman, Kerlkiowske, and Phillips 1997) or in terms of larger cost–benefit analyses (Berry 1998), including the lost opportunity costs of not having the resources spent on mammography available to treat other threats to women's health. Women's risks also include cost effectiveness—since they too pay for their mammograms, one way or another (in, for example, "gender-rated" health insurance costs)—but the other factors on the risk side of their own personal

Table 9.1

Chances of the Development of and Death from Breast Cancer Within the Next Ten Years (per 1,000 women)

Age	Cases of Invasive Breast Cancer	Death from Breast Cancer	Death from Any Cause
40	15	2	21
50	28	5	55
60	37	7	126
70	43	9	309
80	35	11	670

Source: Fletcher and Elmore (2003, 1673, Table 1). Copyright © 2003 Massachusetts Medical Society. All rights reserved.

risk–benefit ledgers include the very high likelihood over time of having a false positive, or a finding of cancer or other abnormality when there is none. The mammography false positive rate is put at anywhere from an estimate of a 10 percent chance of getting a false positive on each mammogram (Fletcher and Elmore 2003), to a cumulative risk of a 43 percent chance of having a false positive after the ninth mammogram (Christiansen 2000). With false positives come additional testing, some of it invasive, and significant and lasting anxiety. Even after further testing reassures women that their falsely "abnormal" mammograms are, in fact, normal, their anxiety about cancer remains higher than is true for women who do not have false positives (Barton 2004).

Another screening mammography risk is that of overdiagnosis, particularly of a form of breast cancer called "ductal carcinoma in situ," which was rarely ever identified before the advent of mammography. Its name is frightening—and it is understandable that the physicians who find it, and the women who are diagnosed with it, want to treat it. The dilemma, however, is that ductal carcinoma in situ may become an invasive cancer—or it may not. Autopsies of women who died of other causes have found "substantial" levels of ductal carcinoma—that is, it was present in these women, but it never advanced to become an invasive cancer or a threat to their health. Thus, a diagnosis of "ductal carcinoma in situ" may cause a diagnosis of "breast cancer" and its subsequent treatment, neither of which was necessary. As Fletcher and Elmore (2003, 1676) note, we just do not know whether such cases save lives or merely increase the number of diagnoses of breast cancer.

Under these circumstances of uncertainty about many aspects of breast cancer screening, one might think that the political system, the health system, and women's opinions would all favor measured observation and careful analysis in the interest of making the most effective health policy. That has not been the case. Twice, in 1997 and again in 2000–2001, public questions about the effectiveness of mammography to prevent breast cancer death have been greeted with outrage.

To take the first case, for most of 1996, scientists, physicians, and surgeons met in what is called a "consensus conference" sponsored by the NIH to try to resolve when and how mammography screening should be used, in the hope of setting a science-based standard to be used in breast cancer care and policy. This group of scientists and physicians, the NIH Consensus Development Conference on Breast Cancer Screening for Women Ages 40 to 49, volunteered to search for and review the scientific literature on the effects of breast cancer screening for the purpose of determining whether such early screening saved lives. On the afternoon of January 23, 1997, the conference panel met to announce its conclusion that "[t]here is insufficient evidence to make an informed decision regarding efficacy of screening as measured by reduction in breast cancer mortality in women aged 40–49 years" (Fletcher 1997, 1180).

Note that the Consensus Conference did *not* say that the evidence was *against* screening among women aged 40 to 49. It merely said that the evidence to date could not conclusively answer the question of whether regular breast cancer screening of women in their forties detected enough curable cancers to outweigh the various economic, emotional, medical, and system costs such as those discussed above of screening this entire population. Should all women in their forties be having regular mammograms, or should they wait? The Consensus Conference found that the balance of the scientific literature did not favor either view. This indeterminate conclusion was not what anyone, on either side of the issue, had been hoping for, but the furor greeting it caught many by surprise.

The furor might have been foreseen: already, by 1997, breast cancer screening had become as much, or more, a political as a scientific question. The president of the Komen Foundation pointedly describes her advocacy of breast cancer research in terms of "priming the market" and "engaging the public" (Braun 2003), a task at which the Komen Foundation and other groups have been extraordinarily successful—so successful, in fact, that the nascent "men's health" movement is attempting to emulate the breast cancer lobby in the case of prostate cancer screening and treatment. Congress, and the Director of the NIH, jointly condemned the Consensus Committee's report. Most people in the breast cancer lobby simply continued to insist that women begin annual mammography screening at age forty.

This notion is challenged by the research of Gotzsche and Olsen of Denmark, who concluded that the evidence on mammography screening to date was flawed and said that a correct evaluation of the findings called into question the efficacy of *all* mammography—not just mammography in younger women—to save lives (Gotzsche and Olsen 2000; Olsen and Gotzsche 2001). Since 2001, most of the Danish researchers' questions have been addressed, but the scientific literature remains full of rebuttals and countercharges. In the meantime, the United States Preventive Services Task Force, charged with helping the government to make sound, science-based policy on preventive health care, as well as the NCI and the American College of Obstetricians and Gynecologists, all continue to recommend that women who do not have any obvious risk factors begin having mammograms "every year or two" beginning in their forties. Fletcher and Elmore (2003) conclude, carefully, that for every 1,000 women who begin having mammograms at age forty and have them each year for ten years, screening mammography will have saved the lives of two of them by the end of the ten-year period.

Breast cancer screening has all the hallmarks of the most bitterly contested political issues. It has become enormously visible. It addresses a problem that has come to be seen as a *public* problem, no longer judged to be a personal or private responsibility, a prerogative of scientific and medical experts, or an inevitable consequence of the free market (as defined by Disch 1996). The prospect of breast cancer frightens women, and that fear stimulates women to take action by organizing into new advocacy groups as "stake challengers" (as defined by Peterson 1993) who enter the political arena and demand policy solutions even though the policy "problem"—the occurrence of breast cancer in younger women—may not be nearly as large or as threatening as are other women's health problems. Women whose breast cancer may or may not be detected early by regular screening have become one of the set of interests. Radiologists and mammography clinics, whose income is partly or wholly derived from interpreting mammography films, are another interest, as is the breast cancer lobby of researchers and advocates. The health insurance lobby conceded the issue long ago, agreeing to pay for younger women's mammography screening—but does this not also contribute to the "gender rating" of insurance costs that ultimately may do women more harm than good?

Even abortion enters the breast cancer debate. In a development probably unwelcome to most breast cancer advocates, anti-abortion forces have begun to play on women's fear of breast cancer by promulgating purported links between abortion and the later development of breast cancer. Secretary of Health and Human Services Tommy Thompson even directed the NCI to put that claim on the NCI website in 2002. Since that time, two different rigorous reviews of the scientific evidence, including one performed by an NCI workshop of over 100 of the world's leading breast cancer researchers (Early Reproductive Events Workshop 2003) and a large international re-analysis of over fifty-three studies (Collaborative Group 2004), have led the NCI and all other mainstream scientific bodies to conclude that there is no connection between either induced or spontaneous abortion and breast cancer.

Figure 9.1 suggests that increasing attempts to make the public aware of breast cancer over the past two decades is associated with an exceptional level of fear on women's part that they will get, and die from, breast cancer. Women understandably react to media portrayals of breast cancer risk—but these media portrayals may have catalyzed an unnecessary level of alarm based on a misunderstanding of true breast cancer risks:

• Women between 40 and 50 years of age have been found to overstate their risk of dying of breast cancer within the next ten years by more than *twentyfold* while simultaneously overestimating their risk reduction from screening by *sixfold* (Black, Nease, and Tosteson 1995).

Figure 9.1   **Reports of Women's Fear of Breast Cancer,
1974, 1992, and 1995**

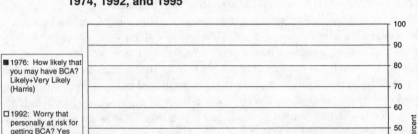

Source: Harris Surveys, 1976 and 1992 (Harris/923009, 12/1992); Gallup Survey 1995 cited in (among others) Burke et al. 2001 and Walsh 1999.

- Stories about breast cancer in the popular media misrepresent the age distribution of the disease, focusing on atypically young women, and possibly increasing women's fears (Burke et al. 2001).
- Media presentations also differ by educational level: messages directed at less educated women are more prescriptive in favor of mammography, while media portrayals at higher educational levels presented more, and more balanced, information (Dobias 2001).

The black line drawn across the bottom of Figure 9.1 shows breast cancer's true mortality. As many as 40 percent of American women believe they will die of breast cancer. The truth, as we know, is quite different. The NCI estimates that breast cancer causes approximately 3.6 percent of female deaths each year. American women's lifetime risk of breast cancer is about 12 percent. Given the reality, as important as breast cancer is, should it dominate women's health concerns, women's health resources, and women's health policy, to the extent that it now does?

Do Men Have "Health" While Women Have "Women's Health"?

Defining "women's health" continues to be a matter of spirited debate.[1] In the meantime, "women's health" has become exceptionally visible and, perhaps, fashionable. From the 104th through the 107th Congresses, as of March 2004, 322 "women's health" bills were introduced. These bills were of all different types, including bills arguing that abortion harms women's health; the point is that "women's health" has entered the policy language as a term of art. During the same period, only ten bills on "men's health" have been introduced. Bills proposing an "Office of Men's Health" in the Department of Health and Human Services have been introduced in the two most recent Congresses, but supporters have not yet succeeded in creating such an office.

In 1991, the National Library of Medicine (NLM) added a "Women's Health" Main Heading, N01.400.900) to the MeSH (Medical Subject Headings) system, its invaluable catalogue of medical subjects. No "Men's Health" MeSH has apparently ever been created.

We can also search the National Library of Medicine's *PubMed* database to determine the subjects of articles published in the scientific journals catalogued by the NLM. Such a search using "women's health" as a key word produces 11,787 articles from 1966 through April 2004. If we use "men's health" as a key word, we produce just 10 percent as many articles, 1,151. The *PubMed* journals database catalogues twenty-five scholarly journals indexed under the Women's Health MeSH heading. There are no scholarly journals catalogued with "men's health" as a keyword, but there are two newsletters on the topic: the Gay Men's Health Crisis Newsletter began publication in 1994, and the Harvard Men's Health Watch Newsletter commenced publication in 1996. All of this activity could be interpreted to argue that we still exist in a world in which there is "health" and "women's health."

Our brief mammography case study shows how limiting even the contemporary openness to "women's health" questions can be. In another illustration of the power of gender roles, both the FDA and the Health Resources Services Administration (HRSA) women's health offices treat women as gatekeepers of family health, and target general health education and outreach programs, including those for men and for children, to women, and especially to women in vulnerable populations, in the expectation that this is the most efficient way to benefit public health generally.[2] Federal health agencies' outreach to women can be viewed in positive terms as a sign that the health system takes women more seriously as significant actors. It is also possible, however, to see such "outreach" as just a modern version of what the British West India Company did in South Carolina: is the federal government holding women responsible for community-building by holding them responsible for the family's health, but without providing women the political and economic resources they need to fulfill such responsibilities?

A simple look at the leading causes of death in Table 9.2 shows clearly that men and women are more likely to be at risk of mortality from similar causes than from dramatically different ones. Heart disease kills men and women at virtually identical rates. The remaining leading killers are more likely to vary in rank order than in kind in their lethality to the two sexes, with the exception that men remain more likely to die by suicide or homicide, and women are more likely to die of Alzheimer's disease and atherosclerosis—and, regrettably, women still die in childbirth.

Table 9.2

Leading Causes of Death for Men and Women, 1980 and 2001

	1980		2001	
Percentage of all deaths from...	Men	Women	Men	Women
Diseases of heart	38	39	29	29
Malignant neoplasms	21	21	24	22
Cerebrovascular diseases	7	11	5	8
Unintentional injuries	7	3	6	3
Diabetes mellitus	2	1	3	3
Chronic obstructive pulmonary/lower respiratory	4	2	5	5
Pneumonia and influenza	3	3	2	3
Suicide	2		2	
Chronic liver disease and cirrhosis	2	1	1	
Homicide	2			
Nephritis, nephritic syndrome, and nephrosis			2	2
Atherosclerosis		1		
Conditions in perinatal period (1980)/Septicemia (2001)		1		1
Alzheimer's disease				3

Sources: Centers for Disease Control and Prevention. National Center for Health Statistics. National Vital Statistics System. *Vital Statistics of the United States,* vol. 2, *Mortality, Part A, 1980,* Washington, DC: Public Health Service, 1985; Centers for Disease Control and Prevention (1985); Anderson and Smith (2003).

Note: Percentages calculated from raw numbers by the author.

Women's own reports of their health status, an example of which is shown in Table 9.3, show that women's most serious health challenges are not always, or even especially, associated with sex—it may be that the politics of gender have distorted our view of "women's health." Should not heart disease, for example, be considered a "women's health" challenge?

The features surrounding breast cancer screening—the perception that something has become a public problem, high visibility and conflict surrounding the problem, potential consequences for large numbers of people, and a broad range of interested parties with high stakes in, and different frames for, the issue—describe the rise onto the policy agenda of *any* difficult political question. When one adds our culture's ambivalence about gender, as breast cancer screening and so many other issues do, the mixture becomes dangerously volatile. The medical profession itself has been all too apt to leave the scientific method behind when it comes to thinking about men and women and the nature of gender roles.

Is this new, fashionable "women's health" entirely to the benefit of women? The fact that the National Library of Medicine formed a MeSH for women's health makes the job of identifying scientific research on women's health much, much easier—but it also continues to say that there is "health" and then there is "women's health." In other words, all health is "men's health" *unless* denoted otherwise, and women are the "otherwise." Similarly, the rise of three scholarly journals devoted

Table 9.3

Self-Reported Health Status Indicators, Women Ages 18–64

	All Women	Ages 18 to 44	Ages 45 to 64
		Age Group	
Fair/poor health	16%	12%*	23%
Disability or condition that limits activity	13	9*	19
Chronic condition requiring ongoing treatment	32	24*	46
Regular prescription drug use	50	40*	66
Diagnosed medical conditions**			
Arthritis	17	8*	33
Asthma	11	11	10
Cancer	3	2*	6
Diabetes	5	2*	11
Heart disease	4	2*	7
Hypertension	17	8*	32
Obesity	11	7*	17
Osteoporosis	4	1*	9
Anxiety/Depression	21	20	23

Source: This information was reprinted with permission from the Henry J. Kaiser Family Foundation. The Kaiser Family Foundation, based in Menlo Park, California, is a nonprofit, independent national health care philanthropy and is not associated with Kaiser Permanente or Kaiser Industries.

Notes: *Significantly different from reference group (ages 45 to 64) at $p < .05$.
**Conditions diagnosed by a physician in past five years.

to women's health offers researchers a place to publish their work, and clinicians and consumers a place to read it. But is the showcase also a marginalization?

Conclusion: Thinking Contextually About Gender

We began this chapter by asking three questions: Have we broken the constraints of a gendered view of women's health? Should reproduction define women's health? Does sex matter? Now we can answer them. Two decades of "women's health" policy activity has *not* meant the end of a gendered view of women's health— gender role stereotypes continue to influence our understanding of "women's health." This gendered view continues to influence us to see reproduction as the sine qua non of women's health, often at the expense of a much broader and more effective understanding of health. Does sex matter? Of course it does—but we are far from a rich and nuanced understanding of *how* and *when* it does. As the Institute of Medicine (2001) says, "every cell has a sex" (4), and meaningful sex differences quite apart from obvious hormonal ones influence the health of men and women—but our research will have limited value unless and until we can "clarify findings of no essential sex differences and [suggest] mechanisms to be pursued when sex differences are found" (10).

In contemporary American culture, the differences between sex and gender are seldom noted. Today, "gender" is the term we most frequently encounter, even when the context obviously calls for sex, as in "What gender [*sic*] are you? Male or female?" The quandaries of health politics and health policy should remind us of the differences between sex and gender—and remind us to ask whether *either* construct is masking a perhaps more medically useful difference. In many cases, as we have seen, sex may influence health, but it is not a limiting factor. For example, although men and women may experience heart disease somewhat differently, heart disease is nonetheless the leading cause of death for each sex.

In other cases, sex is an obviously limiting factor. Obviously, no men become pregnant. Almost no men get breast cancer (those who do are given medical treatments similar to those given to women who have breast cancer). Men are far less likely to be disabled by osteoporosis, while it is the biggest source of disability among women over age seventy-five (HRSA 2004). Of course, no women get prostate or testicular cancer. Sex differences affect health and the body's response to disease outside the reproductive system: heart disease may be the leading killer of both men and women, but men and women experience heart disease differently. Females have more aggressive immune systems, but also get more autoimmune diseases, than do males. The two sexes have different brain organizations for language; men and women respond to toxins differently, and have different sensitivity to pain (Institute of Medicine 2001). Our health policy needs to be informed by a better understanding of the possible health consequences of these differences.

Finally, sometimes it seems to be gender that makes the difference. Because the sexes are socialized differently, their life circumstances are often dramatically different, as can be their access to economic and other resources. Adolescent girls are much less likely to engage in exercise than are adolescent boys. Girls and women are more likely to suffer from depression, while men are more likely to suffer from substance abuse and violent death. Girls and women are more likely to attempt suicide, but men are more likely to succeed in the attempt, because women are more likely to call for help, and men are more likely to use guns as the method of suicide.

The number of women without health insurance is growing at a rate three times that of men, probably as a result of welfare reform and the erosion of employer-sponsored health insurance. If the trend continues, more women than men will be uninsured by 2005—a first. Women are poorer than are men, and poverty is strongly associated with poor health and poor access to quality health care (cf. Collins, Berkson, and Downey 2002; Collins et al. 1999; Meyer et al. 1999; HRSA 2004). The present administration's plan to provide a $1,000 tax credit for the purchase of health insurance will not solve poor or uninsured women's problems, since this level of subsidy will not even buy adequate health coverage for young, single, working women, much less for older women or women with children (Collins, Berkson, and Downey 2002).

These meaningful health status differences between women and men are not organic or physiological. They are the direct or secondary results of differential gender role socialization and the manifestation of gender ideology in public policy. In these cases gender matters, and the *real* "women's health" question may be whether the present system puts too many barriers between women and affordable, high-quality health care.

A broad, deep, and inquiring recognition of when sex matters to health, when gender does, and when *neither* might matter will produce more coherent health policymaking for women and men. It will also assist us in making sense of health politics, and help us to understand how and when to deploy our resources to benefit "men's health," "women's health," and the public's health. The political system's goal of better health outcomes, and superior quality of care, for everyone, is widely shared. We will not reach that goal without continuing to question the gender frames we have placed around it.

Notes

1. I used the following search strategies to gather these data:
   a. For congressional bill introductions, I searched THOMAS, the Library of Congress database of congressional activity, at http://thomas.loc.gov/home/thomas/html (site last visited for this chapter on March 4, 2004), with keyword searches using "women's health" and "men's health" of all introductions (bills, resolutions, and private bills) into the House and Senate in the 104th through 107th Congresses, through March 2004.
   b. For searches of the scientific literature, I verified the absence of "men's health" as a Medical Subject Heading (MeSH) first by searching the MeSH vocabulary for cataloguing the medical literature, maintained at the National Library of Medicine (available at www.nlm.nih.gov/mesh/2004/MBrowser.html; site last visited for this chapter on April 21, 2004), and then verifying my search with health sciences librarians.
   c. For searches of articles and journals, I used the MeSH keyword "women's health" and the keyword "men's health" in the National Library of Medicine's *PubMed* database, the world's largest database of medical literature, to search for all articles and dedicated journals published between 1995 and March 2004 (*Entrez*, the initial *PubMed* search page, is at www.ncbi.nlm.nih.gov/entrez/query.fcgi; site last visited for this chapter on April 21, 2004).
2. See the FDA and HRSA women's health websites, respectively, at www.fda.gov/womens/default.htm (2004) and www.hrsa.gov/WomensHealth/ (2004).

References

Anderson, R.N., and B.L. Smith. 2003. "Deaths: Leading Causes for 2001." *National Vital Statistics Reports*, vol. 52. Hyattsville, MD: National Center for Health Statistics.
Automobile Workers v. Johnson Controls, 499 U.S. 187 (1991).
Baird, Karen L. 1999. "The New NIH and FDA Medical Research Policies: Targeting Gender, Promoting Justice." *Journal of Health Politics, Policy and Law* 24(3): 531–565.
Barton, Mary B., Debra S. Morley, Sara Moore, Jennifer D. Allen, Ken P. Kloeinman, Karen M. Emmons, and Suzanne W. Fletcher. 2004. "Decreasing Women's Anxieties

After Abnormal Mammograms: A Controlled Trial." *Journal of the National Cancer Institute* 96(7): 529–538.

Belmont Report. 1979. Available on line at http://ohsr.od.nih.gov/mpa/belmont.php3; site last reviewed for this chapter on January 21, 2004.

Berkman, Nancy D., John M. Thorp, Kathleen N. Lohr, Timothy S. Carey, Katherine E. Hartmann, Normal I. Gavin, Victor Hasselblad, and Anjolie E. Idicula. 2003. "Tocolytic Treatment for the Management of Preterm Labor: A Review of the Evidence." *American Journal of Obstetrics and Gynecology* 188(6): 1648–1659.

Berkowitz, Gertrude S., and Emile Papiernik. 1993. "The Epidemiology of Preterm Birth." *Epidemiologic Reviews* 15: 2.

Berry, Donald A. 1998. "Benefits and Risks of Screening Mammography for Women in Their Forties: A Statistical Appraisal." *Journal of the National Cancer Institute* 90(19): 1431–1439.

Black, W.C., R.F. Nease, and A.N. Tosteson. 1995. "Perceptions of Breast Cancer Risk and Screening Effectiveness in Women Younger than 50 Years of Age." *Journal of the National Cancer Institute* 17; 87(10): 703–704.

Bleyl, Janet T. 2004. "Subcutaneous Terbutaline Pump Therapy Seriously Threatened." Triplet Connection website; www.tripletconnection.org/jtnote.html; site last visited for this chapter on April 8, 2004.

Braun, Susan. 2003. "The History of Breast Cancer Advocacy." *The Breast Journal* 9 (Suppl. 2): S101–S103.

Buck v. Bell, 274 U.S. 200 (1927).

Burke, W., A.H. Olsen, L.E. Pinsky, S.E. Reynolds, and N.A. Press. 2001. "Misleading Presentation of Breast Cancer in Popular Magazines." *Effective Clinical Practice* (March–April). Printed from ACP [American College of Physicians] Online; www.acponline.org/journals/ecp/marapr01/burke.htm. Site last visited for this chapter on March 3, 2004.

Carroll, William. 2003. *Statistical Brief #11: The Health Insurance Status of U.S. Workers, 2001.* September. Rockville, MD: Agency for Healthcare Research and Quality. Available on line at www.meps.ahrq.gov/printproducts/PrintProd_Detail.asp?ID=487. Site last visited for this chapter on April 8, 2004.

Centers for Disease Control and Prevention. National Center for Health Statistics. National Vital Statistics System. *Vital Statistics of the United States*, vol. 2, *Mortality*, part A, 1980. Washington, DC: Public Health Service, 1985.

Christiansen Cindy L., Fei Wang, Mary B. Barton, William Kreuter, Joann G. Elmore, Alan E. Gelfand, and Suzanne W. Fletcher. 2000. "Predicting the Cumulative Risk of False-Positive Mammograms." *Journal of the National Cancer Institute* 92(20): 1657–1666.

Collaborative Group on Hormonal Factors in Breast Cancer. 2004. "Breast Cancer and Abortion: Collaborative Reanalysis of Data from 53 Epidemiological Studies, Including 83,000 Women with Breast Cancer from 16 Countries." *Lancet* 363 (27 March): 1007–1016.

Collins, Karen Scott, Cathy Schoen, Susan Joseph, Lisa Duchon, Elizabeth Simantov, and Michelle Yellowitz. 1999. *Health Concerns Across a Woman's Lifespan: The Commonwealth Fund 1998 Survey of Women's Health.* New York: The Commonwealth Fund. Publication number 332, available at www.cmwf.org/programs/women/ksc_ whsurvey_ 332.pdf. Site last visited for this chapter on April 20, 2004.

Collins, Sara, Stephanie B. Berkson, and Deirdre A. Downey. 2002. *Health Insurance Tax Credits: Will They Work for Women?* New York: The Commonwealth Fund, Publication number 589, available at www.cmwf.org/programs/insurance/collins_ creditswomen_589.pdf. Site last visited for this chapter on April 20, 2004.

Cubanski, Juliette, and Janet Kline. 2003. "Covering the Uninsured: Prospects and Problems." *Commonwealth Fund Issue Brief #616.* www.cmwf.org/programs/insurance/cubanski_coveringuninsured_ib_616.pdf. Site last visited for this chapter on April 1, 2004.

Cunningham, F.G., P.C. Macdonald, N.F. Gant, K.J. Leveno, and L.C. Gilstrap. 1993. *Williams Obstetrics* 19th ed. Norwalk, CT: Appleton & Lange.

Daniels, Cynthia R. 1993. *At Women's Expense: State Power and the Politics of Fetal Rights.* Cambridge: Harvard University Press.

Disch, Lisa. 1996. "Publicity-stunt Participation and Sound Bite Polemics: The Health Care Debate, 1993–1994." *Journal of Health Politics, Policy and Law* 21 (Spring): 3–33.

Dobias, Karen S., Cheryl A. Moyer, Sarah E. McAchran, Steven J. Katz, and Seema S. Sonnad. 2001. "Mammography Messages in Popular Media: Implications for Patient Expectations and Shared Clinical Decision-Making." *Health Expectations* 4(2): 127–135.

Early Reproductive Events Workshop. 2003. Summary Report. Early Reproductive Events Workshop, February 24–26, 2003. Available at http://cancer.gov/cancerinfo/ere-workshop-report. Site last visited for this chapter on April 26, 2004.

Feldman, Stanley. 2003. "Values, Ideology, and the Structure of Political Attitudes." In *Oxford Handbook of Political Psychology*, ed. David O. Sears, Leonie Huddy, and Robert Jervis. Oxford and New York: Oxford University Press.

Fletcher, Suzanne W. 1997. "Whither Scientific Deliberation in Health Policy Recommendations? Alice in the Wonderland of Breast-Cancer Screening." *New England Journal of Medicine* 336(16): 1180–1183.

Fletcher, Suzanne W., and Joann G. Elmore. 2003. "Mammographic Screening for Breast Cancer." *New England Journal of Medicine* 348(17): 1672–1680.

Food and Drug Administration. 1997. "Dear Colleague" letter warning on terbutaline infusion pump as treatment for preterm labor. www.fda.gov/medwatch/safety/1997/terbut.htm; site last visited for this chapter on April 8, 2004.

———. 2001. Final Guidance for Industry and FDA Reviewers: Class II Special Controls Guidance for Home Uterine Activity Monitors. www.fda.gov/cdrh/ode/guidance/820.pdf; site last visited for this chapter on April 8, 2004.

———. 2004. Office of Women's Health, U.S. Food and Drug Administration. www.fda.gov/womens/programs.html; site last visited for this chapter on April 8, 2004.

Gotzsche, Peter C., and Ole Olsen. 2000. "Is Screening for Breast Cancer with Mammography Justifiable?" *Lancet* 355(January 8): 129–134.

Griswold v. Connecticut, 381 U.S. 479 (1965).

Hazeltine, Florence P. 1997. "Foreword." In *Women's Health Research: A Medical and Policy Primer*, ed. Florence P. Haseltine and Beverly Greenberg Jacobson. Washington, DC: Health Press International.

HCUPNet. 2003. Healthcare Cost and Utilization Project. Agency for Healthcare Research and Quality. Interactive Statistical Tool. At www.ahrq.gov/data/hcup/hcupnet.htm; site last visited for this chapter on May 5, 2004.

Health Resources and Services Administration (HRSA). 2004. "Women's Health: A Lifespan Issue." www.hrsa.gov/WomensHealth/wh_fact.htm; site last visited for this chapter on April 8, 2004.

Institute of Medicine. 1994. *Women and Health Research: Ethical and Legal Issues of Including Women in Clinical Studies.* Volume 1. Washington, DC: National Academy Press.

———. 2001. *Exploring the Biological Contributions to Human Health: Does Sex Matter?* Washington, DC: National Academy Press.

Johnson, Tracy L., and Elizabeth Fee. 1997a. "Women's Health Research: An Introduction." In *Women's Health Research: A Medical and Policy Primer*, ed. Florence P. Haseltine and Beverly Greenberg Jacobson. Washington, DC: Health Press International.

———. 1997b. "Women's Health Research: A Historical Perspective." In *Women's Health Research: A Medical and Policy Primer*, ed. Florence P. Haseltine and Beverly Greenberg Jacobson. Washington, DC: Health Press International.

Kaiser Daily Health Policy Report. 2004. "ConnetiCare in July to Implement Gender-based Premium Rates for Small Employers." Thursday, April 22, "Coverage & Access" section; available on the web at www.kaisernetwork.org/daily_reports/rep_hpolicy.cfm#23334; site last visited for this chapter on April 22, 2004.

Kinder, Donald R. 2003. "Communication and Politics in the Age of Information." In *Oxford Handbook of Political Psychology*, ed. David O. Sears, Leonie Huddy, and Robert Jervis. Oxford and New York: Oxford University Press.

Kingdon, John W. 1995. *Agendas, Alternatives, and Public Policies*. 2d ed. New York: HarperCollins College Publishers.

Levit, Katherine, Cynthia Smith, Cathy Cowan, Art Sensenig, Aaron Catlin, and the Health Accounts Team. 2004. "Health Spending Rebound Continues in 2002." *Health Affairs* 23(1): 147–159.

McDonald, Kim A. 1999. "Studies of Women's Health Produce a Wealth of Information on the Biology of Gender Differences." *Chronicle of Higher Education*, June 25, 1999; available at http://chronicle.com/prm/weekly/v45/i42/42a01901.htm; site last visited for this chapter on April 8, 2004.

McGlynn, Elizabeth A., Eve A. Kerr, Cheryl L. Damberg, and Steven M. Asch, eds. 2000. *Quality of Care for Women: A Review of Selected Clinical Conditions and Quality Indicators*. Santa Monica, CA: RAND.

Meyer, Jane E., Joan M. Leiman, Nina Rothschild, with Marilyn Falik. 1999. *Improving the Health of Adolescent Girls: Policy Report of the Commonwealth Fund Commission on Women's Health*. New York: The Commonwealth Fund.

National Cancer Institute. 2004. *A Snapshot of Breast Cancer*. Available at http://prg.cancer.gov/snapshots/Breast-Snapshot.pdf; site last visited for this chapter on April 26, 2004.

National Women's Health Network Petition to the Food and Drug Administration, Docket No. 96P-0258/CP1 filed July 19, 1996, and FDA Response dated November 7, 1997 (copies of documents supplied to the author by the National Women's Health Network).

Newman, Roger B. 1997. "Subcutaneous Terbutaline Pump Therapy." The Triplet Connection. www.tripletconnection.org/stpt.html. Site last visited for this chapter on April 8, 2004.

Olsen, Ole, and Peter C. Gotzsche. 2001. "Cochrane Review on Screening for Breast Cancer with Mammography." *Lancet* 358 (October 20): 1340–1342.

Peterson, Mark A. 1993. "Political Influence in the 1990s: From Iron Triangles to Policy Networks." *Journal of Health Politics, Policy and Law* 18 (Summer): 395–438.

Salzman, Peter, Karla Kerlkiowske, and Kathryn Phillips. 1997. "Cost-Effectiveness of Extending Screening Mammography Guidelines to Include Women 40 to 49 Years of Age." *Annals of Internal Medicine* 127(11): 955–965.

Sanchez-Ramos, Luis, and John F. Huddleston. 2003. "The Therapeutic Value of Maintenance Tocolysis: An Overview of the Evidence." *Clinical Perinatology* 30(4): 841–854.

Sapiro, Virginia. 2003. "Theorizing Gender in Political Psychology Research." In *Oxford Handbook of Political Psychology*, ed. David O. Sears, Leonie Huddy, and Robert Jervis. Oxford and New York: Oxford University Press.

Schroedel, Jean Reith, and Paul Peretz. 1994. "A Gender Analysis of Policy Formation: The Case of Fetal Abuse." *Journal of Health Politics, Policy and Law* 19 (Summer): 335–360.

Schwartz, Lisa M., Steven Woloshin, Floyd J. Fowler, and H. Gilbert Welch. 2004. "Enthusiasm for Cancer Screening in the United States." *JAMA* 291(1): 71–78.

Sidelines National Support Network. 1997. "Volunteer Organization for High-Risk Pregnant Women Questions Motives of National Women's Health Network." Press release supplied to the author by a researcher at the University of North Carolina at Chapel Hill. Sidelines website, www.sidelines.org/, last visited for this chapter on April 1, 2004.

Spruill, Julia Cherry. [1938] 1972. *Women's Life and Work in the Southern Colonies*. With an introduction to the Norton Library ed. by Anne Firor Scott. New York: Norton.

Taber, Charles S. 2003. "Information Processing and Public Opinion." In *Oxford Handbook of Political Psychology*, ed. David O. Sears, Leonie Huddy, and Robert Jervis. Oxford and New York: Oxford University Press.

Tolleson-Rinehart, Sue. 1987. "Maternal Health Care Policy: Britain and the United States." *Comparative Politics* 19 (January): 193–211.

Walsh, Brian. 1999. "The Individualized Approach to Menopause Management." *Journal of Clinical Endocrinology & Metabolism* 84(6): 1900–1904.

Weisman, Carol S. 1997. "Changing Definitions of Women's Health: Implications for Health Care and Policy." *Maternal and Child Health Journal* 1(3): 179–189.

"Women's Health in the United States: Health Coverage and Access to Care" (#6027). 2002. The Henry J. Kaiser Family Foundation. May.

Part Three

Institutions

10

Cabinet Nominations in the William J. Clinton and George W. Bush Administrations

Gender, Change, and Representation

MaryAnne Borrelli

As presidential nominees and as departmental executives, cabinet secretaries are representatives to and from the Oval Office, the Congress, their departments, and their departments' constituents. Recognizing the power that flows from relationship-building and communication—the definitive functions of representation—political scientists have debated which alliance most decisively affects each secretary's performance. These exchanges have, in turn, revealed the dilemmas of decision making in a system of separated powers, in which no branch is dominant and change is the only constant. Notwithstanding these contributions to our understanding of U.S. politics, cabinet research has generally been blind to the workings of gender.

This chapter utilizes the intellectual tools of gender studies to examine the representation provided by women and men cabinet officers. Greatest attention is given to the William J. Clinton and George W. Bush initial cabinets, as these suggest new developments in cabinet nominations and representation. To place these innovations in historical context, patterns evidenced in the six earlier administrations with women cabinet officers—those of Franklin D. Roosevelt, Dwight D. Eisenhower, Gerald R. Ford, Jimmy Carter, Ronald Reagan, and George H.W. Bush—are also considered. Cumulatively, the eight administrations offer a population of 182 cabinet nominations, of which 23 were awarded to women. As these numbers indicate, women remain statistical tokens in the cabinet. (See Table 10.1 for a listing of the women secretaries-designate.) In the early twenty-first century, however, their presence has been sufficiently normalized so that a president's failure to nominate women to the cabinet would not pass without mention. Still, are these nominations merely showcasing difference or are they indicative of women's inclusion in elite decision making?

Table 10.1

The Women Secretaries-Designate

Secretary-Designate	Race/Ethnicity	Administration	Department
Frances Perkins	White	F.D. Roosevelt	Labor
Oveta Culp Hobby	White	Eisenhower	HEW
Carla Anderson Hills	White	Ford	HUD
Patricia Roberts Harris	African American	Carter	HUD HEW/HHS
Juanita Kreps	White	Carter	Commerce
Shirley M. Hufstedler	White	Carter	Education
Elizabeth H. Dole	White	Reagan	Transportation
		G.H.W. Bush	Labor
Margaret M. Heckler	White	Reagan	HHS
Ann Dore McLaughlin	White	Reagan	Labor
Lynn Martin	White	G.H.W. Bush	Labor
Barbara Franklin	White	G.H.W. Bush	Commerce
Donna E. Shalala	White	Clinton	HHS
Hazel R. O'Leary	African American	Clinton	Energy
Zoë E. Baird*	White	Clinton	Justice
Janet Reno	White	Clinton	Justice
Madeleine K. Albright	White	Clinton	State
Alexis M. Herman	African American	Clinton	Labor
Gale A. Norton	White	G.W. Bush	Interior
Ann M. Veneman	White	G.W. Bush	Agriculture
Linda Chavez*	Hispanic American	G.W. Bush	Labor
Elaine L. Chao	Asian American	G.W. Bush	Labor

Note: *Nomination withdrawn.

This chapter argues three points. First, it maintains that studying the presidents' cabinet nominations provides valuable insights on the U.S. political system. Second, it demonstrates that gender studies provide the requisite concepts to assess the secretaries-designate. Third, it seeks to reveal the extent to which successive administrations have incorporated women into presidential politics as officeholders and as constituents.

Gender, Representation, and Cabinet Nominations

Cabinet members are important both individually and collectively. Individually, they are departmental executives, presiding over extensive bureaucracies with programs encompassing an entire policy arena. Secretaries are expected to demonstrate considerable expertise regarding the programs and the relationships that constitute a department's political environment. Many secretaries, not surprisingly, have served an apprenticeship in the subcabinet, learning the intricacies of executive branch politics. Secretaries have also frequently served as members of Congress, as mayors or governors, or as directors of major interest groups. Thus, individual cabinet members also merit study because of the connections and the priorities that they bring into office. This is representation at its most fundamental, calculated on the basis of past relationships and future access.

Cabinet members are also important as a collectivity. This is a perspective that has seemed less valid in the modern presidency, as decision making has become progressively more centralized in the White House. Presidents have retreated from their promises of cabinet government with almost embarrassing speed, and cabinet meetings have frequently been described as graceless photo opportunities. There are simply too many people in attendance, with too many divergent allegiances and interests, for substantive action. Instead, smaller groupings of cabinet members and administration officers, organized as policy-specific councils or task forces, have been created to develop and advance presidential initiatives (Hult 2003; Walcott and Hult 2003). If the cabinet has been dissected in the policy process, however, it has retained some institutional coherence as a register of a president's commitments. Just as each secretary reflects a president's priorities in a particular arena, the complete cabinet is a commentary on presidential expectations for the wider political agenda—and for his electoral returns.

Recognizing these circumstances, newspaper coverage of a president-elect's cabinet nominations, in particular, has analyzed the "balance" among the secretaries-designate, that is, the extent to which social, economic, and political diversity is evidenced in the cabinet (Martin 1988). Are the secretaries-designate drawn from across the United States? Which party factions, issue networks, and department clients have their loyalists in the cabinet? Which races and ethnicities are included? These queries, and many others, can be mistaken for a superficial showcasing of the nominees. That impression was one that President-elect Bill Clinton sought to foster and to criticize in 1992, when he dismissed as "bean counters" those who were evaluating his nominees in terms of his campaign promise of an administration that "looks like America" (Marcus 1992). In fact, such media coverage—and such campaign promises—tap into an enduring interest in the representativeness of the executive branch. The cabinet secretaries-designate, as a group, are perceived as indicative of the president-elect's (and, later, the president's) responsiveness to pluralism in the United States.

Approaching the secretaries-designate as prospective representatives allows for a finely tuned analysis of this presidential responsiveness. In her classic work *The Concept of Representation* (1967 passim), Hanna Pitkin presents representation as having four distinct aspects.

- Formal representation: The established procedures for selecting individuals who will serve as representatives.
- Descriptive representation: The characteristics that the representative and the represented share, their overlapping identities being expected to result in similar perspectives.
- Substantive representation: The issues and interests advanced by the representative on behalf of the represented.
- Symbolic representation: The fundamental principles that the representative expresses and implements.

Each of these aspects of representation raises important questions relating to women as prospective cabinet members and presidential constituents:

- Formal representation: In what ways does the nomination of women change the nomination and confirmation procedures?
- Descriptive representation: How does the addition of women secretaries-designate affect the political agendas and ambitions of chief executives, departments, issue networks, and constituents?
- Substantive representation: How does the nomination of women secretaries-designate alter the cabinet's policy agenda?
- Symbolic representation: What are the ideological implications of numbering women among the cabinet secretaries-designate?

In order to determine the representation that women secretaries-designate might provide, and thus to determine what changes they might effect, it is necessary first to consider how gender has shaped the executive branch in the past.

To state the obvious, men are gendered creatures. In the same way that social, economic, and political roles have been ascribed to females, they have also been ascribed to males. Femininity has its counterpoint in masculinity, with the two traditionally perceived as mutually exclusive. Thus, in Western European cultures, women have historically been assigned to the private sphere, while men have historically been assigned to the public sphere. Arguably, the executive branch testifies most clearly to the effects of these practices. The notion of a single national leader is celebrated in innumerable Western narratives, both factual and mythological. The warrior king, able to master the fates and direct events, earning unqualified allegiance through his strength and insight, is also a hero in U.S. political traditions (Duerst-Lahti 1997; Di Stefano 1996; see also Jamieson 1995). *Federalist Paper 70*, for example, cites lessons learned from the Romans in support of a unitary, singular, enduring executive office. The constitutional powers granted to the individual in this position, both enumerated and implied, are wholly in keeping with masculine ideals. These conceptions are extremely important for the cabinet. Secretaries, as departmental executives, are expected to demonstrate leadership qualities similar to those of the chief executive. While deferring to presidential priorities, the secretaries are to be self-reliant and resolute in advancing their departments, proactive and even aggressive on behalf of their programs, and masterful in constituency and congressional exchanges. These are not traits that have been historically ascribed to—or acknowledged or valued in—women. A woman with political ambitions to serve in the cabinet therefore faces many obstacles. Even if she is able to enter the public sphere, she is likely to be perceived as presumptively lacking in the qualities deemed requisite to successful leadership (Borrelli 1997). The understanding of who should lead, how they should lead, and to what ends they should lead is masculinist in nature. And these masculinist presumptions are constant across partisan boundaries; they are so elemental that Georgia Duerst-Lahti has labeled masculinism a proto-ideology (Duerst-Lahti 2002).

What, then, do we make of the women who have been secretaries-designate? Are they exceptional individuals who succeed by conforming to masculinist traditions? Or do their accomplishments foreshadow a change in political ideology and practice?

This chapter examines women secretaries-designate in terms of their contributions to regendering or transgendering a cabinet office, to a gender desegregation or integration of the cabinet. To the extent that the prospective roles of women cabinet nominees are circumscribed and delimited, they are part of a *regendering* process. (The terms *regendering* and *transgendering* are first explicated in Duerst-Lahti and Kelly 1995.) Regendering occurs when a woman secretary-designate is nominated to a department whose programs are congruent with traditional conceptions of a woman's role as nurturer, so that her public sphere activism is excused as an extension of private sphere dedication. Other instances of regendering include reserving a particular office as the "woman's seat" in the cabinet, thereby preventing women from expressing the range of their abilities and expertise; nominating women to departments distant from the president's agenda, so that their participation in the administration is minimized; or nominating women "away from" their professional or political expertise, so that they become more dependent on the White House and less likely to offer constructive criticism. In all of these nominations, the women are granted limited power and influence so that they are marginalized within the cabinet, the presidency, and the public sphere. Conversely, *transgendering* occurs as women secretaries-designate are given new and expanding opportunities to contribute to the administration as viable representatives. This occurs as women are nominated to a wider range of departments, including those whose programs are associated with traditionally masculine endeavors, such as foreign affairs and commerce; when women are named to departments important to the president's agenda; or when women are nominated to departments in which they can exercise their expertise, which is then valued by the White House. In these nominations, women are given both power and influence, and are expected to make significant contributions to policymaking. When nominations are regendered, traditional views of women's gender role are reinforced: women are granted little opportunity to contribute to political deliberations, so that their nomination to the cabinet is about showcasing rather than institutional change. When the nominations are transgendered, however, traditional gender roles and barriers are weakened: women are welcomed into the public sphere—previously reserved for men—to participate in its debates and deliberations.

Regendering and *transgendering* are terms that allow us to classify the circumstances of the individual secretaries-designate. To assess the effects of nominating women to the cabinet, as a collectivity, we can speak in terms of *gender desegregation* or *gender integration*. To the extent that regendering predominates in the nomination of women within a presidential administration, the cabinet is experiencing only *gender desegregation*. Women are present, but their contributions are marginalized and the masculinist ideology remains dominant. To the extent, however, that transgendering characterizes the women's nominations, the cabinet

undergoes a *gender integration*. As gender integration proceeds, women are recognized as decision makers and constituents, weakening the power of masculinism.
Unquestionably, gender desegregation and integration shade into one another on a
wide spectrum, as every cabinet is likely to exhibit a mixture of regendering and
transgendering (Borrelli 2002). Still, when applied with care, these terms are useful indicators of the extent to which women are included in the highest ranks of the
presidency. And, as such, they connect the descriptive and substantive representation expected of individual secretaries-designate to the symbolic representation
anticipated from the cabinet as a whole.

Given the power of tradition and the consequent strength of masculinist beliefs,
it is likely that cabinet nominations will evidence more regendering than
transgendering. Women still encounter formal and informal barriers in their professional and political lives, making their candidacy for a cabinet post correspondingly problematic. Yet there have been real changes throughout the polity. Women
have been able to realize more of their ambitions in the public sector, their opportunities and thus their careers becoming more reflective of their distinctive person-
alities. As well, women's nominations to the cabinet are now more common,
suggesting that transgendering may be occurring. Ultimately, then, it seems logi-
cal to hypothesize that women's cabinet nominations have seesawed between
regendering and transgendering, with the cabinet undergoing more of a gender
desegregation than a gender integration.

This expectation is tested in the sections that follow, which examine the
secretaries-designate nominated in the eight administrations with women in the
cabinet. Attention is first given to the Roosevelt, Eisenhower, Ford, Carter, Reagan,
and George H.W. Bush secretaries-designate. This sets a historical context for analysis of the Clinton and George W. Bush cabinet nominations. As this book goes to
press, Bush is beginning his second term and judgments about his administration
must be undertaken with caution. Still, this president has already had a profound
effect on the structure and operation of the executive branch. If there has been
regendering and transgendering in cabinet nominations in the past, with the cabinet undergoing gender desegregation and gender integration, what has happened
in the early stages of the George W. Bush administration?

The Cabinet Nominations of William J. Clinton and His Predecessors

Secretaries-designate are the embodiment of a chief executive's promise of, and
perhaps even commitment to, representation. The president-elect's initial nominations are indicative of which campaign promises will actually be transformed into
programmatic initiatives and of whose interests will be accommodated in political
negotiations. Similarly, the president's midterm or replacement nominees reveal
the will to implement newly enacted programs and reelection concerns (Hershey
1983; King and Riddlesperger 1984). Evaluating cabinet secretaries-designate,
therefore, aids in anticipating the behavior of presidents and presidential advisors.

Yet it is not a purely speculative undertaking—there is a predictability to many of the demands that arise throughout a presidential term and to the responses routinely made by the chief executive.

Two patterns have remained remarkably consistent in regard to the selection of male secretaries-designate in the modern presidency. First, as the presidential term advances, a higher percentage of Washington insiders have been nominated to the cabinet. This can be attributed to a variety of factors: newly elected presidents are indebted to constituencies outside the Beltway, while partisan turnover limits the candidate pool of insiders; midterm presidents need skilled managers to implement new programs and can recruit these individuals from within their own administrations. Second, as the presidential term advances, presidents give higher priority to loyalty and lower priority to political or policy expertise among their cabinet officers. In other words, loyal generalists have become more valued later in the presidential term. These secretaries, who are less independent, effectively abdicate power to the White House and contribute to the centralization of presidential politics (Borrelli 2002; King and Riddlesperger 1984; Best 1981).

Women secretaries-designate have exhibited some consistencies and some inconsistencies with these male-identified patterns. Higher percentages of both women and men nominees have, as the term progressed, been Washington insiders. In many cases, the women have been promoted from within the administrations. Reagan's Transportation Secretary-designate Elizabeth H. Dole is an especially good example of this practice. She was considered and rejected for a cabinet post in the 1980 transition; as a former Democrat, she lacked the requisite ideological credentials and Republican support. Instead, she was named White House public liaison director. In 1983, as the gender gap began to threaten Reagan's reelection, Dole was nominated to the cabinet as part of an outreach to women voters. Since the administration was not particularly interested in transportation policy, her lack of substantive expertise did not pose a problem (Melich 1996; Von Damm 1989). This limitation relates to the second pattern in cabinet nominations, namely, the nomination of higher percentages of policy generalists later in the term. Here, there are sharp contrasts between the women and men secretaries-designate.

In the six earlier administrations, men secretaries-designate have been liaisons to departmental clients and issue networks (52.8 percent) and policy generalists (43.1 percent). Policy specialists who lack a political background are comparatively rare (4.1 percent), as is to be expected in a system whose departmental executives are on call to the Congress and the White House. Even when the timing of the nominations is taken into account, men have been distributed between the liaison and generalist categories. Among initial men secretaries-designate, 62.1 percent have been liaisons and 31.0 percent generalists; among midterm men secretaries-designate, 44.6 percent have been liaisons and 53.8 percent generalists.

The statistical profile of the women secretaries-designate, however, is very different from that of the men. Prior to the Clinton administration, only George H.W. Bush's Commerce Secretary-designate Barbara Franklin could be considered a liaison to her department's clients and issue networks. Franklin, moreover, was nominated so late in the presidential term that she had few opportunities to offer policy feedback to the White House. Thus, across the six earlier administrations, 84.6 percent of women were generalists and 7.7 percent liaisons. (There was also one specialist [7.7 percent], Roosevelt's Labor Secretary-designate Frances Perkins.) With such a high percentage of generalists—with so few prior relationships with department clients and networks, and so little advance expertise in their departmental programs—the women secretaries-designate as a group were correspondingly likely to depend on the White House for guidance and direction.

Study of the individual presidents and the nomination decisions behind these numbers leads to the conclusion that the cabinet underwent only a slight and gradual gender desegregation prior to the Clinton years (Borrelli 2002). Admittedly, there are some similarities in the credentials and circumstances of the women and men secretaries-designate. For instance, the comparable distributions of Washington insiders, among the women and the men nominees, suggest that some transgendering is occurring—and thus there is the possibility of some gender integration. However, the failure to place women in posts where they can exercise their policy and political expertise—and can therefore act more independently of the White House—points to a resistance to women as proactive and masterful departmental executives. Women secretaries-designate in the earlier administrations did not significantly weaken the hold of masculinism on the executive branch. Their credibility as representatives was limited, with the women most often being merely showcased for their sex.

This is a strong conclusion. There are many who would object, noting that women cabinet officers who served prior to the Clinton administration compiled notable records of public service. Still, these women were nominated to departments that were new or young, in the outer cabinet, distant from their presidents' policy agendas. Their contributions were, therefore, on the margins. Further, they were often assigned to policy jurisdictions consistent with traditional understandings of their gender role and/or were slotted into the "woman's seat" in the cabinet. Four women were secretaries-designate of Health, Education and Welfare/Health and Human Services or Education. Labor was the other department with a high proportion of women secretaries: four women held that post in the six administrations, three in Republican administrations that evidenced little interest in the department's strongest clients. The further nomination of women generalists signaled the presidents' desires for a buffer against critical constituencies. Though the women secretaries-designate provided a measure of "protection" for the president, they did not serve as self-reliant policy advisors. The gender power relations endorsed by masculinism were thus reinforced, limiting even the cabinet's gender desegregation.

Did the Clinton nominations change these gender dynamics? Or was there only more showcasing? While there was some regendering in the Clinton nominations, there was in fact more transgendering and more gender integration than had been seen in previous administrations. Electoral factors, as well as the administration's willingness to name women to influential positions, contributed to this outcome.

The political environment of the 1992 presidential transition favored the nomination of women secretaries-designate. The president-elect had promised an administration that "looks like America," a commitment that was sometimes slightly qualified as "looks more like America" (Associated Press 1992; Martin 1997). Shortly after the election, Clinton mentioned that he might nominate a woman as attorney general–designate (Lewis 1992). Searching for something that would bring coherence to their coverage of an unusually disordered transition, the media adopted the campaign promise and the casual remark as hallmarks. The president-elect's indebtedness to women voters reinforced the strength and the appeal of the diversity theme. Women constituted 57 percent of Clinton's voters.[1] By one accounting, 86 percent of African American women had voted for Clinton (Gilliam 1992). Further, the Coalition for Women's Appointments (CFWA), a coalition of approximately seventy women's and "women's issues" organizations, mobilized to remind Clinton of his debt to women voters.[2] They worked to ensure that women had influential representatives in the new administration, forwarding lists of prospective appointees to the transition team, issuing daily newsletters to the national media, and sending faxes to decision makers (CFWA 1992–93). Media and interest group pressure therefore coincided with electoral incentives in favor of women as representatives and as constituents.

Like other presidents-elect, Clinton acknowledged his debts and bowed to situational imperatives only with reluctance. He was self-evidently uninterested in empowering another issue network in Washington; it seemed at first that he avoided nominating or appointing women recommended by the CFWA. By the end of December, however, Clinton had announced all of his cabinet nominations, in carefully executed photo opportunities that matched white male and "diversity" nominees.[3] There were six white male and nine "diversity" secretaries-designate among the original cabinet nominees.

As seen in Table 10.2, Clinton's initial cabinet nominations did evidence some transgendering. Women were named to lead Justice and Energy for the first time. Moreover, the Justice post placed a woman in the inner cabinet, while the Energy post offered a woman a greater role in nuclear disarmament processes. Health and Human Services (HHS) had previously been led by three women secretaries. In the 1992 campaign, however, its programs had been the subject of numerous campaign promises and so the department was expected to be central to the president-elect's agenda. Clinton's woman HHS secretary-designate might therefore play a greater role in policymaking. The women secretaries-designate also had the political and professional credentials to act upon these possibilities. Each had served in the Carter administration—Energy Secretary–designate Hazel R. O'Leary and Attorney General–designate Zoë E. Baird in the departments they were now to lead—and each had proven her abilities in the intervening years. O'Leary and HHS Secretary-designate Donna E. Shalala had ties to the CFWA. Descriptively and

Table 10.2

William J. Clinton and George W. Bush, Initial Secretaries-Designate

Department	Clinton Secretary-Designate	Sex, Race/Ethnicity	Bush Secretary-Designate	Sex, Race/Ethnicity
State	William M. Christopher	Male, White	Colin L. Powell	Male, African American
Treasury	Lloyd Bentsen	Male, White	Paul H. O'Neill	Male, White
Defense	Les Aspin	Male, White	Donald H. Rumsfeld	Male, White
Justice	Zoë E. Baird* Janet Reno	Female, White Female, White	John Ashcroft	Male, White
Interior	Bruce Babbitt	Male, White	Gale A. Norton	Female, White
Agriculture	Mike Espy	Male, African American	Ann M. Veneman	Female, White
Labor	Robert Reich	Male, White	Linda Chavez*	Female, Hispanic American
			Elaine L. Chao	Female, Asian American
Commerce	Ron Brown	Male, African American	Donald L. Evans	Male, White
HHS	Donna E. Shalala	Female, White	Tommy G. Thompson	Male, White
HUD	Henry G. Cisneros	Male, Hispanic American	Melquiades R. Martinez	Male, Hispanic American
Transportation	Federico Peña	Male, Hispanic American	Norman Y. Mineta	Male, Asian American
Energy	Hazel R. O'Leary	Female, African American	Spencer Abraham	Male, White
Education	Richard Reilly	Male, White	Rodney Paige	Male, African American
Veterans' Affairs	Jesse Brown	Male, African American	Anthony J. Principi	Male, White

Note: *Nomination withdrawn.

substantively, then, these women secretaries-designate promised to be strong representatives for women. And then, Baird's promise faltered.

A January 14, 1993, *New York Times* article reported that the attorney general–designate had broken the law in hiring undocumented workers to provide childcare for her young son. She and her husband, Yale law professor Paul Gewirtz, were then in the midst of negotiations, making arrangements to pay the overdue employment taxes. The White House and the confirmation committee senators were prepared to overlook this infraction (Johnston 1993; Isikoff and Kamen 1993). The public, however, was strongly and increasingly critical (Page 1996). For some, there was the irony of nominating a lawbreaker to be one of the nation's chief law enforcement officers.[4] Even more citizens, however, rejected Baird because they judged her a bad mother. Liberals soon adopted what began as a conservative challenge. Suddenly, there was a national debate about what it meant to be a descriptive representative of women. The CFWA, who had not endorsed Baird, did not mobilize on her behalf. Her professional and political accomplishments being viewed as evidence of her lack of fitness for office, Baird was left without credentials or constituents. After two days of confirmation hearings, during which senators announced that telephone calls were running 50–1 and 84–3 against the attorney general–designate, the nomination was withdrawn (U.S. Congress 1993, 100, 132).

Gender roles, careers and children, and descriptive representation continued to be issues in the subsequent search for another attorney general–designate. The suggestion that a man be nominated was floated and dropped, in response to negative public feedback. When Dade County, Florida, State Attorney Janet Reno was nominated, there were those who said her primary qualification was her lack of familial obligations. (Reno had never been married and had never had children, though she was a guardian for two teenagers.) Since the typical attorney general is a close associate of the president who has been an influential member of the campaign organization, and Reno was unknown to Clinton, she was an unusual choice for the post. Lacking experience at the federal level, Reno was a generalist unacquainted with the Justice Department's policies and clients. Her dependence on the president, moreover, promised to be greater than O'Leary's or Shalala's; though neither of these women claimed expertise in their departments' most important programs or had extended relationships with their departments' most influential issue networks, both at least had previously served in the subcabinet—O'Leary in the department that she would now lead. The nomination of a woman to the inner cabinet was therefore not an unqualified advance for women as decision makers or as constituents. The attorney general–designate was given an opportunity, but the likelihood of her success was not great given her apparently limited professional and political resources. It seemed that Justice would be a less important department in the Clinton administration, as the effects of regendering were felt.

Reno, however, became a pivotal figure in the Clinton administration. Her personality and political style, as exhibited at her confirmation, at the time of the Branch Davidian crisis in Waco, and throughout the investigations of Clinton administration officials, were (generally) viewed with approval. Criticisms did surface about her decisions and actions, and the White House did seek to marginalize her in policy negotiations, but Reno kept much of her appeal and credibility. Notwithstanding his apparent wishes to do otherwise, Clinton announced that Reno would continue as attorney general in his second term (Purdum 1996). She and HHS Secretary Donna Shalala served in their posts for Clinton's two terms in office, becoming two of the longer-serving women cabinet members.

Following Hazel O'Leary's 1996 resignation, White House Director of Public Liaison Alexis M. Herman, an African American woman, was named Labor secretary-designate. Identified (and dismissed) as the "woman's seat" in the Reagan and George H.W. Bush administrations, this department's primary constituency was considerably more important to a Democratic president. Director of the Women's Bureau in the Carter administration, Herman had previously served in the Labor Department. Still, her expertise and commitment to affirmative action made her unpopular with organized labor. The intercession of Carter's Labor Secretary F. Ray Marshall was necessary to secure union support. Meanwhile, Senate Republicans imposed their own constraints, first investigating whether Herman had played any part in Clinton's campaign finance irregularities, and then holding her confirmation hostage to Clinton's renunciation of a proposed executive order regulating labor practices in federal contracts (Wines 1997a, 1997b; "Delay" 1997; Gray 1997). Herman's confirmation battles, therefore, focused attention on both the president's politics and the nominee's promise as a representative. If the nomination had been withdrawn, it would have seemed to admit wrongdoing in White House campaign fundraising (thereby implicitly encouraging congressional investigations); to indicate a disregard for the loyal African American voting block (especially for the support of African American women); and to reveal vacillation in labor policymaking (further weakening the administration's relations with organized labor). Thus, the Herman nomination was allowed to stand, despite its consumption of White House political resources.

Also nominated in 1997 was Secretary-designate of State Madeleine Albright, already serving in the Clinton administration as the permanent U.S. representative to the United Nations. As such, Albright had been named plenipotentiary ambassador extraordinaire and given both cabinet rank and National Security Council membership. A former congressional staffer, a member of Carter's National Security Council staff, a well-respected university professor, and the director of two policy foundations, Albright had previously served in most of the arenas in which United States foreign policy was crafted. She was also known to Clinton personally, having met him while he was a governor and having served as a policy advisor in his presidential campaign. She therefore had the knowledge and the experience that distinguishes a secretary who is a liaison to and from a department's established constituents. She also had proven her loyalty to the president, which could ease some concerns about his dependence on her recommendations. Still, this nomination effected a remarkable gender role reversal, challenging the ideology and mythology of the presidency. A woman liaison secretary-designate was nominated to the inner cabinet, at the beginning of a presidential term, with a mandate to bring coherence and credibility to a nation's foreign policy. The Albright nomination was a transgendered cabinet nomination, and it contributed to the gender integration of the cabinet.

But would the transgendering and the gender integration continue in the cabinet after the Clinton administration? Established departmental clients and issue networks had shaped expectations of cabinet representation, and of cabinet nominations, over many previous presidencies. A single administration would not, necessarily, change those standards. Further, the lessons learned in the Clinton years were not entirely to the advantage of women. Janet Reno, for example, was arguably the most independent attorney general seen in the modern presidency. Though this was a reform promised by many presidential candidates, its implementation periodically caused difficulties for the Clinton White House. Then, too, the circumstances of the 1992 transition—campaign promises, media coverage, interest group pressure, electoral indebtedness—were unusually fortuitous for women. What would happen when one, or more, of these influences was lessened? Would women again be nominated to departments in the outer cabinet, distant from the president's agenda and from their own areas of expertise, with policy jurisdictions congruent with their traditional gender roles? What priorities would be set by Clinton's successor in the Oval Office? What would be the implications of those priorities for women as representatives and as constituents of the executive branch?

Old and New Traditions: Patterns in the George W. Bush Cabinet Nominations

Clinton in 1992 and Bush in 2000 were both outsider presidents, and there the resemblance stops in regard to their initial cabinet nomination politics. The election was incredibly close for Bush, so much so that the outcome was uncertain for thirty-six days and then was decided by the Supreme Court. Bush was definitely indebted to the right. Though the close returns could be expected to encourage the nomination of moderates to the cabinet, some acknowledgment would have to be given to conservatives. Further, Bush had made no commitments to nominate or appoint women to leadership positions. The descriptive representation that would be provided by his administration was not a campaign issue, though affirmative action was and it was strongly opposed (Martin and Borrelli 2001). In the past, such stances had created difficulties for "diversity" secretaries-designate, who found their credentials subjected to scrutiny by those wishing to challenge the president's position and by those wishing to reinforce it (see U.S. Congress 1989). Meanwhile, there was comparatively little mobilization on behalf of prospective women nominees among women's and "women's issues" organizations. In sum, the factors that had contributed to transgendering the initial Clinton cabinet were lacking. Singly and cumulatively, these circumstances suggested that Bush would nominate a predominantly (if not exclusively) white and male cabinet.

In fact, as seen in Table 10.2, the initial Bush cabinet nominations both conformed to and contradicted these expectations. In keeping with established practice, senior White House advisors were better known to the president-elect than were the secretaries-designate, but there were no unknowns as there had been among Clinton's initial secretaries-designate. Interior Secretary–designate Gale A. Norton, for example, echoed Janet Reno in stating that she did not know her president-elect well. Norton, however, had worked as a policy advisor in the campaign and Reno had not ("Nonthreatening" 2003). Also following tradition, campaign indebtedness was a part of the nomination politics: it was the rare cabinet nominee who could not offer representation to several constituencies. The media especially highlighted the conservative ties of the individuals named to lead Justice (John Ashcroft), Interior (Gale A. Norton), and Labor (Linda Chavez and, later, Elaine Chao), predicting difficult confirmation hearings for at least the first two of these secretaries-designate (see Jehl 2000). Still, the fireworks were kept to a minimum, the nominees providing the reassurances that the senators demanded while avoiding any real constraints on their future decision making. Ultimately, the Bush cabinet had five (33.3 percent) Washington insiders and ten (66.7 percent) outsiders; these numbers and proportions were similar to those in other initial cabinets. There were also seven (46.7 percent) secretaries-designate who could serve as liaisons to their departments' dominant client or issue network, with eight (53.3 percent) generalists more dependent on the president. The percentage of generalists was high compared to previous administrations; it was also unexpected in light of Bush's self-evident need to strengthen his electoral base after the 2000 election. It may be that the administration believed it was more important to control the cabinet than to use its members for electoral outreach (see Transcript 2003).

The initial nominations also had some surprising elements. Even though he had made no campaign promises relating to cabinet nominations, Bush selected a comparatively significant number of "diversity" secretaries-designate, including an African American man in the inner cabinet (Secretary-designate of State Colin Powell). Among the racial and ethnic cohorts receiving descriptive representation were African Americans, Asian Americans, and Hispanic Americans. With the exception of Colin Powell's nomination, however, these "diversity" secretaries-designate were named to departments that had been previously led by "diversity" secretaries and that were expected to be relatively distant from the president's agenda. Thus, the inclusivity of the initial cabinet, along racial and ethnic lines, was limited.

Women were nominated to lead two departments—Interior and Agriculture—that had previously been led only by men. (Both departments had, however, been led by male "diversity" secretaries.) Further, these departments were important to the administration, the president-elect having made numerous commitments relating to environmental policy (the purview of the Interior Department) and needing to retain the support of mainstream Republicans in the agricultural midwest and west (constituents of the Agriculture Department). Interior Secretary–designate Norton had the political credentials, contacts, and expertise to serve as a liaison to one of her department's dominant issue networks. Her dependence on the president would predictably be lessened, though she would have to exhibit considerable political acumen to counter environmentalist opposition. Agriculture Secretary–designate Ann Veneman lacked ties to midwestern interests, but (like Norton) she had previously served in a subcabinet position in the department she would now lead. Although classified as a generalist, therefore, she was not a newcomer to agricultural policy, having expertise in international trade and state-level policymaking. She was also a Californian, a crucial state for Bush's reelection (see Marinucci 2001). Finally, both departments were distant from women's traditional gender roles. Agriculture had evidenced some concern for consumer issues, but its priorities were centered on agribusiness interests. Interior also had a strongly masculine character; the secretary, for instance, includes "Master of the River" among her titles, in which capacity she administers the law relating to allocation of Colorado River water among seven western and southwestern states. In all of these regards, there was evidence of transgendering and gender integration in the initial Bush cabinet nominations.

What about the women initially nominated to head the Labor Department? This post had been the "woman's seat" in the Reagan and George H.W. Bush administrations. Then, it was a marginalized and even minimized office. It had gained in importance, slightly, during the Clinton administration. George W. Bush, though, was not expected to continue this trend, especially since he nominated conservatives with little sympathy for organized labor. The first Labor secretary-designate was Linda Chavez. When her nomination was withdrawn, she was replaced by an Asian American woman, Elaine L. Chao. Although Chao had an extensive record of service in the executive branch, and had been a successful fundraiser in the 2000 campaign, it seemed unlikely that she would make a strong contribution to the administration. Accordingly, her selection was evidence of regendering. Her circumstances were also indicative of the multiple challenges that confront women of color as they move into elite leadership positions. It seemed that Bush viewed "diversity" secretaries-designate as interchangeable, being more interested in showcasing the "diversity" secretaries-designate than in providing descriptive representation.

A comprehensive assessment of the representation that has been provided by the women members of the initial Bush cabinet cannot yet be given, but a few more general points can be noted. All of the women serve in departments focused on domestic policy, which has meant that their actions received little attention in the wake of September 11 and the war on terrorism (see Hult 2003; Jacobson 2003). This seemed to advantage Interior Secretary Norton, who has avoided major policy confrontations with environmental networks even as she has acted on a pro-development agenda. Though some critique her performance as too incremental, Norton has unquestionably benefited from limiting the scope of policy conflicts. She has even established alliances with some environmental groups, including the Nature Conservancy. Ongoing battles related to the administration of the national forests, the allocation of water in the drought-stricken west, and the Alaska National Wildlife Refuge Area will oblige Norton to either become somewhat more proactive or risk being dismissed as more manager than executive.

At least some reports suggest that Labor Secretary Elaine Chao was active in administration policymaking and in public outreach initiatives. She participated in economic policy through her membership on the related White House councils. (This was a role that Clinton's Labor Secretary Robert Reich had hoped to assume.) Chao fostered alliances with the Teamsters and Carpenters unions, which some believe weakened the AFL-CIO. She also had constructive relationships with the legislative branch. As the wife of Senator Mitch McConnell (R-KY), Chao evidenced an insider's understanding of that chamber's folkways and relationships.

These accomplishments, combined with her past executive and her fundraising expertise, earned her a measure of respect as a conservative Labor secretary ("Giving" 2003).

Among the initial women cabinet officers, Agriculture Secretary Ann Veneman earned the greatest criticism. In a January 25, 2003, article titled "Grading the Cabinet," *National Journal* gave Veneman a "D" for her overall performance. Only Treasury Secretary Paul O'Neill, who had already been forced to resign, received as low a grade. Veneman's limited participation in crafting major farm bills, her poor relationships on the Hill, and her limited success in reaching out to farmers and ranchers in the electorate were all cited as contributing to her poor performance ("Drought" 2003). Veneman previously had posted a midterm report listing her accomplishments on the Agriculture Department website (USDA 2003). This document presented the secretary as facilitating international trade agreements, implementing new programs, and securing increased funding for departmental initiatives. In essence, it seemed that Veneman's prior experience was a poor fit with the expectations directed toward her office. For example, *National Journal* concluded that her interest in and commitment to international trade distanced her from American farmers and ranchers; the *Journal* went so far as to state that she was poaching on the territory of the U.S. Trade Representative. Veneman was unquestionably further disadvantaged by the added scrutiny that is given to women secretaries, especially the "firsts." And yet, women policymakers have stated that her performance is sufficiently problematic that it calls their own credibility into question ("Drought" 2003).

On balance, then, the expectations for the initial women secretaries-designate were generally fulfilled: Norton held her own, while Chao did better and Veneman did worse than predicted. There was a significant level of transgendering, with the initial women secretaries (most notably Norton, but also Veneman) stepping outside the bounds of their traditional gender roles, and it can be said that gender integration is occurring within the Bush cabinet. Women gained some descriptive representation, and the performance of the initial women secretaries pushed the cabinet toward greater inclusivity. Yet the constraints also continue, whether as a function of the president's nomination decisions, or the secretaries' own limitations, or the enduring resistance to "diversity" decision makers in the Washington establishment. This regendering limits women's representation, though not to a greater extent in the George W. Bush than the Clinton administration. Despite the change in partisan control, and with due recognition of the contrasting priorities of the two presidencies, they have offered women comparable levels of descriptive representation in the cabinet in their initial cabinet nominations.

Conclusion

This chapter has examined the patterns in cabinet nominations throughout the modern presidency, exploring whether and how the selection of secretaries-designate has had the potential to change cabinet politics. That change was assessed in terms of the representation provided by and to women. Because this was a study of cabinet nominees, the focus was on possibility and potential, with correspondingly greater attention given to descriptive representation than substantive representation. Symbolic representation, the deeper and ideological impact of the nominees' selection, was also discussed, in terms of gender desegregation and gender integration.

Political institutions are notoriously "sticky." With few exceptions, they change only incrementally and, even then, in ways that are difficult to measure. Given the historic weight of masculinist ideals in executive branch leadership, the change effected by the selection of women secretaries-designate is especially likely to be uncertain and slow (see Duerst-Lahti 2002). In this chapter, the president's women nominees were studied in terms of their professional and political resources, their identity, and their "fit" with their prospective post. The women were classified as liaisons trusted by their departments' established clients and issue networks, or as generalists lacking policy relationships and expertise, who were correspondingly more dependent on the chief executive. Also considered were the departments to which women were named, the congruence of their policy jurisdiction with "women's issues," the centrality of the department to the president's agenda, and the variety of departments to which women were named. To the extent that women secretaries-designate were marginalized within the cabinet—nominated as generalists, to "women's issues" departments distant from the president's agenda, to the "woman's seat"—a process of regendering was identified. Though women held cabinet office, their historic exclusion from the public sphere was continuing. Their inclusion in decision making and policymaking was modest, so that the cabinet underwent only a gender desegregation. As women's participation was enhanced, however, a process of transgendering began to unfold. Women were nominated as liaison secretaries-designate; they began to serve in a wider array of departments, including those associated with previously masculine professions and those essential to the president's agenda. This greater inclusivity, cumulatively, led to gender integration.

Prior to the Clinton administration, cabinet nominations typically evidenced regendering, with the cabinet undergoing a very gradual gender desegregation. With few exceptions, the women secretaries-designate were generalists who buffered the president from critical constituencies. Some of these practices continued in the Clinton presidency, but there was also a decided shift to transgendering. A woman liaison was nominated to the inner cabinet (Albright at State) at the beginning of the second term, with the opportunity and the mandate to make significant policy changes. Other women generalists served in departments central to the administration's performance (Reno at Justice), to the fulfillment of campaign promises (Shalala at HHS), to securing electoral support (Herman at Labor), and in policy arenas distant from traditional gender roles (O'Leary at Energy). In the same administration, the significance and meaning of the women's representation was the subject of a national debate, and the nomination of Attorney General–designate Zoë Baird was withdrawn, in essence, because she lacked constituents. The identity of the women secretaries-designate, always a centerpiece of descriptive representation, was acknowledged as having substantive implications.

The transgendering seen in the Clinton years continued in the initial cabinet nominations of the George W. Bush administration. While Bush did not initially nominate women to the inner cabinet, he did name them to lead departments central to his policy agenda and his electoral success, and at odds with traditional conceptions of women's gender roles and "women's issues." The effects of regendering have continued, as seen in the decision to nominate another Republican woman to the Labor Department and also as evidenced in some of the difficulties encountered by Agriculture Secretary Ann Veneman. Still, there is a push toward gender integration. The next challenges to this development will come with the second term. What role will the women secretaries play in the policymaking and implementation during the second term? How will the connections between descriptive and substantive representation be negotiated? Will lessened electoral pressures cause the lame-duck president to devalue the contributions of "diversity" secretaries-designate? Will these nominees serve as representatives to and from historically marginalized peoples, or will these nominees be chosen for their loyalty to the president and their willingness to serve as buffers against these constituents? These are just a few of the questions that await answers, as the provision of representation in the cabinet is shaped by presidential decisions and political events.

Notes

1. This data comes from Voter Research and Survey Exit Polls; the author is indebted to Mary Bendyna for her statistical analysis.

2. Because the term is more indicative of traditional conceptions of gender roles than of people's interest or concern, "women's issues" is placed in quotations throughout this chapter.

3. With white women and people of color constituting the majority of the U.S. population, "diversity" is placed in quotations when it is used in reference to presidential nominees.

4. Commerce Secretary–designate Ron Brown was subsequently found to have followed practices similar to Baird's in hiring domestic workers. Brown's confirmation hearing, however, occurred before Baird's; he had already received a Senate endorsement. Still, there were newspaper columns that argued a double-standard was at work in assessing women nominees. Virtually all of these articles, however, were published after the nomination had been withdrawn. That there was so little commentary in support of Baird earlier must be attributed to her lack of political connections with Washington "women's issues" and women's organizations networks. Those networks had their own candidate for the attorney general post, who had been interviewed and rejected by the president-elect.

References

Associated Press. 1992. "Current Quotes from the 1992 Campaign Trail." May 22.
Best, James J. 1981. "Presidential Cabinet Appointments, 1953–1976." *Presidential Studies Quarterly* (Winter): 62–67.

Borrelli, MaryAnne. 1997. "Campaign Promises, Transition Dilemmas: Cabinet Building and Executive Representation." In *The Other Elites: Women, Politics, and Power in the Executive Branch*, ed. MaryAnne Borrelli and Janet M. Martin. Boulder, CO: Lynne Rienner.

———. 2002. *The President's Cabinet: Gender, Power, and Representation.* Boulder, CO: Lynne Rienner.

Coalition for Women's Appointments (CFWA). 1992–93. *The Mirror.* Provided to the author by the National Women's Political Caucus.

"Delay in Herman Vote Blocks Bill in Senate." 1997. *The New York Times*, April 30, p. A19.

Di Stefano, Christine. 1996. "Autonomy in the Light of Difference." In *Revisioning the Political, Feminist Reconstructions of Traditional Concepts in Western Political Theory*, ed. Nancy J. Hirschmann and Christine Di Stefano. Boulder, CO: Westview Press.

"Drought of Farm Support." 2003. *National Journal*, January 25, pp. 262–263.

Duerst-Lahti, Georgia. 1997. "Reconceiving Theories of Power: Consequences of Masculinism in the Executive Branch." In *The Other Elites: Women, Politics, and Power in the Executive Branch*, ed. MaryAnne Borrelli and Janet M. Martin. Boulder, CO: Lynne Rienner.

———. 2002. "Governing Institutions, Ideologies, and Gender: Toward the Possibility of Equal Political Representation." *Sex Roles* 47, 7/8 (October): 371–388.

Duerst-Lahti, Georgia, and Rita Mae Kelly, eds. 1995. *Gender Power, Leadership, and Governance.* Ann Arbor: University of Michigan Press.

The Federalist Papers.

Gilliam, Dorothy. 1992. "Black Women Need a Seat at the Table." *Washington Post*, December 19, pp. B1, B4.

"Giving Labor a Raise." 2003. *National Journal*, January 25, pp. 270–271.

"Grading the Cabinet." 2003. *National Journal*, January 25, pp. 232–235.

Gray, Jerry. 1997. "After Impasse, Senate Confirms Clinton's Choice for Labor Post." *The New York Times*, May 1, p. 1.

Heclo, Hugh. 2003. "The Bush Political Ethos." Paper presented at the 2003 Princeton University conference, The George W. Bush Presidency: An Early Assessment.

Hershey, Robert D., Jr. 1983. "Working Profile: Elizabeth H. Dole, Transportation Secretary." *The New York Times*, August 22, sec. II, p. 8.

Hult, Karen M. 2003. "The Bush White House in Comparative Perspective." Revised version of a paper presented at the 2003 Princeton University conference, The George W. Bush Presidency: An Early Assessment.

Isikoff, Michael, and Al Kamen. 1993. "Baird's Hiring Disclosure Not Seen as Major Block." *Washington Post*, January 15, p. A14.

Jacobson, Gary C. 2003. "The Bush Presidency and the American Electorate." Paper presented at the 2003 Princeton University conference, The George W. Bush Presidency: An Early Assessment.

Jamieson, Kathleen Hall. 1995. *Beyond the Double Bind, Women and Leadership.* New York: Oxford University Press.

Jehl, Douglas. 2000. "Interior Choice Sends a Signal on Land Policy." *The New York Times*, December 30, p. A1.

Johnston, David. 1993. "Clinton's Choice for Justice Dept. Hired Illegal Aliens for Household." *The New York Times*, January 14, pp. A1, A20.

King, James D., and James W. Riddlesperger, Jr. 1984. "Presidential Cabinet Appointments: The Partisan Factor." *Presidential Studies Quarterly* (Spring): 231–237.

Lewis, Neil A. 1992. "Getting Things Done, Zoë Baird." *New York Times*, December 25, p. A1.

Marcus, Ruth. 1992. "Clinton Berates Critics in Women's Groups." *Washington Post*, December 22, pp. 1, A12.

Marinucci, Carla. 2001. "Bush Picks Californians for His Team." *San Francisco Examiner*, April 30, p. A11.

Martin, Janet M. 1988. "Frameworks for Cabinet Studies." *Presidential Studies Quarterly* 18 (Fall): 803–814.

———. 1997. "Women Who Govern: The President's Appointments." In *The Other Elites: Women, Politics, and Power in the Executive Branch*, ed. MaryAnne Borrelli and Janet M. Martin. Boulder, CO: Lynne Rienner.

Martin, Janet, and MaryAnne Borrelli. 2001. "Campaign Promises and Presidential Appointments: Women's Issues and Women in the George W. Bush Administration." Paper presented at the 2001 Annual Meeting of the American Political Science Association.

Melich, Tanya. 1996. *The Republican War Against Women: An Insider's Report from Behind the Lines.* New York: Bantam Books.

"The Nonthreatening Face of Development." 2003. *National Journal*, January 25, p. 258.

Page, Benjamin I. 1996. *Who Deliberates? Mass Media in Modern Democracy.* Chicago: University of Chicago Press.

Pitkin, Hanna Fenichel. 1967. *The Concept of Representation.* Berkeley: University of California Press.

Purdum, Todd S. 1996. "Clinton Fills Top Posts, Keeping Reno." *The New York Times*, December 14, 1996, pp. 1, 10.

Transcript of Journalists and Press Secretaries' Statements. 2003. Statements made at the 2003 Princeton University conference, The George W. Bush Presidency: An Early Assessment.

U.S. Congress. Senate. Committee on Finance. 1989. *Nomination of Louis W. Sullivan.* 101st Cong., 1st sess.

U.S. Congress. Senate. Committee on the Judiciary. 1993. *Nomination of Zoë E. Baird to be Attorney General of the United States.* 103rd Cong., 1st sess.

U.S. Department of Agriculture (USDA). 2003. *Midterm Review.* January 7.

Von Damm, Helene. 1989. *At Reagan's Side.* New York: Doubleday.

Walcott, Charles E., and Karen M. Hult. 2003. "The Bush Staff and Cabinet System." In *Considering the Bush Presidency*, ed. Mark J. Rozell and Gary L. Gregg. New York: Oxford University Press.

Wines, Michael. 1997a. "Friends Helped Labor Nominee Move Up, Then Almost Brought Her Down." *The New York Times*, March 12, p. A16.

———. 1997b. "A Nominee Bows Out: Another Hearing." *The New York Times*, March 19, p. B8.

11

Gender and the Federal Judiciary

Susan Gluck Mezey

By 2003, only Presidents Ronald Reagan and Bill Clinton had achieved the distinction of appointing women to the U.S. Supreme Court. Although nominations to the high court are always newsworthy, the selection of Sandra Day O'Connor and Ruth Bader Ginsburg—replacing Potter Stewart and Byron White respectively—attracted more attention than usual from legal scholars, politicians, special interest groups, the media, and the public. As the first and second women to serve as Supreme Court justices, their nominations were accompanied by speculation about how they would vote on issues coming before the Court. More specifically, there was widespread interest in how they would vote on claims involving gender equality and reproductive rights. The assumption that gender affects judicial decision making fueled the preoccupation with the nominations of these two justices; observers believed that as women justices, they would behave differently from their brethren. O'Connor and Ginsburg are, of course, the most visible women on the federal bench, but the appointment of women to the lower federal courts is typically accompanied by a related set of questions, concerns, and assumptions.

This chapter examines the effect of gender on the federal courts in a number of ways. After presenting data on judicial appointments to the federal bench, it discusses the scholarly literature on the impact of gender on judicial behavior, ending with an appraisal of the two women who serve on the highest court of the land.

Appointments to the Federal Bench

Although there were women serving on limited jurisdiction federal courts as early as 1918, they have been absent from the federal bench for most of the nation's history. The first woman was appointed to a federal court of general jurisdiction in 1934 when President Franklin Roosevelt nominated Ohio Supreme Court judge Florence Ellinwood Allen to the Sixth Circuit Court of Appeals. Allen, who served as chief judge of the Sixth Circuit before her retirement in 1959, began her judicial career on the Court of Common Pleas in Cuyahoga County, Ohio, in 1921; a year later, she was the first woman to be elected as a justice on a state supreme court. Despite the active lobbying by women's groups for Allen to fill one of the twelve

Supreme Court vacancies during the Roosevelt and Truman administrations, she was never nominated.

It took more than a decade for the second Article III (life-tenured) woman judge to be named to the bench. In 1949, President Harry Truman appointed Burnita Shelton Matthews, who served as a full-time judge for eighteen years, to the district court of the District of Columbia. A significant time again elapsed until President John F. Kennedy appointed Sarah Hughes to the district court in 1961. Ironically, Hughes was the judge who swore in Kennedy's successor on an airfield in Dallas in November 1963. Then, after a much briefer interval, President Lyndon Johnson named Shirley Hufstedler of the California Court of Appeals to the Ninth Circuit Court of Appeals in 1968 (see Berkson 1982; Martin 1982; Perry 1991; Harrison 1996; Wilson 1996).

The modern era of women appointees to the federal bench began during President Jimmy Carter's tenure in office. In 1978 Congress enacted the Omnibus Judgeship Act (OJA), creating 152 judgeships—117 at the district court level and 35 at the appellate court level. This allowed Carter to place his imprint on the federal judiciary, and by the time his term ended, he had appointed a majority of the appellate judges on the Fifth, Sixth, Ninth, Eleventh, and the District of Columbia Circuits (Gottschall 1983, 167). Although he did not have an opportunity to appoint a Supreme Court justice, Carter took advantage of the increased number of judgeships created by the OJA to name a record number of judges to the lower federal courts, including an unprecedented number of women and minorities.

The history of female appointments to the federal bench before Carter had been dismal. Until 1961, only Allen and Matthews, the Roosevelt and Truman appointees, served on federal courts of general jurisdiction. Between 1961 and 1981, a total of six new women judges were appointed: four during the Kennedy–Johnson administrations and two during the administrations of Presidents Richard Nixon and Gerald Ford (Goldman and Saronson 1994, 68 n. 1). Table 11.1 illustrates the number of judges appointed to the appellate and district courts from 1964 to 2000.

Carter took advantage of his opportunity to diversify the federal bench. When he assumed office, there were 6 women (and 22 nonwhite judges) out of approximately 500 federal court judges (Slotnick 1984, 374). Reflecting a highly visible affirmative action policy as well as an emphasis on merit selection, Carter appointed a record number of women and minorities to federal court judgeships: 93 women, African Americans, and Hispanics out of a total of 258 appointments (*Congressional Quarterly Weekly Report* 1997, 369). He was able to appoint 56 judges to the U.S. Court of Appeals; of these, 11 (19.6 percent) were women (Goldman 1995, Table 4). At the district court level, Carter appointed a total of 202 judges, including 29 (14.4 percent) women. When his administration ended, he had increased the percentage of women on the federal bench from 1 percent to almost 7 percent (Goldman 1981, 349).

Reagan claimed credit for placing a woman on the Supreme Court, but his appointments to the lower federal courts made it clear that he did not wish to

Table 11.1

Presidential Appointments to the U.S. Courts of Appeals and District Courts by Sex, 1964–2000

	President													
	Johnson		Nixon		Ford		Carter		Reagan		Bush		Clinton	
	%	(N)	%	(N)	%	(N)	%	(N)	%	(N)	%	(N)	%	(N)
Women Judges Appointed	1.9	3	0.4	1	1.6	1	15.5	40	7.6	28	19.5	36	29.2	107
Men Judges Appointed	98.1	159	99.6	223	98.4	63	84.5	218	92.4	340	80.5	149	70.8	260
Total Judges Appointed	162		224		64		258		368		185		367	

Sources: Johnson, Nixon, Ford—percentages calculated by author from Goldman (1989, Tables 2 and 4); Carter, Reagan, Bush—Goldman and Saronson (1994, Table 3); Clinton—percentages calculated by author from Goldman, Slotnick, Gryski, and Zuk (2001, Tables 3 and 6).

follow Carter's example of diversifying the federal bench, appointing only 28 women out of a total of 368 appointments. And despite the fact that the percentage of women appointed by Reagan to the district court was almost as high as Carter's, there was a "'dramatic' retreat from Carter's record" on appointments of women to the appellate level (Slotnick 1988, 319).

Some, like Goldman (1983), suggested Reagan was essentially indifferent to the idea of appointing women, but feminists argued that he was actually hostile to it. Martin (1987) believed that Reagan's record with respect to women appointments can be traced to a number of factors: a diminished pool of eligible candidates because of his abolition of the Carter-established circuit nominating panels; his reversion to the practice of "senatorial courtesy" for district court appointments (de-emphasized by Carter); and his insistence on the potential nominee's ideological commitment to traditional family values and opposition to reproductive rights.

Like Carter, President George Bush was aided in leaving his mark on the federal judiciary—although he had only four years to do so—by passage of the 1990 Federal Judgeship Act, creating eighty-five new judicial positions. Although committed to continuing the Reagan policy of appointing judges with conservative views, he also sought to expand the recruitment process to include "appropriately qualified women and minorities" (Goldman 1991, 297). Bush appointed 56 women and racial minorities out of a total of 185 (*Congressional Quarterly Weekly Report* 1997, 369). During his first two years in office, although he outdid Reagan in appointing women to the district and appellate courts, he did not surpass the Carter record despite the increasing number of eligible women in the recruitment pool (Goldman 1991, Tables 1 and 2). But during the last two years of his presidency, Bush exceeded Carter's record of women appointments to the district and appellate courts (Goldman 1993, Tables 2 and 4). Despite these achievements, Bush's judicial legacy has remained tainted by the nomination of Clarence Thomas to the Supreme Court, an appointment vigorously contested by women's groups and liberal organizations, only in part because of the accusations of sexual harassment against Thomas by University of Oklahoma law professor Anita Hill.

Clinton was even more committed than Carter to appointing nontraditional judges to the federal bench, and his nomination of women and minorities reflected the depth of his belief in producing a diversified court (Perry and Abraham 1998). By July 1, 1994, three-fifths of all his appointees were members of racial minority groups and women (Goldman and Saronson 1994, 68). More recent data show that of 198 federal judges he appointed by the end of 1996, 111 were women, African Americans, and Hispanics (*Congressional Quarterly Weekly* 1997, 369).

Like Carter, Clinton followed an affirmative action policy in judicial appointments. Reacting to Clinton's efforts to carry out his pledge, his opponents leveled charges that to meet his self-imposed quota, he appointed less-qualified women and members of racial minority groups. However, after assessing the background characteristics and experience of the earlier Clinton appointees, Goldman and Saronson (1994, 73) concluded that:

Table 11.2

Presidential Appointments to the U.S. Courts of Appeals by Sex, 1976–2000

	President							
	Carter		Reagan		Bush		Clinton	
	%	(N)	%	(N)	%	(N)	%	(N)
Women Judges Apppointed	19.6	11	5.1	4	18.9	7	32.8	41
Men Judges Apppointed	80.4	45	94.9	74	81.1	30	67.2	20
Total Judges Appointed		56		78		37		61

Source: Goldman, Slotnick, Gryski, and Zuk 2001, Table 6).

Table 11.3

Presidential Appointments to the U.S. District Courts by Sex, 1976–2000

	President							
	Carter		Reagan		Bush		Clinton	
	%	(N)	%	(N)	%	(N)	%	(N)
Women Judges Appointed	14.4	29	8.3	24	19.6	29	28.5	87
Men Judges Appointed	85.6	173	91.7	266	80.4	119	71.5	219
Total Judges Appointed		202		290		148		306

Source: Goldman, Slotnick, Gryski, and Zuk (2001, Table 3.

In accord with the concept of affirmative action as widening the recruitment net to bring in highly qualified women and minorities, greater diversity has not come at the expense of qualifications. Clinton's nontraditional appointees are as qualified, if not more so in terms of their ABA ratings and professional experience, as the appointees of Reagan and Bush. . . . The end result is a more diversified federal bench consistent with the principle of merit.

Tables 11.2 and 11.3 illustrate the number and percentage of women and men appointed to the appellate and district courts respectively during the Carter, Reagan, Bush, and Clinton administrations, from 1976 to 2000. When assessing each court level separately and comparing Clinton's record to that of his predecessors, Tables 11.2 and 11.3 show that he exceeded their records of appointing women judges at each court level. And because Supreme Court judges are more likely to be recruited from the U.S. Court of Appeals, it is significant that Clinton appointed an even higher percentage of women to this court than to the District Court.

Representation Theory

Scholars have investigated the effect of gender on the behavior of public office-holders by inquiring whether women in office "act for" women as well as "stand for" them; that is, whether women are more inclined than men to initiate and support women's policy goals. This debate over labeling women as "descriptive" or "substantive" representatives can be traced to Hannah Pitkin's (1967) classification of two types of representation. According to Pitkin's analysis of legislative behavior, "descriptive representation," or "standing for," is accomplished simply by being a member of a group and occupying a seat of power without advocating the group's policy interests. Being defined on the basis of what "he or she is like rather than what he or she does" (Perry 1991, 10), a "descriptive" representative may serve as a role model for the group, but is not necessarily committed to achieving its policy goals. On the other hand, a "substantive representative" is a public official who "acts for" the group by seeking to accomplish goals that purport to benefit the members of the group.

Studies of Gender Effects in Legislatures

For more than three decades, scholars have examined the extent to which women in public office differ from their male counterparts. They have asked whether women voice more concern than men about women's (or feminist) issues, whether women exert greater efforts than men to enact laws and policies that differentially affect women, and whether they serve as role models for other women. Most of this research has focused on state public officials, although scholars have also examined congressional behavior.

The results of this research have been mixed. Taken together, the studies showed that attitudes and voting behavior of politicians were in part attributable to gender differences but that gender *alone* probably did not account for differences in political behavior, with ideology and party also playing a role (see Mezey 1978, 1994). Studies by Welch (1985), Saint-Germain (1989), Thomas and Welch (1991), Reingold (1992), Dolan and Ford (1995), and Swers (2001) reported that women expressed more concern for women's issues and accorded a higher priority to them; women were also more inclined than men to translate these concerns into action by introducing legislation to promote greater equality for women and improve the status of women. Women were also more attentive to legislation that revolved around women's traditional interests, such as children, education, family, and health. Additionally, many women legislators felt they had a special responsibility to represent their women constituents and were more likely to consider their support important.

The research on gender and legislative behavior suggests that many women officeholders believe they must "act for" women in society. Largely because of the different perspectives they bring to their positions, women in elected office are more likely to support a variety of women's policy goals as well as favor a wide range of family-friendly policies. Federal court judges, however, differ from legislators in a number of ways. As lifetime appointees, they do not represent a constituency and are not subject to defeat at the polls. Even more important, their decisions must adhere to legal rules and principles rather than reflect their backgrounds or values. Federal judges also differ from legislators because the latter may be questioned about their policy preferences, which they may manifest in a number of ways. In addition to voting, legislators cosponsor legislation, propose amendments, and speak on the floor of the chamber; judges vote on cases and issue opinions. Hence judicial scholars are typically limited to counting judges' votes and analyzing their written opinions.

Studies of Gender Effects in the Courts

Despite the importance of legal analysis in judicial decision making, scholars have long been aware of the role of extralegal influences, such as political party, gender, region, religion, and age, on the decisions of federal court judges—from the lower district courts to the Supreme Court (see, for example, Goldman 1975; Rowland and Carp 1980; Tate 1981; Carp and Rowland 1983; Songer and Davis 1990). Their studies reflect the belief that social background characteristics affect the way in which judges decide cases and are useful in explaining and/or predicting their votes. Ultimately, therefore, judicial scholars have also addressed the question of whether women judges "act for" women or merely "stand for" them.

In exploring the premise that gender affects a judge's goals, priorities, and, ultimately, behavior on the bench, Gottschall (1983), Walker and Barrow (1985), and Songer, Davis, and Haire (1994) focused on the votes of lower federal court judges. Studies by Gryski, Main, and Dixon (1986), Gryski and Main (1986), Allen and Wall (1987, 1993) and more recently Songer and Crews-Meyer (2000), and Martin and Pyle (2000) examined the effects of gender on voting among state supreme court judges. At the local level, Kritzer and Uhlman (1977) and Gruhl, Spohn, and Welch (1981) examined differences in the sentencing behavior of men and women urban trial court judges.

The Impact of Gender on Judicial Decision Making

The chapter will now explore whether, and to what extent, women judges can be considered "substantive representatives" of women in society. Scholars such as Goldman (1981) and Martin (1982) predicted that as a result of Carter's commitment to diversity and his affirmative action policies, the federal bench would become more activist and liberal and that women judges would manifest a greater sensitivity to issues of race and sex discrimination on the bench. More specifically, they hypothesized that because women experienced societal discrimination, they would be more likely to take a liberal posture in rights and liberties cases. Alternatively, however, it has been argued that because women have been socialized into a common legal subculture, their decisions will closely resemble the decisions of the men with whom they serve (see, for example, Songer, Davis, and Haire 1994).

Martin's (1993) study of members of the National Association of Women Judges

(NAWJ) showed that most of the NAWJ members surveyed at their annual conference in 1989 believed their presence made a difference to women attorneys and that they encouraged other women to seek judgeships; they also thought they helped change the attitudes of men judges toward professional women. Martin's questions, however, related to women judges as role models and gender representatives, and her research, limited to women only, was unable to determine whether gender affected judicial voting behavior.

In his study of votes on federal courts of appeals from July 1, 1979, to June 30, 1981, Gottschall (1983) assessed how Carter's affirmative action policy affected judicial decision making by comparing the votes of appellate judges in cases involving gender and racial discrimination and criminal defendants' rights. Not surprisingly, he found that the Carter-, Johnson-, and Kennedy-appointed judges were more liberal than the Nixon- and Ford-appointed judges in all three issue areas. Comparing Carter's white female appointees to his white male appointees, he found they were alike in prisoners' rights cases, and although the women were slightly more liberal than the men on issues related to gender and racial equality, the differences were not significant.

Walker and Barrow's (1985) study of the diversification of the federal bench also examined the degree to which Carter's affirmative action policy led to greater substantive representation for women and minorities. Their matched sample included twelve pairs of male and female Carter-appointed judges in the same district and of the same race. Their data cast doubt on the degree to which women judges "act for" other women. Although the differences were insignificant, they found that men were more supportive of women's rights claims in cases involving sexual harassment, gender discrimination, maternity rights, affirmative action, equal employment, and reproductive rights. Similarly, men were also slightly more pro-defendant in the criminal rights cases. They found significant differences between women and men in three areas of law: personal liberties (civil liberties and equality); minority policy issues (ethnic and racial discrimination, welfare rights, police brutality, fair housing, and the rights of people with disabilities and elderly people); and economic regulation. But contrary to gender stereotypes, their data showed that men were more liberal in the first two categories, with women more likely to favor the government in the economic regulation cases.

Thus, Walker and Barrow's study indicated that the women judges exhibited greater deference to the political branches of government, hardly evoking the image of activist liberal judges. After conducting the same test on a matched set of white and African American judges, they concluded that "the assumptions that female and African American judges will be more receptive to the policy goals of women and minorities, and more liberal and activist in the use of judicial power find no support in the decision-making patterns of the judges studied" (1985, 614).

Similarly, Davis (1986) examined the voting behavior of appellate judges from July 1, 1981, to June 30, 1983, in eight issue areas: individual rights (freedom of expression and privacy), equality, prisoner petitions, criminal appeals, labor–management, income tax, employee injury, and other personal injury. She found that women were more liberal than men when all the case types were considered together, but they were only significantly more liberal in the areas of income tax and employee injury.

Seeking to reconcile conflicting reports of gender differences on the bench, Songer, Davis, and Haire (1994) examined three types of cases: obscenity, employment discrimination, and search and seizure. Basing their analysis on the decisions of judges in all twelve circuits, they classified the votes in each issue category as liberal or conservative; opinions against censorship were considered liberal. Using separate models for each set of cases, they included the ideology of the appointing president and the judge's region, as well as selected case facts, among their independent variables. They found that there were no significant gender differences in either the obscenity or search-and-seizure cases, but that gender had a strong significant effect on votes in employment discrimination cases. They concluded that "the effect of gender on judicial behavior varies with the context of the decision-making process" (p. 436). Overall, they believed it premature to reach firm conclusions about how gender affects judicial behavior, suggesting that more women must be appointed to the federal bench before more definitive results could emerge.

Not surprisingly, based on studies such as these, scholars have reached different conclusions about the effects of gender on judicial decision making. Smith (1994) argued that increasing the number of women on the courts will affect the outcome of non-gender-specific issues as well as gender-specific ones. Although she acknowledged that there was insufficient evidence to show that gender affected a judge's policy choices, she believed that men and women judges differed in their perspectives, impartiality, and morality.

In their analysis of the studies of sex differences in judicial behavior published during the 1970s and 1980s, Solomine and Wheatley (1995, 919) concluded that "the weight of the evidence demonstrated that most female judges do not decide cases in a distinctively feminist or feminine manner." Because women and men might bring different perspectives to the act of judging, they argued that in the interests of "fairness," it is appropriate to seek to increase the number of women on the bench. Also summarizing the results of the research conducted during this time, Beiner (1998) agreed that, for the most part, scholars found few differences in the voting behavior of men and women judges. Citing the evidence reported in the two studies of the appellate court (Davis, Haire, and Songer 1993; Songer, Davis, and Haire 1994), however, she argued that the results of this later research suggests that sex plays a role in judicial decision making. A few years later, Palmer (2001) cited a general consensus in the literature that women and men judges differed most strongly in their support for women's rights claims. There was less consensus however, she noted, in studies that assessed whether women judges speak in a different voice from men judges and therefore employ a different style of jurisprudence.

"Different Voices" Theory

Carol Gilligan's (1982) approach to sex difference in moral development led her to conclude that women and men exhibit differences in morality and reasoning. Although criticized from several perspectives (see, for example, Baer 1991), Gilligan's work generated a veritable cottage industry of literature on gender differences in legal analysis.

Sherry (1986) classified a type of jurisprudence, emanating from classical Republican (Jeffersonian) thought and exemplified by O'Connor's opinions, as a "feminine" rather than a "feminist" voice. Drawing on Gilligan's analysis of gender differences, Sherry (1986, 582) noted that women emphasized "connection, subjectivity, and responsibility" and men valued "autonomy, objectivity, and rights." She examined O'Connor's opinions in equal protection and religion cases in particular, and compared her votes to those of the ideologically compatible fellow justice, William Rehnquist. She found that O'Connor valued membership in the community and exhibited a preference for communitarian values over individual rights. Sherry believed that the "pattern of disagreement [between O'Connor and Rehnquist] is highly suggestive of the operation of a uniquely feminine perspective" (Sherry 1986, 592). Although she suggested this perspective could have "a revolutionary effect . . . on jurisprudence," she noted that O'Connor voted with the conservatives on most issues (p. 613). Sherry's work implied that the opinions of women judges might differ from those of their men counterparts in a predictable way, although—as O'Connor's votes show—not necessarily tending in a more liberal direction.

Also deriving their approach from Gilligan and from Martha Minow's (1990, 15) "social relations" analysis, Sullivan and Goldzwig (1992, 35) identified another type of judicial decision making. They cited a "female-associated approach" manifested in O'Connor's opinions in abortion cases. Asserting that O'Connor's moral decision making in abortion cases is derived from "female-identified values," they claimed that, among other things, her approach refrained from simple line-drawing and sought to accommodate law to the lives of real people—in this case, women. They noted as well that O'Connor's approach to decision making was not a feminist one and could not be easily categorized on ideological grounds.

In an explicit test of Gilligan's theory, Davis (1992–93) compared the votes of the five women on the Ninth Circuit to seven comparable men. To highlight the gender difference, she matched women with men appointed by the same president, and, as far as possible, by legal education, previous occupation, and previous prosecutorial or judicial experience.

She examined the reasoning of these judges in cases presenting equal protection and Title VII (the Section of the 1964 Civil Rights Act prohibiting employment discrimination on the basis of sex and race) issues, as well as those alleging a deprivation of rights under the federal statute, 42 U.S.C. § 1983. Basing her analysis on the theories expounded by Gilligan and Sherry, she sought evidence confirming that women spoke in different voices in three distinct categories: (1) "equality as connection v. equality as autonomy" (p. 157); (2) "the duty to protect v. freedom from abuse" (p. 165); and (3) "contextual v. rule based decision-making" (p. 168).

Davis's results were far from definitive, and she concluded that "sometimes, some women judges do [speak in a different voice]. But sometimes, some men judges also speak in that different voice." In the end she acknowledged that, contrary to the expectation that placing more women on the bench would affect the legal system, her data did not "provide empirical support for the theory that the presence of women judges will transform the very nature of law" (p. 171). Assessing her research findings, Davis suggested that there were either no gender-based differences or that women had become socialized into the norms of the judicial profession and whatever differences had existed were now faded.

Also reflecting the influence of Gilligan's different voice theory, Allen and Wall's (1993, 158–59) study of state supreme courts examined four possible role orientations of women judges: representatives (adopting "a pro-woman voting record on women's issues cases"), tokens ("characterized by voting records that lie within the central area of any continuum and do not exhibit behavior that differentiates them from other justices"), outsiders ("exhibit[ing] comparatively extreme voting behavior"), and the different voices role ("plac[ing] higher values on relational concerns, such as the community, as opposed to individual rights . . . and exhibit[ing] extremism and isolation in dissenting behavior"). Examining state high court decisions in cases involving criminal appeals, economic liberties (such as landlord–tenant disputes, negligence, and insurance claims), and women's issues (such as sex discrimination, sexual assault damages, and child support), Allen and Wall compared the liberal opinions of the women judges in twenty-one states with the liberal votes of the court as a whole in an attempt to place the women in an appropriate role category.

When they examined the women's rights cases, they found that most of the women judges in their analysis adopted a representative role. Focusing on the economic rights and criminal procedure cases only, they concluded that women were outsiders but that party identification affected their outsider status differentially. Women Democratic judges were significantly more liberal than male Democratic judges, and women Republican judges were more conservative than their party colleagues. The differences, however, were less pronounced among the Republicans. There was also evidence that women judges adopted a different voice in their decisions in criminal procedure and economic liberty cases. However, their measure of a different voice, unlike Gilligan's or Sherry's, was limited to dissenting opinions only.

Notwithstanding the views of these scholars on the question of whether women and men judges speak in different voices, Ginsburg rejected the notion in a 1986 speech, insisting that she "rarely detected any identifiably male or female thinking" (quoted in Kay and Sparrow 2001, 6). Similarly, in delivering the James Madison Lecture at New York University Law School on October 29, 1991, O'Connor (1991, 1557) warned of the danger of the "new feminism," a theory characterized by the belief that men and women have different worldviews. She said that she feared that merely asking whether women and men speak in a different voice risks "setting up the polarity between the feminine virtues of homemaking and the masculine virtues of breadwinning" and threatens a return to the days when women were excluded from the professions and were expected to serve their families at home.

More recently, Cooper Davis and Gilligan (2001) revisited the notion of a different voice in judicial decision making in assessing O'Connor's position on due process issues, such as abortion, the right to die, and grandparent rights. In arguing for a broader and more complex approach than is commonly used to evaluate O'Connor's voice, they sought to explain why she voted to reaffirm *Roe v. Wade* (1973) in *Planned Parenthood of Southeastern Pennsylvania v. Casey*, the 1992 abortion decision, after frequently criticizing *Roe* during her tenure on the high court. In their view, O'Connor's position demonstrates "respect for individual choice in matters that define one's personhood [which is] related to an admirable capacity to appreciate equally the roles of principles or first premises and the role of context in legal decisionmaking" (p. 896). They reject characterizing O'Connor's thinking as stereotypically female, contending that she has succeeded in blending different types of reasoning and analysis in her decisions.

The Women "Brethren"

Following O'Connor's appointment to the U.S. Supreme Court, Behuniak-Long (1992, 417) asked: "What is expected of a justice who is appointed to a 'representational' seat on the Court?" The chapter concludes by assessing the records of O'Connor and Ginsburg, focusing particularly on evidence that they "represent" women by furthering gender equality.

Sandra Day O'Connor

Naming O'Connor to the Supreme Court was one of Reagan's first presidential acts, fulfilling his campaign pledge to "name the most qualified women [he] could possibly find" (Salokar and Wilson 1996, 213). Sworn in on September 25, 1981, she was the first woman to sit on the nation's highest court. Not surprisingly, her views were largely consistent with Reagan's conservative positions, but there was speculation that her experiences as a woman lawyer and judge might make her more favorably disposed to women's concerns.

O'Connor was viewed as a woman justice as well as a woman's justice. There was much discussion over her inability to secure a position as a lawyer, and the humiliation of being considered for a job as a legal secretary, despite her graduating third in her class from Stanford University Law School. It was duly noted that as a legislator she supported the Equal Rights Amendment, opposed laws discriminating against women in employment and child custody, and resisted limits on access to abortion. During questioning in her confirmation hearings, she refused to express an opinion on *Roe* and, although she gave assurances that she was "opposed to abortion as a matter of birth control or otherwise," her nomination to the Supreme Court drew opposition from conservative groups such as the National Right to Life Committee. Conversely, she received support from major women's groups like the NAWJ, the National Organization for Women (NOW), and the National Women's Political Caucus (Salokar and Wilson 1996, 214–15; Maveety 1996, 17). Indeed, a leading women's rights advocate, Eleanor Smeal, characterized her appointment as "a major victory for women's rights" (Wohl, 1989, 44).

Assessing O'Connor's decision making in employment discrimination cases decided by the Court, Palmer (1991) concluded that her support for women's rights was "mixed." Her statistical analysis of O'Connor's voting record showed that although the justice generally voted with the conservative Rehnquist, her votes in sex discrimination cases most often coincided with those of the liberals, William Brennan, Thurgood Marshall, and John Paul Stevens. However, a closer look at her opinions in the eight employment discrimination cases decided between 1983 until 1991 shows that although O'Connor supported the women's rights position in most of the cases, she also often expressed concern for the rights of the employers and the possible negative economic impact on them as a result of these decisions.

In her study of O'Connor's voting, Behuniak-Long (1992, 427) accepted, in part, Sherry's conclusion that judges speak in different voices, but she challenged her assumption that there was a revolutionary potential in the "feminine voice." Unlike a feminist perspective, the "feminine voice" does not strive to create egalitarian changes in society through law. Examining O'Connor's concurring opinions in selected privacy and due process cases, she described the justice's jurisprudence as "feminine," but concluded that she did not use her voice to "act for" women's interests.

Davis (1993, 134) also contended that O'Connor "has neither championed women's rights nor has she engaged in constructing feminist legal theory." Testing Sherry's thesis that O'Connor speaks in the "feminine" voice, Davis compared her votes with Rehnquist's in six issue areas (gender, civil rights, establishment clause, equal protection, race, and criminal procedure) from 1981 to 1991. Some of her findings supported Sherry's analysis of O'Connor's "feminine" voice because they revealed O'Connor's concern for the value of community membership. However, although Davis recognized that O'Connor cast more liberal votes than Rehnquist in civil rights and establishment clause cases, she also showed that O'Connor was more liberal in all issues areas (although not all differences were statistically significant) and that gender appeared irrelevant to her behavior on the Court (see also Aliotta 1995).

Finally, Maveety (1996, 22) also rejected the idea of observing O'Connor through a "Gilliganesque 'feminine voice'" lens. In her view, this approach "conceals as much as it purportedly reveals about the nature of O'Connor's judicial accommodationism, because it fails to focus on the correct jurisprudential and behavioral factors and to identify them specifically as jurisprudential or behavioral and not gender-related factors" (Maveety 1996, 25–26). She found instead that O'Connor displayed a pragmatic, "accommodationist," fact-based approach to law that defied easy analysis and was not based on gender concerns.

Women's rights activists have been very critical of O'Connor for her position in abortion cases. Although she stopped short of voting to overturn *Roe* in her tenure on the Court, she frequently voted with most of the other Reagan-Bush justices to allow states to place additional limits on abortion rights. A different picture emerges when appraising some of O'Connor's opinions in equal protection cases. The two cases discussed below, one at the beginning of her term and one almost twenty years later, seem to demonstrate a concern with women's rights.

O'Connor's opinion in *University of Mississippi v. Hogan* (1982) for a 5–4 majority moved the Court closer to a stricter review of gender discrimination cases by specifying that such classifications required "an extremely persuasive justification" to pass constitutional muster.[1] Although it was surely an easy call to order the University of Mississippi to admit a man to the publicly supported all-women nursing school, O'Connor's opinion was a strong refutation of the maintenance of traditional gender lines (see Mezey 2003, ch. 1).

More recently, in *Nguyen v. INS* (2001), O'Connor was outspoken in her criticism of the majority opinion in a case involving a law at the intersection of immigration policy and equal protection jurisprudence.[2] The law, based on assumptions of societal norms about appropriate sex role behavior, favored children born to unwed citizen mothers over children born to unwed citizen fathers. Writing on behalf of herself, Ginsburg, David Souter, and Stephen Breyer, O'Connor's dissent sharply criticized the majority opinion, arguing that it accepted the sex-based classification too easily, without even inquiring about the possibility of a sex-neutral alternative. In her view, the law assumed the existence of an automatic bond between mother and child, but not between father and child, thus relying on stereotypes about culturally determined sex roles.

In supporting the equal rights claims in *Hogan* and *Nguyen*, O'Connor demonstrated a concern for equal opportunity for men and women and a desire to abandon stereotypical gender roles. However, although she adopted a feminist position in these cases, her views were not radical, remaining within the bounds of the Court's equality jurisprudence, and indeed represented the views of many of her brethren. In sum, O'Connor has fulfilled some of the expectations of her supporters in the women's movement by her votes in gender equality cases. For many, however, her opposition to abortion rights negates the possibility of classifying her as a "representative" justice.

Ruth Bader Ginsburg

When Ruth Bader Ginsburg was sworn in at the nation's highest court on August 10, 1993, she also brought first-hand experience of gender discrimination in employment. Like O'Connor, she was refused a job by the private law firms to which she applied despite her position at the head of her class at both Harvard and Columbia law schools. However, unlike O'Connor, she came with a distinguished record of litigating gender discrimination issues, including six oral arguments before the Supreme Court—five of which she won—and nine appellate briefs. Also unlike O'Connor, who had no experience on the federal bench, Ginsburg had spent thirteen years on the Court of Appeals for the District of Columbia before taking her seat on the high court.

Ginsburg was the first director of the American Civil Liberties Union Women's Rights Law Project (Salokar 1996, 81). Thus, not surprisingly, in the days following her nomination she was characterized as "the Thurgood Marshall of gender equality law" (Lewis 1993a, quoting Janet Benshoof, president of the Center for Reproductive Law and Policy).

Although Ginsburg was an outspoken proponent of women's rights, feminists nevertheless criticized her for making charges—first made public in 1984—that *Roe* was too expansive, had gone too far in sweeping all abortion laws aside, and should have been grounded in principles of equality rather than privacy. A few months before Clinton announced her nomination, she delivered a lecture at New York University School of Law in which she maintained that *Roe* had created a backlash that led to political divisiveness, and the Court should have exhibited greater restraint in deciding it (see Garrow 1993; Greenhouse 1993). In her confirmation hearing, however, she strongly defended women's reproductive rights: "It is essential to a woman's equality with man that she be the decision-maker, that her choice be controlling," adding, "the state controlling a woman would mean denying her full autonomy and full equality" (Lewis 1993b).

Compared with O'Connor, there have been fewer studies of Ginsburg's judicial temperament and her voting record since her appointment to the high court. One exception is Smith et al. (1994; see also Baugh et al. 1994; Perry and Abraham 1998), who assessed her performance as a first-term justice and found that she aligned herself at times with both liberal and conservative camps, most frequently voting with the latter in criminal procedure cases. Although they acknowledged that her views might change over time, they indicated that her "first term clearly did not place her in the mold of the Warren Court justices who consistently advanced broad interpretations of constitutional rights" (Smith et al. 1994, 78). Analyzing her votes in gender discrimination claims, they rejected the comparison with Marshall. Although they found she favored women's rights in the five cases involving women's rights claims, she had only interjected a brief concurring opinion in which she alluded to the level of scrutiny applied to gender-based classifications. They concluded that "she does not presently appear intent on advancing a broad women's rights agenda . . . [and] may not be inclined to seize available opportunities to present her views on women's rights generally" (p. 80).

Recalling Ginsburg's past as a women's rights advocate, Smith (1995) assessed Ginsburg's likely position in future sexual harassment cases. After surveying the state of sexual harassment law as well as Ginsburg's experiences and values, she concluded that Ginsburg would favor sexual harassment plaintiffs only in cases in which "Supreme Court precedent or her interpretation of legislative intent allows it" (Smith 1995, 1945). Nevertheless, she believed that this area of law "may be the best opportunity for Ginsburg to advocate positive change in the women's rights arena" (p. 1945).

In her days as a women's rights litigator, Ginsburg had favored applying the strictest scrutiny to gender-based laws (Baugh et al. 1994, 25). Twenty-five years later, however, although Ginsburg's majority opinion rejected the all-male Virginia Military Institute's (VMI) attempt to justify the policy of excluding women from admission, it stopped short of adopting a higher level of scrutiny for gender-based classifications (see Mezey 2003; Strum 2002). Rejecting the U.S. government's argument that the Courts apply the highest level of scrutiny to sex-based classifications (O'Connor and Palmer 2001, 270), she applied what she termed "skeptical scrutiny" to the school's admission policy.[3] Proclaiming that "physical differences between men and women are . . . enduring," she explained that racial differences and sex differences are not comparable and the Court must apply its most heightened level of scrutiny for racial classifications only.

In their analysis of the Clinton Supreme Court appointees, O'Connor and Palmer (2001) compared the backgrounds and voting records of Ginsburg and Breyer and concluded that their backgrounds were quite similar; they were roughly the same age, the same religion, were graduates of elite colleges and law schools, and had served on the Court of Appeals before being elevated to the Supreme Court. Although the primary purpose of their study was to assess these two Clinton appointees as part of the Clinton legacy rather than to explicitly compare the two, they reported that they shared many views in common; indeed, between 1994 and 1999, Ginsburg and Breyer each agreed with the other more frequently than with any other justice. Despite the feminist hopes that were evident during Ginsburg's nomination, however, neither she nor Breyer had the highest percentage of pro–civil liberties votes on the Court; Stevens and Souter voted in favor of civil liberties more frequently than they did. O'Connor and Palmer concluded that both Clinton justices reflected his political beliefs; both are moderates who are inclined to vote as liberals, but are not inclined to assume a leadership position among the liberals.

Thus although Ginsburg's appointment to the Court greatly cheered women's rights advocates, once on the Court, her support for feminist issues was more restrained than they had hoped. Ginsburg has not appeared to retreat from her feminist principles, but she has not been a strong force for feminist change on the high court.

Conclusion

Twenty-five years ago, there were only a small number of women judges on the federal courts. During the Carter, Bush, and Clinton administrations, especially the latter, an increasing number of women were appointed to the federal bench. The rising tide of women jurists led to speculation that these women would represent the interests of their "sisters" in society. Adopting the principles developed by legislative scholars on whether legislative women "act for" women by supporting women's (that is, feminist) issues, this chapter has explored the degree to which women judges represent the interests of women by furthering the goals that benefit women as a group.

Assessing the results of studies of gender differences on the courts, this analysis showed that although some scholars believe that women judges may act differently from men judges, most judicial scholars remain skeptical about the extent to which judicial decision making is subject to gender influences. The majority of studies reported only slight evidence that women judges differ from their male colleagues, that is, for the most part, scholars found few systematic significant gender-based differences in judicial voting behavior. Moreover, the gender differences that were found were not always in a predictable direction. Women did not always vote in a more liberal, more civil libertarian manner than men, nor were they always more sensitive to issues of sex or race discrimination. Indeed, in some studies, women judges were reported to be even less supportive of women's rights claims than men judges. Finally, there was even less evidence that women judges spoke in a different voice, that is, displayed a unique feminist or feminine perspective that rendered their decision making or their legal analysis different from men judges. Scholars who focused on the voting behavior of the women on the Supreme Court produced little evidence to disturb these conclusions. Both Ginsburg and O'Connor have demonstrated concern for women's rights, but neither has made the feminist agenda her paramount interest on the Court, and indeed, both have expressed uneasiness about overstating the importance of gender differences on the bench.

This inquiry into the judicial scholarship on gender effects on the federal courts suggests that the evidence showing that women judges "act for" women is, at best, mixed. There is little reason to believe in a transformative effect simply by placing women judges on the bench unless these judges share a belief in a feminist agenda.

Notes

1. O'Connor's opinion was not path-breaking, however. In *Personnel Administrator of Massachusetts v. Feeney* (1979), the Court first introduced the phrase, "exceedingly persuasive justification," into the intermediate scrutiny test. Two years later, in *Kirchberg v. Feenstra* (1981), the Court specified that the state's burden under intermediate scrutiny was to provide "an exceedingly persuasive justification" for the sex-based classification.

2. The law treated children of unwed citizen mothers and fathers differently. The Court's

238 SUSAN GLUCK MEZEY

decision in *Miller v. Albright* (1998), the first case on this issue, was split into three different sets of opinions. Because she believed the plaintiff in *Miller* did not have standing to bring the case to court, O'Connor voted to affirm the law; she indicated, however, that she believed it would not survive the heightened scrutiny test.

3. Rehnquist's concurring opinion and Antonin Scalia's dissent in the VMI case both criticized Ginsburg for moving beyond the Court's equal protection jurisprudence in sex discrimination cases.

References

Aliotta, Jilda M. 1995. "Justice O'Connor and the Equal Protection Clause: A Feminine Voice." *Judicature* 78: 232–35.

Allen, David, and Diane Wall. 1987. "The Behavior of Women State Supreme Court Justices: Are They Tokens or Outsiders?" *Justice System Journal* 12: 232–45.

———. 1993. "Role Orientations and Women State Supreme Court Justices." *Judicature* 77: 156–65.

Baer, Judith A. 1991. "Nasty Law or Nice Ladies? Jurisprudence, Feminism, and Gender Difference." *Women and Politics* 11: 1–31.

Baugh, Joyce Ann, Christopher E. Smith, Thomas R. Hensley, and Scott Patrick Johnson. 1994. "Justice Ruth Bader Ginsburg: A Preliminary Assessment." *University of Toledo Law Review* 26: 1–34.

Behuniak-Long, Susan. 1992. "Justice Sandra Day O'Connor and the Power of Maternal Legal Thinking." *Review of Politics* 54: 417–44.

Beiner, Theresa. 1999. "What Will Diversity on the Bench Mean for Justice?" *Michigan Journal of Gender and Law* 6: 113.

Berkson, Larry. 1982. "Women on the Bench: A Brief History." *Judicature* 65: 286–93.

Carp, Robert A., and C.K. Rowland. 1983. *Policymaking and Politics in the Federal District Courts.* Knoxville: University of Tennessee Press.

Congressional Quarterly Weekly Report. 1997. February 8: 367–69.

Cooper Davis, Peggy, and Carol Gilligan. 2001. "A Woman Decides: Justice O'Connor and Due Process Rights of Choice." *McGeorge University Law Review* 32: 895–914.

Davis, Sue. 1986. "President Carter's Selection Reforms and Judicial Policymaking: A Voting Analysis of the United States Courts of Appeals." *American Politics Quarterly* 14: 328–44.

———. 1992–93. "Do Women Judges Speak in a 'Different Voice'? Carol Gilligan, Feminist Legal Theory, and the Ninth Circuit." *Wisconsin Women's Law Journal* 8: 143–73.

———. 1993. "The Voice of Sandra Day O'Connor." *Judicature* 77: 134–39.

Davis, Sue, Susan Haire, and Donald R. Songer. 1993. "Voting Behavior and Gender on the U.S. Courts of Appeals." *Judicature* 77: 129–33.

Dolan, Kathleen, and Lynne E. Ford. 1995. "Women in State Legislatures: Feminist Identity and Legislative Behaviors." *American Politics Quarterly* 23: 96–108.

Garrow, David. 1993. *Washington Post.* June 16, C3.

Gilligan, Carol. 1982. *In a Different Voice: Psychological Theory and Women's Development.* Cambridge: Harvard University Press.

Goldman, Sheldon. 1975. "Voting Behavior on the U.S. Courts of Appeals Revisited." *American Political Science Review* 69: 352–62.

———. 1981. "Carter's Judicial Appointments: A Lasting Legacy." *Judicature* 78: 344–55.

———. 1983. "Reagan's Judicial Appointments: Shaping the Bench in His Own Image." *Judicature* 66: 335–47.

———. 1989. "Reagan's Judicial Legacy: Completing the Puzzle and Summing Up." *Judicature* 72: 318–30.

———. 1991. "The Bush Imprint on the Judiciary: Carrying on a Tradition." *Judicature* 74: 294–306.

———. 1993. "Bush's Judicial Legacy: The Final Imprint." *Judicature* 76: 282–97.

———. 1995. "Judicial Selection Under Clinton: A Midterm Examination." *Judicature* 78: 276–91.

Goldman, Sheldon, and Matthew D. Saronson. 1994. "Clinton's Nontraditional Judges: Creating a More Representative Bench." *Judicature* 78: 68–73.

Goldman, Sheldon, Elliot Slotnick, Gerard Gryski, and Gary Zuk. 2001. "Clinton's Judges: Summing Up the Legacy." *Judicature* 84: 228–54.

Gottschall, Jon. 1983. "Carter's Judicial Appointments: The Influence of Affirmative Action and Merit Selection in Voting on the United States Courts of Appeals." *Judicature* 67: 165–73.

Greenhouse, Linda. 1993. "On Privacy and Equality." *The New York Times.* June 16, A1.

Gruhl, John, Cassia Spohn, and Susan Welch. 1981. "Women as Policymakers: The Case of Trial Judges." *American Journal of Political Science* 25: 308–22.

Gryski, Gerard S., and Eleanor C. Main. 1986. "Social Backgrounds as Predictors of Votes on State Courts of Last Resort." *Western Political Quarterly* 39: 528–37.

Gryski, Gerard S., Eleanor C. Main, and William J. Dixon. 1986. "Models of State High Court Decision Making in Sex Discrimination Cases." *Journal of Politics* 48: 143–52.

Harrison, Cynthia. 1996. "Burnita Shelton Matthews." In *Women in Law*, ed. Rebecca Mae Salokar and Mary Volcansek, pp. 150–58. Westport, CT: Greenwood Press.

Kay, Herma Hill, and Geraldine Sparrow. 2001. "Workshop on Judging: Does Gender Make a Difference?" *Wisconsin Women's Law Journal* 16: 1–14.

Kirchberg v. Feenstra, 450 U.S. 455 (1981).

Kritzer, Herbert M., and Thomas M. Uhlman. 1977. "Sisterhood in the Courtroom: Sex of Judge and Defendant in Criminal Case Disposition." *Social Science Quarterly* 14: 77–88.

Lewis, Neil, A. 1993a. "Rejected as a Clerk, Chosen as a Justice." *The New York Times*, June 15, A1.

———. 1993b. "Ginsburg Affirms Right of a Woman to Have Abortion." *The New York Times*, July 22, A1.

Martin, Elaine. 1982. "Women on the Federal Bench: A Comparative Profile." *Judicature* 65: 306–13.

———. 1987. "Gender and Judicial Selection: A Comparison of the Reagan and Carter Administrations." *Judicature* 71: 136–42.

———. 1993. "The Representative Role of Women Judges." *Judicature* 77: 166–73.

Martin, Elaine, and Barry Pyle. 2000. "Gender, Race, and Partisanship on the Michigan Supreme Court." *Albany Law Review* 63: 1205–36.

Maveety, Nancy. 1996. *Justice Sandra Day O'Connor: Strategist on the Supreme Court.* Boston: Rowman & Littlefield.

Mezey, Susan Gluck. 1978. "Women and Representation: The Case of Hawaii." *Journal of Politics* 40: 369–85.

———. 1994. "Increasing the Number of Women in Office: Does It Matter?" In *The Year of the Woman: Myths and Realities*, ed. Elizabeth Adell Cook, Sue Thomas, and Clyde Wilcox, pp. 255–70. Boulder, CO: Westview.

———. 2003. *Elusive Equality: Women's Rights, Public Policy, and the Law.* Boulder, CO: Lynne Rienner.

Miller v. Albright, 523 U.S. 420 (1998).

Minow, Martha. 1990. *Making All the Difference: Inclusion, Exclusion, and American Law.* Ithaca, NY: Cornell University Press.

Nguyen v. INS, 533 U.S. 53 (2001).

O'Connor, Karen, and Barbara Palmer. 2001. "The Clinton Clones: Ginsburg, Breyer, and the Clinton Legacy." *Judicature* 84: 262–73.

O'Connor, Sandra Day. 1991. "Portia's Progress." *New York University Law Review* 66: 1546–58.

Palmer, Barbara. 1991. "Feminist or Foe? Justice Sandra Day O'Connor, Title VII, and Support for Women's Rights." *Women's Rights Law Reporter* 13: 159–70.

———. 2001. "'To Do Justly': The Integration of Women into the American Judiciary." *PSOnline* (June): 235–39.

Perry, Barbara A. 1991. *A "Representative" Supreme Court?* New York: Greenwood Press.

Perry, Barbara A., and Henry J. Abraham. 1998. "A Representative Supreme Court: The Thomas, Ginsburg, and Breyer Appointments." *Judicature* 81: 158–65.

Personnel Administrator of Massachusetts v. Feeney, 442 U.S. 256 (1979).

Pitkin, Hannah. 1967. *The Concept of Representation*. Berkeley: University of California Press.

Planned Parenthood of Southeastern Pennsylvania v. Casey, 505 U.S. 833 (1992).

Reingold, Beth. 1992. "Concepts and Representation Among Female and Male State Legislators." *Legislative Studies Quarterly* 17: 509–38.

Roe v. Wade, 410 U.S. 113 (1973).

Rowland, C.K., and Robert A. Carp. 1980. "A Longitudinal Study of Party Effects on Federal District Court Policy Propensities." *American Journal of Political Science* 24: 291–305.

Saint-Germain, Michelle A. 1989. "Does Their Difference Make a Difference? The Impact of Women on Public Policy in the Arizona Legislature." *Social Science Quarterly* 70: 956–68.

Salokar, Rebecca Mae. 1996. "Ruth Bader Ginsburg." In *Women in Law*, ed. Rebecca Mae Salokar and Mary Volcansek, pp. 78–87. Westport, CT: Greenwood Press.

Salokar, Rebecca Mae, and Michael Wilson. 1996. "Sandra Day O'Connor." In *Women in Law*, ed. Rebecca Mae Salokar and Mary Volcansek, pp. 210–18. Westport, CT: Greenwood Press.

Sherry, Suzanna. 1986. "Civic Virtue and the Feminine Voice in Constitutional Adjudication." *Virginia Law Review* 72: 543–615.

Slotnick, Elliot E. 1984. "The Paths to the Federal Bench: Gender, Race and Judicial Recruitment Variation." *Judicature* 67: 371–88.

———. 1988. "Federal Judicial Recruitment and Selection Research: A Review Essay." *Judicature* 71: 317–24.

Smith, Christopher E., Joyce Ann Baugh, Thomas R. Hensley, and Scott Patrick Johnson. 1994. "The First-Term Performance of Justice Ruth Bader Ginsburg." *Judicature* 78: 74–80.

Smith, Sheila. 1995. "Justice Ruth Bader Ginsburg and Sexual Harassment Law: Will the Second Female Supreme Court Justice Become the Court's Women's Rights Champion?" *University of Cincinnati Law Review* 63: 1893–1945.

Smith, Susan Moloney. 1994. "Diversifying the Judiciary: The Influence of Gender and Race on Judging." *University of Richmond Law Review* 28: 179–204.

Solomine, Michael E., and Susan E. Wheatley. 1995. "Rethinking Feminist Judging." *Indiana Law Journal* 70: 891–919.

Songer, Donald R., and Kelly Crews-Meyer. 2000. "Does Judge Gender Matter? Decision Making in State Supreme Courts." *Social Science Quarterly* 68: 750–62.

Songer, Donald R., and Sue Davis. 1990. "The Impact of Party and Region on Voting Decisions in the United States Courts of Appeals, 1955–1986." *Western Political Quarterly* 43: 317–34.

Songer, Donald R., Sue Davis, and Susan Haire. 1994. "A Reappraisal of Diversification in the Federal Courts: Gender Effects in the Courts of Appeal." *Journal of Politics* 56: 425–39.

Strum, Philippa. 2002. *Women in the Barracks: The VMI Case and Equal Rights*. Lawrence: University of Kansas Press.

Sullivan, Patricia A., and Stephen R. Goldzwig. 1992. "Abortion and Undue Burdens: Justice Sandra Day O'Connor and Judicial Decision-making." *Women and Politics* 16: 27–54.

Swers, Michele. 2001. "Understanding the Policy Impact of Electing Women: Evidence from Research on Congress and State Legislatures." *PSOnline* (June): 217–20.

Tate, C. Neal. 1981. "Personal Attribute Models of the Voting Behavior of U.S. Supreme Court Justices." *American Political Science Review* 75: 355–67.

Thomas, Sue, and Susan Welch. 1991. "The Impact of Gender on Activities and Priorities of State Legislators." *Western Political Quarterly* 44: 445–56.

University of Mississippi v. Hogan, 458 U.S. 718 (1982).

Walker, Thomas G., and Deborah J. Barrow. 1985. "The Diversification of the Federal Bench: Policy and Process Ramifications." 47: 596–617.

Welch, Susan. 1985. "Are Women More Liberal Than Men in the U.S. Congress?" *Legislative Studies Quarterly* 10: 125–34.

Wilson, Sarah. 1996. "Florence Ellinwood Allen." In *Women in Law*, ed. Rebecca Mae Salokar and Mary Volcansek, pp. 17–24. Westport, CT: Greenwood Press.

Wohl, Alexander. 1989. "O'Connor, J., Concurring." *ABA Journal* (December): 42–48.

12

Cracking the Glass Ceiling
The Status, Significance, and Prospects of Women in Legislative Office

Sue Thomas

I'm not finished yet. I've been waiting over 200 years. . . . I didn't run as a woman. I ran, again, as a seasoned politician and experienced legislator. It just happens that I am a woman and we have been waiting a long time for this moment.

—*Congresswoman Nancy Pelosi, (D-CA), Minority Leader, U.S. House of Representatives (Rogers 2002)*

Nearly 13,000 people have served in the Congress since the founding of the Republic. But only 216 have been women—and of those, none has been the leader of a political party. This is "definitely smashing the glass ceiling."

—*Former GOP Representative Margaret Heckler (R-MA), co-founder, Congressional Caucus for Women's Issues*

The words of Minority Leader Nancy Pelosi and former Representative Margaret Heckler are infused with both the excitement of long-pursued historical achievement and the acknowledgment that, despite its magnitude and import, comparatively few women serve in state or federal legislatures. Indeed, parity for women is still a relatively distant dream. As such, the purpose of this chapter is to assess women's status in legislative life. Its first focus is to illuminate the richness of the results of more than thirty years of scholarly investigation of women in legislatures, including analyses of their preparation, motivation, ascent, impact, and obstacles. The second focus of the chapter is to address the meaning of the following juxtaposition of events: at the same time that Representative Pelosi became the first woman to hold a high-level leadership position in the U.S. Congress, women's legislative gains at the state and federal levels have become stagnant. The context or environment producing these results is the perspective through which this analysis is shaped.

The Evolution of Inquiry

Prior to the 1960s, what little scholarly attention was paid to women's political inclinations occurred within an accepted understanding that they were substantially

242

less political or even apolitical compared to men. Study of women's impact on political processes or policies was considered unnecessary, since it was assumed to be negligible. Accordingly, analyses of women as political actors at the mass level were rare, and interest in politically elite women was virtually nonexistent. Apart from stories or even biographies of some early "exceptional" women such as Senator Margaret Chase Smith (R-ME), Representative Helen Gahagan Douglas (D-CA), or Representative Claire Boothe Luce (R-CT), women legislators were not topics of interest to political scientists.

Attention to how women experienced the political grew as the modern feminist movement of the 1960s and 1970s brought more women to the academy. As a result, a new area of inquiry concerning the world of elite-level political women flourished. Initial research questions about women legislators were basic. Scholars wanted to know who they were; what sort of educational, occupational, and political experience they brought to office; the contours of their life situations—especially with respect to marriage and family; their levels of political ambition, and the advantages and constraints of being individual and collective newcomers and part of a small minority of legislators.[1] Questions were often framed in the context of how women compared to men who held office. Because men had been the political and legislative norm, or, reversing the perceptual lens, because women as a group had been largely excluded from elite-level politics, the most compelling questions about legislative women were distilled into how they pierced the barriers to their participation and how they compared to their male counterparts.

As the numbers of women in legislative office grew, and as the types of women who held office became more diverse, a second avenue of inquiry generated additional, more sophisticated questions. While continuing to pursue the topics addressed in the preceding paragraph, scholars increasingly explored the extent to which women made a distinctive impact on legislative outcomes and processes. A large amount of information was gathered about women's ideologies, voting behavior, legislative priorities, committee assignments, bill introductions and sponsorships, success rates, activity levels on routine tasks, and individual and collective obstacles to success. And, presaging the ascent of Minority Leader Pelosi, as women began to gain leadership roles at both the committee and institutional levels, studies designed to clarify their styles and impact advanced.

This second avenue of inquiry into the experiences of legislative women also introduced two additional analytical lenses through which they were viewed. Beyond questions of individual impact, the extent to which women collectively contribute to legislative life has been of interest. The concept of critical mass and its effect on distinctive contributions emerged as a significant focus of this area of inquiry. Finally, the tension between analysis of women as one relatively homogeneous group and the reality of the diversity among women has become centrally important. In particular, the backgrounds, priorities, and impact of legislative women of color are increasingly addressed in research.

A third set of questions, explicated more recently, concerns not women themselves in isolation or in comparison to men, but the environment in which they operate. The continuing extreme minority status of women in the U.S. Congress and in most state legislatures coupled with clear, consistent, and ongoing reports of disparate obstacles to success signaled a need for nuanced analysis of the bi-directionality of influence. Beyond questions of women's impact lie questions about how, and how much, context or environment structures and limits progress toward greater representation and increased success levels. Scholarly focus has increasingly been devoted to the effects of gendered political institutions and gendered societal roles on the possibilities and choices of legislative women.

Legislative Women: Who Are They?

In 1975, women comprised 4 percent of Congress and 8 percent of state legislatures. From the mid-1970s until the current time, women have generally incrementally increased their presence in the legislative arena. Table 12.1 illustrates the results of electoral cycles of the past decade. In 1993, women were 10 percent of Congress and 21 percent of state legislatures. A decade later, women comprised 13.6 percent of Congress and 22.3 percent of state legislatures. As Table 12.2 shows, in 1993, 14 women of color held seats in Congress and 202 held seats in state legislatures. By 2003, the numbers in Congress had risen marginally to 18 while the number of women of color in state legislatures grew to 299 (CAWP 2003).

Beyond the numbers, what have over three decades of systematic study of legislative women told us about the contours of their professional and personal lives? What general patterns exist? Do patterns reveal differences between women and men and differences among women? Have the patterns altered with the passage of time? And, what, if any, unique challenges do women in politics face? Explorations of the life experiences of female legislators coupled with their political attitudes and choices reveal a set of enduring patterns and, simultaneously, a set of dramatic changes. Table 12.3 provides an overview of the patterns of change and stability introduced in the coming pages.

The professional and political profiles that legislative women bring to office have reflected gendered disparities in wider society. As such, women have tended to come to their positions from somewhat lesser levels of education than men; from different, usually less high-status and high-paying professions; and from less high-status political experiences. For example, men make up a greater portion of legislators who are college graduates and who complete graduate and professional school. They are also more likely to come to legislatures from professional or business/management positions, whereas women are more likely to join legislatures from teaching and social work. With respect to prior political experience, men are more likely than women to have served on city councils or as mayors, whereas women are more likely to have served on school boards. While asymmetries between the sexes have diminished over time as gender-based socialization has ebbed, even recent studies have confirmed an enduring pattern (Kirkpatrick

Table 12.1

Women in the U.S Congress and State Legislatures, 1993–2003

		WOMEN IN THE U.S. CONGRESS, 1993–2003			
Congress	Year	Number of Women in the House of Representatives	Number of Women in the Senate	Total Number of Women in the U.S. Congress	Women as a Percentage of Congress
103rd	1993–1995	47	7	54	10.1
104th	1995–1997	48	9	57	10.6
105th	1997–1999	54	9	63	11.8
106th	1999–2001	56	9	65	12.1
107th	2001–2003	60	13	73	13.6
108th	2003–2004	59	14	73	13.6

Note: Figures for the 107th Congress include Representative Patsy Mink (D-HI), who died on September 19 before the 2002 elections. None of the figures include nonvoting delegates from Washington, DC, the Virgin Islands, or Guam.

	WOMEN IN STATE LEGISLATURES, 1993–2003	
Year	Number of Women in State Legislatures	Proportion of Women in State Legislatures (in %)
1993	1,524	20.5
1994	1,526	20.6
1995	1,535	20.7
1996	1,546	20.8
1997	1,593	21.5
1998	1,607	21.6
1999	1,664	22.4
2000	1,672	22.5
2001	1,666	22.4
2002	1,680	22.6
2003	1,645	22.3

Source: The data for these tables come from the Center for American Women and Politics, Eagleton Institute of Politics, Rutgers University.
Note: The total number of state legislators across the fifty states is 7,424.

1974; Diamond 1977; Carroll and Strimling 1983; Dodson and Carroll 1991; Dolan and Ford 1998; Gertzog 1995, 2002; van Assendelft and O'Connor 1994; Thomas 1994, 2002; Dodson 1997; Dolan and Ford 1995, 1997; Takash 1997). With at least one exception, these patterns hold true for subgroups of women as well as the whole. For example, Prestage (1991) found that African American women state legislators have become more highly educated than their male counterparts.

The private sphere lives of female and male legislators reflect another enduring pattern of gender-based dissimilarity. Entrenched gender roles have meant that legislative women have been and still are less likely than legislative men to be married and more likely to be childless. Of those legislators with children, women

Table 12.2

Women of Color in Legislatures, 1993–2003

Year	Number of Women in Congress	Party Breakdown in Congress	Number of Women in State Legislatures	Party Breakdown in State Legislatures
1993	14	13 Democrats 1 Republican	202	196 Democrats 6 Republicans
1994	14	13 Democrats 1 Republican	206	201 Democrats 5 Republicans
1995	15	14 Democrats 1 Republican	221	210 Democrats 9 Republicans 2 Independents
1996	16	15 Democrats 1 Republican	223	211 Democrats 9 Republicans 3 Independents
1997	18	17 Democrats 1 Republican	230	224 Democrats 5 Republicans 1 Independents
1998	18	17 Democrats 1 Republican	232	226 Democrats 5 Republicans 1 Independents
1999	18	17 Democrats 1 Republican	250	241 Democrats 9 Republicans
2000	18	17 Democrats 1 Republican	253	245 Democrats 8 Republicans
2001	20	19 Democrats 1 Republican	267	259 Democrats 8 Republicans
2002	20	19 Democrats 1 Republican	277	268 Democrats 9 Republicans
2003	18	17 Democrats 1 Republican	299	281 Democrats 18 Republicans

Source: The data for this table come from the Center for American Women and Politics, Eagleton Institute of Politics, Rutgers University.

Note: Details of 2003: Of the 18 women of color in Congress in 2003, 17 are Democrats and 1 is a Republican. Eleven are African American, and 7 are Latinas. Together, women of color are 24.7 percent of women members of Congress and 3.4 percent of the total members of the United States Congress. Of the 299 women of color in state legislatures, 281 are Democrats and 18 are Republicans. Two hundred and eight are African American, 23 are Asian Americans/Pacific Islanders, 59 are Latinas, and 9 are Native American. Together, women of color are 18.1 percent of women state legislators and 4.1 percent of state legislators overall.

Table 12.3

Enduring Patterns Versus Significant Changes—Early Modern Era Versus Current Legislative Women

CHANGES

Presence	In 1993, women were 10 percent of Congress and 21 percent of state legislatures. A decade later, women comprised 13.6 percent of Congress and 22.3 percent of state legislatures. In 1993, 14 women of color held seats in Congress and 202 seats in state legislatures. By 2003, the numbers in Congress had risen marginally to 18 while the number of women of color in state legislatures grew to 299.
Education/ Occupation/ Ambition	Whereas women were once much less educated than men, less participatory in professional occupations, had less political experience, and were less politically ambitious than men, today, they are more highly educated than in the past, more likely to pursue a range of occupations, and are equally or more politically experienced and ambitious.
Legislative Activity, Participation, and Leadership	Early women legislators showed a certain amount of reticence about participating fully in all aspects of legislative life. They were not as active in terms of giving floor speeches, speaking in committees, bargaining with lobbyists and colleagues. Today, however, women are equal to men in all these categories. They also have made serious strides expanding legislative agendas and the range of issue debate. After little presence in legislative leadership, women are claiming increasing numbers of committee and institutional leadership positions.
Policy Priorities	Evidence from the past suggests that women did not have different policy priorities than men. Today, however, women are more likely to make priorities out of issues dealing with women and children and the family than are men, and this is reflected in committee assignments, bill introductions and sponsorships, bill passage, and pride in accomplishments.

ENDURING PATTERNS

Education/ Occupation/ Political Experience	While women have made gains, there are still differences in educational and occupational attainment, with men being more highly educated and serving in a wider range of occupations. While women and men have generally equal amounts of prior political experience, women tend to come from lower-level positions than men.
Family Life/Perceptions of Status	Women have been and still are less likely to be married, and likely to have fewer children. If they have children, they are likely to get into politics later in life. Women also continue to perform double duty in the household and the workplace. There are persistent disparities between women and men in the way they see their acceptance levels in the political world, and their desire to increase their numbers in office. Women also consistently hold an alternative vision of the ways in which power can be used in legislative operations.
Ideology/Issues/ Voting Records	Women have been and are still more liberal than their male counterparts, more supportive of issues related to women and children and the family, and they make these views manifest in differential voting records.

Source: Table created by author.

tend to have fewer offspring than men. Further, delayed entry due to child rearing is notably more common for women (Werner 1966, 1968; Kirkpatrick 1974; Githens 1977; Mezey 1978a; Carroll 1989, 1993; Carroll and Strimling 1983; Dodson 1997; Dodson and Carroll 1991; Dolan and Ford 1998). Illustratively, in a recent study, Thomas (2002) found that 56 percent of married state legislators were men and 43 percent were women. Of those representatives who were childless, 55 percent of women were childless, whereas only 6 percent of men were childless. Patterns found among women as a whole are equally, if not more, prevalent among women of color. For example, Takash (1997) reports that the tension between family responsibilities and political service is especially serious for Latinas with political aspirations.

One reason married women with children are less active in legislatures than similarly situated men may be family expectations that their primary attention will be devoted to private life. An indicator of this possibility is clear evidence throughout the modern era that a supportive spouse is a much more prominent feature of women's career path than men's (Carroll 1989). Without one, women are more likely than men to forgo political pursuits altogether (Mezey 1978a; Sapiro 1982; Stoper 1977). Beyond decisions to run for or continue in office, the support levels of spouses and families differentially affect satisfaction levels of women and men in office. Herrick reports that among former members of Congress, women's "job satisfaction was most greatly influenced by whether their families benefited from the job whereas family benefits had only a modest effect on men's job satisfaction" (Herrick 2001, 85).

If socialization affects women's educational and occupational opportunities and choices, does it follow that women have diminished levels of political ambition compared to men? The answer is yes when it comes to the early modern era (Costantini 1990; Stoper 1977; Sapiro and Farah 1980; Githens 1977; Gertzog 1995). However, among current legislative women in general, and among African American legislative women, gender-based ambition level differentials have all but disappeared. Recent studies find very small differences in favor of men, no differences whatever between the sexes, or small differences in favor of women (Carroll 1984, 1993; Prestage 1991; Carey, Niemi, and Powell 1998; Bledsoe and Herring 1990). It appears that socialization has constrained individual choices and societal opportunities, but it has not dampened women's interest in politics or their ambition to contribute to the public sphere. Indeed, Dolan and Ford (1995) discovered that differences in ambition among women are related in the expected direction to age, the presence of minor children, intentional political careers, and previous officeholding. This is indicative of the juxtaposition of interest and ambition, on one hand, and opportunity on the other.

Legislative Women: What Has Been Their Impact?

In style and philosophy, the new senators were as diverse as America itself, yet the experiences that formed their ideals were often quite similar. The practical daily problems that confronted women—issues related to careers, wages, housing, day care, health care, education, and public safety—were of burning urgency to them. These issues had often been pushed to the back burner in male-dominated senates and legislatures, especially when they involved matters that were gender-specific, such as job equity, sexual harassment, maternity leave, and rape shield laws. (Mikulski et al. 2001, 123)

Once information of sufficient depth and breadth had been gathered about the backgrounds and ambitions women bring to legislative life, questions inevitably turned to the difference they might make as officeholders. If deeply embedded cultural assumptions about women and men's proper roles result in asymmetrical socialization, it follows that women could bring distinctive perspectives to legislative deliberation. What scholars uncovered was that women's ideologies, voting records, levels and types of legislative engagement and effectiveness, issue concentration, leadership abilities, and collective impact were indeed distinctive, and that they have had an increasingly significant impact on the work of legislatures.

As Table 12.3 displays, an enduring indicator of women's distinctive perspective concerns issue attitudes and voting records. Studies of each reveal that legislative women tend to be more liberal than men and more supportive of women's issues defined either traditionally or from a feminist perspective. Their voting records reflect these attitudes even when taking party and ideology into account (Diamond 1977; Johnson and Carroll 1978; Frankovic 1977; Carver 1979; Welch 1985; Saint-Germain 1989; Dodson and Carroll 1991; Thomas 1990, 1994, 2002; Barrett 1995; Clark 1998; Carey, Niemi, and Powell 1998; Leader 1977; Dolan 1997; Reingold 2000; Vega and Firestone 1995; Tamerius 1995; Swers 2002; but see Barnello 1999 for a New York State Assembly exception). Further, explorations of the variation apparent when women are compared to each other rather than to men indicate that African American women officeholders are more liberal than either white women or men (Barrett 2001).

Perhaps because gender socialization differentially influences perceptions of urgent need, legislative women have directed and continue to direct their energy to aspects of constituencies in a distinctive fashion. In particular, female state legislators appear to be more focused than males on constituent work (Diamond 1977; Thomas 1992, 1994; Richardson and Freeman 1995; Carey, Niemi, and Powell 1998; Reingold 2000), and are particularly concerned with the women of their constituencies and beyond (Carroll 2002). This latter pattern holds when women are compared to men and when they are compared to each other. Takash (1997) and Prindeville and Gomez (1999) find respectively that Latina and Native American women pay particular attention to women in their constituencies.

One dramatically evolving category of political behavior of women concerns legislative activity engagement and priority setting. Whereas women legislators were once reluctant to participate fully in routine legislative activities, today they are as active as men. This includes bill introduction and passage, committee work, legislative bargaining, and floor presentations (Blair and Stanley 1991a, 1991b;

Friedman 1993; Thomas 1994; Norton 1995; Tamerius 1995; Dolan and Ford 1998; Shogan 2001; Wolbrecht 2002). Further, while no evidence from the early modern era exists to suggest that women's legislative priorities differed from men's (Mueller 1982; Mezey 1978b), women today are more likely to target their work toward bills related to women, children, and the family. They are also more likely than their male counterparts to be successful passing these bills through legislatures and obtaining gubernatorial signatures (Saint-Germain 1989; Thomas 1994; Dodson and Carroll 1991; Vega and Firestone 1995; Tamerius 1995; Dodson 1998, 2001; Dolan and Ford 1997, 1998; Swers 2002; Bratton and Haynie 1999). Relatedly, when asked about the accomplishments of which they are most proud, women, much more than men, select bill passage on issues related to women, children, and families (Thomas 1994).[2]

Another key aspect of policymaking, related to women's policy priorities and their successes, concerns the diversity of the issues put on legislative agendas and the range of debate about proposals. As the quote offered at the start of this section suggests, whether by bringing previously private-sphere issues to public agendas (such as domestic violence), transforming issues long hidden from public view from whispered conversations to public crimes (such as sexual harassment), or expanding the education of men and influencing their policy choices on topics with which they are unfamiliar (such as funding for breast cancer research), women have made strides in creating space for public consideration of issues that, in an earlier time, were concealed. Further, scholars have found that individual and collective experience in legislatures and placement on key committees and in leadership positions enhances efforts toward agenda expansion (Levy, Tien, and Aved 2001; Kedrowski and Sarow 2002; Walsh 2002; Norton 2002; Thomas 1994; Dolan 1997; Dodson 1998).

As women have moved increasingly into committee and institutional leadership positions, questions have arisen about their styles and priorities. While no systematic research exists for the early modern era (as numbers of women leaders were far too small), current exploration reveals distinctive leadership choices (Thomas 2003). Illustratively, women leaders in state legislatures are more likely than men to exhibit a consensual rather than a command-and-control style. They also tend to place more emphasis on getting the job done in a team-oriented way; collaboration and consensus are emphasized over more aggressive tactics (Rosenthal 1998; Whicker and Jewell 1998). Similarly, Kathlene (1994) found that female committee chairs in Colorado were more likely to facilitate open discussions among hearing participants, whereas men were more likely to use their position to control hearings. These behaviors persist among subgroups of women.[3] For example, women tribal leaders on Indian reservations have been found to be inclusive managers who are more likely than men to compromise (Prindeville and Gomez 1999).[4] One still-emerging set of questions related to women's distinctive impact concerns theories of critical mass. That is, are women more likely to have an impact or a stronger impact in legislatures with higher proportions of women? The evidence to date is somewhat mixed. Some studies show that the presence of either a formal women's legislative caucus or a relatively high percentage of women in the legislature is associated with higher rates of bill passage on issues of women, children, and families (Thomas 1994; Berkman and O'Connor 1993). However, other studies find little or no difference (Tolbert and Steuernagel 2001; Reingold 2000). In light of women's still small proportions in most legislatures and the short spans of time surrounding their collective presence, it may be that critical mass theories cannot yet be adequately tested. It is also possible that increases in women's numbers, at least in the short term, are not enough by themselves to create deeper transformations in legislative life. It is to these possibilities that we turn next.[5]

Legislative Life: Environmental Factors

The third avenue of inquiry regarding the experiences, successes, and challenges of legislative women concerns the environment in which they operate. While attention continues to be paid to questions having their origins in the first two phases, most recently, scholars have focused on the effect of institutional and societal norms, rules, and expectations on women's legislative choices and impact.

Turning first to institutional context, the extent to which tacit assumptions about the nature of policymaking, legislative procedures, and expectations for excellence result in gender-based obstacles is the cutting edge of research. Scholars have sought to deconstruct the assumptions of neutrality underlying legislative organization. In particular, two types of evidence have pointed toward the need for deepening exploration. The first consists of long-standing reports of discriminatory atmospheres in legislatures. The second concerns women's unease with frameworks for legislative business that are ostensibly impartial, but decidedly at odds with conditions for their optimal effectiveness.

While women's rise to high-profile leadership positions, such as the ascension of Nancy Pelosi to the minority leadership of the House of Representatives, implies that discrimination against women is a thing of the past, the exceptions often train our gaze away from more general conditions. It is true that women's increased presence in and leadership of state and federal legislatures signals that the days of overt, absolute exclusion are largely over. However, research findings make it clear that inchoate remnants of discrimination persist.

One indicator of discriminatory environments is responses of legislators to queries about benefits and hurdles experienced in careers. A recent example from the state level reveals divergent responses from women and men. Fully one-quarter of legislative women responded to an open-ended question about career challenges by introducing discussions of discrimination. No men responded similarly (Thomas 2002). Among women's comments regarding the challenges were these:

- "Being a woman and proving your qualifications."
- "Having my male counterparts deal with me on their level."
- "Discrimination against women legislators," or "sexism," or "prejudice against women," or "gender prejudices."
- "Racism and sexism." "Being Black and a Woman."
- "Getting people to respect me as a woman."
- "Being a woman in a good old boys club."
- "No recognition of female leadership."
- "Doing away with the male dominated environment."
- "Isolation of women members."

These comments confirm patterns in evidence throughout the modern era (Diamond 1977; Kirkpatrick 1974; Mezey 1978a; Carroll 1984) and reflect the expectations of legislative identities built on male-centered values and prerogatives. The veneers of neutrality in the evaluation of successful legislators belie the reality that, even today, men's "socially designed biographies define workplace expectations and successful career patterns" (MacKinnon 1987).

Additionally, the available literature on within-group analysis strongly indicates that gender-based discrimination is intensified for women of color. Isolation beyond that which is experienced by white women or men of color makes the experience of atmospheric discrimination doubly palpable (Cohen 2002). Writing about African American women legislators, Gill (1997, 1) notes, "Not only would their efforts not be rewarded, but their invisibility would result from a country that viewed African American progress as male and feminist progress as white. . . . Theirs had been the struggle within the struggle."

A second body of evidence pointing toward the disparate impact of seemingly neutral institutional norms and rules is available from analysis of women's preferred way of conducting legislative business. Women officeholders consistently report feeling out of sync with routine operations. In particular, women operationalize power less as "power over" and more as "power to" (Cantor and Bernay 1992). They envision a standard under which influence is used for responsiveness to colleagues and constituents rather than for personal gain. Specific examples of the type of structure under which women feel they can achieve optimal effectiveness are available from interviews of state legislators (Thomas 1994). Responses revealed that women emphasized long-range planning, considered the views of others equally with their own, and looked out for what is good for their constituencies, rather than just their own self-interest. As the women themselves characterized the alternative:

- "There would be more consensus politics. Women are better at consensus building."
- "The legislature would change. Legislation would be more considered and more refined, more in-depth. The process would be more organized and there would be better communication."

- "Women see practical, not just political applications. They are cooperative and nonconfrontational."
- "Women look at benefits for society and men look at how [it] will benefit them politically."

Gendered Institutions

The evidence of persistent experiences of atmospheric discrimination and structures designed to entrench male privilege provide clues to deeper, less immediately visible processes at work in legislative environments. The issue is not just that rules—formal and informal, tacit and explicit—privilege some over others; it is that they do so in a discriminatory fashion. A leading theory to emerge from the third phase of research on legislative women is the concept of gendered institutions. Scholars point out that gender adheres not just to individuals but also to the organizations and institutions to which they belong. Those structures and behaviors that conform to the gendered expectations (the male norm) of the institution—in this case, legislatures—are rewarded. Further, to the extent that women's preferences are distinctive, they are likely to be devalued and attenuated (Duerst-Lahti 2002a, 2002b; Duerst-Lahti and Kelly 1995; Kathlene 1994, 1998; Kenney 1996). As Duerst-Lahti (2002a, 380) explains:

> [Analysis of gendered institutions] can turn the gaze toward the institution itself if formal and informal structures, practices, norms, rules tenaciously block congresswomen's desired policy outcomes. Because sometimes women and men do have different policy preferences, cite different life experiences based upon gender, or different assumptions about appropriate behaviors, rules, and practices, institutions predicated upon masculinity are not as responsive to women as to men. Masculine ideology functions as a cultural system that curtails women's capacity to represent. . . . Thus, even when women win a place in the institution, they remain outsiders.

Applying the theory of gendered institutions to women's experiences in legislatures is best seen in Lyn Kathlene's work concerning gender-based policy prescriptions (1994, 1998). In a study of the Colorado legislature, she found that legislative women were more likely than men to be contextual in their political outlook (the perception that people's lives are interdependent, based on a continuous web of relationships). Men were more likely to be instrumental (see people as autonomous individuals in a hierarchical, competitive world). Consequently, when formulating policy solutions, legislative women relied on different and more sources of information and created prescriptions that reflected not just an individual aberrant action, but also the impact of societal opportunities and lifelong experiences. The complexity of their legislative proposals and their contextual nature also meant lower success rates for bill passage. As Kathlene notes, women's approach was "at odds with the instrumental institutionalized discourse" that devalued or marginalized contextualism in legislative institutions.

The establishment of a research agenda that explores the effects of gendered institutions on women's success leaves two remaining questions. First, if gendered institutions place barriers in the way of their success, how can evidence of women's distinctive impact on agendas, debates, and outcomes be explained? The relatively simple answer is the exertion of disproportionate effort. Throughout the modern era, women have consistently reported that to achieve the same level of success as men and to be perceived as effective and credible, they have to produce more, display more patience, pay greater attention to detail, and deliver higher levels of preparation for daily tasks. These perceptions hold true regardless of party identi- fication, ideology, or region from which women are elected (Githens 1977; Main, Gryski, and Schapiro 1984; Diamond 1977; Dodson and Carroll 1991; Johnson and Carroll 1978; Kirkpatrick 1974; Reingold 2000; Thomas 1994, 1997). In short, in gendered institutions the playing field is not equal; while women can achieve success, it comes at a higher cost.

The last question is, how can institutionally systemic gendering be reversed? The conventional answer is to increase the proportions of women in legislatures beyond critical mass levels to full parity. However, scholars of gendered institu- tions suggest that while increasing the number of women in office and reaping the benefits of collectivization in the form of caucuses and coalitions are necessary conditions to transforming institutions, they may not be sufficient in and of them- selves. As Duerst-Lahti (2002a, 380) concludes, "The preferences of women, there- fore, must receive the full attention of the institution. . . ." In other words, routine operations have to be re-conceptualized; business as usual has to be transformed.[6]

From Gendered Institutions to Gendered Societal Roles

Along with explorations of the ways in which institutional arrangements create gendered experiences in legislatures, attention is increasingly being paid to con- straints on women's political pursuits resulting from sex-based divisions of soci- etal labor. If, for example, private-sphere workloads disproportionately fall to women, women's contributions to legislatures may be diluted. It has been estab- lished that sex-role socialization keeps married women with children away from political office at greater rates than their male counterparts, but what about the effects of socialization on private-sphere tasks? Are persistent gendered experi- ences in the private sphere prevalent even for those women who have sought and won the most public of professions? In addition to paying a higher cost for public- sphere success, do they bear disproportionate responsibility at home?

While few early studies directly examined the effects of private-sphere duties of legislators on public life, what exists suggests that, despite holding public of- fice, women bore the brunt of work inside the home. This was not true for men. In fact, the general conclusion of the most direct early study of this phenomenon noted, "even women who have broken free of sex roles sufficiently to run for political office are limited by the same sex roles, particularly, the family-related ones, from shaping a full political career" (Stoper 1977, 335).

Two more recent studies suggest that little progress on this front has been made. First, Thomas's (2002) study of the intersection of the personal and the political in state legislative careers offers evidence of unequal private sphere duties of public women and men. For example, legislative women were much more likely than legislative men to be primarily responsible for everyday household tasks such as cleaning, cooking, shopping, dishes, and laundry. The gap on each of these variables ranged from 35 to 52 percentage points. Most centrally, women were the primary caretakers of children (60 percent versus 40 percent). Even when legislators' partners worked outside the home, women were the ones who most often stayed home with ill children (59 percent versus 41 percent). In part, these findings reflect the fact that men are more likely to have stay-at-home partners, but they hold even in situations in which that is not true.

In what ways, if any, do unequal family duties affect the contours of legislative careers? One answer comes from responses to queries about career dreams and career timing. Thomas (2002) found that women state legislators were much less likely than men to dream of careers at early ages and less likely to run for office early. For example, of those who dreamed of a political career in their twenties, 79 percent were men and only 21 percent were women. Consequently, of those state legislators who ran for office for the first time in their forties, 61 percent were women and 39 percent were men. Explanations for timing are found in responses to open-ended questions. Women's reasons were much more likely than men's to concern their marital status or the age of their children. In short, women are more likely to fit public sphere activity around their private responsibilities.

Further evidence of the effects of gendered divisions of private-sphere labor on women's political careers comes from another recent study—this one exploring decisions to seek legislative seats. In New York State, among those women who fit within the pool of expected candidates and who have considered running, "traditional family structures and historically socialized gender roles may continue to discourage women from seeking public office" (Fox and Lawless 2003, 19). Consequently, the proportion of women in office may be inconsistent with the proportion of those otherwise interested and prepared to serve.

As suggested, gender-based public/private imbalance can have serious deleterious consequences for women's presence and effectiveness in legislatures. Under the present circumstances, the higher cost to serve means that women have disproportionate reasons to delay entry into politics, decline to enter at all, enter on a very limited basis, and/or stay for shorter periods than men. This means that women's ability to reverse their minority status in legislatures, obtain sufficient collective experience, and maximize their impact is compromised.[7] What's more, it is possible that until women's entry into the public sphere is matched by men's entry into the private sphere, it is unlikely that their numbers will dramatically rise. Indeed, the first book of the modern era on women state legislators predicted that cultural and social revolution would be required before women attained numerical equality (Kirkpatrick 1974).

Progress and Plateaus

The environmental context in which legislative women set their priorities and share their contributions serves to attenuate their efforts. Unequal playing fields experienced both at home and in legislatures limit women's political choices and contributions. One relatively recent consequence of these phenomena concerns levels of women's representation. After more than twenty-five years of incremental progress elevating the proportion of women in legislatures, it appears that a plateau has been reached. For the first time since the late 1960s/early 1970s, the election cycles of the twenty-first century are not continuing to produce steady gains for women. As Table 12.1 shows, by 2003, state legislative election cycles had produced fewer women in office than we had in 1999, and the 2002 congressional election resulted in no increase whatsoever. Also, as Table 12.2 shows, the number of women of color in Congress declined with the 2002 elections. Says Debbie Walsh, director of the Center for American Women and Politics, "It's been a story of stagnation . . . . Women have barely held their early 1990s gains in Congress" (Women's enews 3/14/03). The story coming out of the 2004 electoral cycle continues this general trend. Since some races are still being contested at this writing, it is only safe to say that, at the state legislative level, women's representation for 2005 will be no greater than it was before the election. Also, at the congressional level, women's Senate representation remains at 14 percent—as was the case before the election. The only heartening news is that women gained five seats in the U.S. House of Representatives. In sum, women's progress in the modern era has come to a virtual halt.

While women candidates running for election and reelection win at comparable rates to men (see Fiber and Fox, this volume), there appears to be a drop-off in the number of women running for legislative office.[8] Elaborating on this trend, Susan Estrich, the first woman to run a presidential campaign, notes: "Those of us in our 50s and 60s are looking around for women in their 30s and 40s to try to lead the Democratic party in California, for example, and we can't think of anyone," said Estrich. The same thing is starting to happen in Congress (Hutchison 2002). The disproportionate cost of success required of women legislators appears to be having an effect on women's desires to serve.

If women's gains in state legislatures and the U.S. Congress continue to stagnate or decline, is this a situation with which we should be inordinately concerned? As long as the women who choose to run for legislative office have an equal opportunity to win, are redoubled efforts to increase the number of women candidates warranted? From broad concerns about the cultivation of healthy democracy to the details of practical policymaking, the answer is yes. Vibrant and stable democracies derive, in part, from perceptions and experiences of legitimacy. A government that is democratically organized is only truly legitimate if all of its citizens are provided with the same opportunities for full participation. If gender-based atmospheres differentially affect aspirations or the ability to make political contributions, the quality of democracy suffers. If a variety of voices are not sustained and encouraged, public policy agendas and decisions will be circumscribed, thereby serving ever smaller segments of society.

Conclusions and Implications

This survey of the shape of inquiry about legislative women of the modern era and its results suggests that women can make distinctive and meaningful contributions to legislative work, but to do so, they must incur disparate costs. Among the effects of gendered institutions are persistent perceptions of discriminatory environments, constrained policy approaches, and the need to work harder and more precisely to achieve the same levels of success as men. Additionally, among the effects of gendered divisions of societal labor are double duty and attenuated career service. The results of these forces may well be stagnation in the proportions of women who hold legislative office. If so, women's status as minorities within legislatures, collective newcomers, and outsiders may be more entrenched and longer lasting than previously recognized. At the very least, a temporary plateau has been reached.

In light of the evidence provided in this chapter, it would be facile to predict that the ongoing gendering of institutions and society will preclude steady, meaningful growth in the proportions of women serving in legislatures. However, I assert that it is premature to conclude that these unresolved challenges are insurmountable. If nothing else, as Table 12.4 encapsulates, the story of legislative women over the last thirty years shows that when they have encountered obstacles, they have found ways to succeed around them and to create increasingly more equal playing fields.[9] That they can continue this trajectory seems not only plausible, but also probable. Since women are active, not just passive agents of politics, their impact, though limited by gendered environments, cannot be completely nullified by them. The point, however, may be the extent to which they will need to operate unilaterally (and therefore achieve slow progress at high cost), or whether the benefits of diversity and equality of representation will spur more widely cooperative (and thereby more rapid) efforts for which costs are shared. Put another way, will it take external cultural and institutional revolutions to achieve uniformity of opportunity and experience, or will the efforts of legislative women foreshorten those revolutions?

Table 12.4

Women's Obstacles and Strategies for Success

OBSTACLES	STRATEGIES FOR SUCCESSES
Socialization	✓ Increased educational and occupational opportunities ✓ Increases in professional ambition ✓ Targeted outreach, recruitment, workshops, training, fundraising ✓ Mentoring
Discrimination ✓ Gender ✓ Women of Color ✓ Dual Oppression	✓ Performance Success: introduction and bill passage on general legislation and on policy priorities ✓ Performance Success: winning committee and institutional leadership roles ✓ Performance Success: equal activity levels in committees, on floor, influence with colleagues ✓ Performance Success: harder working ✓ Resistance to homogenization: distinctive ideology, roll-call voting behavior, policy priorities, pride in accomplishments on women's issues ✓ Resistance to homogenization: different leadership voice ✓ Group efforts such as caucuses and coalition building ✓ Outreach, recruitment, workshops, training, fundraising ✓ Alternative recruitment, training, fundraising organizations for women of color
Gendered Institutions ✓ Power Over Versus Power To	✓ Distinctive legislative policy priorities; expanding agendas, debates ✓ Attention to constituency—greater levels than men and specific focus on women constituents ✓ Education efforts toward male colleagues ✓ Caucuses and other coalition efforts ✓ Increasingly more diverse committee assignments ✓ Increased representation in committee and institutional leadership posts ✓ Efforts to increase the proportion of women in legislatures
Gendered Societal Roles ✓ Private Sphere	✓ Sequential life choices—politics worked around family life ✓ Double duty
Stagnation ✓ Federal level ✓ State level	✓ Renewed efforts at recruitment, mentoring, fundraising, training, reversing unwelcome environments

Source: Table created by author.

Notes

1. As articulated in this volume's chapter on women candidates, questions about the viability of women's candidacies and reelection prospects also abounded.

2. For anecdotal accounts of the difference women's presence makes in legislative outcomes, see Boxer 1994; Kunin 1994; and Margolies-Mezvinsky 1994.

3. Further, one study of state legislative leaders finds that women can make a difference by influencing some men's perspectives, votes, and styles. Over time, men have begun to adopt "female" leadership styles centered on collaboration and consensus (Whicker and Jewell 1998). Hence, women's impact on legislatures may extend to effects of men's legislative behaviors.

4. Women currently hold committee chair positions in proportion to their representation in state legislatures (Carroll and Taylor 1989; Thomas 1994; Darcy 1996; Whistler and Ellickson 1999; Rosenthal 2002; Whicker and Jewell 1998). Evidence also suggests that women are represented across the board on committees in the U.S. Congress (Friedman 1996; Arnold and King 2002).

5. Legislative women appear to subscribe to theories of critical mass. They spend considerable time and effort recruiting and training women candidates, fundraising to increase their chances of success, and mentoring women who achieve office (Thomas 1994, 1997; Gierzynski and Burdreck 1995; Dolan and Ford 1998).

6. An underexplored but related analysis concerns the ways in which race privilege is embedded in institutional foundations. The intersection of race and gender must be centrally located in future study of institutional constraints.

7. Anecdotal research supports these conclusions. Former representatives such as Susan Molinari have commented extensively about the extent to which family responsibilities affected her retirement decision (Molinari 1998). These findings are statistically significant and, when appropriate, confirmed in multivariate analysis.

8. Term limits have exacerbated this trend. Carroll and Jenkins (2001) have found that the interaction of term limits on seats held by women and the drop-off in the number of women running for office results in fewer women in the lower chambers of statehouses.

9. Fox and Fiber's chapter in this volume amplifies this interpretation with respect to women candidates.

References

Arnold, Laura W., and Barbara M. King. 2002. "Women, Committees, and Institutional Change in the Senate." In *Women Transforming Congress*, ed. Cindy Simon Rosenthal. Norman: University of Oklahoma Press.

Barnello, Michelle A. 1999. "Gender and Roll Call Voting in the New York State Assembly." *Women & Politics* 20: 77–94.

Barrett, Edith J. 1995. "The Policy Priorities of African American Women in State Legislatures." *Legislative Studies Quarterly* 20: 223–247.

———. 2001. "Black Women in State Legislatures: The Relationship of Race and Gender to the Legislative Experience." In *The Impact of Women in Public Office*, ed. Susan J. Carroll. Bloomington: Indiana University Press.

Berkman, Michael B., and Robert E. O'Connor. 1993. "Do Women Legislators Matter? Female Legislators and State Abortion Policy." *American Politics Quarterly* 21: 102–124.

Blair, Diane D., and Jeanie R. Stanley. 1991a. "Gender Differences in Legislative Effectiveness: The Impact of the Legislative Environment." In *Gender and Policymaking: Studies of Women in Office*, ed. Debra L. Dodson. New Brunswick, NJ: Center for the American Woman and Politics.

———. 1991b. "Personal Relationships and Legislative Power: Male and Female Perceptions." *Legislative Studies Quarterly* 16: 495–507.

Bledsoe, Timothy, and Mary Herring. 1990. "Victims of Circumstances: Women in Pursuit of Political Office in America." *American Political Science Review* 84: 13–224.

Boxer, Barbara, with Nicole Boxer. 1994. *Strangers in the Senate: Politics and the New Revolution of Women in America.* Washington, DC: National Press Books.

Bratton, Kathleen, and Kerry L. Haynie. 1999. "Agenda Setting and Legislative Success in State Legislatures: The Effects of Gender and Race." *Journal of Politics* 61: 658–679.

Cantor, Dorothy W., and Toni Bernay, with Jean Stoess. 1992. *Women in Power: The Secrets of Leadership.* Boston: Houghton Mifflin.

Carey, John M., Richard G. Niemi, and Lynda W. Powell. 1998. "Are Women State Legislators Different?" In *Women and Elective Office: Past, Present, and Future,* ed. Sue Thomas and Clyde Wilcox. New York: Oxford University Press.

Carroll, Susan J. 1984. "Women Candidates and Support for Feminist Concerns: The Closet Feminist Syndrome." *Western Political Quarterly* 37: 307–323.

———. 1989. "The Personal Is Political: The Intersection of Private Lives and Public Roles Among Women and Men in Elective and Appointive Office." *Women & Politics* 9: 51–67.

———. 1993. "The Political Careers of Women Elected Officials: An Assessment and Research Agenda." In *Ambition and Beyond: Career Path of American Politicians,* ed. Shirley Williams and Edward L. Lascher, Jr. Berkeley: Institute of Governmental Studies Press.

———. 2002. "Representing Women: Congresswomen's Perceptions of Their Representational Roles." In *Women Transforming Congress,* ed. Cindy Simon Rosenthal. Norman: University of Oklahoma Press.

Carroll, Susan J., and Krista E. Jenkins. 2001. "Unrealized Opportunity? Term Limits and the Representation of Women in State Legislatures." *Women & Politics* 23: 1–30.

Carroll, Susan J., and Wendy S. Strimling, with the assistance of John J. Cohen and Barbara Geiger-Parker. 1983. *Women's Routes to Elective Office: A Comparison with Men's.* New Brunswick, NJ: Center for the American Woman and Politics.

Carroll, Susan J., and Ella Taylor. 1989. "Gender Differences in the Committee Assignments of State Legislators: Preferences or Discrimination?" Paper presented at the annual meeting of the Midwest Political Science Association, Chicago.

Carver, Joan S. 1979. "Women in Florida." *Journal of Politics* 41: 941–955.

Center for American Women and Politics (CAWP). 2003. Fact Sheets.

Clark, Janet. 1998. "Women at the National Level: An Update on Roll Call Voting Behavior." In *Women and Elective Office: Past, Present, and Future,* ed. Sue Thomas and Clyde Wilcox. New York: Oxford University Press.

Cohen, Cathy J. 2002. "A Portrait of Continuing Marginality: The Study of Women of Color in American Politics." In *Women and American Politics: New Questions, New Directions,* ed. Susan J. Carroll. New York: Oxford University Press.

Costantini, Edmond. 1990. "Political Women and Political Ambition: Closing the Gender Gap." *American Journal of Political Science* 34: 741–770.

Darcy, Robert. 1996. "Women in the State Legislative Power Structure: Committee Chairs." *Social Science Quarterly* 77: 888–898.

Diamond, Irene. 1977. *Sex Roles in the State House.* New Haven, CT: Yale University Press.

Dodson, Debra L. 1997. "Change and Continuity in the Relationship Between Private Responsibilities and Public Officeholding: The More Things Change, the More They Stay the Same." *Policy Studies Journal* 25: 569–584.

———. 1998. "Representing Women's Interests in the U.S. House of Representatives." In *Women and Elective Office: Past, Present, and Future,* ed. Sue Thomas and Clyde Wilcox. New York: Oxford University Press.

———. 2001. "Acting for Women: Is What Legislators Say, What They Do?" In *The Impact of Women in Public Office,* ed. Susan J. Carroll. Bloomington: University of Indiana Press.

Dodson, Debra L., and Susan J. Carroll. 1991. *Reshaping the Agenda: Women in State Legislatures*. New Brunswick, NJ: Center for the American Woman and Politics.

Dolan, Julie. 1997. "Support for Women's Interests in the 103rd Congress: The Distinct Impact of Congressional Women." *Women & Politics* 18: 81–94.

Dolan, Kathleen, and Lynne E. Ford. 1995. "Women in the State Legislatures: Feminist Identity and Legislative Behavior." *American Politics Quarterly* 23: 96–108.

———. 1997. "Change and Continuity Among Women State Legislators: Evidence from Three Decades." *Political Research Quarterly* 50: 137–151.

———. 1998. "Are All Women State Legislators Alike?" In *Women and Elective Office: Past, Present, and Future*, ed. Sue Thomas and Clyde Wilcox. New York: Oxford University Press.

Duerst-Lahti, Georgia. 2002a. "Governing Institutions, Ideologies and Gender: Toward the Possibility of Equal Political Representation." *Sex Roles: A Journal of Research* 47: 371–388.

———. 2002b. "Knowing Congress as a Gendered Institution: Manliness and the Implications of Women in Congress." In *Women Transforming Congress*, ed. Cindy Simon Rosenthal. Norman: University of Oklahoma Press.

Duerst-Lahti, Georgia, and Rita Mae Kelly, eds. 1995. *Gender Power, Leadership, and Governance*. Ann Arbor: University of Michigan Press.

Fox, Richard L., and Jennifer L. Lawless. 2003. "Family Structure, Sex Role Socialization, and the Decision to Run for Office." *Women & Politics* 24: 19–48.

Frankovic, Kathleen A. 1975. "Sex and Voting in the U.S. House of Representatives 1961–1977." *American Politics Quarterly* 5: 315–331.

Friedman, Sally, A. 1993. "Committee Assignments of Women and Blacks in Congress—1964–1990." *Legislative Studies Quarterly* 21: 73–81.

Gertzog, Irwin N. 1995. *Congressional Women: Their Recruitment, Integration, and Behavior*. 2d ed. Westport, CT: Praeger.

———. 2002. "Women's Changing Pathways to the U.S. House of Representatives: Widows, Elites, and Strategic Politicians." In *Women Transforming Congress*, ed. Cindy Simon Rosenthal. Norman: University of Oklahoma Press.

Gierzynski, Anthony, and Paulette Burdreck. 1995. "Women's Legislative Caucus and Leadership Campaign Committees." *Women & Politics* 15: 37–54.

Gill, LaVerne McCain. 1997. *African American Women in Congress: Forming and Transforming History*. New Brunswick, NJ: Rutgers University Press.

Githens, Marianne. 1977. "Spectators, Agitators or Lawmakers: Women in State Legislatures." In *A Portrait of Marginality: The Political Behavior of the American Woman*, ed. Marianne Githens and Jewel Prestage. New York: McKay.

Herrick, Rebekah. 2001. "Gender Effects on Job Satisfaction in the House of Representatives." *Women & Politics* 23: 85–98.

Hutchison, Sue. 2002. "Great will be the day when 'I Am Woman' is a dying cry." *San Jose Mercury News*. November 15.

Johnson, Marilyn, and Susan J. Carroll, with Kathy Stanwyck and Lynn Korenblit. 1978. *Profile of Women Holding Office II*. New Brunswick, NJ: Center for the American Woman and Politics.

Kathlene, Lyn. 1994. "Power and Influence in State Legislative Policymaking: The Interaction of Gender and Position in Committee Hearing Debates." *American Political Science Review* 88: 560–576.

———. 1998. "In a Different Voice: Women and the Policy Process." In *Women and Elective Office: Past, Present, and Future*, ed. Sue Thomas and Clyde Wilcox. New York: Oxford University Press.

Kedrowski, Karen, and Marilyn Stine Sarow. 2002. "The Gendering of Cancer Policy: Media Advocacy and Congressional Policy Attention." In *Women Transforming Congress*, ed. Cindy Simon Rosenthal. Norman: University of Oklahoma Press.

Kenney, Sally J. 1996. "Field Essay: New Research on Gendered Political Institutions." *Political Research Quarterly* 49: 445–466.

Kirkpatrick, Jeane. 1974. *Political Woman*. New York: Basic Books.

Kunin, Madeleine. 1994. *Living a Political Life*. New York: Knopf.

Leader, Shelah G. 1977. "The Policy Impact of Women Elected Officials." In *The Impact of the Electoral Process*, ed. Joseph Cooper and Louis Maisels. Beverly Hills: Sage.

Levy, Dena, Charles Tien, and Rachell Aved. 2001. "Do Differences Matter? Women Members of Congress and the Hyde Amendment." *Women & Politics* 23: 105–128.

MacKinnon, Catharine A. 1987. *Feminism Unmodified: Discourses on Life and Law*. Cambridge: Harvard University Press.

Main, Eleanor C., Gerard S. Gryski, and Beth Schapiro. 1984. "Different Perspectives: Southern State Legislators' Attitudes About Women in Politics." *Social Science Journal* 21: 21–28.

Margolies-Mezvinsky, Marjorie, with Barbara Feinman. 1994. *A Woman's Place . . . The Freshman Women Who Changed the Face of Congress*. New York: Crown.

Mezey, Susan Gluck. 1978a. "Does Sex Make a Difference? A Case Study of Women in Politics." *Western Political Quarterly* 31: 492–501.

———. 1978b. "Women and Representation: The Case of Hawaii." *Journal of Politics* 40: 369–385.

Mikulski, Barbara, Kay Bailey Hutchison, Dianne Feinstein, Barbara Boxer, Patty Murray, Olympia Snowe, Susan Collins, Mary Landrieu, and Blanche L. Lincoln, with Catherine Whitney. 2001. *Nine and Counting: The Women of the Senate*. New York: Perennial.

Molinari, Susan, with Elinor Burkett. 1998. *Representative Mom: Balancing Budgets, Bills, and Baby in the U.S. Congress*. New York: Doubleday.

Mueller, Carol M. 1982. "Feminism and the New Women in Public Office." *Women and Politics* 2: 7–21.

Norton, Noelle H. 1995. "Women, It's Not Enough to Be Elected: Committee Position Makes a Difference in Georgia." In *Gender Power, Leadership, and Governance*, ed. Georgia Duerst-Lahti and Rita M. Kelly. Ann Arbor: University of Michigan Press.

———. 2002. "Transforming Policy from the Inside: Participation in Committee." In *Women Transforming Congress*, ed. Cindy Simon Rosenthal. Norman: University of Oklahoma Press.

Prestage, Jewel L. 1991. "In Quest of African-American Political Women." *The Annals* 515: 88–103.

Prindeville, Diane-Michele, and Teresa Braley Gomez. 1999. "American Indian Women Leaders, Public Policy, and the Importance of Gender and Ethnic Identity." *Women & Politics* 20: 17–32.

Reingold, Beth. 2000. *Representing Women: Sex, Gender, and Legislative Behavior in Arizona and California*. Chapel Hill: University of North Carolina Press.

Richardson, Lilliard E., and Patricia K. Freeman. 1995. "Gender Differences in Constituency Service Among State Legislators." *Political Research Quarterly* 48: 169–179.

Rogers, David. 2002. *The Wall Street Journal*, November 15.

Rosenthal, Cindy Simon. 1998. *When Women Lead: Integrative Leadership in State Legislatures*. New York: Oxford University Press.

———. 2002. *Women Transforming Congress*. Norman: University of Oklahoma Press.

Saint-Germain, Michelle A. 1989. "Does Their Difference Make a Difference? The Impact of Women on Public Policy in the Arizona Legislature." *Social Science Quarterly* 70: 956–968.

Sapiro, Virginia. 1982. "Private Costs of Public Commitments or Public Costs of Private Commitments? Family Roles Versus Political Ambition." *American Journal of Political Science* 26: 265–279.

Sapiro, Virginia, and Barbara Farah. 1980. "New Pride and Old Prejudice: Political Ambition and Role Orientations Among Female Partisan Elites." *Women & Politics* 1: 13–36.

Shogan, Colleen J. 2001. "Speaking Out: An Analysis of Democratic and Republican Women-Invoked Rhetoric of the 105th Congress." *Women & Politics* 23: 129–146.

Stoper, Emily. 1977. "Wife and Politician: Role Strain Among Women in Public Office." In *A Portrait of Marginality: The Political Behavior of the American Woman*, ed. Marianne Githens and Jewell Prestage. New York: McKay.

Swers, Michelle L. 2002. *The Difference Women Make: The Policy Impact of Women in Congress*. Chicago: University of Chicago Press.

Takash, Paule Cruz. 1997. "Breaking Barriers to Representation: Chicana/Latina Elected Officials in California." In *Women Transforming Politics: An Alternative Reader*, ed. Cathy J. Cohen, Kathleen B. Jones, and Joan C. Tronto. New York: New York University Press.

Tamerius, Karin L. 1995. "Sex, Gender, and Leadership in the Representation of Women." In *Gender Power, Leadership, and Governance*, ed. Georgia Duerst-Lahti and Rita Mae Kelly. Ann Arbor: University of Michigan Press.

Thomas, Sue. 1990. "Voting Patterns in the California Assembly: The Role of Gender." *Women & Politics* 9: 43–56.

———. 1992. "The Effects of Race and Gender on Constituency Service." *Western Political Quarterly* 45:169–180.

———. 1994. *How Women Legislate*. New York: Oxford University Press.

———. 1997. "Why Gender Matters: The Perceptions of Women Officeholders." *Women & Politics* 17: 27–53.

———. 2002. "The Personal Is Political: Antecedents of Gendered Choices of Elected Representatives." *Sex Roles: A Journal of Research* 47: 343–353.

———. 2003. "The Impact of Women in Political Leadership Positions." In *Women and American Politics: New Questions, New Directions*, ed. Susan J. Carroll. Oxford, UK: Oxford University Press.

Tolbert, Caroline J., and Gertrude A. Steuernagel. 2001. "Women Lawmakers, State Mandates and Women's Health." *Women & Politics* 22: 1–39.

van Assendelft, Laura, and Karen O'Connor. 1994. "Backgrounds, Motivations and Interests: A Comparison of Male and Female Local Party Activists." *Women & Politics* 14: 77–92.

Vega, Arturo, and Juanita M. Firestone. 1995. "The Effects of Gender on Congressional Behavior and Substantive Representation of Women." *Legislative Studies Quarterly* 20: 213–222.

Walsh, Katherine Cramer. 2002. "Enlarging Representation: Women Bringing Marginalized Perspectives to Floor Debate in the House of Representatives." In *Women Transforming Congress*, ed. Cindy Simon Rosenthal. Norman: University of Oklahoma Press.

Welch, Susan. 1985. "Are Women More Liberal Than Men in the U.S. Congress?" *Legislative Studies Quarterly* 10: 125–134.

Werner, Emmy E. 1966. "Women in Congress: 1917–1964." *Western Political Quarterly* 19: 16–30.

———. 1968. "Women in the State Legislatures." *Western Political Quarterly* 21: 40–50.

Whicker, Marcia Lynn, and Malcolm Jewell. 1998. "The Feminization of Leadership in State Legislatures." In *Women and Elective Office: Past, Present, and Future*, ed. Sue Thomas and Clyde Wilcox. New York: Oxford University Press.

Whistler, Donald E., and Mark C. Ellickson. 1999. "The Incorporation of Women in State Legislatures: A Description." *Women and Politics* 20(3): 81–97.

Wolbrecht, Christina. 2002. "Female Legislators and the Women's Rights Agenda: From Feminine Mystique to Feminist Era." In *Women Transforming Congress*, ed. Cindy Simon Rosenthal. Norman: University of Oklahoma Press.

Women's enews. 2003. www.womensenews.org. March 14.

13

Gender Bias?
Media Coverage of Women and Men in Congress

David Niven

> She went to Wal-Mart and Kmart to shop for blue jeans and sneakers for her twin sons, Reece and Bennett, who turn 7 later this month. She registered the boys for Little League and bought their uniforms. She sent checks to their school to cover two months' worth of cafeteria lunches, and paid for their summer camp.
>
> —Sheryl Gay Stolberg

While the precise details might vary, an account such as this one could have been written about a day in the life of any of millions of women in the United States. The subject here, however, is a day in the life of U.S. Senator Blanche Lincoln (D-Arkansas). We learn in this account from the *New York Times* not only about Senator Lincoln, but also about Patty Murray (D-Washington), Lisa Murkowski (R-Alaska), Kay Bailey Hutchison (R-Texas), and Mary Landrieu (D-Louisiana), who have in common the fact that they are senators and mothers.

What difference does it make if the media cover motherhood in the Senate, or the House, or some other elected body? A number of analysts have considered the potential implications of this kind of coverage and cite several concerns.

First, every article focused on family life is an article not focused on the actual accomplishments of the senator in office. Second, it is frequently the case that family life is portrayed as being in conflict with the responsibilities of a senator. The *Times* describes how these senators "juggle pediatricians' appointments with Cub Scout meetings with fund-raisers and late-night roll call votes." The challenge can prove too much, as the *Times* noted that Senator Hutchison was late to a meeting because her two-year-old slept late, and that Senator Landrieu refuses to work most nights because she wants to be with her two children.

Third, the association with motherhood seems to encourage reporters to use childish language to describe the senators and their behavior. Senator Lincoln, who led the effort in the Senate to extend a tax credit to include low-income families, was described in that same *Times* article as having "kicked up a fuss" on the tax issue. Senator Murkowski, meanwhile, was admonished in the article for missing a Senate vote to attend her son's sixth-grade graduation. The *Times* labeled the decision "a definite no-no."

Fourth, experience as a mother seems to encourage crediting women senators with expertise in women-oriented issues while often serving to limit their voice on other issues. To wit, the article mentions that Senator Bill Frist (R-Tennessee) was a heart surgeon before winning a Senate seat, and that he speaks with great credibility on issues related to medicine and health care. By contrast, women senators "have a certain credibility on matters that affect women." The article does not mention that in addition to being a surgeon, Senator Frist is also a man and a father, or that he has any special credibility on issues affecting men. Nor does it mention, for example, that in addition to being a woman and a mother, Senator Murkowski is also a lawyer, or that she has any special credibility on legal issues.

Finally, coverage of women senators as mothers offers a vastly different picture than the coverage of men senators as fathers. Which is to say, the men in the Senate seem less apt to have to justify their ability to be both senators and fathers and less likely to have their family role interfere with their political portrayal. Indeed, the *Times* directly states that political fatherhood is less important than political motherhood because "men do not carry precisely the same child-rearing burdens as women."

Impressively, in just one article, the *New York Times* was able to include many aspects of the main complaints and fears women in politics have about the media. This chapter reviews the major allegations of gender bias in coverage of politics, and considers a sample of newspaper coverage of women and men members of the U.S. Senate and the U.S. House to explore to what extent women are treated differently. Then, using the websites of members, the question of whether men and women in office might seek different coverage is considered.

Gender Bias in the Media: Allegations and Evidence

Members of the House and Senate need the media. They seek to communicate positive messages about their efforts and their accomplishments through the media to the voters back home. Congressional offices are communication centers, geared to respond to media requests for interviews, comments, and information (Cook 1989).

Academic research leaves no doubt that this effort matters. Media coverage of congressional candidates and incumbents has been found to influence recognition, emotional connections, evaluations, and, ultimately, vote choice (Herrnson 1995; Payne 1980; Parker 1981; Goidel and Shields 1994; Niven and Zilber 1998).

Though the media are a crucial link to the voters for candidates and officeholders, many would argue that the media abuse this power by employing stereotypes in political coverage (Witt, Paget, and Matthews 1995). Specifically, women seem to be portrayed quite differently and in some cases quite dismissively (Devitt 1999; Kahn and Goldenberg 1991).

My study of press secretaries to members of the U.S. House of Representatives (described more fully in Niven and Zilber 2001) suggests the potential depth of the problem. Press secretaries are the staff members charged with encouraging positive press coverage of the representative and responding to all press inquiries. Press secretaries to both men and women members of the House were asked a variety of questions about the kind of reception their member receives from the media.

In short, press secretaries working for women members were considerably more likely to complain about unfair coverage. Whereas 90 percent of the press secretaries to men stated that the media generally treated their bosses fairly, only 32 percent of the press secretaries for women members agreed with that sentiment.

Moreover, when asked about their disappointments with media coverage, there was a tendency for press secretaries to men and women to emphasize different concerns. For the most part, secretaries to men complained about a particular story or issue. For example, one press secretary felt that his boss was not getting enough credit for his efforts on issues such as economic assistance.

In contrast, press secretaries to women were more likely to cite a general lack of press coverage as their greatest disappointment. Many suggested that the reason their representative received less coverage is that the media afford women lawmakers less respect. One press secretary to a woman member said, "time and again, she is underestimated by the media." Another added that her boss "might as well be invisible for all the attention they pay to her leadership on issues."

When asked if their representative had been subject to any media stereotypes, the vast majority of press secretaries to women complained specifically about categorizations having to do with gender (press secretaries to female African American members typically decried stereotypes of both their gender and race). Indeed, there were several strong reactions to this line of inquiry:

> [The media] see her as a woman, and they come to us when they think they have a "woman's issue" and need to hear a woman's view.

> She's a woman first to the media, and it's always as if she was elected to be in some kind of special woman's seat, like her job is somehow different from that of the men in the delegation.

Others focused on the media's fascination with women members' family situations:

> The next time [our local paper] puts together a story that doesn't mention she's a mom with young children it will be a first.

> A reporter once asked me, "How does she have time for kids and Congress?" I asked him if he had ever posed the same question to a man.

In stark contrast, press secretaries to male members were often hard-pressed to think of stereotypes they had encountered. Some press secretaries to men stated flatly that their member had not been subject to *any* media stereotypes. Of those who did mention a stereotype, virtually all complained about either a political characterization ("liberal," "right wing," "Washington bureaucrat," etc.) or an unflattering personality trait ("hot-tempered," "confrontational," "nerdy," etc.). In not one case did a press secretary from a male office complain about gender stereotyping.

When asked what they would seek to change about the media, press secretaries to women were clear that they sought a chance to speak for themselves and present the true nature of their office's agenda. As one press secretary put it, "The day the media spend as much time pointing out that [Senator] Trent Lott was a cheerleader in college, spend as much time worrying about how the men in this body take care of their young kids while they're in office, and start asking why these men don't care about family issues instead of why we [women representatives] do, then you can ask me if the media are fair and I won't have to laugh out loud."

Of course, complaints of media unfairness do not necessarily show that the media are unfair. Indeed, several studies have found that people on opposite sides of an issue can be shown the same newspaper article and both sides can conclude that it is biased against their position (Lord, Ross, and Lepper 1979). Nevertheless, academic research does tend to find differences in media coverage for women and men both in general and specifically with regard to politics.

Some argue that in its unrelenting portrayal of women as "others" the media are making a powerful contribution to American notions of sex roles (Desjardins 1989). Such portrayals not only reinforce traditional gender identity patterns, but powerfully support a tradition of imbalanced political power in which the male is not only the relevant but the appropriate political voice (Desjardins 1989; Frye 1996; McClelland 1993; Signorielli 1989).

Lind and Salo (2002) examined media treatment of the sexes in news coverage, including network, cable, public television, and radio news. They found an emphasis on the personal (romance/marital status, clothing and appearance, motherhood, sex, body parts) when women were mentioned. When women were featured in a political context, their concerns were often trivialized and portrayed as not quite "normal" or "regular."

The main thrust of academic attention to women in politics has examined coverage of election campaigns—especially those that pit a woman against a man. Kahn (1994), for example, examined newspaper coverage of campaigns for the U.S. Senate and for governor. She found that women tended to receive less coverage overall. Women also received disproportionate attention to their horserace position—that is, how likely they were to win the race, where they stood in the polls, and other indicators of their standing in the race. This pattern is potentially harmful to women candidates for two reasons. First, much of the horserace coverage was negative, suggesting women were unlikely to win and thus discouraging voters, volunteers, and campaign contributors from supporting the candidate. Second, every article focused on the horserace means there is less room for issues or other matters of substance that candidates need to communicate to demonstrate their competence. In what issue coverage there was, Kahn found women received more attention for "women's issues"[1] and had a harder time getting the media to cover the issues they were emphasizing in their campaigns.

Findings from a number of scholars studying elections for various levels of office continue to show women receiving less coverage (Gidengil and Everitt 2000), receiving more negative attention (Rausch, Rozell, and Wilson 1999; Ross 1995), receiving more horserace coverage (Rausch, Rozell, and Wilson 1999), being portrayed as inherently different from men candidates (Vavrus 1998), being portrayed in family situations (Banwart, Bystrom, and Robertson 2003; Gilmartin 2001; Ross 1995), having their sex, age, appearance, or personality discussed (Banwart, Bystrom, and Robertson 2003; Braden 1996; Witt, Paget, and Matthews 1995; Gidengil and Everitt 2000; Devitt 1999), and having more trouble getting coverage on the issues they have actually emphasized (Gidengil and Everitt 2000). Ultimately, the portrait of women that emerges from the press reinforces stereotypes (Banwart, Bystrom, and Robertson 2003) and suggests women are simply less weighty players in the political game (Devitt 1999).

Men, meanwhile, can expect greater attention to their experience and accomplishments, as well as greater attention to their issue stands (Devitt 1999; Davis 1982; Jamieson 1995). Not only do male candidates receive more issue coverage, but that issue coverage is more likely to suggest men are prepared, qualified, and understand the logic and evidence of the issues at hand (Devitt 1999).

There has been relatively less attention paid to women once they have been elected to office. Some scholars have found, however, that women in office received attention on "women's issues" such as abortion and family leave (Carroll and Schreiber 1997) while being ignored on most other matters of substance (Braden 1996; Clawson and Tom 1999).

Content Analysis of Newspaper Coverage

This chapter examines media coverage of women elected to the U.S. House and the U.S. Senate and compares it to coverage of men elected to those bodies. Examining coverage of women in office, instead of candidates, is of particular significance in understanding the position of women in modern politics for two reasons. First, this coverage is constant rather than seasonal. While campaign coverage might be available in the month or two preceding an election, coverage of officeholders (women and men) continues year-round, every year. Second, officeholders represent the face of politics for most voters, thus the media depictions of officeholders affect not only their current and future political standing, but also the political context in which future candidates must compete.

We will now examine newspaper coverage over a two-year span (May 1, 2001–April 30, 2003) received by all the women serving in 2003 in the U.S. Senate (14 members) and U.S. House of Representatives (59 members).[2] For the purposes of comparison, each woman was matched to the man in the same office who most closely resembled her political traits (with regard to party, ideology, and region). Thus, all the results regarding coverage of the 73 women in office are compared to coverage of 73 politically similar men in office.

Ten newspaper articles on each member were selected for analysis. To ensure a reliable sample of articles from large newspapers and more representative smaller papers (Shaw and Sparrow 1999), five of the ten articles were randomly chosen from the "major newspaper" database in Nexis, and five of the ten were randomly chosen from the home state newspapers of the member that were available in the Nexis state database.

Based on the results of previous studies and the comments of congressional press secretaries, the articles were examined in the following six areas. Except where noted, each measure was recorded as a yes/no response.[3]

- *Amount of coverage.* For each member in the sample, a count of the number of articles published in major newspapers and in-state newspapers mentioning them in the headline or first three paragraphs was recorded. This simple measure represents the amount of attention each member receives, and according to previous research, is likely to be higher for men than for women.
- *Priorities.* After randomly selecting articles for analysis, each article in the sample was then scrutinized to determine how the member's priorities were presented. For example, is the member depicted as working on any particular issue? Is the member working on behalf of any particular group or constituency? Is the member physically in Washington in the article's description? These questions capture the kind of work the member is performing. According to previous research, women are likely to receive less attention for the work they do in Washington on issues, but are more likely than men to receive attention for women's issues and for associating themselves with particular groups.
- *Qualifications/Accomplishments.* Each article in the sample was also read for its portrayal of the member's abilities and the outcomes that resulted. Does the article mention that the member has accomplished something? Does the article mention the member's abilities, leadership, or strong connections in the legislature? Does the coverage portray the member as interacting with the president? Conversely, does the coverage suggest the member is locked out of power, or in any way incapable of pursuing legislative work? Is the member in any way unfit for office? These questions get at the competence of the member for office and suggest whether the member belongs in the job. Previous research suggests men will receive more positive attention in this area, and women more negative attention.
- *Politics.* The political motivations of members in each article were also noted. Does the coverage portray the member as being motivated by ideology or partisanship? These questions get at whether the member is portrayed

Table 13.1

Newspaper Coverage of Women and Men in Congress, 2001–2003

	Women (in-state) N = 365	Women (major papers) N = 365	Men (in-state) N = 365	Men (major papers) N = 365
I. Amount				
Number of articles	259	106	281	121
II. Priorities				
Issue Mentioned (% yes)	53	62	76	72
Top 3 Issues Mentioned	*Jobs/Economy *Medicine/Health Care *Environment	*Foreign Policy/Terrorism *Taxes/Budget *Medicine/Health Care	*Jobs/Economy *Medicine/Health Care *Foreign Policy/Terrorism	*Foreign Policy/Terrorism *Jobs/Economy *Taxes/Budget
Group mentioned (% yes)	39	27	29	23
Top 3 Groups Mentioned	*Poor/Jobless *Children *Women	*Poor/Jobless *Women *Senior Citizens	*Children *Terrorism Victims *Poor/Jobless	*Poor/Jobless *Senior Citizens *Veterans
Member in Washington (% yes)	37	63	48	64
III. Qualifications/Accomplishments				
Accomplishment (% yes)	12	4	17	13
Insider/Capable (% yes)	7	5	12	10
President (% yes)	4	6	8	15
Outsider (% yes)	8	4	1	2
Unfit (% yes)	9	1	1	1

271

IV. Politics				
Ideology (% yes)	5	1	5	3
Partisanship (% yes)	5	7	3	3
V. Personal Portrayal				
Sex (% yes)	27	36	8	13
Family (% yes)	7	24	2	3
Age/Appearance (% yes)	11	10	6	3
Personality/Personal Traits (% yes)	6	15	4	4
VI. Overall Tone				
Tone (−1 = negative, 0 = neutral, 1 = positive)	0.12	0.08	0.21	0.26

as independently thinking through a situation or as reflexively locked into a position. Previous research suggests women are more likely to be portrayed as automatically following their party or ideology rather than thinking through the issue.

- *Personal portrayal.* Articles were also examined for their comments on the members outside of the scope of their office. Is the member's sex mentioned? Is the member's family life mentioned? Is the member's age or any aspect of their appearance mentioned? Is the member's personality or other personal traits mentioned? These questions all relate to whether details of the member's personal life were featured in the article, and according to previous work, they are more likely to be mentioned in coverage of women.

- *Overall tone.* Finally, the overall tone of the article is recorded. Each paragraph of each article was assessed as being either positive, negative, or neutral. Positive paragraphs include anything suggesting the member's accomplishment, ability, or results. Negative paragraphs include anything suggesting inability or failure. Neutral paragraphs lacked information on the member's ability, or included both positive and negative information. Each article was then characterized on a three-point scale (-1 = more negative paragraphs than positive, 0 = equal positive and negative paragraphs, or no positive and negative paragraphs, and 1 = more positive paragraphs than negative). Previous work suggests men should expect an overall more positive tone in their coverage.

Results

Amount of Coverage

The amount of coverage received by women and men is not equal (see Table 13.1, section I). Women were the subject of 8 percent fewer articles in major newspapers, and 14 percent fewer articles in in-state newspapers. As an example of the sometimes extreme imbalances of coverage for similar members, consider Senators Debbie Stabenow and Carl Levin (both liberal Democrats from Michigan), and Representatives Sue Kelly and Sherwood Boehlert (both conservative Republicans from New York). Senator Stabenow was the subject of 19 articles in major newspapers, while Levin, her close political colleague, was the subject of 154. Senator Stabenow was the subject of 45 articles in in-state newspapers, while Senator Levin was the subject of 156. Similarly, Representative Kelly was the subject of 6 articles in major newspapers, while Boehlert, her close political colleague, was the subject of 91. In-state newspapers dedicated 32 articles to Kelly and 495 to Boehlert. The amount of coverage received by women and men is as previous work and the comments of political professionals have suggested—women in the House and Senate receive less attention than men.

Priorities

Coverage of the priorities of members reveals several stark differences and some clear similarities (Table 13.1, section II). First, in both in-state and major newspapers, men are more likely to receive issue-centered coverage than women. The gap is particularly large for in-state papers, where just over half of the coverage of women includes political issues, while more than three-fourths of the coverage of men includes political issues. That having been said, the particular issues associated with women and men in Congress do not vary greatly. For example, for both men and women, the most frequently mentioned topic in major newspapers is foreign policy/terrorism. Meanwhile, the most frequently mentioned topic in in-state newspapers is jobs/the economy, which is also the same for men and women. While the second and third most frequently mentioned issues are not precisely the same, there is considerable overlap. The only issue that uniquely appears among women is the environment. Thus, the types of issues covered offers little support to the notion that women are locked out of major issues and assigned roles limited to women's and children's concerns. However, the total amount of issue coverage is out of balance, as women are not only less likely to see their coverage focused on issues, but are less likely to attract coverage in the first place.

Coverage of group ties is quite different, however. By a slim margin in major papers, and a somewhat larger margin in in-state papers, women are more likely to have their efforts tied to a particular group. This is generally viewed as a double-edged sword by political professionals. On the positive side, such coverage can link the member to accomplishments that will attract the loyalty of the affected group. On the negative side, such coverage can serve to isolate the member from the majority of voters who are not affiliated with the group in question.

Nevertheless, the particular groups mentioned are also significant. As was the case with specific issues mentioned, again there is some notable overlap. The poor/jobless are the most frequently mentioned group for women (in both in-state and major papers) and for in-state paper coverage of men (in major papers, it was the third most mentioned group for men). Other groups, such as senior citizens and, notably, children, appear among the most mentioned groups for both women and men members. The presence of children as a group among the most mentioned for men is a notable departure from previous research findings and from the perceptions of some political participants. It suggests perhaps that the political value of appearing pro-child is currently so great that an area that might once have been consigned to women is now highly valued enough that men in office seek coverage highlighting their advocacy on behalf of children. Even with this general overlap, advocacy on behalf of women draws much greater coverage for women members than for men members.

As interesting as the *presence of women* on the list of groups women elected officials care about is the *absence of men* on the list of groups men elected officials care about. Indeed, not a single article in the entire sample linked a senator or representative to advocacy of behalf of men.

It is a situation analogous to that seen when comparing media coverage of African American elected officials to coverage of white officials. In that case, coverage of African Americans in office frequently links their efforts to their concern for African Americans, while coverage of whites in office never links their efforts to their concern for whites (Zilber and Niven 2000). The effect, in that case, allows white elected officials to present themselves as having inclusive concerns that incorporate not only whites, but every racial and ethnic group. African American members, meanwhile, are portrayed by the media as having exclusive concerns that include African Americans while ignoring other groups. This coverage is shown to be electorally damaging when African American officeholders attempt to win the support of white voters (Zilber and Niven 2000). The effect is potentially even greater for women, because unlike African American candidates who might run in a majority-minority district, there is no such thing as a majority-women district. Thus, to win or remain in office, women must appeal to both women and men voters.

In addition to coverage of issues and groups, attention to the members' work was also measured by whether the article placed the member in Washington. Obviously if they are not in Washington, then the members will have a harder time linking themselves to the work they are doing on behalf of their district. Here, women are as likely to be portrayed as being in Washington in major papers, but less likely than men to be in Washington in in-state papers.

Overall, coverage of members' priorities and work conforms to several expectations and diverges from a few. As expected, women receive less issue coverage and their coverage is less likely to place them in Washington. Also as expected, their coverage is more likely to link them to specific groups. However, their issue specialties are not limited to women's and children's issues and instead share much of the same emphasis of the coverage received by men. There are similarities in the specific groups advocated for as well, and—in a divergence from expectation— both men and women were linked to working on behalf of children. Conversely, only women were linked to working on behalf of women. This suggests that what was once conventionally lumped together in research as "women's and children's issues" might need to be more carefully examined, as children may have become politically valuable enough to draw more universal political attention, while women's needs continue to be seen as being solely in the care of women officials.

Qualifications/Accomplishments

Apart from the question of what members were doing, according to the media, is the question of how they were doing it. Are women portrayed as having the same abilities to succeed in legislative politics? In a word, no.

A quick look at section III of Table 13.1 shows that women are consistently more likely to receive coverage suggesting an inability to function in the legislature and consistently less likely to receive coverage suggesting accomplishments or capabilities. That is, men are more likely to receive attention describing something they accomplished. Indeed, in major papers, men are almost four times more likely than women to have an accomplishment described. Men are more likely to be described as being experts or well connected or masters of the legislative process. In major papers, for example, men are twice as likely as women to have their capabilities highlighted. Interactions with the president, a sure sign of legislative significance, also produces a disparity, with men twice as likely to be linked to the president in both major and in-state papers.

Meanwhile, the results for the negative portrayal of being described as inexperienced, lacking connections, or generally unable to pass legislation showed women to be far more likely to attract such attention. Even more damagingly, being portrayed as unfit for office is vastly more likely for women in in-state papers than men.

Examples abound of the respectful coverage uniquely afforded men. One that stood out is the coverage of Senator Charles Grassley (R-Iowa). Senator Grassley, it seems, has undergone some kind of unofficial name change in the eyes of the media. Consider his description in the following articles: "Sen. Charles Grassley, R-Iowa, the most influential Senate voice on taxes" (Thompson 2003, 4a), or "Mr. Grassley, the most influential senator on tax matters" (Rosenbaum 2003b, 1A), or, "Senator Charles E. Grassley, the Iowa Republican who is chairman of the Finance Committee and who is the most influential voice in the Senate on taxes" (Rosenbaum 2003a, 22A), or, "Senator Charles E. Grassley, the Iowa Republican who is the most influential senator on tax legislation" (Bumiller 2003b, 25A), or, "Mr. Grassley, who is the chairman of the Finance Committee and the most influential senator on tax legislation" (Bumiller 2003a, 26A).

Interestingly, by any realistic measure, the 2003 debate on tax cuts in the Senate hinged on the decisions of George Voinovich (R-Ohio) and Olympia Snowe (R-Maine). Those two senators held decisive votes that could have derailed the tax cut proposal, but which they ultimately leveraged to make the tax cut more palatable to their priorities by reducing its size by half. Nevertheless, no paper referred to Senator Snowe as the most influential senator on the tax bill.

While media coverage is obviously and legitimately affected by members' status in the legislature, even allowing for that disparity makes it hard to account for differences in coverage between men and women. Representative Nancy Pelosi (D-California), for example, is the minority leader of the House, the top-ranking Democrat in the body. A *Los Angeles Times* article (Barabak 2003, 12) on her ascendancy to the leadership position was headlined "Triumph of the 'Airhead.'" The article went on to state that Pelosi "has been routinely dismissed" as "a legislative lightweight." Moreover, the article notes that when she opens her mouth to say something, she is "plastic and superficial." It is nearly impossible to conceive of a man assuming such a high position of leadership in the Congress being dismissed in such terms.

Similarly, even in a situation in which a female legislator has achieved a victory—as was the case in two instances when Senator Patty Murray successfully objected to a federal court nominee and sought changes in a port security measure—the language used to describe the situation can be demeaning. In both controversies, different writers referred to Senator Murray as having a "spat" with those with whom she disagreed (Fryer 2003b, B1; Pfleger, 2002). Senator Murray was also said to be "bickering" with her opponents (Pfleger 2002). Instead of referring to a disagreement in terms suggesting thoughtfulness or even passion, those phrases suggest that the senator was involved in nothing more than a childish tiff.

Overall, coverage of the qualifications and accomplishments of members clearly conforms to expectations that women are afforded less respect by the media. In various measures, women are subject to fewer positive and more negative portrayals than men.

Politics

In terms of the political portrayal of their actions, women and men drew the same amount of attention in in-state papers for their ideological behavior (acting on behalf of their political beliefs). In major newspapers, men drew more attention. By contrast, women drew more coverage for their partisan behavior (acting on behalf of their political party) than did men in both in-state and major newspapers. By portraying women as being more likely to be led by their partisanship, there is a message sent that women are less independent, less likely to think for themselves.

Personal Portrayal

While differences in descriptions of their work and their politics are important, differences in personal portrayals are perhaps the most galling media habit in covering women. Indeed, the results (Table 13.1, section V) show that differences in personal portrayals of members are clear and stark. Women are three times more likely to be characterized by their sex than are men. Women are much more likely to be written about in the context of their family than are men. Women are twice as likely to have age or appearance mentioned than men. Women are much more likely to have their personality or personal traits discussed than are men.

As one article noted (Barabak 2003, 12), Representative Nancy Pelosi has a "high-beam smile" and that if she has "a negative in her political career, it's that she's too attractive." The article further mentioned that Pelosi's "wide brown eyes suggest a perpetual state of wonderment" and that she has "high cheekbones, sharp features" and "small fists." Meanwhile, Senator Hillary Rodham Clinton (D-New York), one article explained, must compensate for her "thick ankles" when choosing what to wear (Brown 2003a, F1).

Indeed, observations on the physical size of women in Congress are frequently reported. According to the *Seattle Times*, Senator Patty Murray is a "diminutive Democrat" (Fryer 2003a, B1). The *Times-Picayune* reports that Senator Barbara Mikulski is "a diminutive but ornery member of the Senate" (Alpert and Walsh 2001, 21). Meanwhile, *USA TODAY* characterizes Representative Nancy Pelosi as a "diminutive grandmother" (Stone 2003, 13A). Meanwhile, the *Pittsburgh Post-Gazette* notes that Representative Melissa Hart (R-Pennsylvania), "at 5 feet, 10 inches [does] indeed stand out" (Smolkin 2001, G1).

Clothing choices of women lawmakers are also regularly commented upon. The *Washington Post* reported that in 1993 Senator Mikulski was among the first to break with the tradition that had women in Congress wearing dresses in the Capitol building. "Mikulski took a stand and wore trousers on the Senate floor," the paper announced ("Evolution," 2002, L14).

Ten years later it remained noteworthy when Senator Clinton appeared in variously described pantsuits (*Baltimore Sun*: "Dressed in a crisp navy pant suit and a white silk scarf, the senator, 55, looked well-coiffed and cheery" [Knight 2003, 1E]; *Washington Post*: "Clinton is wearing a canary yellow pantsuit and crosses her cream-colored pumps. . ." [Leibovich 2003, C1]). However, these fashion decisions are not without psychological underpinnings. According to the *Washington Post*, "trousers still have not completely shattered their link to masculinity" ("Evolution," 2002, L14). Meanwhile, the *Denver Post* reports that Senator Clinton's fashion choices reveal her to be "a woman who is comfortable with herself" (Brown 2003a, F1).

In contrast to Clinton and Mikulski, Representative Nancy Pelosi wears "stylish dresses" (Barabak 2003, 12). However, as the *Los Angeles Times* reports, she doesn't buy the dresses herself! "Despite a fashion-plate image, Pelosi actually hates to shop. Her husband bought most of the children's clothing, and he continues to buy many of his wife's outfits" (Barabak 2003, 12).

Hair is another frequent topic in personal discussions of women in office. In a discussion of Senator Clinton's fashion and hair decisions, the *Palm Beach Post* ran eleven separate pictures of her to accompany the story (Brown 2003b, 1D).

The role of family is not only more prevalent in descriptions of women in office, it is also portrayed as being a more determinative factor. While there are many fathers and grandfathers in the House and Senate, it is the mothers and grandmothers who are more often identified as such. And while raising a family may have shaped the thinking of many men in the Congress, it is women who are seen as products of their family experience. To wit, for Representative Nancy Pelosi, "The skills Pelosi learned while running a bustling household . . . would find great application in Congress." Meanwhile, the then childless Senator Kay Bailey Hutchinson was noted to be an "iron lady" (Battaile 2001, 8A).

Even in an article saying that Representative Melissa Hart does not speak to the media about her personal life, we nevertheless must learn about her inclinations in the kitchen: "It's no secret that she enjoys cooking, especially Italian dishes. When aides call her on weekends, Hart invariably is cooking for friends and family," the reporter notes (Smolkin 2001, G1).

Men are not fully free from attention to their age, appearance, or personality. But what is striking in examining the coverage of men in Congress is the number of comments that use their personal attributes as evidence of their high stature and suitability for the job. Senator Frank Lautenberg (D-New Jersey), for example, has a "regal swatch of white hair" (Jacobs 2002, 1B). Senator John Cornyn's "shock of white hair gives a senatorial impression" (Martin 2003 1A). Robert Byrd (D-West Virginia) appears so senatorial that he's come to be compared to our nation's symbol. According to the *Washington Post*, Byrd, "with his white feathery hair and his beak nose . . . looks like a bald eagle" (Carlson 2003, C1). Meanwhile, the *Hartford Courant* notes that Byrd has a "brushed-back mane of snow-white hair, and an eagle-faced imperiousness" (Halloran 2003, A1).

Overall, consistent with expectations, women were more frequently the subject of personally oriented attention. Perhaps the most significant implication of that attention is simply that it accomplishes nothing for the representative or senator in getting her message across. Comments on dress, size, and personality serve as a distraction from the issue commitments elected officials seek to communicate. Of course, this attention can also be belittling as it suggests the superfluity of women elected officials' concerns or undermines their professional stature by dwelling on their physical stature.

Overall Tone

The final area examined is the overall tone of the articles (Table 13.1, section VI). While this represents a much more subjective judgment than many of the other items reported here, it nevertheless gives an estimation of the impression left when the pieces of an article are examined together as a whole. For both men and women, the overall tone score is near the neutral mark—suggesting that most articles balance positive and negative information, or consist of mostly neutral information. However, in both in-state and major newspapers, men received a higher (more positive) score. Considering the overall scale, men's coverage was 4.5 percent more positive than women's in in-state papers, and 9 percent more positive than women's in major papers.

Website Analysis

The most obvious defense to criticisms of media coverage is to assert that the coverage reflects reality. That is, less issue coverage is not the media's fault if women officials say less about issues. Or, more coverage depicting women officials concerned about women's welfare can hardly be evidence of a media bias if women in office are more concerned about women.

To explore how women and men in Congress wish to be portrayed—rather than how they are portrayed—the official congressional websites of each member of the sample were analyzed. The value of these websites as a source of information is that they represent a forum of communication under complete control of the congressional office. Members' websites can mention as many or as few issues as they want, and present the members in any terms desired. These sites represent the actual messages members circulate (Owen, Davis, and Strickler 1999).

During the summer of 2003, two coders read the biographical statements and the issues sections of the website for each member in the sample. Following the lines of the content analysis results, depictions of priorities, accomplishments, and personal life details were noted.

On issues, the results are striking in their similarity. Women and men mention almost the same number of issues (women 13, men 12). Jobs/economic issues are the most frequently mentioned issue on the websites of both women and men. While women are more likely to mention a women's issue (83 percent mentioned at least one), the majority of men also mention their commitment to at least one women's issue (67 percent). In terms of effectiveness, women and men use similar terms to convey their commitment and accomplishments on issues (using phrases such as "fought for," "leading the way," "the most effective voice") and women provide more details than men about their accomplishments and experience (the mean number of accomplishments in the biography section was 15 for women, 11 for men).

The most notable finding comes in regard to personal life. In contrast to a media that pays more attention to women's personal lives, the websites show that women dedicate less space to discussing their family and family life than men (the number of family paragraphs for women was 3, and for men 5).

Thus the websites offer little support to the notion that women are trying to communicate a vastly different message through the media that results in the imbalances in coverage shown in the content analysis. Instead, the results suggest women are generally trying to communicate much the same information through the media, and that it is the media's choice to construct vastly different images of women and men in Congress.

Conclusion

The results of the content analysis show that women in Congress receive less coverage and less issue coverage. They are less likely to be portrayed as successful in their legislative efforts and less likely to be portrayed as competent. Women are more likely to be portrayed as advocating for a specific group, more likely to be portrayed as partisan, and more likely to be portrayed as ineffective. And, women are more likely to have their personal life details—their age, appearance, family life, personality—discussed in the media. In sum, women in Congress receive less of the coverage that would clearly be sought (that discussing accomplishments and ideas) and more of the coverage that is either irrelevant (such as appearance) or would clearly be avoided if possible (such as being unfit for office). An analysis of congressional websites does not suggest that women seek or are responsible for such differing images.

The implications of differences in media coverage for men and women are great. Koch (1999) reports that better informed voters have more rigid stereotypes of women candidates, presumably because of their constant exposure to media stereotyping of women. Indeed, Kahn and Goldenberg (1991) argue, and experimental research has shown (Kahn 1992; Dayhoff 1983), that typical media coverage of women candidates can serve to undermine their credibility with voters. Even some potentially benign stereotypes, such as the portrayal of women as concerned about women, may not be particularly useful. Leeper (1991) argues that women already have the edge with regard to women's issues, and instead need to shore up their credentials in other areas.

Ultimately, a fair media would not treat women as the exact and indistinguishable clones of men in office. There are important differences between women and men in issue commitments (Thomas 1994), leadership styles (Rosenthal 1997), and communication practices (Canary and Dindia 1998). However, a fair media— one that gave women and men in office the same opportunity to communicate their goals and achievements—would also recognize fundamental similarities between women and men.

Notes

1. The definition of "women's issues" generally used in research encompasses initiatives that exclusively affect women (such as funding for women's health research), initiatives that primarily affect women (such as sexual harassment laws), and initiatives that fall at the intersection of family, children, and compassion (including education, family leave, child care, child-safe gun laws).

2. There are also four women who serve as nonvoting delegates to the House of Representatives. They were not included in the analysis.

3. Two trained coders analyzed the articles. A subsample of the articles were analyzed by both, producing an intercoder agreement of at least 90 percent for each measure.

References

Alpert, Bruce, and Bill Walsh. 2001. "On the Hill." *Times-Picayune*, August 3, 21.
Banwart, Mary C., Dianne G. Bystrom, and Terry Robertson. 2003. "From the Primary to the General Election: A Comparative Analysis of Candidate Media Coverage in Mixed-Gender 2000 Races for Governor and US. Senate." *American Behavioral Scientist* 46(5): 658–676.
Barabak, Mark. 2003. "Triumph of the 'Airhead.'" *Los Angeles Times*, January 26.
Battaile, Janet. 2001. "A Tough Texas Senator is a Crusader Against Cancer." *The New York Times*, July 9, 8A.

Braden, Maria. 1996. *Women Politicians and the Media*. Lexington, KY: University Press of Kentucky.

Brown, Suzanne. 2003a. "Sen. Clinton Removes the White Gloves." *Denver Post*, July 23, F1.

———. 2003b. "Sen. Clinton's Winning Style." *Palm Beach Post*, July 29, 1D.

Bumiller, Elisabeth. 2003a. "Bush Gains Crucial Backer for his Tax Cut Plan in Senate." *The New York Times*, February 12, 26A.

———. 2003b. "With Help from Democrat, Bush Pitches Tax Cut Plan." *New York Times*, February 21, 25A.

Canary, D., and K. Dindia. 1998. *Sex differences and similarities in communication*. Mahwah, NJ: Erlbaum.

Carlson, Peter. 2003. "The Senator Votes Nay." *The Washington Post*, May 24, C1.

Carroll, Susan, and Ronnee Schreiber. 1997. "Media Coverage of Women in the 103rd Congress." In *Women, Media, and Politics*, ed. Pippa Norris. New York: Oxford University Press.

Clawson, Rosalee, and Ryan Tom. 1999. "Invisible Lawmakers: Media Coverage of Black and Female State Legislators." Unpublished manuscript.

Cook, Timothy. 1989. *Making Laws and Making News*. Washington, DC: Brookings.

Davis, J. 1982. "Sexist Bias in Eight Newspapers." *Journalism Quarterly* 59: 456–460.

Dayhoff, Signe. 1983. "Sexist Language and Person Perception: Evaluation of Candidates from Newspaper Articles." *Sex Roles* 9: 527–539.

Desjardins, Mary. 1989. "(Re)Presenting the Female Body." *Quarterly Review of Film & Video* 11: 67–73.

Devitt, James. 1999. "Framing Gender on the Campaign Trail: Women's Executive Leadership and the Press." Report for the Women's Leadership Fund.

"Evolution of the Pantsuit." 2002. *Washington Post*, June 5, L14.

Frye, David. 1996. "The Gendered Senate: National Politics and Gender Imagery After the Thomas Hearing." In *Outsiders Looking In: A Communication Perspective on the Hill/ Thomas Hearings*, ed. Paul Siegel. Cresskill, NJ: Hampton Press.

Fryer, Alex. 2003a. "Senators' Teamwork Pays Off For State." *The Seattle Times*, March 23, B1.

———. 2003b. "Murray Wins Fight to Fund Port Measure; Security Initiative Intact; Months of Squabbling End." *The Seattle Times*, June 12, B1.

Gidengil, Elisabeth, and Joanna Everitt. 2000. "Filtering the Female: Television News Coverage of the 1993 Canadian Leaders' Debate." *Women and Politics* 21(4): 105–131.

Gilmartin, Patricia. 2001. "Still the Angel in the Household: Political Cartoons of Elizabeth Dole's Presidential Campaign." *Women and Politics* 22(4): 51–67.

Goidel, Robert, and Todd Shields. 1994. "The Vanishing Marginals, the Bandwagon, and the Mass Media." *Journal of Politics* 56: 802–810.

Halloran, Liz. 2003. "Byrd Enjoys Ruffling Feathers." *Hartford Courant*, May 18, A1.

Herrnson, Paul. 1995. *Congressional Elections: Campaigning at Home and in Washington*. Washington, DC: Congressional Quarterly Press.

Jacobs, Andrew. 2002. "For Lautenberg, Another Shot at the Limelight and the Fray." *The New York Times*, October 28, 1B.

Jamieson, Kathleen Hall. 1995. *Beyond the Double Bind: Women and Leadership*. New York: Oxford University Press.

Kahn, Kim. 1992. "Does Being Male Help?" *Journal of Politics* 54: 497–517.

Kahn, Kim Fridkin. 1994. "The Distorted Mirror: Press Coverage of Women Candidates for Statewide Office." *Journal of Politics* 56(1): 154–173.

Kahn, Kim, and Edie Goldenberg. 1991. "Women Candidates in the News: An Examination of Gender Differences in U.S. Senate Campaign Coverage." *Public Opinion Quarterly* 55: 180–199.

Knight, Molly. 2003. "Book-Signing a Capital Event." *Baltimore Sun*, June 13, 1E.

Koch, Jeffrey. 1999. "Candidate Gender and Assessments of Senate Candidates." *Social Science Quarterly* 80: 84–96.

Leeper, Mark. 1991. "The Impact of Prejudice on Female Candidates: An Experimental Look at Voter Inference." *American Politics Quarterly* 19: 248–261.

Leibovich, Mark. 2003. "Lady of 'History.'" *The Washington Post*, June 12, C1.

Lind, Rebecca Ann, and Colleen Salo. 2002. "The Framing of Feminists and Feminism in News and Public Affairs Programs in U.S. Electronic Media." *Journal of Communication* 52(1): 211–228.

Lord, C., L. Ross, and M. Lepper. 1979. "Biased Assimilation and Attitude Polarization: The Effects of Prior Theories on Subsequently Considered Evidence." *Journal of Personality and Social Psychology* 37: 2098–2109.

McClelland, John. 1993. "Visual Images and Re-Imaging: A Review of Research in Mass Communication." In *Women in Mass Communication*, ed. Pamela Creedon. Newbury Park, CA: Sage.

Martin, Gary. 2003. "San Antonio's First U.S. Senator." *San Antonio-Express News*, January 19, 1A.

Niven, David, and Jeremy Zilber. 1998. "'What's Newt Doing in *People Magazine*?' The Changing Effect of National Prominence in Congressional Elections." *Political Behavior* 20: 213–224.

———. 2001. "How Does She Have Time for Kids and Congress? Views on Gender and Media Coverage from House Offices." *Women and Politics* 23: 147–165.

Owen, Diana, Richard Davis, and Vincent James Strickler. 1999. "Congress and the Internet." *Harvard International Journal of Press/Politics* 4: 10–29.

Parker, Glenn. 1981. "Interpreting Candidate Awareness in U.S. Congressional Elections." *Legislative Studies Quarterly* 6: 219–234.

Payne, James. 1980. "Show Horses and Work Horses in the United States House of Representatives." *Polity* 12: 428–456.

Pfleger, Katherine. 2002. "Senators, White House Might be Close to Resolution on Federal Judicial Nominee." Associated Press, March 18.

Rausch, John David, Mark Rozell, and Harry Wilson. 1999. "When Women Lose: A Study of Media Coverage of Two Gubernatorial Campaigns." *Women and Politics* 20(4): 1–21.

Rosenbaum, David. 2003a. "House Budget Chairman Vows Tax Cuts and Balanced Budget." *The New York Times*, March 12, 22A.

———. 2003b. "Senate Vote Could Sharply Reduce Bush Tax Cut." *The New York Times*, April 12, 1A.

Rosenthal, Cindy S. 1997. "A view of their own: Women's committee leadership styles and state legislatures." *Policy Studies Journal* 25: 585.

Ross, Karen. 1995. "Gender and Party Politics: How the Press Reported the Labour Leadership Campaign, 1994." *Media, Culture, & Society* 17: 499–509.

Signorielli, Nancy. 1989. "Television and Conceptions about Sex Roles: Maintaining Conventionality and the Status Quo." *Sex Roles* 21 (5/6): 341–360.

Smith, Kevin. 1997. "When All's Fair: Signs of Parity in Media Coverage of Female Candidates." *Political Communication* 14: 71–82.

Smolkin, Rachel. 2001. "Ms. Hart Goes to Washington." *Pittsburgh Post-Gazette*, December 16, G1.

Stolberg, Sheryl Gay. 2003. "Working Mothers Swaying Senate Debate, as Senators." *The New York Times*, June 7, 1A.

Stone, Andrea. 2003. "Pelosi Surprises Critics." *USA TODAY*, July 3, 13A.

Thompson, Jake. 2003. "Scaled-Down Tax-Cut Plan Draws Kudos from Grassley." *Omaha World Herald*, March 13, 4A.

Vavrus, Mary Douglas. 1998. "Working the Senate from the Outside in: The Mediated Construction of a Feminist Political Campaign." *Critical Studies in Mass Communication* 15: 213–235.

Witt, Linda, Karen Paget, and Glenna Matthews. 1995. *Running as a Woman: Gender and Power in American Politics*. New York: Free Press.

Zilber, Jeremy, and David Niven. 2000. *Racialized Coverage of Congress: The News in Black and White*. Westport, CT: Praeger.

14

Conclusion
Gender and the Future of
American Political Life

Sue Tolleson-Rinehart and Jyl J. Josephson

The essays in this volume raise questions for all who study American politics, in which gender continues to play a critical but often incompletely understood role. The volume offers a set of challenges to the discipline of political science regarding the integration of the study of gender into the study of American political life. In each of the three arenas addressed by this volume—political behavior, public policy, and institutions—gender is often an afterthought, if it is thought of at all, for many American politics researchers despite the fact that, as this volume indicates, gender is a significant element in politics in all of these areas. Political science still has much to learn from feminist approaches to research, and here we wish to suggest some fruitful directions for this inquiry. As we suggested in the Introduction, gender politics scholarship has most often been done by scholars, both women and men, who are themselves feminist, and who have a normative as well as an intellectual interest in women's political life. In that spirit, the foregoing chapters also raise a series of questions for those concerned with the feminist movement and with women's political progress and equality.

The scholars who began the study of women and politics three decades ago—not to mention the lonely pioneers of the field, like Sophonisba Breckenridge in the 1930s—certainly hoped for more "gender mainstreaming" in the discipline than has occurred to date. Our twofold intent in this concluding chapter is to provide grist for the mill of "gender mainstreaming" by suggesting ways that the study of American politics can benefit from the use of gender as an analytical, theoretical, and methodological construct, and, at the same time, to note some of the policy and political recommendations the foregoing chapters seem to suggest to those who seek the full integration of women into all aspects of American political life.

As the essays in this volume indicate, the problem of both scholarship and activism regarding women and American political life is considerably more complicated than simply to "add women and stir." In the literature on women, gender, and the sciences, feminist concerns are usefully seen as encompassing concerns about "women in science" and concerns about gender and the philosophy and practice of science (Hammonds and Subramaniam 2003). Similarly, in research on gender and American political life, we might see the concerns of feminists as in these two broad realms: the study of women's participation in political life, including as political leaders, and the separate, though not entirely unrelated, problem of gendered political institutions.

But even these two realms are more complicated than they look: while increasing the number of women in elected office and the participation of women in political decision making is important for the representation of what might be seen as women's interests, there is no simple linear relationship between descriptive and substantive representation. Nor, of course, is there uniformity among women in what women perceive to be in their interests. In fact, women themselves may be more polarized than they have been since the days of the suffrage movement. In many ways feminist research is far ahead of political science as a discipline in this respect. For example, its development of intersectional analysis could contribute much to the study of women in political life (Crenshaw 1991; Cohen 2003; Carroll and Liebowitz 2003; Hawkesworth 2003). Women differ not only in terms of characteristics such as race, ethnicity, class, sexual orientation, national origin, and religious beliefs, but also, very importantly, in terms of political ideology (including differing configurations of "women's issues") and party affiliation.

This point, related as it is to points made by many of the chapters in this book about descriptive versus substantive representation, deserves further explication at two different levels of analysis. The more global, or perhaps more abstract, level is that of democratic representation. Do all women represent the interests of all women? Can "women's interests" *only* be represented by women (and, conversely, can only men represent men)? Many of the essays in this volume illuminate the increasing integration of women into positions of political leadership, and then ask how the presence of women decision makers has changed, or failed to change, political processes and policy outcomes. As Sue Thomas points out, the literature on women in legislative office indicates that the presence of a "critical mass" of women legislators does make a difference in terms of the representation of issues important to women. Yet it is also true, as Thomas points out, as well as Mary Anne Borelli and Susan Gluck Mezey, that women in the legislative, executive, and judicial branches do not necessarily represent women's interests or issues. This issue of representation is not unique to women; among other demographic groups, as well, the interaction between descriptive and substantive representation is complex (Haider-Markel, Joslyn, and Kniss 2000; Johnson 2002; Gay 2002; Simien 2004; Pantoja and Segura 2003). Nor is it desirable to expect that women in public life will represent "women's interests" only, or exclusively. That would doom women to less than full integration into political life, including or especially into the exercise of political power. Apart from the fact that not all issues can or should be construed as "women's issues," or the even more intriguing view that many issues originally introduced as "women's issues" should evolve into issues of moment to all, artificial constraints on what women are expected to represent would seem to lead to undesirable outcomes for women and for the polis. One possible outcome is that of persisting marginalization, despite women's recent advances. If women are seen as capable only of representing "women's interests," they are unlikely to be successful in an electoral system that was and still is overwhelmingly male. Instead, popular political culture would be one of "Interests" writ large, and "women's interests" writ small. No woman appearing to represent only women could ever be elected president, for example, but nor could such women expect to increase their share of other offices in a system that favors incumbents over challengers. This is not to say that women do not bring alternative perspectives to the political arena, because we know that they can and do. Living in a gendered world means that women and men continue to have certain different experiences, and of course those different experiences can have meaning for politics. We must not assume, however, that the differences always or even usually trump the similarities in the two sexes' lives and political needs.

But even if we considered a "women's representation" limited to "women's interests" to be a desirable thing, which definition of "women" and "women's interests" would we choose? This leads us to the second level of analysis, that of individual-level, intra-sex diversity in location, beliefs, and policy preferences. Scholars, the women's movement, and popular culture alike have often spoken of "women's interests" when the interests in question might more accurately be thought of as those of white, middle-class, heterosexual women. Even this class of women contains politically significant divisions—such women are liberal Democrats and conservative Republicans, with very different worldviews; superficially similar women, for example, are found on either side of the abortion divide.

When we disaggregate "women" further, the issues become considerably more complex. Here a great deal more work is needed in the subfield of gender and politics and in the discipline as a whole. Unfortunately, much of the work in the area of gender and American political life has not been intersectional, but rather, additive. This is partly an artifact of the data most readily available to us, as with National Election Study data, and of the dominance of certain quantitative approaches in political science. As other scholars have pointed out, we need both better data and a broader range of methodological approaches (Carroll and Liebowitz 2003; Cohen 2003; Simien 2004), and we need both the expectation of, and the belief that, those different methods can be equally rigorous. It is nothing short of shocking that in 2004 political scientists are still removing race from analyses where race is surely an important factor simply because the available data lack enough cases in different subgroups for valid statistical analysis. We as scholars and researchers simply must do better.

What follows is a brief summary of some directions for future research, as well as feminist activism, based on the recommendations of our authors in the three main sections of this text. We then conclude with a few comments on gender mainstreaming in the discipline and in political life.

Political Behavior

We have learned a great deal about women, men, and gender in political behavior in the last several decades. The gender gap in voting behavior, the persistence of a gender gap in political knowledge, differences between men and women in the interaction between party loyalty and voting behavior, and changes in gendered voting patterns over time are all much more clearly understood as a result of scholarship in this area. Yet much remains to be done as well to flesh out knowledge regarding the operation of gender in voting, in perceptions of candidates by voters, in the treatment of candidates by the media, and in how gender consciousness affects both men's and women's political behavior. Further, we need better data, as well as improved measures, to understand the intersectional effects of gender, race, class, and other characteristics on political engagement and behavior.

As the chapter by Michael Delli Carpini and Scott Keeter makes particularly clear, the gap in political knowledge has real consequences in terms of how men and women vote, and, ultimately, in policy outcomes. If women had comparable political knowledge to men, and voted on the basis of that knowledge, the effect on electoral outcomes, they suggest, would be significant. The gap in political knowledge, and the importance of knowledge to citizens who wish to translate their political concerns into public policy outcomes or engagement with political institutions, also has implications for feminist activism. For example, how can women use their knowledge advantage in local politics to advance women's political interests? How can the political knowledge gap at other levels be closed or at least narrowed? Delli Carpini and Keeter reaffirm Jennings's (1979) finding that women's knowledge and participation can also be seen as "domain-specific." Twenty-five years ago, Jennings found that women are more likely to be both more knowledgeable about and more participatory in local politics—especially school politics—than are men. Clearly, when women see relevant reasons for political engagement, they become engaged. How does the larger system continue to fail women by failing to engage them? How can political scientists contribute not only innovative research but civic education to reverse this disappointing finding?

One of the things we may need to change is our approach to measuring men's and women's knowledge and attitudes. We do know that men and women respond differently to survey questionnaires and to the entire survey environment. We know, for example, that the sex of the interviewer influences responses, with women who are interviewed by women giving more feminist responses to questions than are women who are interviewed by men (Huddy et al. 1997). We know that men persistently offer more comments in response to open-ended invitations to give reasons for liking or disliking parties and candidates, and that women are persistently less likely to say they have tried to persuade someone to their own political views (Atkeson and Rapoport 2003); these findings have been the basis of past assertions that women are neither as politically sophisticated nor as instrumental as are men.

We know that gender gaps in attitudes and policy preferences are dependent on the formulation of the questions, and we know that apparent gender gaps can change dramatically in response to emphasis on different aspects of target policies—for instance, in the difference between wording about "cutting" versus "spending more" on a policy area (Sapiro 2003). Of course, we should also take heed of Sapiro's warning that we may *not* in fact "know" as much as we think we do about gendered survey responses, because we lack rigorous, comprehensive, systematic reviews of the literature, and because publication bias, or researchers' tendency to try to publish findings such as gender gaps, rather than "nonfindings" such as results that show the sexes to be similar, may lead us to overestimate difference.

With that warning in mind, however, one of the most notable and enduring sex differences in survey research, and one that may have the most relevance to gender gaps in knowledge, is the continued sex difference in the selection of the "don't know" response. Examinations of sex differences in "don't know" responses show that women's propensity to choose "don't know" on questions of political knowledge, and even on questions about issues and about candidates, is significantly greater than is men's (Rapoport 1982; Atkeson and Rapoport 2003)—or perhaps we should rephrase that summary to say that men are significantly more reluctant to say they "don't know" in a response to a question about politics. In short, for whatever reason, men are much more likely to guess at an answer, and accounting for men's greater propensity to guess and women's greater propensity to say they don't know might do away with as much as 50 percent of the gender gap in political knowledge (Mondak and Anderson 2004). In a test of objective political knowledge with multiple choice responses, a guess gives one a considerable chance of being given credit for a correct answer. Even in "fill in the blank" tests, guessing has at least some probability of getting a right answer. In contrast, if one says "I don't know," one is invariably credited for having given the wrong answer.

In other words, the work of scholars like Rapoport and his associates Mondak and Anderson, and others, makes it possible for us to conclude that survey research is "rigged" to favor male response preferences in many ways, or to inflate modest gender differences into more important ones. This finding has echoes of reports of differently gendered experiences in schools, where, as the American Association of University Women (AAUW) report on gender bias in education reported more than ten years ago (Greenberg Lake Analysis Group 1991), girls were not considered to have been encouraged to assert what they knew. In the AAUW study and others like it, boys were found to be the recipients of significantly more classroom attention than were girls, with particular ramifications for differences in girls' and boys' willingness to try to assert knowledge. Such early socialization patterns could play a role in shaping the imminent adults' response to being questioned.

Note, however, that while accounting for men's guessing reduces the gender gap in objective political knowledge, it does not eliminate it. The fact that forty years of women's movement activity has not sufficed to elevate women's level of political knowledge is sobering, and all the more so because, as Delli Carpini and Keeter's work ingeniously emphasizes, political knowledge is critical to individual women's ability to represent their interests in the political arena. We have argued that women must not be treated as a single, undifferentiated group, but in this we can comfortably do so: all women, regardless of the differences among them, need knowledge of the political system that can so powerfully affect their lives.

To understand why women remain comparatively less engaged by politics, we must continue to expand our measurement capacity. In her chapter on gender and political participation, M. Margaret Conway argues that we need better measures of gender role orientation, as well as of perceptions of candidates, parties, and issues with respect to gender, since current measures do not seem adequately to capture these phenomena. Claudine Gay and Katherine Tate have made explicit arguments about the need for better analysis and understanding of the interaction of gender and race consciousness for African American women (Gay and Tate 1998). Further, Conway's finding that women who do not identify with the women's movement are more active in politics bears further scrutiny and study. The lack of adequate measures of gender consciousness in contemporary data leaves us unable to ascertain whether these are highly conscious, mobilized *anti-feminist* women of the sort that Tolleson-Rinehart (Rinehart 1992) identified in data from the 1970s and 1980s, but Conway's findings suggest that the same phenomenon may be at work. Is the present climate one in which anti- or nonfeminist forces are more successful in stimulating women's political engagement than is the women's movement? Certainly the buoyant expectations of women's contribution to electoral outcomes in the 1980s and early 1990s seem more muted at the time of this writing, but we are no longer well equipped to measure attitudes toward gender roles in order to associate them with attitudes toward political roles.

Our single most common survey measure is the so-called "equal roles" question, asked in the National Election Studies (NES) and in other surveys since 1972: "Recently there has been a lot of talk about women's rights. Some people feel that women should have an equal role with men in running business, industry, and government. Others feel that women's place is in the home. And other people have opinions somewhere in between." Respondents are asked to choose the number, from 1, "equal roles," to 7, "women's place is in the home," that comes closest to their own views (Sapiro et al. 1948–2002). The question has been exhaustively analyzed and criticized. The most pertinent concern about it is that it may no longer accurately reflect people's views of gender roles, especially because of social desirability. Even if contamination by the desire to give an acceptable response is not a problem, and people are responding sincerely, this indicator's variance has diminished steadily and dramatically over time. For instance, Jennings (2000) uses his unique multigenerational panel study to demonstrate that men and women of all three of the generations he has studied have converged on the more liberal position on the equal roles question over the last two decades, with one exception: the youngest generation of men in Jennings's panel is actually more conservative on the question than were their fathers fifteen years earlier. As intriguing as this finding is, we are left dissatisfied by the limits on our ability to probe it further in the major political science survey databases.

The need for better analytical tools is even more obvious when we consider women's multiple identifications. Measuring the feminist consciousness of African American women using questions based on white women's identities likely leads to significant misunderstanding regarding African American women's views of feminism (Simien 2004). Similarly, measuring race consciousness for African American women using questions based on African American men's identities fails to capture the interaction of gender and race for African American women (Cohen 2003; Dawson 2001; Simien 2004).

We also need more sensitive measures of gender consciousness among women of other racial and ethnic minority groups, where the literature in political science is even less developed (Cohen 2003). Work such as that by Mary Pardo and Carol Hardy-Fanta needs to be replicated and expanded in the discipline (Pardo 1998; Hardy-Fanta 2002). Other disciplines have been more attentive to Latina women's political activism and leadership than has political science. For example, a recent volume entitled *Chicana Leadership*, consisting of essays from the feminist journal *Frontiers*, contains no essays by scholars trained in political science (Niemann et al. 2002). Political science's comparative neglect of women of color may be the result, in part, of some discipline norms. Scholars in disciplines such as sociology, anthropology, and literature may submit their work to interdisciplinary feminist journals more often than do political scientists because those disciplines are more likely to give credit for this kind of work in hiring, tenure, and promotion decisions. This is a loss to political science, and also a loss to interdisciplinary inquiry generally, since the latter is deprived of the insights into politics and power that political science is uniquely equipped to provide.

To illustrate the lacunae, take studies of Asian American women's political life. Two full-text searches of JSTOR, using the two terms "women" and "Asian American," and then "gender" and "Asian American," yielded a total of only nineteen articles. Of these, only six actually addressed U.S. political behavior or institutions in a way that attended to both race and gender, and only three of these actually included Asian Americans in the analysis. Of the original nineteen, three actually showed up in the analysis only because the article included a footnote indicating that Asian Americans were eliminated from the analysis because of the low number of Asian American respondents in the data set. None of these studies analyzed Asian American women in any substantive way. The JSTOR database lags publication by two or more years in several journals, so it is possible (but unlikely) that JSTOR searches are missing a recent burst of scholarship on Asian American women. One might also argue that many political science journals are not archived by JSTOR, including *Women & Politics*. The journals that are represented in JSTOR, however, are widely regarded in the discipline as the most important journals in which to publish.

The literature on the politics of Native American women is also small. Diane-Michele Prindeville has been the primary political scientist pursuing this work. Her work is particularly interesting because of her rich data set of qualitative interviews (Prindeville 2003b) and because she examines the intersection of race and ethnicity with gender for Native American and Latino women political leaders (Prindeville 2003a, 2003b). She also has engaged in theory-building in the area of gender consciousness and racial/ethnic identity, developing a classification system that might be used by both quantitative and qualitative researchers (Prindeville 2003a).

The point of this discussion is to suggest that many methodological approaches, and cross-fertilization from work that is proceeding in other disciplines, would help to advance the study of the diversity of women's experiences in U.S. political life. The work by scholars in history, American studies, sociology, anthropology, and other disciplines represented in a recent anthology on Asian and Pacific Islander American women is an example from which political scientists might draw (Hune and Nomura 2003).

Further explication of all of these issues would be useful not only to political scientists interested in how people's understandings of their intersectional identities affect voting behavior and political participation. It would also be useful for feminist groups seeking a broad mobilization of women around candidates and issues. Organizers of the March for Women's Lives, for example, mobilized a broader coalition of women in 2004 than for previous marches, in part by expanding the range of women's health issues to reach beyond abortion (Clemetson 2004; Elliott 2004).

We have emphasized that this book is about gender and politics, not just "women and politics," and men have gender roles too. The history of the discipline might be said to be a history of research on the political life of men—especially that of white men—but precisely *because* men have been so dominant, both as the researchers and the researched, few have questioned whether particular constructions of masculinity have shaped men's politicization. In the foregoing pages, we pointed to an example—men's socialization toward answering political questions, even with a guess. Some recent research asks other such questions. A small but persuasive body of gender gap research has demonstrated changes in men's voting patterns that are as large as, and even larger than, changes in the voting patterns of women. Southern white men, for example, appear to have begun a flight to the Republican party that can be traced to the Goldwater campaign in 1964, but became virtually a stampede by the mid-1980s (Hood 1997; see also Tien and Tronto 2003; Norrander 1999; Kaufmann and Petrocik 1999; Kaufmann 2002). To the limited extent that we can measure the phenomenon, much of this Southern white male migration may be the result of a kind of male gender consciousness resulting from feelings that they are simultaneously disadvantaged relative to men of color and all women, because of movements to advance those groups, at the same time that they are held responsible for the historic discrimination suffered by those groups (Hood 1997). Such men, especially those who have few resources themselves, may feel they have been unfairly targeted as "oppressors" and they may feel that the contemporary Democratic party has led the charge. Nor is the South the only area in which such feelings—that groups other than white men are now perceived to have the political advantage—are at play. Charles Tien and Joan Tronto (2003) found similar phenomena in a study of urban Northeastern ethnic white men.

The traditional literature on partisanship and voting behavior has assumed that increasing partisan conflict on one issue leads to decreasing partisan conflict on others, in what is known as the "conflict displacement" process. Layman and Carsey (2002) argue that, on the contrary, the parties have become more polarized on more issues, and that the polarization far exceeds what the "conflict displacement" model can accommodate. They contend, instead, that we have witnessed "conflict extension." Their careful examination of three NES panel studies (surveys of the same individuals at different points in time), those of 1956–1958–1960, 1972–1974–1976, and 1992–1994–1996, clearly shows that the comparative interparty agreement on social welfare issues and civil rights in the 1950s was ended by the Democrats' movement toward the left by the 1970s and the Republicans' even sharper movement to the right by the 1990s.

Within the data from the panel studies, Layman and Carsey's analysis elucidates a picture of some partisans in both parties changing party identification in response to their party's movement on these issues, but even more partisans changing their own issue positions, to remain in harmony with their party. Of particular relevance for this discussion, Republican partisans have become dramatically more conservative on the issues of the scope of government, civil rights, and abortion over time; these are the very issues most gender politics scholars target in explanations of the gender gap.

Layman and Carsey, among many others, do not take specific note of the gender gap as a factor in increasing party polarization or of the role of feminism as a cleaver of interparty agreement, and yet their findings seem to lead us inevitably back to some of the core findings of gender gap research. Similarly, gender politics scholars have not always attempted to integrate their research on women's electoral behavior with other findings from the work of party politics and electoral behavior scholars. The findings of this volume, taken together with other new research on partisanship and electoral behavior, tell us that we urgently need two new research initiatives. First, clearly, we need more valid, reliable measures of gender role beliefs and gender identification or consciousness—measures that would enable us to understand the relationship of gender to the political behavior of women *and* men. Second, we need to integrate streams of research. The parties and elections literature can benefit by employing the theoretical, analytical, and empirical findings of gender politics research. Gender politics research, in turn, will profit from newly invigorated efforts to study women's political behavior *and* that of men, while also considering how gendered political behavior is actually reshaping the most important American political institutions.

We need also to prepare for analysis of future developments: the present level of polarization in American politics is almost unprecedented. Will what appears to be a gendering of pertinent political issues continue to be one of the drivers of that polarization, or can a more reflective, less reflexive evaluation of the public understandings of gender offer strategies for the creation of a polis that is more engaged, but less bitterly divided?

Understanding differences in politicization may require more than better measures, as these pages suggest, though it clearly does require that. We may also simply need more and better data. The American National Election Studies, as we have already mentioned, contain too few respondents who are African American, Latino, or Asian American voters to permit us to draw conclusions about the ways that intersecting identities might affect voting patterns over time. We have noted some promising work in the area (Cohen 2003; Simien 2004; Smooth forthcoming), and we have stressed, with Susan Carroll, the need for more methodological tools. Although their chapters primarily describe institutional rather than behavioral processes, Sue Thomas's and Susan Gluck Mezey's work gives us a useful reminder of the importance of recognizing institutional constraints on individual political behavior as we attempt to understand the behavior of all women, and of men of color. Empirical work on differences in the individual's engagement with the political world can profit from rich theoretical analyses of the political self-understanding of identity groups as developed by Cynthia Burack, as well as a range of other methodological and theoretical approaches (Burack 2004; Carroll and Liebowitz 2003; Cohen 2003).

Understanding gender and politicization also means understanding the role of gender in electoral processes from the point of view of the candidates, and the electoral institutions that choose and support the candidates (Dolan 2004). Pamela Fiber and Richard Fox, in their chapter on congressional campaigns, show us a surprising level of regional variation in the interactions of gender and political culture. These variations correspond to variations in women's presence in state- and national-level offices. Research on this variation remains somewhat limited in scope as of yet, and the variation is not well understood. We have not yet delineated the factors that lead, at the state level, to the presence of more or fewer women in legislative office, which then influences the electoral environment for women seeking congressional seats. Changing partisan dynamics of state legislatures have created greater ideological polarization of male and female state legislators. While women state legislators and women in Congress have not become more conservative in the main, their male counterparts in both parties have become more likely to describe themselves as conservative (Carroll 2002). Because state legislative seats are still important "base offices," the implications of this shift for the trajectories of candidates' political ambition may also be profound. Both major political parties' recruitment of male and female candidates, and the effect this will have on the presence of women as legislators—and women as seekers of higher office—seem subject to an unusually high level of gendering, even though it is happening outside the glare of Year of the Woman–style media attention.

Furthermore, as Fiber and Fox argue, "the electoral environment continues to treat women and men differently," and the way in which this matters to electoral experiences and outcomes remains opaque to view. Fiber and Fox note that the differences between how the Republican and Democratic parties recruit candidates result in some differences in the presence of women candidates. To understand the process of candidate recruitment, we need to look further up the "pipeline" toward the recruitment and advancement of women in professions that most frequently lead to political officeholding. Fox, in collaboration with Jennifer Lawless, has begun research that addresses the "pipeline" for men and women prior to running for political office; much more work of this kind is needed (Fox and Lawless 2004).

We also need a better understanding of the ways in which men and women go about making difficult decisions that are personal and yet are deeply inflected by political life. Eric Plutzer argues here that examining real men and women in actual moral decision-making situations helps people to see the complexity of moral reasoning, and to see that in fact, both men and women are concerned about care and justice. As his chapter shows, simplistic notions about men's and women's moral reasoning do not withstand scrutiny. Plutzer suggests that we must investigate the role that men play as participants in and supporters of women's reproductive decision making. As the widely noted greater presence of young men at the recent March for Women's Lives than at previous marches might indicate, men's gender role socialization regarding women's rights in political life could be deeply affected by taking supportive roles in such decisions (Stuever 2004).

Plutzer also suggests that the dissemination of research such as that represented by his chapter might have political effects. Specifically, the thoughtfulness with which women approach these decision-making situations can be used as an argument in favor of encouraging citizens to understand and respect women's right to make these decisions for themselves, and to recognize the harm of denying women these decisions. In this way, the citizenry's deeper understanding and appreciation of the complexity of women's moral decision making about reproduction would have powerful political implications—not the least of which would be to reclaim civic debate from angry sloganeering.

Public Policy

The study of international relations and foreign policy was the last subfield in the discipline of political science to be subjected to feminist analysis. Even as scholars focusing on postcolonial relations, the politics of diasporic communities, or on globalization have begun to alter the way that international relations is studied, many political scientists still fail to take account of gender in their analyses and in their teaching. A recent review of international relations syllabi shows that gender is largely absent from the way many international relations scholars teach the basic courses in their subfield (Hurrell 2004).

Yet feminist work has shown how crucial gender is in organizing the international political system. This is true whether one's concern is military operations, the organization of the global labor market, gender and international development policies, or international human rights (Cohn 2004; Enloe 1990, 1993, 2000; Moghadam 1998; Peterson 2003). Certainly any concern with economic development in a global context must consider the organization of families, work, and gender relations in particular cultural contexts. Globalization has led to underground markets that exploit women and children, particularly in the sex trade, but also to the spread of organizing among women (Ehrenreich and Hochschild 2003).

U.S. foreign policy is gendered, but simply placing women in foreign policymaking roles does not necessarily change this picture (Borelli 2000; Cohn and Enloe 2003). As Janie Leatherman's chapter in this volume suggests, a foreign policy based on institutionalized hegemonic masculinity means that placing women such as Margaret Thatcher or Madeleine Albright in leadership positions does not change the fundamental structure of foreign policy institutions. Of course, after many years of feminist organizing to influence the United Nations and other international bodies, advocates for women have succeeded in making some progress for women's interests (Meillon and Bunch 2001). Examples include the Convention on the Elimination of All Forms of Discrimination Against Women (CEDAW)—which the United States in its usual fashion has refused to ratify—as well as Resolution 1325, which Leatherman analyzes, and which requires the inclusion of women's concerns and gender perspectives in peacekeeping, as well as gender mainstreaming in the United Nations (Poehlman-Doumbouya and Hill 2001). The use of international instruments such as CEDAW and Resolution 1325 can transform institutional decision making, but the solutions will require long-term and ongoing advocacy on the part of feminist groups. International feminist nongovernmental organizations (NGOs) played a crucial role in convincing the Security Council to adopt Resolution 1325 and are actively involved in making sure that it is implemented.

This phenomenon of feminist organizations influencing international policymaking is echoed at the level of nation-states. For example, in the area of public policy, an interesting line of research has looked at the effects of "state feminism"—that is, official state bodies that are intended to represent the interests of women in public policy decision making—on public policy outcomes (Mazur 2001). Other researchers have looked at the presence of feminist organizations in civil society, and how the strength of such bodies affects policymaking (Weldon 2002). Dorothy E. McBride, one of the founding scholars of "state feminism" research, points out in her study of three policies of particular relevance to women that, despite U.S. feminist groups' political engagement with these policies, winning was by no means assured. In order to retain the "gendered frame" of the debate that would help feminists win on their issues, political actors need both allies and access. The lesson that feminist activists can take from the McBride chapter is that it is important for feminists to maintain allies in both parties, as the policy losses of the 1990s illustrate.

The policy chapters in this volume all address the importance of framing to policy outcomes. McBride's chapter is most explicit in its application of framing, noting that feminist groups lost on policy outcomes when they lost the political power to frame the debate. Further, she notes that policies that are framed as important to women may not result in outcomes seen as desirable by feminist groups, as was demonstrated by the shifting ground of the abortion debate in the 1990s. McBride's analysis points again to the importance of agenda setting, and of language and symbolic framing in shaping policy outcomes (Kingdon 1995). Her analytical approach works especially well to explain policies aimed at reproduction; in addition to "partial-birth abortion," recent political conflicts over fetal rights have also demonstrated how useful it is for those who oppose reproductive rights for women to frame the feminist reproductive rights community as anti-mother and anti-fetus (Roth 2000; Daniels 1993).

As both Jyl Josephson and Dorothy McBride point out, policy debates over social welfare in the U.S. reflect dominant frames of gender, race, and appropriate gender roles. Certainly the history of social policymaking in the United States has been shaped by the relative political power of whites in relation to other racial and ethnic groups, as well as by social constructions of race, gender, and class (Mettler 1998; Smith 2001; Williams 2003). In addition, contemporary public attitudes toward welfare policy are fairly negative and reinforce stereotypes of low-income people (Neubeck and Cazenave 2001; Smiley 2001; Sparks 2003). But these opinions do not come from nowhere. They are shaped by the efforts of advocacy groups to influence policy outcomes that are to their liking (Williams 1997). In the debate over the 1996 welfare reform law, social science evidence played almost no role. Rather, the debate was in many ways overdetermined by the way that welfare recipients were depicted. As Mary Hawkesworth (2003) points out, congresswomen of color tried, unsuccessfully, to bring social science evidence to bear on the congressional welfare reform debates. In part because of the "racing and gendering enactments" of Congress as an institution (Hawkesworth 2003, 534), the welfare bill was based on a series of false assumptions about policy recipients.

In the scholarly literature on welfare reform, the consensus seems to be that welfare reform has been overwhelmingly successful, but this is partly a measurement problem (Moffitt 2002). In fact, we simply do not know what has happened with many families that have left Temporary Assistance to Needy Families (TANF), especially those families who are the most disadvantaged (Zedlewski and Loprest 2001). We know the least about outcomes for those families who might have additional barriers to employment besides low levels of educational attainment and work skills, such as families coping with domestic violence, psychiatric problems, or physical disabilities (Josephson 2002). Feminist critiques of welfare policy have had little effect on policymaking (Hirschmann 2003; Mink 2003). Women members of

Congress have had some impact on policy (Hawkesworth 2003; Carroll 2001), but it is at the margins and has not changed the overall direction of policymaking for low-income women. Here is where welfare policy analysis provides some insights for feminist activists: only if coalitions of groups concerned about the multitude of issues that affect low-income women find common cause in a policy arena such as welfare are feminist concerns with this policy likely to have any effect. Changes in welfare policy will likely require changes in public opinion and economic conditions, as well as a coalitional political movement (Zoelle and Josephson 2005). Without such a movement, low-income women will remain politically convenient targets of punitive public policies.

Yet even an active and well-equipped political movement may face a significant lag time in terms of policy impacts. Despite the advent of a women's health movement contemporaneously with the modern or second-wave women's movement, Sue Tolleson-Rinehart's chapter shows how long it took to get women's health on the national policymaking agenda. Further, health policy shows the power of gender in shaping the imagination and practice even of scientifically trained health care researchers and practitioners. Women, too, may have responded to the force of gender by so readily identifying "women's health" almost solely with reproductive and breast health. Until very recently, the whole policymaking and health care systems, when they have considered "women's health" at all, have seemed not to acknowledge that women have "health" apart from their reproductive systems. Until we can treat reproductive and breast health as merely parts of women's health—as we now may be beginning to do—we will be unprepared to understand the potentially different influences of sex and gender on health, and we may not adequately provide for women's health in the many areas where neither sex nor gender matters in critical ways.

Certainly, there are many arenas of public policy where gender matters, and sex matters, that are not covered by the chapters in this volume. There is still need for a great deal more gender mainstreaming with respect to the study of public policy.

Institutions

Political scientists still do not understand well what happens to political institutions when historically underrepresented groups begin to enter them in significant numbers. As MaryAnne Borelli points out, the Cabinet seems to evidence processes of both transgendering and regendering. That is, some Cabinet nominations and nominees seem to show evidence of changing institutional processes in ways that challenge traditional understandings of gender roles; at other times, traditional gender roles are reinforced even when women are present. The literature on black political leadership shows that many institutional forces work to limit the transformative effects of black elected officials (Johnson 2002; Stone 1989; Orr 1999). Sue Thomas notes in her chapter that "business as usual has to be transformed" in order for women's presence to actually change the traditionally gendered practices of political institutions. Counting the number of women present in an institution, while important, is not a transformation of it.

MaryAnne Borrelli's chapter argues for more scholarly analysis of transgendering and regendering as more women are appointed to top government posts. We need such analysis of all three branches of government, and of institutions at all levels of government, from federal to local. But this kind of analysis has only recently become possible with respect to the Cabinet, as Borelli points out, since it is only in the last two presidential administrations that women have been present in significant enough numbers to warrant such study. Many further questions present themselves: What is the gender, race, and ethnicity makeup of the top advisors to the secretaries? How does this affect the processes of transgendering and regendering? What role do ideology and party affiliation play in these processes? How does media coverage of Cabinet personnel affect gender integration?

Borrelli also suggests some further questions:

> What role will the women secretaries play in the policymaking and implementation during the second term? How will the connections between descriptive and substantive representation be negotiated? Will lessened electoral pressures cause the lame-duck president to devalue the contributions of "diversity" secretaries-designate? Will these nominees serve as representatives to and from historically marginalized peoples, or will these nominees be chosen for their loyalty to the president and their willingness to serve as buffers against these constituents? These are just a few of the questions that await answers, as the provision of representation in the cabinet is shaped by presidential decisions and political events.

For some of these questions, the lessons may become clear only over the course of many decades and many administrations. Other questions about gender and the Cabinet may become clear within the next several presidential administrations.

The first woman Cabinet secretary, Frances Perkins, antedates the first woman to serve on a federal court of general jurisdiction, Florence Ellinwood Allen, by one year—and both were appointed by Franklin Delano Roosevelt (Perkins in 1933, Allen in 1934). Susan Gluck Mezey's questions regarding gender and judicial behavior have received more scholarly attention than have Borelli's, however, because of women's somewhat earlier entrance to the bench in notable numbers. Carter's appointment of 152 women to the federal bench (he also appointed two women to his Cabinet) began to make systematic analysis of gender in the federal judiciary possible. In this volume, Mezey seeks to identify the circumstances under which we find a difference in the voting behavior of male and female judges. How does "feminist consciousness" matter? This may require a study of judges' feminist or gender consciousness that compares women judges to each other as well as to men, and, as Conway's chapter points out, better measures of feminist or gender consciousness are needed if we are to do this. Debra Dodson has suggested that consciousness of gender may be more important for judicial decision making than whether the judge is male or female (Dodson 2001). Further, we need more study of the interaction between party affiliation, gender or feminist consciousness, and the identity characteristics of judges on specific issues. For example, there is some evidence that on issues such as gay rights, the judge's race and sex may be significant indicators of decision making (Pinello 2003).

For Mezey, the evidence suggests that hopes for women judges who might act for or on behalf of women is, at best, mixed. There is little reason to believe that a transformative effect will arise simply from placing women judges on the bench, unless these judges share a belief in a feminist agenda. Feminist organizations might take lessons from Mezey's analysis: a judge's policy orientations and political ideology may be more important for the pursuit of feminist goals than is his or her sex. Mezey's chapter also reminds us of the complexity of the question of representation with which we began this concluding essay.

The presence of women in legislative bodies has brought changes to the agenda and policymaking processes of those bodies. Sue Thomas finds some validation for the theory of critical mass, but as women legislators have become increasingly diverse in race, ethnicity, and party affiliation, we should be prepared to analyze those intersections, and should not assume that identifications as women are always women legislators' most important identifications. We must also remember that many state legislatures do not yet *have* a critical mass of women members. When and if latecomer states—those with the smallest numbers of women in their legislatures—achieve critical mass, will they behave as did the states that crossed the thresholds first? Southern legislatures populate most of the latecomer ranks, and New England, upper Midwest, and Pacific Northwest states were in the vanguard. We know that those states differ in myriad ways other than the proportion of legislators who are women—not least in their cultures' views of the proper scope of government: will a critical mass of women in office change Southern legislatures in expected ways?

Other questions regarding gender and legislative bodies are more complex, of course, and require much more than counting the presence of women and studying their behavior as legislators in comparison to men. As Thomas points out, legislative bodies remain deeply gendered in many ways; the power of the gendering may be seen in the degree to which progress toward parity now seems stalled. How will the legislative environment be changed by changes in sex, gender, racial, and ethnic composition in the twenty-first century? Will the social expectations regarding women's gender roles continue to limit the number of women who run or consider running for political office? How much change might women legislators bring about through, for example, women's legislative caucuses? Will it, as Thomas notes, "take external cultural and institutional revolutions to achieve uniformity of opportunity and experience" for men and women? Will legislative women continue to be able to be innovative in the face of discrimination? All of these questions merit our continuing attention.

David Niven's chapter suggests that we cannot yet be certain of the fundamental source of disparity between media coverage of women members of Congress and their male counterparts. Is the disparity a function of simple bias on the part of reporters and editors? Is it a perception about what readers want to see? Or is this bias the result of some combination of these and other factors? How, precisely, does this coverage affect voter perceptions and decisions? Would simple awareness of these biases on the part of the media prompt changes in coverage, or would other sorts of changes in the institutional structure of the press or in the training of journalists be required?

As Niven points out, "a fair media would not treat women as the exact and indistinguishable clones of men in office," but rather would recognize actual policy differences as well as similarities between male and female officeholders. Can studies such as Niven's be used to encourage the media to alter their coverage? If the press is responding to reader expectations regarding gendered coverage, would changes be implemented by ratings- and readership-conscious media outlets?

The chapters on political institutions show that the inclusion of women in positions of political power is important, not to say normatively desirable, but insufficient for producing equality between women and men in American political life. As Mary Hawkesworth (2003) shows in her analysis of the treatment of congresswomen of color in the welfare debates of the 103rd and 104th Congress, male political elites are not necessarily enlightened in their treatment of their female peers. In the welfare debates, male members of Congress interacted with their female colleagues in ways that reinforced racial and gender stereotypes and reinscribed gender and racial hierarchies. All of the chapters in this volume's section on institutions indicate that the mechanisms driving what Borrelli terms the "regendering" of institutions are complex, nuanced, and often subtle. Political scientists must continue to attend to the way in which these institutions actually operate in practice, and not simply to the presence of increased diversity among the actors in them.

Conclusions

Much remains to be done in the study of gender and American political life. We need to understand how gender operates at all levels of social and political analysis. The chapters in this volume testify abundantly to the fact that political science already has a fine body of gender politics research within the traditional boundaries of the discipline, but to which the larger discipline has not often paid enough attention. To some extent, political scientists can use the rich work produced by other social science disciplines, particularly sociology and anthropology, as well as to some intriguing approaches developed by women's studies, queer studies, and cultural studies scholars.

But political science has its own unique and powerful contribution to make to the study of gender, power, and politics, including a keen understanding of how scholarly research can be translated for, and used by, policymakers. To make these contributions, political scientists need to refine old tools and develop new ones in the ongoing effort to develop the discipline's own particular insights into gender. The work of gender mainstreaming, initiated with such intrepid enthusiasm by scholars who first developed the subfield of women and politics, has only just begun.

References

Atkeson, Lonna Rae, and Ronald B. Rapoport. 2003. "The More Things Change the More They Stay the Same: Examining Differences in Political Communication by Men and Women, 1952 through 2000." *Public Opinion Quarterly* 67: 495–521.

Borrelli, MaryAnne. 2000. "Gender, Politics, and Change in the United States Cabinet: The Madeleine Korbel Albright and Janet Reno Appointments." In *Gender and American Politics: Women, Men, and the Political Process*, ed. Sue Tolleson-Rinehart and Jyl Josephson. Armonk, NY: M.E. Sharpe.

Burack, Cynthia. 2004. *Healing Identities: Black Feminist Thought and the Politics of Groups.* Ithaca, NY: Cornell University Press.

Carroll, Susan J., ed. 2001. *The Impact of Women in Public Office.* Bloomington: Indiana University Press.

———. 2002. "Partisan Dynamics of the Gender Gap Among State Legislators." *Spectrum: The Journal of State Government* (Fall): 18–21.

Carroll, Susan J., and Debra J. Liebowitz. 2003. "New Challenges, New Questions, New Directions." In *Women and American Politics: New Questions, New Directions*, ed. Susan J. Carroll. New York: Oxford University Press.

Clemetson, Lynette. 2004. "For Abortion Rights Cause, a New Diversity." *The New York Times*, April 24, 2004, A14.

Cohen, Cathy. 2003. "A Portrait of Continuing Marginality: The Study of Women of Color in American Politics." In *Women and American Politics: New Questions, New Directions*, ed. Susan J. Carroll. New York: Oxford University Press.

Cohn, Carol. 2004. "Feminist Peacemaking: In Resolution 1325, the United Nations Requires the Inclusion of Women in All Peace Planning and Negotiation." *Women's Review of Books* 21, 5 (February): 8–9.

Cohn, Carol, and Cynthia Enloe. 2003. "A Conversation with Cynthia Enloe: Feminists Look at Masculinity and the Men Who Wage War." *Signs* 28: 1187–1207.

Crenshaw, Kimberle. 1991. "Demarginalizing the Intersection of Race and Sex: A Black Feminist Critique of Antidiscrimination Doctrine, Feminist Theory, and Antiracist Politics." In *Feminist Legal Theory: Readings in Law and Gender*, ed. Katharine T. Bartlett and Roseanne Kennedy. Boulder, CO: Westview Press.

Daniels, Cynthia R. 1993. *At Women's Expense: State Power and the Politics of Fetal Rights.* Cambridge: Harvard University Press.

Dawson, Michael C. 2001. *Black Visions.* Chicago: University of Chicago Press.

Dodson, Debra L. 2001. "Acting for Women: Is What Legislators Say, What They Do?" In *The Impact of Women in Public Office*, ed. Susan J. Carroll. Bloomington: Indiana University Press.

Dolan, Kathleen A. 2004. *Voting for Women: How the Public Evaluates Women Candidates.* Boulder, CO: Westview Press.

Ehrenreich, Barbara, and Arlie Russell Hochschild, eds. 2003. *Global Woman: Nannies, Maids, and Sex Workers in the New Economy.* New York: Metropolitan Books.

Elliott, Andrea. 2004. "Against Abortion but in Favor of Choice." *The New York Times*, April 26, 2004, A17.

Enloe, Cynthia. 1990. *Bananas, Beaches and Bases: Making Feminist Sense of International Politics.* Berkeley: University of California Press.

———. 1993. *The Morning After: Sexual Politics at the End of the Cold War.* Berkeley: University of California Press.

———. 2000. *Maneuvers.* Berkeley: University of California Press.

Fox, Richard L., and Jennifer L. Lawless. 2004. "Entering the Arena? Gender and the Decision to Run for Office." *American Journal of Political Science* 48(2): 264–280.

Gay, Claudine. 2002. "Spirals of Trust? The Effect of Descriptive Representation on the Relationship Between Citizens and Their Government." *American Journal of Political Science* 46, 4 (October): 717–732.

Gay, Claudine, and Katherine Tate. 1998. "Doubly Bound: The Impact of Gender and Race on the Politics of Black Women." *Political Psychology* 19(1): 169–184.

Greenberg Lake Analysis Group. 1991. *Shortchanging Girls, Shortchanging America.* Washington, DC: American Association of University Women.

Haider-Markel, Donald P., Mark R. Joslyn, and Chad J. Kniss. 2000. "Minority Groups Interests and Political Representation: Gay Elected Officials in the Policy Process." *Journal of Politics* 62, 2 (May): 568–577.

Hammonds, Evelynn, and Banu Subramaniam. 2003. "A Conversation on Feminist Studies." *Signs* 28: 923–942.

Hardy-Fanta, Carol. 2002. "Latina Women and Political Leadership: Implications for Latino Community Empowerment." In *Latino Politics in Massachusetts: Struggles, Strategies, and Prospects*, ed. Carol Hardy-Fanta and Jeffrey N. Gerson, pp. 193–212. New York: Routledge.

Hawkesworth, Mary. 2003. "Congressional Enactments of Race-Gender: Toward a Theory of Raced-Gendered Institutions." *American Political Science Review* 97, 4 (November): 529–550.

Hirschmann, Nancy J. 2003. *The Subject of Liberty: Toward a Feminist Theory of Freedom.* Princeton, NJ: Princeton University Press.

Hood, M.V. III. 1997. "Capturing Bubba's Heart and Mind: Group Consciousness and the Political Identification of Southern White Males, 1972–1992." Unpublished doctoral dissertation, Texas Tech University.

Huddy, Leonie, Joshua Billig, John Bracciodieta, Lois Hoeffler, Patrick J. Moynihan, and Patricia Pugliani. 1997. "The Effect of Interviewer Gender on the Survey Response" *Political Behavior* 19(3): 197–220.

Hune, Shirley, and Gail Nomura. 2003. *Asian/Pacific Islander American Women.* New York: New York University Press.

Hurrell, Andrew. 2004. "America and the World: Issues in the Teaching of U.S. Foreign Policy." *Perspectives on Politics* 2, 1 (March): 101–111.

Jennings, M. Kent. 1979. "Another Look at the Life Cycle and Participation." *American Journal of Political Science* 23, 4 (November): 755–771.

———. 2000. "The Gender Gap and the Place of Women in Political Life: A Longitudinal, Cross-Generational Analysis." Paper prepared for delivery at the Dilemmas of Democracy 2000 Conference, Loyola Marymount University, Los Angeles, February 17.

Johnson, Valerie C. 2002. *Black Power in the Suburbs: The Myth or Reality of African American Suburban Political Incorporation.* Albany: State University of New York Press.

Josephson, Jyl. 2002. "The Intersectionality of Domestic Violence and Welfare in the Lives of Poor Women." *Journal of Poverty* 6(1): 1–20.

Kaufmann, Karen M. 2002. "Culture Wars, Secular Realignment, and the Gender Gap in Party Identification." *Political Behavior* 24, 3 (September): 283–307.

Kaufmann, Karen M., and John R. Petrocik. 1999. "The Changing Politics of American Men: Understanding the Sources of the Gender Gap." *American Journal of Political Science* 43, 3 (July): 864–887.

Kingdon, John W. 1995. *Agendas, Alternatives, and Public Policies.* 2d ed. New York: HarperCollins College Publishers.

Layman, Geoffrey C., and Thomas M. Carsey. 2002. "Party Polarization and Party Structuring of Policy Attitudes: A Comparison of Three NES Panel Studies." *Political Behavior* 24, 3 (September): 199–236.

Mazur, Amy, ed. 2001. *State Feminism, Women's Movements, and Job Training: Making Democracies Work in the Global Economy.* New York: Routledge.

Meillon, Cynthia, and Charlotte Bunch, eds. 2001. *Holding on to the Promise: Women's Human Rights and the Beijing + 5 Review*. New Brunswick, NJ: Center for Women's Global Leadership, Rutgers University.

Mettler, Suzanne. 1998. *Dividing Citizens: Gender and Federalism in New Deal Public Policy*. Ithaca, NY: Cornell University Press.

Mink, Gwendolyn. 2003. "From Welfare to Wedlock: Marriage Promotion and Poor Mothers' Inequality." In *Fundamental Differences: Feminists Talk Back to Social Conservatives*, ed. Cynthia Burack and Jyl Josephson, pp. 207–218. Lanham, MD: Rowman & Littlefield.

Moffitt, Robert. 2002. "A Return to Categorical Welfare." *Joint Center for Poverty Research Newsletter* 15(6): 15–17.

Moghadam, Valentine. 1998. "Feminisms and Development." *Gender & History* 10, 3 (November): 590–597.

Mondak, Jeffery J., and Mary R. Anderson. 2004. "The Knowledge Gap: A Reexamination of Gender-Based Differences in Political Knowledge." *The Journal of Politics* 66(2): 492–512.

Neubeck, Kenneth J., and Noel A. Cazenave. 2001. *Welfare Racism: Playing the Race Card Against America's Poor.* New York: Routledge.

Niemann, Yolanda Flores, Susan H. Armitage, Patricia Hart, and Karen Weathermon, eds. 2002. *Chicana Leadership: The "Frontiers" Reader*. Lincoln: University of Nebraska Press.

Norrander, Barbara. 1999. "The Evolution of the Gender Gap." *The Public Opinion Quarterly* 63, 4 (Winter): 566–576.

Orr, Marion. 1999. *Black Social Capital: The Politics of School Reform in Baltimore 1986–1998*. Lawrence: University Press of Kansas.

Pantoja, Adrian, and Gary M. Segura. 2003. "Does Ethnicity Matter? Descriptive Representation in Legislatures and Political Alienation Among Latinos." *Social Science Quarterly* 84, 2 (June): 441–461.

Pardo, Mary S. 1998. *Mexican American Women Activists: Identity and Resistance in Two Los Angeles Communities*. Philadelphia: Temple University Press.

Peterson, V. Spike. 2003. *A Critical Rewriting of Global Political Economy: Integrating Reproductive, Productive and Virtual Economies*. New York: Routledge.

Pinello, Daniel. 2003. *Gay Rights and American Law*. Cambridge: Cambridge University Press.

Poehlman-Doumboya, Sara, and Felicity Hill. 2001. "Women and Peace in the United Nations." *New Routes* 6(3): 1–6.

Prindeville, Diane-Michele. 2003a. "Identity and the Politics of American Indian and Hispanic Women Leaders." *Gender & Society* 17, 4 (August): 591–608.

———. 2003b. " 'I've Seen Changes': The Political Efficacy of American Indian and Hispanic Women Leaders." *Women & Politics* 25: 1–2, 89–113.

Rapoport, Ronald B. 1982. "Sex Differences in Attitude Expression: A Generational Explanation." *Public Opinion Quarterly* 46, 1 (Spring): 86–96.

Rinehart, Sue Tolleson. 1992. *Gender Consciousness and Politics*. New York: Routledge.

Roth, Rachel. 2000. *Making Women Pay: The Hidden Costs of Fetal Rights*. Ithaca, NY: Cornell University Press.

Sapiro, Virginia. 2003. "Theorizing Gender in Political Psychology Research." In *Oxford Handbook of Political Psychology*, ed. David O. Sears, Leonie Huddy, and Robert Jervis. New York: Oxford University Press.

Sapiro, Virginia, Steven J. Rosenstone, and the National Election Studies. 2001. 1948–2002 Cumulative Data File. Ann Arbor: University of Michigan, Center for Political Studies.

Simien, Evelyn M. 2005. "Black Feminist Theory: Charting a Course for Black Women's Studies in Political Science." *Women & Politics* 26: 81–93.

Smiley, Marion. 2001. "'Welfare Dependency': The Power of a Concept." *Thesis Eleven*, no. 64 (February): 21–38.

Smith, Anna Marie. 2001. "The Politicization of Marriage in Contemporary American Public Policy: The Defense of Marriage Act and the Personal Responsibility Act." *Citizenship Studies* 5(3): 303–320.

Smooth, Wendy. Forthcoming. "African American Women State Legislators and the Politics of Legislative Incorporation." New Brunswick, NJ: Center for American Women and Politics, Rutgers University.

Sparks, Holloway. 2003. "Queens, Teens, and Model Mothers: Race, Gender and the Discourse of Welfare Reform." In *Race and the Politics of Welfare Reform*, ed. Sanford Schram, Joe Soss, and Richard C. Fording, pp. 171–195. Ann Arbor: University of Michigan Press.

Stone, Clarence. 1989. *Regime Politics: Governing Atlanta 1946–1988*. Lawrence: University Press of Kansas.

Stuever, Hank. 2004. "Body Politics: Today's Feminist, It Turns Out, Looks Like a Lot of People—Maybe a Million." *The Washington Post*, April 26, 2004, C1.

Tien, Charles, and Joan C. Tronto. 2003. "Whose Gender Gap Is It, Anyway? Regional Differences in the Gender Gap." Paper presented at the Annual Meeting of the Midwest Political Science Association, Chicago, April.

Weldon, S. Laurel. 2002. *Protest, Policy, and the Problem of Violence Against Women: A Cross-National Comparison*. Pittsburgh: University of Pittsburgh Press.

Williams, Linda. 2003. *The Constraint of Race: Legacies of White Skin Privilege in America*. University Park: Pennsylvania State University Press.

Williams, Lucinda. 1997. "Decades of Distortion: The Right's Thirty-Year Assault on Welfare." Somerville, MA: Political Research Associates.

Zedlewski, Sheila R., and Pamela Loprest. 2001. "Will TANF Work for the Most Disadvantaged Families?" In *The New World of Welfare*, ed. Rebecca Blank and Ron Haskins, pp. 311–334. Washington, DC: Brookings Institution Press.

Zoelle, Diana, and Jyl Josephson. 2005. "Making Democratic Space for Poor People: The Kensington Welfare Rights Union." In *Charting Transnational Democracy: Beyond Global Arrogance*, ed. Julie Webber and Janie Leatherman. New York: Palgrave Macmillan.

Index